A SHAKESPEARE
BIBLIOGRAPHY

SÄCHSISCHE FORSCHUNGSINSTITUTE IN LEIPZIG
FORSCHUNGSINSTITUT FÜR NEUERE PHILOLOGIE

III. ANGLISTISCHE ABTEILUNG

EXTRA VOLUME

A SHAKESPEARE BIBLIOGRAPHY

By

WALTHER EBISCH, Ph.D.

LIBRARIAN OF THE ENGLISH SEMINAR
UNIVERSITY OF LEIPZIG

in collaboration with

LEVIN L. SCHÜCKING

PROFESSOR AT THE UNIVERSITY OF
LEIPZIG

OXFORD

AT THE CLARENDON PRESS

1931

OXFORD UNIVERSITY PRESS
Amen House, E.C. 4
London Edinburgh Glasgow
Leipzig New York Toronto
Melbourne Capetown Bombay
Calcutta Madras Shanghai
Humphrey Milford
Publisher to the
University

PRINTED IN GREAT BRITAIN

PREFACE

A SHAKESPEARE bibliography that meets the demands of recent research has long been one of the most urgent desiderata of Modern Philology. The reason why this task has nevertheless up till now not been taken in hand consists in the almost inexhaustible riches of Shakespearian literature. It is a subject to which every new year brings new material. To register all of it would be neither desirable nor indeed possible. In other words, the task entails the dangers of *selection*. Selection, however, implies the necessity of more or less intimate knowledge of the available work. Now although the authors of this bibliography cannot boast of having read every book and article of which the title has here been given, their ambition has been to form some opinion as to the relative value of all Shakespearian investigation and criticism known to them and not to leave out any title indispensable for scientific Shakespearian study. That a first attempt of this kind will in many ways fall short of the mark aimed at, they are of course conscious.

With regard to the collaboration of the authors, whilst the idea originated with Professor Schücking, Dr. Ebisch has carried out the bulk of the actual work.

Nothing published after 1929 has been included.

W. E.
L. L. S.

October, 1930.

1

5

CONTENTS

A. GENERAL

B. THE WORKS OF SHAKESPEARE EXAMINED INDIVIDUALLY

ABBREVIATIONS

1. PERIODICALS

Arch. = Archiv für das Studium der neueren Sprachen und Literaturen.
Bbl. = Beiblatt zur Anglia.
CHEL. = The Cambridge History of English Literature.
Dt. Litztg. = Deutsche Literaturzeitung
Dt. Vjschr. = Deutsche Vierteljahrsschrift für Literaturwissenschaft und Geistesgeschichte.
E. St. = Englische Studien.
Euph. = Euphorion.
Fortn. Rev. = Fortnightly Review.
GRM. = Germanisch-romanische Monatsschrift.
JEGPh. = Journal of English and Germanic Philology.
Libr. = The Library.
Litbl. = Literaturblatt für germanische und romanische Philologie.
Lit. Zbl. = Literarisches Zentralblatt.
Litt. = Litteris.
MLN. = Modern Language Notes.
MLR. = Modern Language Review.

Mod. Phil. = Modern Philology.
N. Spr. = Die neueren Sprachen.
N. & Q. = Notes and Queries.
PMLA. = Publications of the Modern Language Association of America.
Phil. Quart. = Philological Quarterly.
Quart. Rev. = Quarterly Review.
RDM. = Revue des Deux Mondes.
RESt. = The Review of English Studies.
Rev. de litt. comp. = Revue de littérature comparée.
Rom. Forsch. = Romanische Forschungen.
Sh. Jb. = Jahrbuch der deutschen Shakespeare-Gesellschaft.
Stud. in Phil. = Studies in Philology.
TLS. = The Times Literary Supplement.
Z. f. e. U. = Zeitschrift für französischen und englischen Unterricht.
Zs. f. vgl. Lit.gesch. = Zeitschrift für vergleichende Literaturgeschichte.

2. SHAKESPEARE'S DRAMAS AND POEMS

Ado = Much Ado about Nothing.
All's = All's Well that Ends Well.
Ant. = Antony and Cleopatra.
As = As You Like It.
Caes. = Julius Caesar.
Compl. = A Lover's Complaint.
Cor. = Coriolanus.
Cymb. = Cymbeline.
Err. = The Comedy of Errors.
Gent. = The Two Gentlemen of Verona.
1 H. IV = The First Part of King Henry IV.
3 H. VI = The Third Part of King Henry VI.
H. VIII = King Henry VIII.
Haml. = Hamlet.
John = King John.
L.L.L. = Love's Labour's Lost.
Lear = King Lear.
Lucr. = The Rape of Lucrece.
Macb. = Macbeth.

Meas. = Measure for Measure.
Merch. = The Merchant of Venice.
Mids. = A Midsummer Night's Dream.
Oth. = Othello.
Per. = Pericles.
Phoen. = The Phoenix and the Turtle.
Pilgr. = The Passionate Pilgrim.
R. II = King Richard II.
R. III = King Richard III.
Rom. = Romeo and Juliet.
Shr. = The Taming of the Shrew.
Sonn. = Sonnets.
Tim. = Timon of Athens.
Tit. = Titus Andronicus.
Temp. = The Tempest.
Troil. = Troilus and Cressida.
Tw. = Twelfth Night, or, What You Will.
Ven. = Venus and Adonis.
Wint. = The Winter's Tale.
Wiv. = The Merry Wives of Windsor.

3. APOCRYPHAL DRAMAS

Arden = Arden of Feversham.
Cromw. = The Life and Death of Thomas Lord Cromwell.
Edw. III = King Edward III.
Em = Fair Em.
Kins. = The Two Noble Kinsmen.
Locr. = Locrine.
Merl. = The Birth of Merlin.

Merry D. = The Merry Devil of Edmonton.
More = The Book of Sir Thomas More.
Muced. = Mucedorus.
Oldc. = Sir John Oldcastle.
Prod. S. = The London Prodigal Son.
Yorksh. = A Yorkshire Tragedy.

4. OTHER ABBREVIATIONS (not included under 1–3)

Abhdl. = Abhandlungen.
Beih. = Beiheft.
Beil. = Beilage.
C.U.P. = Cambridge University Press.
Diss. = Dissertation.
Dt. = Deutsch.
F 1 = Folio 1.
H. = Heft.

Jb. = Jahrbuch.
Jbb. = Jahrbücher.
Jg. = Jahrgang.
O.U.P. = Oxford University Press.
Progr. = Schulprogramm.
Q 1 = Quarto 1.
Rdsch. = Rundschau.
Rev. = Reviews.

A. GENERAL

I. SHAKESPEARE BIBLIOGRAPHY

[JOHN WILSON]: Catalogue of all the books, pamphlets, etc. relating to Shakespeare. London, printed for John Wilson, 1827. (xlii, 70 pp.)

J. O. HALLIWELL: Shakesperiana. A catalogue of the early editions of Shakespeare's plays and of the commentaries and other publications illustrative of his works. London, 1841. (46 pp.)

P. H. SILLIG: Die Shakespeare-Literatur bis Mitte 1854. Ein bibliographischer Versuch, eingeführt von H. Ulrici. Leipzig, 1854. (viii, 99 S.)

FRANZ THIMM: Shakespeariana from 1564 to 1864. An account of the Shakespearian literature of England, Germany, France, and other European countries during three centuries, with bibliographical introductions. London, 1865 (vi, 92 pp.); 1872² (viii, 120 pp.).

Shakespeare-Bibliographie in: Jahrbuch der Deutschen Shakespeare-Gesellschaft. Compiled by: ALBERT COHN 1865–99, RICHARD SCHRÖDER 1900–6, HANS DAFFIS 1907–18, EDUARD HARTL 1919–28.

Catalogue of the works of William Shakespeare, original and translated, together with the Shakespeariana embraced in the Barton Collection of the *Boston Public Library*, by JAMES MASCARENE HUBBARD. Boston, 1880. (227 pp.)

LUDWIG UNFLAD: Die Shakespeare-Literatur in Deutschland. Versuch einer bibliographischen Zusammenstellung der in Deutschland erschienenen Gesamt- und Einzel-Ausgaben Shakespeares und der literarischen Erscheinungen über Shakespeare und seine Werke von 1762 bis 1879. München, 1880. (57 S.) Rev.: Litbl. 2, Sp. 285.

British Museum. Catalogue of printed books. William Shakespeare. [By G. FORTESCUE.] London, 1897. (232 pp.) Rev.: Bbl. 11, 1900, pp. 33–5, R. Fischer.

City of *Birmingham.* An index to the *Shakespeare Memorial Library,* by A. CAPEL SHAW. Birmingham, 1903. (viii, 265 pp.) Rev.: Bbl. 15, 1904, pp. 123–6, H. G. Fiedler.

Katalog der Bibliothek der Deutschen Shakespeare-Gesellschaft. Weimar, 1909. (vi, 88 S.)

ALBERT H. TOLMAN: Select general bibliography [of Shakespeare]. In the same writer's Questions on Shakespeare, Part I, Chicago (1910), pp. 103–97. Rev.: Sh. Jb. 47, 1911, pp. 292/3, Schücking.

Shakespeare-bibliography. In: Cambr. Hist. of Engl. Literature, vol. 5, 1910, pp. 426–72.

WILLIAM JAGGARD: Shakespeare bibliography. A dictionary of every known issue of the writings of our national poet and of recorded opinion thereon in the English language. Stratford-on-Avon, 1911. (xxiii, 729 pp.) Rev.: Libr. 3rd ser., vol. 2, 1911, pp. 331–5.

Very detailed bibliography of English Shakespearean literature, arranged alphabetically.

H. H. B. MEYER: A brief guide to the literature of Shakespeare. American Library Assoc. Publishing Board. Chicago, 1915. (61 pp.)

HENRIETTA C. BARTLETT: Catalogue of the exhibition of Shakespeare held at the New York Public Library, April to June 1916. New York, 1917. (161 pp.)

C. H. HERFORD: A sketch of recent Shakesperian investigation < 1893–1923 > London, n.d. (vii, 58 pp.)

A critical survey.

SIDNEY LEE and EDMUND CHAMBERS: A Shakespeare reference library. London, 1925². (18 pp.)=The English Assoc. Pamphl. no. 61.

SAMUEL A. TANNENBAUM: A classified Shakespeare bibliography for 1927. New York, 1928.

The bibliography is continued and supplemented in The Shakespeare Assoc. Bulletin, publ. by The Shakespeare Assoc. of America, New York, vol. 1, 1926 seq.

PERCY SIMPSON: The bibliographical study of Shakespeare. In: Oxford Bibliogr. Soc. Proc. and Papers, Part I, 1922–23, Oxford, 1923, pp. 19–53.

II. ELIZABETHAN LITERATURE

(1) BIBLIOGRAPHY

W. H. LOWNDES: The bibliographer's manual of English literature, containing an account of rare, curious and useful books . . . from the invention of printing. New ed. by H. G. BOHN. 6 vols. London, 1864.

J. PAYNE COLLIER: A bibliographical and critical account of the rarest books in the English language. 4 vols. New York, 1866.

British Museum. Catalogue of books in the library of the British Museum printed in England, Scotland, and Ireland, and of books in English printed abroad to the year 1640. Compiled by A. H. BULLEN. 3 vols. London, 1884.

ROBERT W. LOWE: A bibliographical account of English theatrical literature from the earliest times to the present day. London, 1888. (xii, 384 pp.)

Catalogue of original and early editions of some of the poetical and prose works of English writers from Langland to Wither. New York, Grolier Club, 1893. (xiii, 240 pp.)

SIDNEY LEE: A catalogue of Shakespeareana. With a prefatory essay. London, 1899. (xlviii, 504 pp.)

Annual *bibliography* of English language and literature. Ed. for the Modern Humanities Research Assoc. by A. C. PAUES, vol. 6 seq. by D. EVERETT, E. Seaton and M. S. Serjeantson. 1920 et seq.

The Year's *Work* in English Studies. Ed. for the English Assoc. by SIR SIDNEY LEE, F. S. BOAS and C. H. HERFORD. London, 1921 et seq.

HARDIN CRAIG: Recent literature of the English Renaissance. In: Stud. in Phil. [In the April number of each volume.]

JAMES B. CHILDS: Sixteenth century books. A bibliography of literature describing books printed between 1501 and 1601. Chicago Univ. Pr. 1925= Bibliogr. Soc. of America Papers, 17, pp. 73–152.

A. W. POLLARD and G. R. REDGRAVE: A short-title catalogue of books printed in England, Scotland and Ireland, and of English books printed abroad, 1475–1640. London, for the Bibliogr. Soc. 1926. (xvi, 609 pp.)

(2) DICTIONARIES OF PLAYS AND DRAMATISTS

GERARD LANGBAINE: Momus triumphans, or, the plagiaries of the English stage, exposed in a catalogue of all the comedies, tragicomedies, masques, and tragedies, operas, pastorals, interludes, etc. both ancient and modern that were ever yet printed in English, the names of their known and supposed authors, their several volumes and editions. London, 1688. (32 pp. and index.)

GERARD LANGBAINE: An account of the English dramatick poets, or, some observations and remarks on the lives and writings of all those that have publish'd either comedies, tragedies, tragicomedies, pastorals, masques, interludes, farces, or operas in the English tongue. Oxford, 1691. (556 pp. and index.)

GERARD LANGBAINE: The lives and characters of the English dramatick poets. Also an exact account of all the plays that were ever yet printed in the English tongue. Improved and continued down to this time by a careful hand [CHARLES GILDON]. London, 1698.

GILES JACOB: The poetical register, or the lives and characters of the English dramatick poets, with an account of their writings. London, 1719, 1720.

WHINCOP: Compleat list of all the English dramatic poets and of all the plays ever printed in the English language to the present year, 1747.

G. LANGBAINE: The lives of the English poets, digested in alphabetical order. With a particular account of their dramatick performances, whether tragedies, tragi-comedies. . . . London, 1751.

[DAVID ERSKINE BAKER]: The companion of the play-house, or, an historical account of all the dramatic writers (and their works) that have appeared in Great Britain and Ireland, from the commencement of our theatrical exhibitions, down to the present year 1764. Composed in the form of a dictionary. In 2 vols. London, 1764.

Vol. 1, Authors; Vol. 2, Plays; both arranged alphabetically.

[DAVID ERSKINE BAKER]: Biographia dramatica, or, a companion to the play-house. . . . A new edition, originally compiled to the year 1764, by D. E. BAKER, continued thence to 1782 by ISAAC REED, and brought down to the end of Nov. 1811 by STEPHEN JONES. 3 vols. London, 1812.

JAMES O. HALLIWELL: A dictionary of old English plays, existing either in print or in manuscript, from the earliest times to the close of the seventeenth century; including also notices of Latin plays written by English authors during the same period. London, 1860. (viii, 296 pp.)

FREDERICK G. FLEAY: Biographical chronicle of the English drama, 1559–1642. 2 vols. London, 1891. (387 and 405 pp.)

WILLIAM CAREW HAZLITT: A manual for the collector and amateur of old English plays. London, 1892.

WALTER W. GREG: A list of English plays, written before 1643, and printed before 1700. London, for the Bibliogr. Soc., 1900.

WILLIAM DAVENPORT ADAMS: A dictionary of the drama. A guide to the plays, playwrights . . . of the United Kingdom and America from the earliest times to the present. Vol. 1, A–G. London, 1904. (viii, 627 pp.)
No further volumes have appeared.

REGINALD CLARENCE: 'The stage' cyclopaedia. A bibliography of plays. An alphabetical list of plays and other stage pieces of which any record can be found since the commencement of the English stage, together with descriptions, authors' names, dates and places of production, and other useful information. London, 1909. (503 pp.)

WALTER W. GREG: Notes on dramatic bibliographers. In: Malone Soc. Coll. I, 1911, parts 4 and 5, pp. 324–40.

FELIX E. SCHELLING: A list of plays and like productions written, acted, or published in England between the years 1558 and 1642. In the same author's Elizabethan drama, 1558–1642, vol. 2. London, 1911, pp. 538–624.

WILHELM CREIZENACH: Verloren gegangene englische Dramen aus dem Zeitalter Shakespeares. In: Sh. Jb. Jg. 54, 1918, S. 42–9.
Supplements and completes Schelling's list.

(3) COLLECTIONS AND SPECIMENS OF THE DRAMA

ROBERT DODSLEY: A select collection of old [English] plays. Publ. by ROBERT DODSLEY. 12 vols. London, 1744. 2nd ed. by I. REED. 12 vols. 1780. New ed. [by J. P. COLLIER]. 12 vols. 1825–27. 4th ed., now first chronologically arranged, revised, and enlarged by W. C. HAZLITT. 15 vols. London, 1874–6.

CHRISTIAN HEINRICH SCHMID: Englisches Theater. Bd. 1–6. Frankfurt, Danzig und Leipzig, 1769–77.

CHARLES LAMB: Specimens of English dramatic poets who lived about the time of Shakespeare. London, 1808. New ed. by I. GOLLANCZ. 2 vols. 1893.

FR. BODENSTEDT: Shakespeares Zeitgenossen und ihre Werke. In Charakteristiken und Übersetzungen. 3 Bde. Berlin, 1858–60.

RICHARD SIMPSON: The school of Shakespere. 2 vols. London, 1878. (xxii, 359 and 492 pp.)

R. PRÖLSS: Altenglisches Theater. 2 Bde. Leipzig (1881).

A. H. BULLEN: A collection of old English plays. 4 vols. London, 1882–5. New series, 3 vols. 1887–90.

ADOLF FRIEDR. GRAF VON SCHACK: Die englischen Dramatiker vor, neben und nach Shakespeare. Stuttgart, 1893. (xii, 500 S.)

ALFRED W. POLLARD: English miracle plays, moralities and interludes. Specimens of the Pre-Elizabethan drama. Oxford, 1898[3], 1923[7]. (lxxii, 250 pp.)

JOHN MATTHEWS MANLY: Specimens of the Pre-Shakesperean drama. With an introd., notes, and a glossary. 2 vols. Boston, 1897, 1898. Rev.: Sh. Jb. 36, 1900, S. 308–9, W. Keller.

ALOIS BRANDL: Quellen des weltlichen Dramas in England vor Shakespeare. Ein Ergänzungsband zu Dodsley's Old English plays. Strassburg, 1898. (cxxvi, 667 S.)=Quellen u. Forschungen, 80. Rev.: Sh. Jb. 35, 1899, S. 339–41, W. Keller; JEGPh. 2, 1900, S. 389–428, J. M. Manly.

W. BANG:

Materialen zur Kunde des älteren englischen Dramas. Louvain, 1902 et seq. The following volumes have been published:

Vol. I. The Blind Beggar of Bednall Green, by HENRY CHETTLE and JOHN DAY, ed. from the quarto of 1659 by W. BANG. (x, 80 pp.)
II. The King and Queenes Entertainement at Richmond, ed. from the quarto of 1636 by W. BANG and R. BROTANEK. (x, 35 pp.)
III. THOMAS HEYWOOD's Pleasant Dialogues and Dramma's, ed. from the octavo of 1637 by W. BANG. (xii, 380 pp.)
IV. *Everyman*, reprinted by W. W. GREG from the edition by John Skot preserved at Britwell Court. (viii, 32 pp.)
V. A newe Enterlude of Godly Queene Hester, ed. from the quarto of 1561 by W. W. GREG. (xvi, 62 pp.)
VI. The Devil's Charter, by BARNABE BARNES, ed. from the quarto of 1607 by R. B. MCKERROW. (xxiii, 144 pp.)
VII. BEN JONSON's Dramas, reprinted from the folio of 1616 by W. BANG. 1st part (276 pp.); 2nd part (276 pp.)
VIII. *Pedantius*, a Latin comedy formerly acted in Trinity College, Cambridge, ed. by G. C. MOORE SMITH. (lvi, 164 pp.)
IX. E. KOEPPEL: Studien über Shakespeares Wirkung auf zeitgenössische Dramatiker. (xi, 103 pp.)
X. BEN JONSON's Every Man in his Humor, reprinted from the quarto of 1601 by W. BANG and W. W. GREG. (88 pp.)
XI. BEN JONSON's Sad Shepherd, with Waldron's Continuation, ed. by W. W. GREG. (xxv, 99 pp.)
XII. The Enterlude of Youth, with fragments of the Playe of Lucres and of Nature, ed. by W. BANG and R. B. MCKERROW. (xxiv, 108 pp.)

XIII. The Queen, or the Excellency of her Sex, ed. from the quarto of 1653 by W. BANG. (ix, 60 pp.)

XIV. Victoria, a Latin comedy, by ABRAHAM FRAUNCE, ed. from the Penshurst MS. by G. C. MOORE SMITH. (xl, 130 pp.)

XV. CH. CRAWFORD: A concordance to the works of Thomas Kyd. 1st part (200 pp.); 2nd part (200 pp.); 3rd part (290 pp.).

XVI. BEN JONSON's Every Man out of his Humor, reprinted from Holme's Quarto of 1600 by W. BANG and W. W. GREG . (viii, 128 pp.)

XVII. BEN JONSON's Every Man out of his Humor, reprinted from Linge's Quarto of 1600 by W. BANG and W. W. GREG. (v, 128 pp.)

XVIII. ANTHONY BREWER's The Love-Sick King, ed. from the quarto of 1655 by A. E. H. SWAEN. (xv, 64 pp.)

XIX. H. MAAS: Äussere Geschichte der englischen Theatertruppen in dem Zeitraum von 1559 bis 1642. 1. Teil. (x, 283 S.)

XX. Satiro-Mastix, or the Untrussing of the Humorous Poet, by THOMAS DEKKER, reprinted from the editions of 1602 by H. SCHERER. (xvi, 136 pp.)

XXI. A. FEUILLERAT: Documents relating to the Office of the Revels in the time of Queen Elizabeth. (xvii, 512 pp.)

XXII. BEN JONSON's The Fountain of Self-Love, or Cynthias Revels, reprinted from the quarto of 1601 by W. BANG and L. KREBS, (92 pp.)

XXIII. JOHN FORDE's Dramatic Works, reprinted from the original quartos by W. BANG. 1st part: with an introductory essay: Forde's contribution to the decadence of the drama, by S. P. SHERMAN, and a reprint of DEKKER's Penny-Wise, Pound-Foolish. (xix, 210 pp.)

XXIV. *Everyman*. Reprinted by W. W. GREG from the edition by John Skot in the possession of Mr. A. H. Huth. (viii, 32 pp.)

XXV. BALE's Kynge Johan, from the MS. in the Chatsworth Collection, ed. in facsimile by W. BANG.

XXVI. Sir Gyles Goosecappe, ed. from the quarto of 1606 by W. BANG and R. BROTANEK. 1st part (75 pp.)

XXVII. E. ECKHARDT: Die Dialekt- u. Ausländertypen des älteren engl. Dramas. Teil 1: Die Dialekttypen. (xv, 159 S.)

XXVIII. *Everyman*. Reprinted by W. W. GREG from the fragments of two editions by PYNSON, preserved in the Bodleian Library and the British Museum, together with critical apparatus. (vi, 69 pp.)

XXIX. C. C. STOPES: William Hunnis and the Revels of the Chapel Royal. A study of his period and the influences which affected Shakespeare. (xiv, 363 pp.)

XXX. NATHANAEL RICHARDS' Tragedy of Messallina, the Roman Emperesse, ed. by A. R. SKEMP. (xv, 63 and 160 pp.)

XXXI. DANIEL's The Tragedy of Cleopatra, reprinted from the edition of 1611 by M. LEDERER. (xvi, 99 pp.)

XXXII. E. ECKHARDT: Die Dialekt- und Ausländertypen des älteren engl. Dramas. 2. Teil: Die Ausländertypen. (xxxii, 190 S.)

XXXIII. A Newe Interlude of Impacyente Pouerte, ed. from the quarto of 1560 by R. B. MCKERROW. (xix, 70 pp.)

XXXIV. CH. CRAWFORD: The Marlowe concordance. 1st part (xx, 220 pp.); 2nd part (160 pp.); 3rd part (160 pp.).

XXXV. How a Man may chuse a Good Wife from a Bad, ed. by A. E. H. SWAEN. (xliii, 120 pp.)

XXXVI. EDWARD SHARPHAM's The Fleire, ed. from the quarto of 1607 by
H. NIBBE. (47, 89 pp.)

XXXVII. JOHN MASON's The Turke, ed. from the quartos of 1610 and 1632 by
J. Q. ADAMS, JR. (xxv, 104 pp.)

XXXVIII. STUDLEY's Translations of Seneca's Agamemnon and Medea, ed.
from the octavos of 1566 by E. M. SPEARING. (xxiii, 252 pp.)

XXXIX. A Tale of a Tub, reprinted from the edition of 1640 by H. SCHERER.
(xv, 90 pp.)

XL. WILLIAM HEMING's The Jewes Tragedy, ed. from the quarto of 1662
by H. A. COHN. (xi, 106, 91 pp.)

XLI. JASPER HEYWOOD and his translations of Seneca's Troas, Thyestes
and Hercules Furens, ed. from the octavos of 1559, 1560 and 1561
by H. DE VOCHT. (lvii, 355 pp.)

XLII. WILLIAM SAMPSON's Vow-Breaker, ed. by H. WALLRATH (60, 82 pp.)

XLIII. THOMAS MAY's Tragedy of Julia Agrippina, Empresse of Rome, with
an essay about the Tragedy Nero and Thomas May by F. E. SCHMID.
(lxxxv, 217 pp.)

XLIV. A. FEUILLERAT: Documents relating to the Revels at Court in the time
of King Edward VI and Queen Mary, ed. from the Loseley MSS.,
with notes and indexes. (xv, 340 pp.)

New Series:

I. JOHN FORDE's Dramatic Works, reprinted from the original quartos.
2nd part. Ed. by H. DE VOCHT. 1928.

The Malone Society Publications. Oxford, 1907 et seq.:

1907

The Battle of Alcazar, by G. PEELE, 1594.

The History of Orlando Furioso, by R. GREENE, 1594.

The Interlude of Johan the Evangelist. (Waley's undated edition.)

The Interlude of Wealth and Health. (Waley, 1557?)

The History of King Leir, 1605.

Collections, Vol. I, Part i, containing Notes on the Publications, 'Love Feigned
and Unfeigned', 'The Prodigal Son', The Elizabethan Lords Chamberlain,
and Dramatic Records from the City Remembrancia.

1908

The Interlude of Calisto and Melebea, by J. RASTELL? (J. Rastell's undated
edition.)

The Tragedy of Locrine, by W. S., 1595.

The Life of Sir John Oldcastle, by MUNDAY, DRAYTON, WILSON, and HATHWAY,
1600.

The Tragical Reign of Selimus, by R. GREENE?, 1594.

The Old Wives Tale, by G. P(EELE), 1595.

Collections, Vol. I, Part ii, containing Notes on the Publications, Rules for
Editors, 'Robin Hood and the Sheriff of Nottingham', 'A Play of Robin Hood
for May-Games', 'The Play of Lucrece' (a fragment of 'Fulgens and Lucres'),
and Dramatic Records from the Lansdowne Manuscripts.

1909

The Play of Patient Grissell, by JOHN PHILLIP. (Colwell's undated edition.)

Iphigenia at Aulis, translated by LADY LUMLEY. Ed. from the original MS.
(Royal 15 A. ix).

The Virtuous Octavia, by s. BRANDON. (Undated edition [1598].)

Fidele and Fortunio, the two Italian Gentlemen, by A. MUNDAY? (Devonshire copy (imperfect) of the edition of 1585.)

The Second Maiden's Tragedy. Edited from the playhouse MS. (Lansd. 807), licensed October 31, 1611.

Collections, Vol. I, Part iii, containing Notes on the Publications, 'Albion Knight', 'Temperance and Humility', James I at Oxford in 1605, and Royal Patents for Players.

1910

The Arraignment of Paris, by G. PEELE, 1584.

Tom Tyler and His Wife, 1661 ('The second impression').

The Wounds of Civil War, by T. LODGE, 1594.

A Knack to Know an Honest Man, 1596.

The Birth of Hercules. Edited from the MS. (B.M. Add. 28722).

1911

Apius and Virginia, by R. B., 1575.

King Edward the First, by G. PEELE, 1593.

The Comedy of George a Green, 1599.

The Tragedy of Caesar's Revenge (Caesar and Pompey). (Undated edition [1606? reissued 1607].)

The Book of Sir Thomas More, edited from the playhouse MS. (Harl. 7368).

Collections, Vol. I, Parts iv and v, containing Notes on the Publications, Quotations in Bodenham's 'Belvedere', 'The Hunting of Cupid', 'The Cruel Debtor', Notes on Dramatic Bibliographers, A Jotting by J. Aubrey, Two Early Player-Lists, Commissions for the Chapel, Plays of the King's Men in 1641, and Dramatic Records from the Privy Council Register, 1603–42, with four plates.

1912

The Love of King David and Fair Bethsabe, by G. PEELE, 1599.

The Two Angry Women of Abington, by H. PORTER. (Hunt and Ferbrand's edition of 1599).

The Weakest Goeth to the Wall, 1600.

Wily Beguiled, 1606.

Englishmen for my Money, by W. HAUGHTON, 1616.

The Resurrection of Our Lord, edited from an imperfect MS. (belonging to Mr. B. Dobell).

1913

Clyomon and Clamydes, 1599.

Look about you, 1600.

A Larum for London, 1602.

The Contention between Liberality and Prodigality, 1602.

The Wit of a Woman, 1604.

Collections, Vol. II, Part i, containing Blackfriars Records, edited by ALBERT FEUILLERAT.

1914

The Tragedy of Mariam, by LADY E(LIZABETH) C(ARY), 1613.

The Cobler's Prophecy, by R. WILSON, 1594.

The Pedlar's Prophecy, 1595.

Gesta Grayorum (1594). Reprinted from the edition of 1688, together with the Masque of Proteus from MS. Harl. 541.

The Tragedy of Tancred and Gismund, by R. WILMOT and others, 1591–2.
The Tragedy of Tiberius (Claudius Tiberius Nero), 1607.

1920

The Welsh Embassador, edited from the Cardiff MS.
Every Man out of his Humour, by B. J(ONSON). Reprinted from Holme's first edition.

1921

The Scottish History of James the Fourth, by R. GREENE, 1598.
Antonio and Mellida and Antonio's Revenge, by J. M(ARSTON), 1602.

1922

The Christmas Prince (1607–8). Edited from the original MS. (at St. John's College, Oxford).
[Extra Volume.] W. W. GREG: Two Elizabethan Stage Abridgements: The Battle of Alcazar and Orlando Furioso.

1923

John a Kent and John a Cumber. Edited from the Mostyn MS. (now in the Henry E. Huntington Library).
Collections, Vol. II, Part ii, containing Notes on the Publications, 'The Cruel Debtor' (addition), Four Letters on Theatrical Affairs, and The Academic Drama at Cambridge, extracts from the college records edited by G. C. M. Smith.

1924

Designs by INIGO JONES for Masques and Plays at Court. A descriptive catalogue of drawings for scenery and costumes mainly in the Duke of Devonshire's collection, with introduction and notes by P. SIMPSON and C. F. BELL.

1925

The Spanish Tragedy (by T. KYD) with additions, 1602.
Edward the Second, by C. MARLOWE, 1594.

1926

Alphonsus King of Aragon, by R. G(REENE), 1599.
Friar Bacon and Friar Bungay, by R. GREENE, 1594.

1927

Believe as you list, by PHILIP MASSINGER, 1631.
Fair Em.
Edmond Ironside, or, War hath made all friends.

1928

The Blind Beggar of Alexandria, by GEORGE CHAPMAN, 1598.
The Parliament of Love.
The Massacre of Paris, by CHRISTOPHER MARLOWE.

1929

The True Tragedy of Richard III, 1594.
The 1st part of the Reign of King Richard II, or, Thomas of Woodstock.

Tudor Facsimile Texts.

Exact collotype reproductions of old English plays, printed and MS. rarities, under the general editorship of JOHN S. FARMER. 1907–14. The following volumes have been published:

R. A—: The Valiant Welshman, or The True Chronicle History of the life and valiant deeds of Caradoc the Great, 1615.

ROBERT ARMIN: History of the Two Maids of More-Clacke, 1609.

BARNEBE BARNES: The Devil's Charter: a Tragedie, conteining the Life and Death of Pope Alexander the Sixt, 1607.

SAMUEL BRANDON: The Tragi-comoedi of the vertuous Octavia, 1598.

GEORGE CHAPMAN: Eastward Hoe, as it is Played in the Blackfriars, by the Children of Her Maiesties Revels made by Geo. Chapman, Ben Jonson, Joh. Marston, 1605.

JOHN COOKE: Greene's Tu-quoque, or the Cittie Gallant, 1614.

T. D—: The Bloodie Banquet: a Tragedie, 1620.

JOHN DAY: The Blind Beggar of Bednal Green, or the merry humour of Tom Strowd, the Norfolk Yeoman, 1659.

DEKKER and WEBSTER: the Famous History of Sir Thomas Wyat, 1607.

THOMAS DEKKER and JOHN WEBSTER: Northward Hoe, 1607.

GEORGE GASCOIGNE: The Glasse of Gouernement: a tragicall Comedie, 1575.

ROBERT GREENE: George a Greene, the Pinner of Wakefield, 1599.

ROBERT GREENE: The Honorable History of Frier Bacon and Frier Bongay, 1594.

WILLIAM HAUGHTON: Englishmen for my Money, or a Pleasant Comedy, called, 'A Woman will have her Will', 1616.

JOHN HEYWOOD: The Play, called, 'The Four PP.', c. 1545.

JOHN HEYWOOD: Of Gentleness and Nobility, c. 1535.

JOHN HEYWOOD: John John the Husband, Tib his Wife, and Sir John the Priest, c. 1533.

JOHN HEYWOOD: The Pardoner and the Frere, c. 1521.

JOHN HEYWOOD: Play of the Weather, 1533.

JOHN HEYWOOD: The Play of Love, 1533.

T. HUGHES: Certaine Deuises and Shewes presented to Her Maiestie by the Gentlemen of Grayes-Inne [The Misfortunes of Arthur], 1587.

THOMAS LODGE and ROBERT GREENE: A Looking Glasse for London and Englande, 1598.

JOHN LYLY: The Maydes Metamorphosis, 1600.

CHR. MARLOWE: The Tragicall History of D. Faustus, 1604.

MARLOWE and NASHE: the Tragedie of Dido, Queene of Carthage, played by the Children of Her Maiestie's Chappell, 1594.

MIDDLETON and DEKKER: The Roaring Girle, or Moll Cut-Purse, 1611.

ANTHONY MUNDAY: The Death of Robert, Earle of Huntington, otherwise called, 'Robin Hood of Merry Sherwodde', 1601.

ANTHONY MUNDAY: The Downfall of Robert, Earl of Huntington . . . with his love of chaste Matilda, the Lord Fitzwater's daughter, afterwardes his faire Maide Marion, 1601.

HENRY PORTER: The Pleasant Historye of the two angrye women of Abington, with the humourous mirth of Dickie Coomes, 1599.

S. ROWLEY: The Noble Souldier, or a Contract broken justly reveng'd, 1634.

SHAKESPEARE: The Tragedy of King Richard the Third, 1597.

NATHANIEL WOODES: The Conflict of Conscience, 1581.

R. WILMOT: The Tragedy of Tancred and Gesmund, compiled by the Gentlemen of the Inner Temple, 1592.

ROBERT WILSON: The Three Ladies of London, 1584.

ROBERT WILSON: The Three Lordes and three Ladies of London, 1590.

ROBERT WILSON: The Cobler's Prophecie, 1594.

ROBERT WILSON: The Pedler's Prophecie, 1595.

ROBERT YARINGTON: Two Lamentable Tragedies, 1601.

Anonymous Plays

Caesar and Pompey, or Caesar's Revenge, privately acted by the Studentes of Trinity Colledge in Oxford, 1607.

The Famous Historye of the Life and Death of Captain Thomas Stukeley, 1605.

Everie Woman in her Humor, 1609.

Grim, the Collier of Croyden, or The Devil and his Dance, by J. T., 1662.

The Famous Victories of Henry the Fift, containing the Honourable Battell of Agin-Court, 1598.

Life and Death of Jacke Straw, a notable Rebell in England, who was kild in Smithfield, 1593.

Knacke to Know an honest Man, 1596.

A Larum for London, or the Siedge of Antwerpe, 1602.

Lingua, or The Combat of the Tongue and the five Senses for Superiority, 1607.

The Tragedie of Claudius Nero, Rome's greatest Tyrant, 1607.

Nobody and Somebody, with the true Chronicle Historie of Elydure, who was fortunately three severall times crowned King of England (*circa* 1592).

A Mery Geste of Robyn Hoode, and of hys lyfe (*circa* 1558).

The True Tragedie of Richarde, Duke of Yorke, and the death of good King Henrie the Sixt, 1600.

The Historie of the Two valiant Knights Sir Clyomon . . . and Clamydes, the White Knight, 1599.

Sir Gyles Goosecappe, Knight. A Comedie, presented by the Children of the Chappell, 1606.

Solimon and Perseda; wherein is laid open Loues constancie, Fortunes inconstancie, and Death's Triumphs, 1599.

Swetnam: The Woman-Hater arraigned by Women, 1620.

Thersytes: thys Interlude . . . Dothe Declare howe the greatest boesters are not the greatest doers (*circa* 1550).

Tryall of Chevalry, with the Life and Death of Cavaliero, Dicke Bowyer, 1605.

Two Wise Men and all the Rest Fooles, or a Comicall Morall censuring the follies of this age, 1619.

A Warning for Fair Women, containing the most tragical and lamentable murther of Master George Sander, of London, Marchant, nigh Shooters hill, 1599.

Warres of Cyrus, King of Persia, against Antiochus, King of Assyria, 1594.

The Weakest goeth to the Wall, 1600.

Wily Beguilde. A Pleasant Comedie, 1606.

The Wit of a Woman, 1604.

J. QUINCY ADAMS: Chief Pre-Shakespearean dramas. London, n.d. (iv, 712 pp.)

WILLIAM ALLAN NEILSON: The chief Elizabethan dramatists excluding Shakespeare. Selected plays by Lyly, Peele, Greene, Marlowe, Kyd, Chapman, Jonson, Dekker, Marston, Heywood, Beaumont, Fletcher, Webster, Middleton, Massinger, Ford, Shirley. Ed. from the original quartos and folios, with notes, biographies, and bibliographies. Boston, 1911. (vi, 880 pp.), Rev.: Sh. Jb. 48, 1912, S. 291, Churchill.

FELIX E. SCHELLING: Typical Elizabethan plays by contemporaries and immediate successors of Shakespeare. New York & London, 1926. (x, 797 pp.)

E. H. A. C. OLIPHANT: Shakespeare and his fellow dramatists, a selection of plays illustrating the glories of the golden age of English drama. 2 vols. New York, 1929. (xx, 1177 and xiii, 1173 pp.) Rev.: Rev. anglo-amér. 7, 1929, pp. 149–50, A. Brulé.

45 plays, arranged in chronological order.

(4) GENERAL ACCOUNTS OF THE ELIZABETHAN DRAMA

J. PAYNE COLLIER: The history of English dramatic poetry to the time of Shakespeare, and annals of the stage to the Restoration. 3 vols. London, 1831, 1879. (xxxvi, 454; vi, 488; vi, 508 pp.)

A. MÉZIÈRES: Prédécesseurs et contemporains de Shakespeare. Paris, 1863, 1881³. (xv, 367 pp.)

A. MÉZIÈRES: Contemporains et successeurs de Shakespeare. Paris, 1864², 1897⁴.

J. L. KLEIN: Geschichte des Dramas. 13 Bde. Leipzig, 1865–86.

Vols. 12 and 13 deal with the English Drama.

W. C. HAZLITT: The English drama and stage under the Tudor and Stuart princes, 1543–1664. Illustrated by a series of documents, treatises and poems. Printed for the Roxburghe Library, 1869.

ADOLPHUS WILLIAM WARD: A history of English dramatic literature to the death of Queen Anne. 2 vols. London, 1875. New and rev. ed. 3 vols. London, 1899. (xiii, 575; xii, 766; xix, 599 pp.) Rev.: Sh. Jb. 36, 1900, S. 288–90, W. Keller; Bbl. 12, 1901, S. 49–59, R. Brotanek.

English standard work on the drama treated biographically.

J. J. JUSSERAND: Le théâtre en Angleterre depuis la conquête jusqu'aux prédécesseurs immédiats de Shakespeare. Paris, 1878, 1881².

W. HERTZBERG: Shakespeare und seine Vorläufer. In: Sh. Jb. Jg. 15, 1880, S. 360–409.

A. MÉZIÈRES: Contemporains de Shakespeare. Paris, 1881.

R. PRÖLSS: Geschichte des neueren Dramas. 3 Bde. 1881–3.

J. ADD. SYMONDS: Shakspere's predecessors in the English drama. London, 1884, 1900. (xx, 552 pp.)

WILHELM CREIZENACH: Geschichte des neueren Dramas. 5 Bde. Halle a. S., 1893 seq., 1911 seq.[2] Engl. transl. of the 4th vol. under the title: The English drama in the age of Shakespeare. London, 1916. (467 pp.) Rev.: Sh. Jb. 54, 1918, S. 141–4, Brie; Bbl. 7, 1897, S. 4–7, W. Wetz; Bbl. 28, 1917, S. 161–71, Ph. Aronstein.
Vols. 4 and 5 deal with the drama of Shakespeare's time in chronological order.

FREDERICK S. BOAS: Shakespeare and his predecessors. London, 1896. (viii, 556 pp.) Rev.: Bbl. 7, 1897, S. 195–209, R. Fischer.

SIDNEY LANIER: Shakespeare and his forerunners. Studies in Elizabethan poetry and its development from Early English. 2 vols. New York, 1902. (xxiv, 324 and xix, 329 pp.) Rev.: Sh. Jb. 39, 1903, S. 266–7, A. Brandl.

THOMAS SECCOMBE and J. W. ALLEN: The age of Shakespeare (1579–1631). Vol. i: Poetry and prose. Vol. ii: The drama. London, 1903. Rev.: Sh. Jb. 40, 1904, S. 237, Sarrazin.

FELIX E. SCHELLING: Elizabethan drama, 1558–1642. A history of the drama in England from the accession of Queen Elizabeth to the closing of the theaters, to which is prefixed a résumé of the earlier drama from its beginnings. 2 vols. London, 1908, 1911. (xliii, 666 and x, 685 pp.) Rev.: JEGPh. 12, 1913, pp. 677–82, R. A. Law; MLR. 5, 1910, pp. 211–20, W. W. Greg.
Description of the drama from the point of view of contents and according to the different types of drama.

FELIX E. SCHELLING: English literature during the lifetime of Shakespeare. New York and London, 1910, 1927[2]. (xv, 486 pp.), 1928[3]. Rev.: Sh. Jb. 48, 1912, S. 291–3, A. Brandl.

Cambridge history of English literature. Gen. editors: A. W. WARD and A. R. WALLER. Vols. 5, 6. Cambridge, 1910.

W. J. COURTHOPE: A history of English poetry. Vol. 4: Development and decline of the poetic drama; influence of the court and the people. London, 1911. (xxix, 476 pp.)

C. F. TUCKER BROOKE: The Tudor drama. A history of English national drama to the retirement of Shakespeare. London, 1912. (xiii, 461 pp.) Rev.: Sh. Jb. 49, 1913, S. 250–1, M. Förster; JEGPh. 12, 1913, pp. 677–82, R. A. Law.

CHARLES WILLIAM WALLACE: The evolution of the English drama up to Shakespeare. With a history of the first Blackfriars Theatre. Berlin, 1912. (xxi, 246 S.)=Schriften d. Dt. Sh. Ges., Bd. 4. Rev.: Sh. Jb. 49, 1913, S. 210–14, W. Keller.

VILHELM GRØNBECH: Shakespeare og det førshakespeareske drama. In: Edda, Bd. 6, 1916, S. 75–91. Rev.: Sh. Jb. 54, 1918, S. 150–1, Jantzen.

ARTHUR SYMONS: Studies in the Elizabethan drama. London, 1920. (261 pp.)

JANET SPENS: Elizabethan drama. London (1922). (ix, 148 pp.)

G. B. HARRISON: Shakespeare's fellows; being a brief chronicle of the Shakespearean age. London, 1923. (207 pp.)

G. B. HARRISON: The story of Elizabethan drama. Cambridge, 1924. (xii, 134 pp.)

FELIX E. SCHELLING: Elizabethan playwrights. A short history of the English drama from the beginning to the closing of the theaters in 1642. London, 1925. (xiv, 335 pp.) Rev.: Sh. Jb. 63, 1927, S. 208, W. Keller; MLN. 42, 1927, pp. 133–4, F. M. Padelford.

EDUARD ECKHARDT: Das englische Drama im Zeitalter der Reformation und der Hochrenaissance. Vorstufen, Shakespeare und seine Zeit. Berlin, 1928. (xii, 291 S.) Rev.: Sh. Jb. 65, 1929, S. 196–7, W. Keller.

PHILIPP ARONSTEIN: Das englische Renaissancedrama. Leipzig u. Berlin, 1929. (x, 336 S.) Rev.: Sh. Jb. 65, 1929, S. 198–9, W. Keller; E. St. 65, 1930, S. 98–100, W. Franz.
Treated chronologically and in relation to contemporary society.

EDUARD ECKHARDT: Das englische Drama der Spätrenaissance. (Shakespeares Nachfolger). Berlin und Leipzig, 1929. (202 S.)

A. d' ANCONA: Origini del teatro italiano. 1891.

E. RIGAL: Le théâtre français avant la période classique. 1901.

H. A. RENNERT: The Spanish stage in the time of Lope de Vega. 1909.

(5) VARIOUS TYPES OF DRAMA
(a) TRAGEDY

H. W. SINGER: Das bürgerliche Trauerspiel in England (bis zum Jahre 1800). Diss. Leipzig, 1891. (128 S.)

RUDOLF FISCHER: Zur Kunstentwicklung der englischen Tragödie von ihren ersten Anfängen bis zu Shakespeare. Strassburg, 1893. Rev.: Bbl. 5, 1895, S. 1–3, L. Proescholdt.

ASHLEY H. THORNDIKE: The relations of Hamlet to contemporary revenge plays. In: PMLA., vol. 17, n.s. vol. 10, 1902, pp. 125–220.

LUDWIG WINCKLER: Über die Blutrachetragödien in der elisabethanischen Literatur. Diss. Halle, 1907. (33 S.)

ASHLEY H. THORNDIKE: Tragedy. Boston & New York, 1908. (vi, 390 pp.)= Types of English literature, ed. by W. A. Neilson. Rev.: Sh. Jb. 45, 1909, S. 319–20, W. Keller.

OSCAR BALLWEG: Das klassizistische Drama zur Zeit Shakespeares. Heidelberg, 1909. (120 S.)=Beitr. z. neueren Lit. gesch., hrsg. W. Wetz, Bd. 1, H. 3. Rev.: Sh. Jb. 47, 1911, S. 325, Schücking.

JOHN W. CUNLIFFE: Early English classical tragedies. Ed. with introduction and notes. Oxford, 1912. (c, 352 pp.) Rev.: Sh. Jb. 49, 1913, S. 251–2, M. Förster.
With detailed introduction.

ALWINE WINKLER: Thomas Heywood's A Woman killed with kindness und das Ehebruchsdrama seiner Zeit. Diss. Jena, 1915. (67 S.) Rev.: Sh. Jb. 55, 1919, S. 170–1, W. Keller.

L. M. ELLISON: The early romantic drama at the English court. 1917.

A. W. REED: The beginnings of the English secular and romantic drama. Oxford, 1922. (31 pp.)

ALEXANDER M. WITHERSPOON: The influence of Robert Garnier on Elizabethan drama. New Haven & London, 1924. (vi, 197 pp.)
For the influence of Seneca on the English drama cf. Section VI.

(b) COMEDY

WINIFRED SMITH: Italian and Elizabethan comedy. In: Mod. Phil., vol. 5, 1907/8, pp. 553–67.

F. S. BOAS: Early English comedy. In: CHEL., vol. 5, 1910, pp. 89–120.
With very full bibliography.

CHARLES M. GAYLEY: Representative English comedies. With introductory essays and notes. Vol. i: From the beginnings to Shakespeare. Vols. ii, iii: The later contemporaries of Shakespeare. New York, 1912, 1913, 1914. (xcii, 686; lix, 586; xcvii, 663 pp.) Rev.: Sh. Jb. 50, 1914, S. 227–8, M. Förster.

OLA ELIZABETH WINSLOW: Low comedy as a structural element in English drama from the beginnings to 1642. Diss. Chicago, 1926. (186 pp.)

(c) SCHOOL AND UNIVERSITY DRAMA

GEORGE B. CHURCHILL und WOLFGANG KELLER: Die lateinischen Universitätsdramen Englands in der Zeit der Königin Elisabeth. Mit Vorwort von A. Brandl. In: Sh. Jb. 34, 1898, S. 221–323.
Contents: (i) Religious Drama; (ii) Classical Tragedy; (iii) Imitations of Seneca; (iv) Historical Plays; (v) School Comedy; (vi) National Comedy; (vii) Italian Comedy; (viii) Pastoral Plays.

G. P. BAKER: The plays of the university wits. In: CHEL., vol. 5, 1910, pp. 121–41.
With detailed bibliography.

FREDERICK S. BOAS: University plays. In: CHEL., vol. 6, 1910, pp. 293–327.
With detailed bibliography.

LOUISE B. MORGAN: The Latin university drama. By way of supplement to the article by George B. Churchill and Wolfgang Keller in Jb. 34. In: Sh. Jb. 47, 1911, S. 69–91.

FREDERICK S. BOAS: University drama in the Tudor age. Oxford, 1914. (xi, 414 pp.) Rev.: JEGPh. 14, 1915, pp. 620–24, C. R. Baskervill; MLR. 11, 1916, pp. 358–60, E. K. Chambers.

G. C. MOORE SMITH: The academic drama at Cambridge. Extracts from college records. 1923=Malone Soc. Coll., vol. ii, part ii, pp. 150–230.

G. C. MOORE SMITH: College plays performed in the university of Cambridge. Cambridge, 1923. (viii, 110 pp.)

T. H. VAIL MOTTER: The school drama in England. London & New York, 1929. (325 pp.)

(d) CHRONICLE PLAYS

FELIX E. SCHELLING: The English chronicle play. A study in the popular historical literature environing Shakespeare. New York, 1902. (xi, 310 pp.) Rev.: Sh. Jb. 39, 1903, S. 310–13, Churchill; JEGPh. 4, 1902, pp. 94–100, J. W. Tupper.

Marlowe's Edward II. Edited by WILLIAM D. BRIGGS. London, 1914. (cxxx, 221 pp.) Rev.: Bbl. 25, 1914, S. 312–14, E. Einenkel; Sh. Jb. 50, 1914, S. 235, M. Förster.

The introduction contains a good and detailed account of the history of the chronicle plays.

(e) MASQUES

ALFRED SOERGEL: Die englischen Maskenspiele. Diss. Halle, 1882.

H. A. EVANS: English masques. 1897.

RUDOLF BROTANEK: Die englischen Maskenspiele. Wien und Leipzig, 1902= Wiener Beitr. z. engl. Phil., hrsg. von Schipper, 15. Rev.: Sh. Jb. 40, 1904, S. 250–2, W. Keller; Bbl. 14, 1903, S. 257–8, v. Westenholz.

WALTER W. GREG: A list of masques, pageants, etc. supplementary to A List of English plays. London, for the Bibliogr. Soc., 1902.

J. W. CUNLIFFE: Italian prototypes of the masque and dumb show. In: PMLA., vol. 22, n.s. vol. 15, 1907, pp. 140–56.

F. E. SCHELLING: The English masque. In his: Elizabethan drama. London, 1908. Vol. 2, pp. 93–138.

PAUL REYHER: Les masques anglais. Étude sur les ballets et la vie de cour en Angleterre (1512–1640). Paris, 1909. (x, 563 pp.) Rev.: Sh. Jb. 47, 1911, S. 313–22, Brotanek; MLR. 6, 1911, pp. 529–30, W. W. Greg.

EDWARD DOWDEN: The English masque. In the same writer's Essays modern and Elizabethan. London, 1910, pp. 334–50.

RONALD BEYNE: Masque and pastoral. In: CHEL., vol. 6, 1910, pp. 328–72.

With detailed bibliography.

MARY SULLIVAN: Court masques of James I. Their influence on Shakespeare and the public theatres. New York & London, 1913. (xi, 259 pp.) Rev.: Sh. Jb. 50, 1914, S. 228–9, M. Förster.

PERCY SIMPSON: The masque. In: Shakespeare's England, 1917, vol. ii, pp. 311–33.

ENID WELSFORD: Italian influence on the English court masque. In: MLR., vol. 18, 1923, pp. 394–409.

PERCY SIMPSON and C. F. BELL: Designs by Inigo Jones for masques and plays at court. A descriptive catalogue of drawings for scenery and costumes mainly in the Collection of the Duke of Devonshire. Oxford, printed for the Walpole and Malone Societies, 1924. (viii, 158 pp. and 51 plates.) Rev.: MLR. 20, 1925, pp. 200–5, W. J. Lawrence.

C. R. BASKERVILL: Mummers' wooing plays in England. In: Mod. Phil., vol. 21, 1923/4, pp. 225–72.

MARY SUSAN STEELE: Plays and masques at court during the reigns of Elizabeth, James, and Charles. New Haven, 1926. (xiii, 300 pp.)=Cornell Studies in English, 10. Rev.: RESt. 4, 1928, p. 468, P. S.; MLN. 43, 1928, p. 492, L. B. Wright.

ENID WELSFORD: The court masque. A study in the relationship between poetry and the revels. Cambridge, 1927. (xv, 434 pp.) Rev.: RESt. 4, 1928, pp. 463–7, P. Simpson; MLN. 43, 1928, pp. 492–3, L. B. Wright; Sh. Jb. 63, 1927, S. 207, W. Keller; MLR. 23, 1928, pp. 70–2, E. K. Chambers.

J. A. GOTCH: Inigo Jones. A modern view. In: Essays by divers hands. Being the Trans. Roy. Soc. of Lit. of the United Kingdom, n.s., vol. 7, 1927.

(f) ELIZABETHAN JIG AND SONG DRAMA

CHARLES READ BASKERVILL: The Elizabethan jig and related song drama. Chicago and London, C.U.P. 1929. (x, 642 pp.) Rev.: TLS., May 16, 1929, p. 399; JEGPh. 28, 1929, pp. 551–5, H. E. Rollins; MLN. 45, 1930, pp. 47–9, W. J. Lawrence.

(g) PASTORAL DRAMA

FRED. W. MOORMAN: William Browne and the pastoral poetry of the Elizabethan age. Diss. Strassburg, 1896. (vi, 67 S.)=Quellen und Forsch., 81.

HOMER SMITH: Pastoral influence in the English drama. In: PMLA., vol. 12, 1897, pp. 355–460. Rev.: Bbl. 9, 1899, S. 223–4, R. Brotanek.

A. H. THORNDIKE: The pastoral element in the English drama before 1605. In: MLN., vol. 14, 1899, pp. 228–46.

JOSEPHINE LAIDLER: A history of pastoral drama in England until 1700. In: E. St., Bd. 35, 1905, S. 193–259.

WALTER W. GREG: Pastoral poetry and pastoral drama. A literary inquiry, with special reference to the Pre-Restoration stage in England. London, 1906.

(xii, 464 pp.) Rev.: Sh. Jb. 43, 1907, S. 241–3, A. Brandl; MLR. 4, 1909, pp. 110–15, H. J. C. Grierson; Bbl. 18, 1907, S. 75–7, Ph. Aronstein.
With good bibliography.

V. M. JEFFERY: Italian and English pastoral drama of the Renaissance. In: MLR., vol. 19, 1924, pp. 56–62, 175–87 and 435–44.

V. M. JEFFERY: La fortuna del dramma pastorale italiano in Inghilterra. In: Nuova Antologia, 1925.

H. GENOUY: L'élément pastoral dans la poésie narrative et le drame en Angleterre, de 1579 à 1640. Paris, 1929. (444 pp.)

(h) BIBLICAL DRAMA

LOUIS B. WRIGHT: The Scriptures and the Elizabethan stage. In: Mod. Phil. vol. 26, 1928, pp. 47–56.

(6) THE ELIZABETHAN DRAMATISTS AND THEIR MUTUAL RELATIONS

(a) COLLABORATION

JAMES T. FOARD: Joint authorship of Marlowe and Shakespeare. In: Gentleman's Mag., vol. 288, 1900, pp. 134–54.

ELBERT N. S. THOMPSON: Elizabethan dramatic collaboration. In: E. St., Bd. 40, 1909, S. 30–46.

O. L. HATCHER: Fletcher's habits of dramatic collaboration. In: Anglia, Bd. 33, 1910, S. 219–31.

WILLIAM J. LAWRENCE: Early dramatic collaboration. In his: Pre-Restoration stage studies. Harv. Univ. Pr. 1927, pp. 340–72.

E. H. C. OLIPHANT: Collaboration in Elizabethan drama. Mr. W. J. Lawrence's theory. In: Philol. Quart., vol. 8, 1929, pp. 1–10.

(b) PROBLEMS OF AUTHORSHIP

E. H. C. OLIPHANT: Problems of authorship in Elizabethan dramatic literature. In: Mod. Phil., vol. 48, 1910/11, pp. 411–59. Rev.: Sh. Jb. 48, 1912, S. 217–18, Grabau.

J. M. ROBERTSON: The Shakespeare canon. P. I–IV. London, 1922, 1923, 1925, 1930. (xvi, 205; xx, 216; xv, 206; xvi, 137 pp.) Rev.: Dt. Vjschr. 6, 1928, S. 182, L. L. Schücking.

H. DUGDALE SYKES: Sidelights on Elizabethan drama. A series of studies dealing with the authorship of 16th and 17th century plays. Oxford, 1924. (231 pp.) Rev.: MLN. 42, 1927, pp. 545–6, Briggs.

Cf. E. H. C. OLIPHANT: How not to play the game of parallels. In: JEGPh., vol. 28, 1929, pp. 1–15.
Criticism of the researches of H. D. Sykes and S. R. Goldings.

(c) THE WAR OF THE THEATRES

J. H. PENNIMAN: The war of the theatres. Boston & Halle, 1897=the Univ. of Pennsylvania. Series in Phil., Lit. and Archaeology, iv. 3. Rev.: Sh. Jb. 35, 1899, S. 311–13, W. Dibelius.

R. A. SMALL: The stage-quarrel between Ben Jonson and the so-called poetasters. Breslau, 1899. (x, 204 S.)=Forsch. z. engl. Spr. und Lit., hrsg. von Kölbing, H. 1. Rev.: Sh. Jb. 36, 1900, S. 311–13, W. Dibelius; Bbl. 12, 1901, S. 294–302, Ph. Aronstein.

W. LÜHR: Die drei Cambridger Spiele vom Parnass (1598–1603) in ihren literarischen Beziehungen. Eine literarhistorische Studie. Diss. Kiel, 1900. (107 S.) Rev.: Sh. Jb. 37, 1901, S. 261, A. Brandl.

G. SARRAZIN: Nym und Ben Jonson. In: Sh. Jb. 40, 1904, S. 213–22.

MORSE S. ALLEN: The satire of John Marston. Diss. Princeton. Columbus, Ohio, 1920. Rev.: JEGPh. 21, 1922, pp. 703–4, H. N. Hillebrand.

ARTHUR GRAY: How Shakespeare 'purged' Jonson. A problem solved. Cambridge, 1928. (34 pp.) Rev.: TLS., May 3, 1928, p. 330.

(7) ELIZABETHAN LYRIC

(a) LYRICAL ANTHOLOGIES OF THE XVIth CENTURY

Tottel's Miscellany (1557–87). Ed. by HYDER EDWARD ROLLINS. Vol. i. Harv. Univ. Pr. 1928. (xx, 346 pp.) Rev.: RESt. 4, 1928, S. 374; Bbl. 40, 1929, S. 9–10, W. Schirmer.

A Hundreth Sundrie Flowres, from the original edition [1573]. Ed. by B. M. WARD, 1926. (xl, 198 pp.)=Haslewood Books. Rev.: MLR. 22, 1927, pp. 214–20, G. Ambrose; RESt. 3, 1927, pp. 111–14, McKerrow.
  B. M. WARD: Further research on A hundreth sundrie flowers. In: RESt., vol. 4, 1928, S. 35–48.

The Paradise of Dainty Devices (1576^1–1606^{10}). Ed. by HYDER EDWARD ROLLINS. Cambridge, Harv. Univ. Pr., 1927. (lxx, 299 pp.) Rev.: RESt. 4, 1928, pp. 480–2, McKerrow; JEGPh. 27, 1928, pp. 96–100, C. S. Northup; MLR. 23, 1928, pp. 68–70, Moore Smith.

A Gorgeous Gallery of Gallant Inventions (1578). Ed. by HYDER E. ROLLINS. O.U.P., 1926. (xxvi, 245 pp.) Rev.: MLR. 22, 1927, pp. 98–9, F. Sidgwick; RESt. 3, 1927, pp. 242–3, McKerrow.

A Handfull of Pleasant Delights, 1584, by Clement Robinson and divers others. Ed. by HYDER E. ROLLINS. Harvard Univ. Pr. 1924. (xix, 145 pp.) Rev.: Mod. Phil. 23, pp. 119–25, Ch. R. Baskervill.

The Phoenix Nest. Reprinted from the original edition of 1593. With introd. and notes by HUGH MACDONALD. London, 1927. (xvi, 117 pp.) Rev.: TLS. Jan. 20, 1927, p. 41.

Willobie his Avisa [1594]. With an essay towards its interpretation by CHARLES HUGHES. London, 1904. (xxviii, 164 pp.) Rev.: Sh. Jb. 41, 1905, S. 269–70, A. Brandl.

Willobie his Avisa, or, the true picture of a modest maide and of a chast and constant wife, 1594. With a critical essay by G. B. HARRISON. London, 1926. (271 pp.)=Bodley Head Quartos.

England's Helicon. A collection of lyrical and pastoral poems, published in 1600. Ed. by A. H. BULLEN. London, 1899. (xxxvii, 262 pp.) Rev.: Sh. Jb. 36, 1900, S. 313–14, W. Keller.

England's Helicon. Reprinted from the edition of 1600 with additional poems from the edition of 1614. London, 1925. (ix, 256 pp.)=Haslewood Books.

England's Parnassus. Compiled by Robert Allot, 1600. Ed. by CHARLES CRAWFORD. Oxford, 1913. (xliii, 560 pp.) Rev.: Sh. Jb. 50, 1914, S. 245–6, M. Förster.

(b) MODERN ANTHOLOGIES

W. SANDYS: Festive songs, principally of the 16th and 17th centuries. In: Percy Soc. Publ., vol. 23, London, 1848.

A. H. BULLEN: Lyrics from the dramatists of the Elizabethan age. London, 1889, 1901.

EWALD FLÜGEL: Liedersammlungen des 16. Jhrh., besonders aus der Zeit Heinrichs VIII. I. II. III. In: Anglia, Bd. 12, 1889, S. 225–72 und S. 585–97; Bd. 26, 1903, S. 94–285.
Reprints of the collections of songs mentioned.

A. H. BULLEN: Poems, chiefly lyrical, from romances and prose-tracts of the Elizabethan age. London, 1890.

F. J. CARPENTER: English lyric poetry, 1500–1700. London, 1897.

EDWARD ARBER: British anthologies. Vol. iii: The Spenser anthology, 1548–1591. iv: The Shakespeare anthology, 1592–1616. v: The Jonson anthology, 1617–1637. London, 1899. Rev.: Sh. Jb. 37, 1901, S. 262–3, A. H. Tolman.

BERNHARD FEHR: Die Lieder des Fairfax MS. (Add. 5465 Brit. Mus.). In: Arch. Jg. 55, Bd. 106, 1901, S. 48–70. Reprint.

A. H. BULLEN: Songs from the dramatists. London, 1907.

F. M. PADELFORD: Early 16th century lyrics. London, 1907. (lviii, 174 pp.)
The preliminary chapter contains a good introduction to early modern English lyric.

WILLIAM BRAITHWAITE: The book of Elizabethan verse. London, 1908. (xii, 823 pp.)=The Shakespeare Library. Rev.: Sh. Jb. 44, 1908, S. 387–8, M. Förster.

J. WILLIAM HEBEL and HOYT H. HUDSON: Poetry of the English Renaissance (1509–1660), selected from early editions and manuscripts. New York, 1929. (1068 pp.)

(c) STUDIES IN THE ELIZABETHAN LYRIC

HERMANN ISAAC: Wie weit geht die Abhängigkeit Shakespeares von Daniel? Eine Studie zur englischen Renaissancelyrik. In: Sh. Jb. Jg. 17, 1882, S. 165–200.

The Elizabethan lyric. In: Quart. Rev. 1902, Oct. Rev.: Sh. Jb. 39, 1903, S. 324–5, Dibelius.

JOHN ERSKINE: The Elizabethan lyric. A study. New York, 1903. (xvi, 344 pp.)=Columbia Univ. Stud. in Engl., vol. 2. Rev.: Bbl. 15, 1904, S. 356–9, Ph. Aronstein.

F. M. PADELFORD: Early 16th century lyrics. London, 1907. (lviii, 174 pp.)
The preliminary chapter contains a good introduction to the early modern English lyric.

M. DAMETZ: Englische Volkslieder und Moriskentänze. Progr. Wien, 1912. (26 S.)

T. K. WHIPPLE: Martial and the English epigram from Sir Thomas Wyatt to Ben Jonson=Univ. of California Publ. in Mod. Philol., vol. 10, 1925, pp. 279–414. Rev. JEGPh. 26, 1927, pp. 598–9, Fletcher.

LOUIS B. WRIGHT: Extraneous song in Elizabethan drama after the advent of Shakespeare. In: Stud. in Phil., vol. 24, 1927, pp. 261–74.

(*d*) MADRIGALS

A. H. BULLEN: Lyrics from the song books of the Elizabethan age. London, 1891.

O. BECKER: Die englischen Madrigalisten William Byrd, Thomas Morley u. John Dowland. Diss. Bonn, 1901. (70 pp. and 32 pp. musical supplements.)

WILHELM BOLLE: Die gedruckten englischen Liederbücher bis 1600. Ein Beitrag zur Geschichte der sangbaren Lyrik in der Zeit Shakespeares. Berlin, 1903=Palaestra 29. Rev.: Sh. Jb. 41, 1905, S. 267–9, Dibelius; JEGPh. 10, 1911, pp. 483–6, J. Erskine; Bbl. 18, 1907, S. 176–8, O. Ritter.

MARIANNE FISCHER: Zum Stil des elisabethanischen Madrigals. In: Arch., 133, 1915, S. 1–44. Rev.: Sh. Jb. 53, 1917, S. 210–11, Grabau.

EDMUND H. FELLOWES: The English madrigal composers. London, 1921. (364 pp.)

The English madrigal school. Ed. by EDMUND H. FELLOWES. 1923.

EDMUND H. FELLOWES: William Byrd. A short account of his life and work. London, 1923. (124 pp.)

SIR W. HENRY HADOW: William Byrd, 1623–1923. In: Brit. Acad. Proceedings, vol. 11, London, 1923. (22 pp.)

EDMUND H. FELLOWES: Orlando Gibbons. A short account of his life and work. London, 1925. (120 pp.)

EDMUND H. FELLOWES: The English madrigal. O.U.P., 1925. (112 pp.)

(*e*) THE SONNET

SIDNEY LEE: Elizabethan sonnets. Newly arranged and indexed. With an introduction. 2 vols. London, 1904. (cx, 316 and 448 pp.)=An English Garner.
Valuable anthology.

K. LENTZNER: Über das Sonett und seine Gestaltung in der englischen Dichtung bis Milton. Diss. Halle, 1886. (vi, 83 S.)

IRENE ZOCCO: Petrarchismo e Petrarchisti in Inghilterra. Palermo, 1906.

SIDNEY LEE: The Elizabethan sonnet. In: CHEL., vol. 3, Cambridge, 1909.

E. KAUN: Konventionelles in den elisabethanischen Sonetten mit Berücksichtigung der französischen und italienischen Quellen. Diss. Greifswald, 1915. (122 S.)

RAYMOND M. ALDEN: The lyrical conceits of the Elizabethans. In: Stud. in Philol., vol. 14, 1917, pp. 130 seq.

WALTER L. BULLOCK: The genesis of the English sonnet form. In: PMLA., vol. 38, 1923, pp. 729–44.

WALTER F. SCHIRMER: Das Sonett in der englischen Literatur. In: Anglia, Bd. 49, 1926, S. 1–31.

HERM. KARL HASSELKUSS: Der Petrarkismus in der Sprache der englischen Sonettdichter der Renaissance. Diss. Münster, 1927. (249 S.). Rev.: Litbl. 1928, Sp. 469; Sh. Jb. 65, 1929, S. 196, W. Keller; Engl. Studies, 11, 1929, pp. 225–7, M. Praz.

JANET G. SCOTT: Les sonnets élisabéthains, les sources et l'apport personnel. Paris, 1929. (343 pp.)=Bibl. de la Revue de litt. comparée, t. 60. Rev.: Rev. anglo-amér. 7, 1929, pp. 66–67, É. Legouis; Engl. Studies, 11, 1929, pp. 227–31, M. Praz; MRN. 45, 1930, pp. 328–9, Ch. G. Osgood.

J. VIANEY: Le Pétrarquisme en France au 16ᵉ siècle. Montpellier, 1909.

(f) PASTORAL POETRY

H. O. SOMMER: Erster Versuch über die englische Hirtendichtung. 1888.

K. WINDSCHEID: Die englische Hirtendichtung von 1579–1625. Diss. Heidelberg, 1895. (66 S.) Rev.: Bbl. 8, 1898, S. 41–4, R. Brotanek.

FREDERIC W. MOORMAN: William Browne. His Britannia's pastorals and the pastoral poetry of the Elizabethan age. Strassburg, 1897. (x, 159 pp.)= Quellen u. Forsch., H. 81. Rev.: Bbl. 8, 1898, S. 44–6, R. Brotanek.

(g) THE BALLAD

F. J. CHILD: The English and Scottish popular ballads. In 5 vols. Boston & London, 1882–98.

RICHARD SIEVERS: Thomas Deloney. Eine Studie über Balladenliteratur der Shakspere-Zeit, nebst Neudruck von Deloneys Roman 'Jack of Newbury'. Berlin, 1904. (viii, 244 S.)=Palaestra, 36. Rev.: Sh. Jb. 41, 1905, S. 227–8, W. Keller; Bbl. 15, 1904, S. 359–62, Ph. Aronstein.

C. H. FIRTH: Ballads and broadsides. In: Shakespeare's England, 1917, vol. ii, pp. 511–38.

Old English ballads, 1553–1625. Ed. by HYDER E. ROLLINS. C.U.P., 1920. (xxi, 423 pp.)

HYDER E. ROLLINS: An analytical index to the ballad-entries (1557–1709) in the Registers of the Company of Stationers of London. Chapel Hill, U.S.A., 1924. (324 pp.) Rev.: Bbl. 36, 1925, S. 167–8, M. F. Mann.

The Pack of Autolycus. Ed. by HYDER E. ROLLINS. Cambridge, Harv. Univ. Press, 1927. (xvii, 270 pp.) Rev.: JEGPh. 28, 1929, pp. 294–9, H. M. Belden.

(8) ELIZABETHAN NARRATIVE LITERATURE

J. J. JUSSERAND: Le roman au temps de Shakespeare. Paris, 1887. Engl. translation: The English novel in the time of Shakespeare, translated by ELIZABETH LEE. London, 1890. (434 pp.) 1899³.

FRIEDR. BRIE: Roman und Drama im Zeitalter Shakespeares. In: Sh. Jb. 48, 1912, S. 125–47.
Deals with the mutual influences of the novel and the drama.

EDWARD DOWDEN: Elizabethan romance. In the same writer's Essays modern and Elizabethan. London, 1910, pp. 351–80.
A valuable survey.

ARUNDELL ESDAILE: A list of English tales and prose romances printed before 1740. London, Bibliogr. Soc. 1912.

ERNEST A. BAKER: The history of the English novel. The Elizabethan age and after. London, 1929. (302 pp.) Rev: RESt. 6, 1930, pp. 360–2, H. Williams.

III. SHAKESPEARE'S LIFE

(1) DOCUMENTARY EVIDENCE

D. H. LAMBERT: Cartae Shakespeareanae. Shakespeare documents. A chronological catalogue of extant evidence relating to the life and works of William Shakespeare. London, 1904. (xxi, 107 pp.) Rev.: Sh. Jb. 42, 1906, S. 247, W. Keller.

CHARLES W. WALLACE: New Shakespearean discoveries. Shakespeare as a man among men. In: Harper's Monthly Magazine, vol. 120, 1910, pp. 489–510.

TUCKER BROOKE: Shakespeare of Stratford. A handbook for students. New Haven & London, 1926. (viii, 177 pp.)
Reprint of documents.

SAMUEL A. TANNENBAUM: A new study of Shakspere's will. In: Stud. in Phil., vol. 23, 1926, pp. 117–41.

CHARLOTTE C. STOPES: Early records illustrating the personal life of Shakespeare. Shakespeare through the Ardens. In: The Shakespeare Assoc. 1925–26, London, 1927, pp. 217–39.

(2) SHAKESPEARE'S HANDWRITING

(Cf. also works on Sir Thomas More, pp. 277–278 and on Elizabethan
Handwriting, p. 47.)

RICHARD SIMPSON: Are there any extant manuscripts in Shakespeare's handwriting? In: N & Q., 4th ser., vol. 8, London, 1871, pp. 1 seq.

Here for the first time the Addition in Sir Thomas More is attributed to Shakespeare.

JAMES SPEDDING: Shakespeare's handwriting. In: N. & Q., 4th ser., vol. 10,
London, 1872, pp. 227 seq.

SIR EDWARD M. THOMPSON: Shakespeare's handwriting. A study. Oxford,
1916. (xii, 63 pp.) Rev.: Libr. 3rd ser., vol. 8, 1917, pp. 97–100, J. A. Herbert; Sh. Jb. 55, 1919, S. 183–4, A. Schröer; Bbl. 35, 1924, S. 97–102,
B. Fehr.

SIR EDWARD M. THOMPSON: Shakespeare's handwriting. In: Shakespeare's
England, Oxford, 1916, vol. i, pp. 284–311.

SIR EDWARD M. THOMPSON: Two pretended autographs of Shakespeare. In:
Libr., 3rd ser., vol. 8, 1917, pp. 193–217.

Refers to Shakespeare's autographs in Florio's translation of Montaigne and in Ovid's
Metamorphoses.

FALCONER MADAN: Two lost causes, and what may be said in defence of them.
(a) The Oxford Jerome of '1468'. (b) The supposed Shakespeare autograph
in the Bodleian 'Ovid'. In: Libr., 3rd ser., vol. 9, 1918, pp. 89–105.

GEORGE GREENWOOD: Shakespeare's handwriting. London, 1920. (36 pp.)

SIR GEORGE GREENWOOD: The Shakespeare signatures and 'Sir Thomas More'.
London, 1924. (130 pp.)

SAMUEL A. TANNENBAUM: Shakspere's unquestioned autographs and the addition to 'Sir Thomas Moore'. In: Stud. in Phil., vol. 22, 1925, pp. 133–60.

SAMUEL A. TANNENBAUM: Reclaiming one of Shakspere's signatures. In: Stud.
in Philol., vol. 22, 1925, pp. 392–411.

Contrary to the view of Thompson the author considers the 'Montaigne' signature
genuine.

SAMUEL A. TANNENBAUM: Problems in Shakespeare's penmanship, including
a study of the poet's will. New York, 1927. (241 pp.) Rev.: MLR. 23, 1928,
pp. 231–4, Ch. Sisson.

The most thorough examination of Thompson's views.

SAMUEL A. TANNENBAUM: Genuine and putative autographs of William Shakespeare. Columbia Univ. Press, 1930. [announced].

SUPPLEMENT : SHAKESPEARE FORGERIES

(a) THE IRELAND FORGERIES

S. IRELAND: Miscellaneous papers and legal instruments under the hand and
seal of W. Shakespeare, including the tragedy of King Lear, and a small
fragment of Hamlet, from the original MSS. in the possession of Samuel
Ireland. London [1795].

WILLIAM HENRY IRELAND: An authentic account of the Shakesperian MSS. London, 1796. (ii, 44 pp.)

E. MALONE: An inquiry into the authenticity of certain miscellaneous papers and legal instruments, published Dec. 24, 1795, and attributed to Shakespeare. London, 1796.

JAMES BOADEN: A letter to G. Steevens containing a critical examination of the papers of Shakspeare, published by Mr. S. Ireland. London, 1796. (iv, 72 pp.)

GEORGE CHALMERS: An apology for the believers in the Shakespeare papers, which were exhibited in Norfolk Street. London, 1797. (iv, 628 pp.)

GEORGE CHALMERS: A supplemental apology for the believers in the Shakespeare papers, being a reply to Mr. Malone's answer, which was early announced, but never published, etc. London, 1799. (viii, 656 pp.)

WILLIAM HENRY IRELAND: The confessions of W. H. Ireland, containing the particulars of his fabrication of the Shakspeare MSS., etc. London, 1805. Reprint: New York, 1874.
Admits authorship of the forgeries.

C. VORBRODT: Ireland's forgeries. Progr. Meissen, 1885. (13 S.)

(b) THE COLLIER FORGERIES

J. PAYNE COLLIER: History of English dramatic poetry to the time of Shakespeare, and annals of the stage to the Restoration. 3 vols. London, 1831[1], 1879[2].

J. PAYNE COLLIER: New facts regarding the life of Shakespeare. London, 1835.

J. PAYNE COLLIER: New particulars regarding the works of Shakespeare. London, 1836.

J. PAYNE COLLIER: Further particulars regarding Shakespeare and his works. London, 1839.

J. PAYNE COLLIER: Notes and emendations to the text of Shakespeare's plays, from early manuscript corrections in a copy of the folio 1632. London, 1853. (xxvi, 528 pp.)

N. DELIUS: Alte handschriftliche Emendationen zum Shakspere gewürdigt. Bonn, 1853.

S. W. SINGER: The text of Shakespeare vindicated from the interpolations and corruptions advocated by J. P. Collier in his Notes and Emendations. London, 1853. (xx, 312 pp.)

TYCHO MOMMSEN: Der Perkins-Shakespeare. Berlin, 1854.

C. M. INGLEBY: The Shakespeare fabrications, or the MS. notes of the Perkins Folio shown to be of recent origin; with an appendix on the Ireland forgeries. London, 1859. (156 pp.)
With bibliography.

N. E. S. H. HAMILTON: An inquiry into the genuineness of the MS. corrections in Mr. Payne Collier's annotated Shakspere Folio 1632, and of certain Shaksperian documents likewise published by Mr. Collier. London, 1860. (iv, 156 pp.)

J. PAYNE COLLIER: Reply to Mr. Hamilton's 'Inquiry' into the imputed Shakespeare forgeries. London, 1860.

C. M. INGLEBY: A complete view of the Shakspere controversy concerning the authenticity and genuineness of the MS. matter affecting the works and biography of Shakspere, published by Mr. J. Payne Collier as the fruits of his researches. London, 1861.

HENRY B. WHEATLEY: Notes on the life of John Payne Collier, with a complete list of his works and an account of such Shakespeare documents as are believed to be spurious. London, 1884=Repr. from the Bibliographer, v, 108 seq.

SAMUEL A. TANNENBAUM: Another Shakspere forgery. In: MLN., vol. 44, 1929, pp. 13–15.
Cf. also Textual Criticism, pp. 58–61.

(c) THE CUNNINGHAM FORGERIES

PETER CUNNINGHAM: Extracts from the accounts of the revels at court in the reigns of Queen Elizabeth and King James I, from the original office books of the masters and yeomen. With introduction and notes. London, 1842. (lii, 228 pp.)

ERNEST LAW: Some supposed Shakespeare forgeries. An examination into the authenticity of certain documents affecting the dates of composition of several of the plays. London, 1911. (80 pp.)

CHARLOTTE C. STOPES: The 17th century accounts of the Masters of the Revels. Oxford, 1922. (36 pp.)=The Shakespeare Assoc. Pamphl., no. 6.

W. J. LAWRENCE: Was Peter Cunningham a forger? In: MLR., vol. 19, 1924, pp. 25–34.

D. T. B. WOOD: The Revels Books. The writer of the 'Malone Scrap'. In: RESt., vol. 1, 1925, pp. 72–4.

D. T. B. WOOD: The suspected Revels Books. In: RESt., vol. 1, 1925, pp. 166–72.

SAMUEL A. TANNENBAUM: Shakspere forgeries in the Revels Accounts. New York, 1928. (xiv, 109 pp. and 22 facs.) Rev.: RESt., vol. 5, 1929, pp. 344–58, W. W. Greg; Arch. 156, 1929, S. 127–8, A. Brandl.

(3) SHAKESPEARE'S NAME

KARL ELZE: Die Schreibung des Namens Shakespeare. In: Sh. Jb. Jg. 5, 1870, S. 325–32.

KARL ELZE: Die Schreibung des Namens Shakespeare. In the same author's William Shakespeare. Halle, 1876. Appendix 1.

CHARLOTTE C. STOPES: The earliest official record of Shakespeare's name. In: Sh. Jb. Jg. 32, 1896, S. 182-9.

JOHN L. HANEY: The name of William Shakespeare. A study in orthography. Philadelphia, 1906. (68 pp.) Rev.: Sh. Jb. 43, 1907, S. 261-2, A. Brandl; Bibl. 18, 1907, S. 322-3, M. F. Mann.

(4) THE MOST IMPORTANT BIOGRAPHIES

(including general studies of Shakespeare's Life and Works)

NATHAN DRAKE: Shakespeare and his times. 2 vols. London, 1817. (xii, 735 and v, 677 pp.)

JAMES O. HALLIWELL: The life of William Shakespeare. London, 1848. (xvi, 336 pp.)

RUDOLPH GENÉE: Shakespeare's Leben und Werke. Hildburghausen, 1872. (408 S.)=Bibliothek ausländischer Klassiker. New edition under the title: William Shakespeare in seinem Werden und Wesen. Berlin, 1905. (xii, 472 S.)

HENRY N. HUDSON: Shakespeare, his life, art, and characters. 2 vols. Boston, 1872, 1895[4].

KARL ELZE: William Shakespeare. Halle, 1876. (viii, 651 S.) Rev.: Anglia, 1, 155 seq., Leo; E. St. 2, 235 seq., Köppel; Archiv. 57, 317 seq., D. Asher.
CONTENTS: I. Home and Childhood; II. Youth and marriage; III. London; IV. The Theatre; V. Shakespeare's Works; VI. Shakespeare's Education; VII. Shakespeare's Character; his conception of the world and attitude towards life; VIII. Retirement to Stratford and Death; Appendix I. The Writing of the Name Shakespeare; Appendix II. Shakespeare Portraits.

JAMES O. HALLIWELL-PHILLIPPS: Illustrations of the life of Shakespeare. London, 1874. (viii, 128 pp.)

C. M. INGLEBY: Shakespeare, the man and the book, being a collection of occasional papers on the bard and his writings. 2 vols. London, 1877-81. (viii, 172 and x, 194 pp.)

JAMES O. HALLIWELL-PHILLIPPS: Outlines of the life of Shakespeare. London, 1882, 1885[5]. (640 pp.)

HENRIK SCHÜCK: William Shakspere. Hans lif och värksamhet. En historisk framställning. Stockholm (1883). (iv, 160 S.) Cf. WILHELM BOLIN: Eine schwedische Shakespeare-Monographie. In: Sh. Jb. Jg. 22, 1887, S. 202-16.

MAX KOCH: Shakespeare. Stuttgart (1885)=Cottasche Bibl. d. Weltliteratur.

FREDERICK G. FLEAY: A chronicle history of the life and work of William Shakespeare, player, poet, and playmaker. London, 1886. (viii, 364 pp.)

GEORG BRANDES: Englische Persönlichkeiten. 2. Teil: William Shakespeare. Teil 1-3. München, 1896. (1001 S.) 1904[3]. (311, 306 u. 300 S.)=Gesammelte Schriften. Bd. 6. Teil 2. Rev.: Bbl. 7, 1897, S. 129-40, W. Wetz.

GREGOR SARRAZIN: William Shakespeares Lehrjahre. Eine literarhistorische Studie. Weimar, 1897. (xii, 233 S.) Rev.: Bbl. 10, 1900, S. 117-19, R. Fischer.

SIDNEY LEE: A life of William Shakespeare. London, 1898, 1922³. (xlvii, 776 S.) 1925⁴. German translation: William Shakespeare, sein Leben und seine Werke. Rechtmäss. dt. Übers., durchges. und eingel. von Richard Wülker. Leipzig, 1901. (xxiv, 469 S.) Rev.: Sh. Jb. Jg. 35, 1899, S. 303–4, A. Brandl; Bbl. 15, 1904, S. 337–40, Rud. Fischer.

SIDNEY LEE: Shakespeare's life and work, being an abridgment, chiefly for the use of students, of a Life of William Shakespeare. London, 1900. (xv, 232 pp.) Rev.: Sh. Jb. 44, 1908, S. 363, M. Förster; Bbl. 13, 1902, S. 97–100, R. Brotanek.

LEON KELLNER: Shakespeare. Leipzig, Berlin, und Wien, 1900. (238 S.) Rev.: Sh. Jb. 37, 1901, S. 243–6, H. Spies.

EDWARD DOWDEN: Shakespeare. London, 1903, 1905=Literature Primers.

WILLIAM J. ROLFE: A life of William Shakespeare. Boston, 1904, 1905². (viii, 552 pp.)

GREGOR SARRAZIN: Aus Shakespeares Meisterwerkstatt. Stilgeschichtliche Studien. Berlin, 1906. (vii, 226 S.) Rev.: Sh. Jb. 43, 1907, S. 246 –57, E. Koeppel; Bbl. 21, 1910, S. 4–7, G. Binz.

MAX J. WOLFF: Shakespeare. Der Dichter und sein Werk. 2 Bde. München, 1907. (v, 477 u. 470 S.). 1926⁶. Rev.: Sh. Jb. 44, 1908, S. 320–22, Churchill; Bbl. 20, 1909, S. 321–6, G. Binz.

WALTER RALEIGH: Shakespeare. London, 1907. (232 pp.)=Engl. Men of Letters. Rev.: Sh. Jb. 44, 1908, S. 322–4, A. Brandl, and 45, 1909, S. 398, M. Förster.

GEORGE SAINTSBURY: Shakespeare, life and plays. In: CHEL., vol. 5, 1910, pp. 165–222.
With detailed bibliography.

WILHELM WETZ: Die Lebensnachrichten über Shakespeare mit dem Versuch einer Jugend- und Bildungsgeschichte des Dichters. Heidelberg, 1912. (xi, 272 S.) Rev.: Sh. Jb. 48, 1912, S. 319–23, M. Förster.

OLIPHANT SMEATON: Shakespeare, his life and work. London [1912]. (xii, 562 pp.)=Everyman's Library. Rev.: Sh. Jb. 48, 1912, S. 309, M. Förster.

HENRIK SCHÜCK: Shakspere och hans tid. 2 Bde. Stockholm (1916). (viii, 412 u. 408 S.) Rev.: Z. f. e. U. 17, 1918, S. 21–4, Jantzen; MLR. 12, 1917, pp. 390–1, Herbert Wright.

ALOIS BRANDL: Shakespeares Leben-Umwelt-Kunst. Neue Ausgabe. Berlin, 1922. 1929⁴. (xvi, 517 S.)=Geisteshelden, Bd. 8. Rev.: JEGPh. 22, 1923, pp. 294–8, W. E. Leonard.

RAYMOND M. ALDEN: Shakespeare. New York, 1922. (xix, 377 pp.)=Master Spirits of Literature. Rev.: JEGPh. 22, 1923, pp. 294–8, W. E. Leonard.

JOSEPH QUINCY ADAMS: A life of William Shakespeare. With illustrations. London, 1923, 1925. (xvi, 561 pp.) Rev.: JEGPh. 23, 1924, pp. 594–9, H. N. Hillebrand; Bbl. 35, 1924, S. 72–6, B. Fehr.

SIDNEY LEE: A life of William Shakespeare. London, 1925[4]. Rev.: Sh. Jb. 61, 1925, S. 129–30, W. Keller.

A standard authority.

(5) SHAKESPEARE—ACTOR AND MAN OF THE THEATRE

HERMANN KURZ: Shakespeare der Schauspieler. In: Sh. Jb. Jg. 6, 1871, S. 317–42.

ERNEST LAW: Shakespeare as a Groom of the Chamber. London, 1910. (viii, 64 pp.) Rev.: Sh. Jb. 47, 1911, S. 342–4, M. Förster.

CHARLES W. WALLACE: Shakespeare's money interest in the Globe Theater. Newly discovered records of a suit-at-law which show that his profits as part owner were smaller than has been supposed. In: Century Magazine, vol. 80, 1910, pp. 500–12.

CHARLES W. WALLACE: Shakespeare and the Blackfriars, based on documents lately discovered by the writer. In: Century Magazine, 1910, pp. 742–52.

BRANDER MATTHEWS: Shakespeare as an actor. In: North American Rev. 1912, pp. 392–403. Rev.: Sh. Jb. 49, 1913, S. 190.

ALBERT EICHLER: Shakespeares Regiekunst. In: Dt. Revue 1912, S. 213–18.

JOH. E. SCHMIDT: Shakespeares Dramen und sein Schauspielerberuf. 1914.

ALWIN THALER: Shakespeare's income. In: Stud. in Philol., vol. 15, 1918, pp. 82–97.

HELENE RICHTER: [Shakespeare], der Schauspieler. In the same writer's Shakespeare der Mensch, Leipzig, 1923, S. 7–44.

CLARA LONGWORTH-CHAMBRUN: Shakespeare acteur-poète. Paris, 1926. (316 pp.) English translation: Shakespeare, actor-poet, as seen by his associates, explained by himself, and remembered by the succeeding generation. New York, 1927. (357 pp.)

J. ISAACS: Shakespeare as a man of the theatre. In: The Shakespeare Association 1925–26, London, 1927, pp. 88–119.

(6) SHAKESPEARE'S FAMILY

GEORGE R. FRENCH: Shakespeareana genealogica. London, 1869. (xiv, 590 pp.)

CHARLOTTE C. STOPES: Shakespeare's family, being a record of the ancestors and descendants of William Shakespeare, with some account of the Ardens. New York, 1901. (260 pp.)

CHARLES I. ELTON: William Shakespeare, his family and friends. Ed. by A. HAMILTON THOMPSON. London, 1904. (x, 521 pp.). Rev.: Sh. Jb. 41, 1905, S. 231–2, A. Brandl.

J. W. GRAY: Shakespeare's marriage, his departure from Stratford and other incidents in his life. London, 1905. (vii, 285 pp.) Rev.: Sh. Jb. 42, 1906, S. 257–8, A. Brandl.

RICHARD SAVAGE and EDGAR I. FRIPP: Minutes and accounts of the Corporation of Stratford-upon-Avon and other records 1553–1620. Vol. i: 1553–66, ii: 1566–77, iii: 1577–86. London, 1921, 1924, 1926. (lx, 152; l, 119 and lx, 171 pp.)=Publ. of the Dugdale Soc., vols. i, iii, v.

Specially important for research into the circumstances of Shakespeare's father.

(7) SHAKESPEARE'S SOCIAL ENVIRONMENT

(a) FRIENDS AND ACQUAINTANCES

CHARLOTTE C. STOPES: Shakespeare's Warwickshire contemporaries. Stratford-upon-Avon, 1897. (iv, 114 pp.); 1907 (viii, 273 pp.) Rev.: Sh. Jb. 44, 1908, S. 350–2, A. Brandl.

CHARLOTTE C. STOPES: Shakespeare's fellows and followers. A special set of facts collected from the Lord Chamberlain's Papers. In: Sh. Jb. Jg. 46, 1910, S. 92–105.

CHARLES W. WALLACE: Shakespeare and his London associates as revealed in recently discovered documents. Lincoln, Nebraska, 1910=Univ. of Nebraska Stud., vol. 10, no. 4.

CHARLES W. WALLACE: New Shakespeare discoveries. In: Harper's Magazine, vol. 120, 1910, pp. 489 seq.

Deals with the Mountjoys.

CHARLOTTE C. STOPES: Shakespeare's environment. London, 1914, 1918[2]. (xii, 369 pp.)

DODGSON H. MADDEN: Shakespeare and his fellows. New York, 1916.

CLARA LONGWORTH-CHAMBRUN: Giovanni Florio, un apôtre de la renaissance en Angleterre. Diss. Paris, 1921. (271 pp.)

G. B. HARRISON: Shakespeare's fellows, being a brief chronicle of the Elizabethan age. London, 1923. (207 pp.)

V. STAMPANATO: Un amico del Bruno in Inghilterra [i.e. John Florio]. In: La Critica, vol. 21, 1923, pp. 56, 113, 189, 313.

EDGAR I. FRIPP: Master Richard Quyny, bailiff of Stratford and friend of William Shakespeare. O.U.P., 1924. (215 pp.)

A valuable study.

HANS HEIDRICH: John Davies of Hereford (1565?–1618) und sein Bild von Shakespeares Umgebung. Leipzig, 1924 = Palaestra 143. Rev.: Sh. Jb. 59–60, 1924, S. 197–8, W. Keller.

G. E. BENTLEY: Shakespeare's fellows. In: TLS. Nov. 15, 1928, p. 856.

Documentary evidence about players, musicians, or bear-wards from church records in Southwark.

B. M. WARD: The 17th Earl of Oxford, 1550–1604, from contemporary documents. London, 1928. (xvi, 408 pp.) Rev.: Sh. Jb. 64, 1928, S. 198–9, W. Keller; MLR. 24, 1929, pp. 216–21, W. W. Greg.

EDGAR I. FRIPP: Shakespeare's haunts near Stratford. O.U.P., 1929. (160 pp.)

(b) COURT AND PATRONS

WOLFGANG KELLER: Shakespeare und sein König. Festvortrag. In: Sh. Jb. Jg. 54, 1918, S. xiii–xxxiii.

TUCKER BROOKE: Shakespeare's Queen. In: The Yale Review, 1927 (Jan.).

R. W. GOULDING: Wriothesley iconography. 1920.

CHARLOTTE C. STOPES: The life of Henry, third Earl of Southampton, Shakespeare's patron. C.U.P., 1922. (xii, 544 pp.) Rev.: Sh. Jb. 58, 1922, S. 128–30, W. Keller.
Good source-book.

CLARA LONGWORTH-CHAMBRUN: Lord Southampton, protecteur de Shakespeare. In: Rev. de Paris, 1923, pp. 857–90.

(c) LONDON AND SHAKESPEARE'S HOME
(Cf. also pp. 180–181)

JOHN R. WISE: Shakespeare, his birthplace and its neighbourhood. London, 1861. (x, 164 pp.)

CAROLA BLACKER: Stratford-on-Avon and Shakespeare. In: Sh. Jb. Jg. 32, 1896, S. 44–86.

H. T. STEPHENSON: Shakespeare's London. New York, 1905.

GEORGE MORLEY: Sweet Arden, a book of the Shakespeare country. London, 1906. (190 pp.) Rev.: Sh. Jb. 44, 1908, S. 363, M. Förster.

G. DUVAL: Londres au temps de Shakespeare. Paris, 1907. (340 pp.)

H. SNOWDEN WARD and CATHARINE W. WARD: Shakespeare's town and times. London [1909³]. (184 pp.) Rev.: Sh. Jb. 46, 1910, S. 316, M. Förster.

BERNHARD FEHR: Shakespeare and Coventry. In: Bbl., Bd. 31, 1920, S. 85-7.

FREDERICK C. WELLSTOOD: Catalogue of the books, manuscripts, works of art, antiquities and relics exhibited in Shakespeare's birthplace. With 58 illustr. Stratford-upon-Avon, 1925. (176 pp.)

N. ZWAGER: Glimpses of Ben Jonson's London. Amsterdam, 1926. Rev.: Bbl. 38, 1927, S. 204–5, Ph. Aronstein; RESt. 3, 1927, pp. 481–2, Cl. Byrne.

EDGAR I. FRIPP: Shakespeare's Stratford. O.U.P., 1928. (96 pp. and 36 illustr. and a map.)

EDGAR I. FRIPP: Shakespeare's haunts near Stratford. O.U.P., 1929. (160 pp.)

(8) SHAKESPEARE ICONOGRAPHY
(a) PORTRAITS AND BUSTS

KARL ELZE: Shakespeares Bildnisse. In: Sh. Jb. Jg. 4, 1869, S. 308–26. Cf. also KARL ELZE: William Shakespeare, Halle, 1876, Anhang II.

GUSTAV KRUEGER: Shakespeares Grabbüste. In: Sh. Jb. Jg. 41, 1905, S. 124–34.

A. BRANDL: O. Lessings zweiter Shakespeare. In: Sh. Jb. Jg. 41, 1905, S. 182–3.

M. H. SPIELMANN: The title-page of the First Folio of Shakespeare's plays. A comparative study of the Droeshout portrait and the Stratford monument. London, 1924. (xi, 56 pp. and 47 illustr.)

Cf. also the reprint in 'Studies in the First Folio', London, 1924. The best-informed treatment.

SIR GEORGE GREENWOOD: The Stratford bust and the Droeshout engraving. London, 1925. (71 pp.)

The author opposes the theory of M. H. Spielmann and contests the authenticity of both works.

(b) THE DEATH MASK

HERMANN SCHAAFFHAUSEN: Über die Totenmaske Shakespeares. In: Sh. Jb. Jg. 10, 1875, S. 26–49.

PAUL WISLICENUS: Shakespeares Totenmaske. Darmstadt, 1910. (107 S. u. Abb.) Further studies by the same author: Shakespeares Totenmaske. Jena, 1911.—Dokumente zu Shakespeares Totenmaske. Darmstadt, 1911. (42 S.)—Shakespeares Totenmaske. In: Sh. Jb. Jg. 48, 1912, S. 116–24.—Nachweise zu Shakespeares Totenmaske. Jena, 1913. (100 S. u. 50 Taf.)—Über Shakespeares Totenmaske. In: GRM., Jg. 6, 1914, S. 358 ff.

ALOIS BRANDL: Zu 'Shakespeares Totenmaske' und 'Ben Jonsons Totenbild'. In: Sh. Jb. Jg. 47, 1911, S. 156–69.

Brandl doubts the genuineness of the death mask.

JOSEPH FEST: Zu 'Shakespeares Totenmaske' und 'Ben Jonsons Totenbild'. In: GRM. Jg. 5, 1913, S. 147–55.

Opposes the theory of Wislicenus.

ERNST BENKARD: Das ewige Antlitz. Berlin, 1927.

ERNST GUNDOLF: Zur Beurteilung der Darmstädter Shakespeare-Maske. In: Sh. Jb., Bd. 64, N.F. Bd. 5, 1928, S. 132–40.

IV. SHAKESPEARE'S PERSONALITY

(1) GENERAL ACCOUNT OF SHAKESPEARE'S CHARACTER

E. VEHSE: Shakespeare als Protestant, Politiker, Psycholog und Dichter. 2 Bde. Hamburg, 1851.

GUSTAV RÜMELIN: Shakespeares Individualität und Bildungsgang. In the same writer's Shakespeare—Studien. Stuttgart, 1874[2], S. 167–192.

EDWARD DOWDEN: Shakspere, his mind and art. London, 1875. German translation: E. DOWDEN: Shakspere. Sein Entwicklungsgang in seinen Werken. Übers. von WILHELM WAGNER. Heilbronn, 1879. (xii, 327 S.)

GEORG BRANDES: William Shakespeare. A critical study. 2 vols. London, 1896.

GOLDWIN SMITH: Shakespeare the man. An attempt to find traces of the dramatist's personal character in his dramas. Toronto, 1899. (77 pp.) Rev.: Sh. Jb. 38, 1902, S. 247, W. Keller.

WILHELM MÜNCH: Shakespeare als Mensch, nach Leslie Stephen. In: Sh. Jb. Jg. 39, 1903, S. 223–32.

RUDOLPH GENÉE: William Shakespeare in seinem Werden und Wesen. Berlin, 1905. (xiii, 472 S.)

HERMANN CONRAD: Was erkennen wir von Shakespeares Wesen in seinem Brutus? In: Preuss. Jbb., Bd. 125, 1906, S. 462–92.

LORENZ MORSBACH: Shakespeare als Mensch. Festvortrag. In: Sh. Jb. Jg. 44, 1908, S. xiii–xxviii.

FRANK HARRIS: The man Shakespeare and his tragic life-story. New York, 1909. (xviii, 422 pp.) German translation: Der Mensch Shakespeare und seine tragische Lebensgeschichte. Berlin, 1928. (384 S.)

A. C. BRADLEY: Shakespeare the man. In Bradley's Oxford lectures on poetry. London, 1909, pp. 311–57.

WILHELM CREIZENACH: Religiös-sittliche und politisch-soziale Anschauungen der Theaterdichter. In his: Geschichte des neueren Dramas, Bd. 4, Halle, 1909, S. 115–72.

SIDNEY LEE: The impersonal aspect of Shakespeare's art. Oxford, 1909. (20 pp.)=The Engl. Assoc., no. 13. Rev.: Sh. Jb. 46, 1910, S. 310–11, M. Förster.

EDWARD DOWDEN: Is Shakespeare self-revealed? In the same author's Essays, modern and Elizabethan. London, 1910, pp. 250–81.
Opposes Lee's view.

DAVID MASSON: Shakespeare personally. Ed. by ROSALINE MASSON. London, 1914. (243 pp.) Rev.: Sh. Jb. 51, 1916, S. 262–3, Creizenach.

W. T. BREWSTER: The restoration of Shakespeare's personality. In: Columbia Univ. Shakespearian Studies, 1916.

H. C. BEECHING: The character of Shakespeare. London, 1921. (Annual Shakespeare lecture, 1917).=Proc. Brit. Acad. 1917–18, pp. 157–79.

EDWARD G. HARMAN: The 'impersonality' of Shakespeare. London, 1925. (326 pp.)

PHILIPP ARONSTEIN: Shakespeares Persönlichkeit in seinen Dramen. In: GRM. Jg. 17, 1929, S. 111–30.

(2) SHAKESPEARE'S CONCEPTION OF LIFE AND THE WORLD

(a) SHAKESPEARE'S PHILOSOPHICAL IDEAS IN GENERAL

GUSTAV RÜMELIN: Shakespeares Lebensansichten. In the same author's Shakespeare-Studien. Stuttgart, 1874², S. 193–225.

KARL ELZE: Shakespeares Charakter, seine Welt- und Lebensanschauung. In: Sh. Jb. Jg. 10, 1875, S. 75–126.

SIDNEY LEE: Aspects of Shakespeare's philosophy. In Lee's Shakespeare and the modern stage. London, 1907, pp. 142–69.
Contrasts Shakespeare's practical outlook on life with Bacon's academic philosophy.

FRANZ LÜTGENAU: Shakespeare als Philosoph. Leipzig, 1909. (116 S.) Rev.: Sh. Jb. 47, 1911, S. 291, R. Petsch.

ALFRED HOYER: Eine historisch-genetische Analyse der Begriffe *nature* und *fortune* bei Shakespeare bis Abschluss der 'Hamlet'-Periode. Diss. Halle, 1913. (viii, 82 S.) Rev.: Sh. Jb. 51, 1915, S. 268, Creizenach.

CHRISTEN COLLIN: Fra Shakespeare-tidens idékamp. In: Edda, Bd. vi, 1916, S. 1–43. Rev.: Sh. Jb. 54, 1918, S. 148–9, Jantzen.

BERNHARD MÜNZ: Shakespeare als Philosoph. Halle, 1918. (105 S.) Also in: Anglia, Bd. 42, 1918, S. 225–329. Rev.: Litbl. 44, 1923, Sp. 246–7.

HELENE RICHTER: [Shakespeare], Der Weltmann und Weltweise. In H. Richter's Shakespeare der Mensch. Leipzig, 1923, S. 111–44.

LEVIN L. SCHÜCKING: Shakespeares Persönlichkeitsideal. In: Neue Jbb. f. Wiss. und Jugendbildung, Jg. 3, 1927, S. 324–34.

HARDIN CRAIG: Shakespeare and formal logic. In: Studies in English philology. A miscellany in honor of Frederick Klaeber. Minneapolis, 1929, pp. 380–96.

A. MARQUARDSEN: Christopher Marlowes Kosmologie. In: Sh. Jb. Jg. 41, 1905, S. 54–80.

(b) SHAKESPEARE'S PSYCHOLOGY AND ETHICS

J. C. BUCKNILL: The psychology of Shakespeare. London, 1859. (viii, 264 pp.)

ONIMUS: La psychologie dans les drames de Shakespeare. Paris, 1876.

C. C. HENSE: Die Darstellung der Seelenkrankheiten in Shakespeares Dramen. In: Sh. Jb. Jg. 13, 1878, S. 212–47.

RICHARD LOENING: Über die physiologischen Grundlagen der Shakespeare-schen Psychologie. Festvortrag. In: Sh. Jb. Jg. 31, 1895, S. 1–37.

HANS LAEHR: Die Darstellung krankhafter Geisteszustände in Shakespeares Dramen. Stuttgart, 1898.

S. SINGER: Über die physiologischen Grundlagen der Shakespeareschen Psychologie. In: Sh. Jb. Jg. 36, 1900, S. 65–94.
With copious examples and quotations from Shakespeare's dramas.

FRANK CH. SHARP: Shakespeare's portrayal of the moral life. New York, 1902. (xiii, 232 pp.) Rev.: Sh. Jb. 40, 1904, S. 267–8, Churchill.

RICHARD G. MOULTON: The moral system of Shakespeare. New York, 1903. (viii, 381 pp.) Rev.: Sh. Jb. 40, 1904, S. 270–5, McClumpha; JEGPh. 7, 1907/8, pp. 133–5, R. K. Root.

BRUNO KIEHL: Wiederkehrende Begebenheiten und Verhältnisse in Shake-speares Dramen. Ein Beitrag zur Shakespeare-Psychologie. Diss. Berlin, 1904. Rev.: Sh. Jb. 41, 1905, S. 241–2, Hale.

ROBERT PETSCH: Die Volksszenen in Shakespeares Dramen. In: Frankf. Ztg. v. 19. Sept. 1905. Rev.: Sh. Jb. 42, 1906, S. 315–16.
Deals with mass-psychology in Shakespeare's works.

RICHARD G. MOULTON: Shakespeare as a dramatic thinker, a popular illustration of fiction as the experimental side of philosophy. New York & London, 1907. (viii, 381 pp.) Rev.: Sh. Jb. 44, 1908, S. 362, M. Förster.

Being a new edition of his work, 'The moral system of Shakespeare' (1903).

EDWARD DOWDEN: Elizabethan psychology. In: Dowden's Essays, modern and Elizabethan. London, 1910, pp. 308–33.

HAROLD FORD: Shakespeare, his ethical teaching. Smith's Publishing Co., 1922. (112 pp.)

MURRAY W. BUNDY: Shakespeare and Elizabethan psychology. In: JEGPh., vol. 23, 1924, pp. 516–49.

SIR HENRY JONES: The ethical idea in Shakespeare. In the same author's Essays on literature and education, ed. by H. J. W. HETHERINGTON, No. 4. London, 1924. (288 pp.)

HARDIN CRAIG: Shakespeare's depiction of passions. In: Phil. Quart., vol. 4, 1925, pp. 289–301.

Author compares Charron's 'Book of Wisdom', Burton's 'Anatomy of Melancholy', and Bacon's 'Advancement of Learning'.

RENÉ BERTHELOT: La sagesse shakespearienne. In: Rev. de métaphysique et de morale, 1926, pp. 145–80.

RUTH LEILA ANDERSON: Elizabethan psychology and Shakespeare's plays. Iowa, 1928. (182 pp.)=Univ. of Iowa Humanistic Studies, vol. iii, no. 4. Rev.: PMLA. 48, 1928, p. 22; Litbl., 1928, Sp. 468; JEGPh. 28, 1929, pp. 438–9, M. W. Bundy.

CARROLL CAMDEN: Marlowe and Elizabethan psychology. In: Philol. Quart., vol. 8, 1929, pp. 69–78.

(3) SHAKESPEARE'S ATTITUDE TOWARDS RELIGION AND THE CHURCH

(Cf. also pp. 175–176)

A. F. RIO: Shakespeare. Paris, 1864. Aus dem Französ. übers. von KARL ZELL. Freiburg i. Br., 1864. (xvi, 303 S.)

Represents Shakespeare as a Catholic.

BISHOP WORDSWORTH: On Shakespeare's knowledge and use of the Bible. London, 1864. (xii, 310 pp.) 1892[4].

MICHAEL BERNAYS: Shakespeare ein katholischer Dichter. (Shakespeare von A. F. Rio. Aus d. Französ. übers. v. Karl Zell.) In: Sh. Jb., Bd. 1, 1865, S. 220–99.

Refutes Rio's view.

A. REICHENSPERGER: William Shakespeare, insbesondere sein Verhältnis zum Mittelalter und zur Gegenwart. Münster, 1872.

Regards Shakespeare as a Catholic.

C. J. PLUMPTRE: Religion and morality of Shakespeare's works, 1873.

J. M. RAICH: Shakespeares Stellung zur katholischen Religion. Mainz, 1884.

FRED. G. FLEAY: Shakespeare and Puritanism. In: Anglia, Bd. 7, 1884, S. 223–31.

THOMAS CARTER: Shakespeare, puritan and recusant. Edinburgh and London, 1897. (208 pp.) Rev.: Sh. Jb. 35, 1899, S. 307–11, Dibelius.
Shakespeare's father as a puritan. Cf. also four essays by Th. Carter and George Wyndham in the Saturday Review, vol. 84, 1897.

HENRY S. BOWDEN: The religion of Shakespeare, chiefly from the writings of the late Mr. Richard Simpson. London, 1899. (xvi, 428 pp.). Rev.: Sh. Jb. 36, 1900, S. 290–2, A. Brandl.
Regards Shakespeare as a Catholic.

H. R. D. ANDERS: Shakespeare's books. Berlin, 1904.
Cf. the section: The Bible and the Prayer Book.

EMIL KOEPPEL: Konfessionelle Strömungen in der dramatischen Dichtung des Zeitalters der beiden ersten Stuart-Könige. Festvortrag. In: Sh. Jb. Jg. 40, 1904, S. xvi–xxix.

THOMAS CARTER: Shakespeare and Holy Scripture, with the version he used [i.e. the Genevan Bible]. London, 1905. (498 pp.)

H. C. BEECHING: On the religion of Shakespeare. In: Shakespeare's works in 10 vols., Stratford, 1904–7=The Stratford Town Edition, vol. 10.
The article contains a review of all opinions on the subject up to 1907.

W. BURGESS: The Bible in Shakespeare. A study of the relation of the works of William Shakespeare to the Bible; with numerous parallel passages, quotations, references, paraphrases, and allusions. New ed. New York (1918). (xiv, 288 pp.)

CAMILLE LOOTEN: Shakespeare et la religion. Paris, 1924. (311 pp.)

GEORGE SEIBEL: The religion of Shakespeare. London, 1924. (76 pp.)

S. O. ADDY: Shakespeare's puritan relations. In: N. & Q., vol. 154, 1928, pp. 273–6.

E. I. FRIPP: The religion of Shakespeare's father. In: Hibbert Journal, vol. 26, 1928, pp. 535–47.

(4) SHAKESPEARE'S ATTITUDE TOWARDS THE SUPERNATURAL

(Cf. also Ghosts, p. 114, and Folk-lore, p. 179)

LEWES LAVATER: Of ghostes and spirites walking by nyght, 1572. Edited with introduction and appendix by J. DOVER WILSON and MAY YARDLEY. Oxford, for the Shakespeare Association, 1929. (xxxi, 251 pp.) Introduction: J. DOVER WILSON: The ghost-scenes in Hamlet in the light of Elizabethan spiritualism. Appendix: MAY YARDLEY: The Catholic position in the ghost controversy of the 16th century, with special reference to Pierre Le Loyer's IIII livres des spectres (1586).

REGINALD SCOT: The discoverie of witchcraft. 1584. Edited by B. NICHOLSON, 1886.
With valuable introduction.

LUDWIG TIECK: Shakespeares Behandlung des Wunderbaren. 1793. Also in: Krit. Schriften 1, 1898, S. 39 ff.

THOMAS A. SPALDING: Elizabethan demonology. An essay in illustration of the belief in the existence of devils . . . with special reference to Shakespeare and his works. London, 1880. (xiv, 152 pp.)

T. F. THISELDON DYER: Folk-lore of Shakespeare. London [1883].

ALFRED NUTT: The fairy mythology of Shakespeare. London, 1900. (40 pp.) Rev.: Sh. Jb. 37, 1901, S. 249–50, A. Brandl; Bbl. 16, 1905, S. 289–91, G. Binz.

WILLIAM WILSON: Shakespeare and astrology from a student's point of view. Boston, 1903. (12 pp.)

R. ZENDER: Die Magie im englischen Drama des elisabethanischen Zeitalters. Diss. Halle, 1907. (111 S.)

J. PAUL GIBSON: Shakespeare's use of the supernatural. Cambridge, 1908. (143 pp.) Rev.: Sh. Jb. 45, 1909, S. 396–7, M. Förster; Bbl. 20, 1909, S. 175–7, Ph. Aronstein.

HELEN H. STEWART: The supernatural in Shakespeare. London, 1908. (159 pp.) Rev.: Sh. Jb. 45, 1909, S. 396, M. Förster.

MARGARET LUCY: Shakespeare and the supernatural. A brief study of folk-lore, superstition, and witchcraft in 'Macbeth', 'Midsummer Night's Dream', and 'The Tempest'. Liverpool, 1908. (40 pp.)

J. E. PORITZKY: Shakespeares Hexen, ein literarisches Kulturbild. Neue Shakespeare-Bühne, 1909.

HELENE RICHTER: Shakespeare, der Naturalist des Übernatürlichen. In: E. St., Bd. 42, 1910, S. 363–80.

WALLACE NOTESTEIN: A history of witchcraft in England from 1558 to 1718. Washington, 1911. (xiv, 442 pp.)

PHILIPP ARONSTEIN: Die Hexen im englischen Renaissancedrama. I, II. In: GRM., Jg. 4, 1912, S. 536–49 u. 582–97. Rev.: Sh. Jb. 39, 1913, S. 196–7, Grabau.

FLORIS DELATTRE: English fairy poetry from the origins to the 17th century. London, 1912. (235 pp.) Reprint of 'A Description of the King and Queen of Fairies, their habit, fare, their abode, pomp, and state' (1635). Rev.: Sh. Jb. 49, 1913, S. 240–41, M. Förster.
Deals with instances of belief in fairies in English literature up to the XVIIth century.

ALBERT DE BERZEVICZY: Le surnaturel dans le théâtre de Shakespeare. Traduit du hongrois. Paris [1913]. (179 pp.) Rev.: Sh. Jb. 50, 1914, S. 190–91, M. Förster.

F. WEBER: Volkskundliche Streifzüge durch Shakespeare. In: Bayerische Hefte f. Volkskunde, Jg. 1, 1914, S. 187–200.

AUGUST ACKERMANN: Der Seelenglaube bei Shakespeare. Eine mythologisch-literarwissenschaftliche Abhandlung. Diss. Zürich. Frauenfeld, 1914. (vi, 151 S.) Rev.: Sh. Jb. 52, 1916, S. 225–29, M. Förster; Bbl. 26, 1915, S. 99–102, A. Eichler; Arch. 134, 1915, S. 471, A. Brandl.

ERNST FRIEDRICH: Die Magie im französischen Theater des 16. und 17 Jhrh. Leipzig, 1908. (xxxvi, 344 S.)=Münchener Beitr. z. rom. und engl. Philol., hrsg. v. Breymann und Schick, H. 41. Rev.: Sh. Jb. 45, 1909, S. 397, M. Förster.

(5) SHAKESPEARE'S ATTITUDE TOWARDS THE STATE
(Cf. Works on Machiavelli, p. 71)

BENNO TSCHISCHWITZ: Shakespeares Staat und Königtum. Nachgewiesen aus der Lancaster-Tetralogie. Halle, 1866. (iv, 89 S.)

SIDNEY LEE: Shakespeare and patriotism. In Lee's Shakespeare and the modern stage. London, 1907, pp. 170–87.

CHRISTEN COLLIN: Fra Shakespeare-tidens idékamp. In: Edda, 1916, S. 1–43. Rev.: Z. f. e. U. 15, 1916, S. 437, Jantzen.

FRANZ KAIBEL: Dichter und Patriotismus. Die Betrachtung eines Deutschen zum 300. Todestag eines Engländers. In: Sh. Jb. Jg. 52, 1916, S. 36–63.

R. BROTANEK: Shakespeare über den Krieg. Festvortrag. In: Sh. Jb. Jg. 52, 1916, S. xvi–xlviii.

JOSEPH KOHLER: Die Staatsidee Shakespeares in 'Richard II'. Sh. Jb. Jg. 53, 1917, S. 1–12.

SIR WALTER RALEIGH: Shakespeare and England. London=The Brit. Acad. The annual Shakespeare lecture, 1918. (18 pp.)

J. A. R. MARRIOTT: Shakespeare and politics. In: Cornhill Magazine, 1927, pp. 678–90.

ILSE DÜRR: Die Vaterlandsliebe Shakespeares. Diss. Tübingen, 1929. (116 S.)

H. B. CHARLTON: Shakespeare, politics, and politicians. London, 1929. (24 pp.) =Engl. Assoc. Pamphlet 72.

A H. SMITH: Les événements politiques de la France dans le théâtre anglais du siècle d'Élisabeth. 1906.

PHILIPP ARONSTEIN: Das nationale Erlebnis im englischen Renaissance-drama. In: Sh. Jb. Jg. 55, 1919, S. 86–128.

(6) SHAKESPEARE'S ATTITUDE TOWARDS THE SOCIAL CLASSES

(Cf. also pp. 176–177)

ERNEST H. CROSBY: Shakespeare's attitude towards the working classes. New York [*ca.* 1900]. (32 pp.)

BERNARD SHAW: Better than Shakespeare. In Shaw's Three plays for puritans. London, 1901 (pp. 27–38).

HUGO VON HOFMANNSTHAL: Shakespeares Könige und grosse Herren. In: Sh. Jb. Jg. 41, 1905, S. x–xxvii.

LEO N. TOLSTOI: Shakespeare. Eine kritische Studie. Nebst dem Essay Ernest Crosbys über die Stellung Shakespeares zu den arbeitenden Klassen und einem Brief Bernard Shaws. Übers. von M. ENCKHAUSEN. Hannover, 1906². (148 S.) Rev.: Südd. Monatshefte 1910, S. 548, L. L. Schücking.

THEODOR VETTER: Shakespeare und das Volk. Festvortrag. In: Sh. Jb. Jg. 46, 1910, S. xiv–xxxii.
Depicts Shakespeare as friend of the lower classes.

FREDERICK TUPPER: The Shakespearean mob. In: PMLA., vol. 27, N.S. vol. 20, 1912, pp. 486–523.

ALBERT H. TOLMAN: Is Shakespeare aristocratic? In: PMLA., vol. 29, N.S. vol. 22, 1914, pp. 277–98.

CHARLES M. GAYLEY: Shakespeare and the founders of liberty in America. New York, 1917.

WOLFGANG KELLER: Shakespeare und sein König. Festvortrag. In: Sh. Jb. Jg. 54, 1918, S. xiii–xxxiii.
Expresses view that Shakespeare was a Court playwright.

PHILIPP ARONSTEIN: Der soziologische Charakter des englischen Renaissance-dramas. In: GRM., Jg. 12, 1914, S. 155–71 u. 214–24. Rev.: Sh. Jb. 62, 1926, S. 174.

FELIX E. SCHELLING: The common folk of Shakespeare. In the same author's Shakespeare and 'demi-science'. Papers on Elizabethan topics. Philadelphia, 1927.

(7) SHAKESPEARE'S ATTITUDE TOWARDS THE LAW

WILLIAM L. RUSHTON: Shakespeare's legal maxims. London, 1859 (34 pp.), 1907² (61 pp.). Rev.: Sh. Jb. 44, 1908, S. 330–2, R. Eberstadt.

LORD CAMPBELL: Shakespeare's legal acquirements. London, 1859. (118 pp.)

JOSEPH KOHLER: Shakespeare vor dem Forum der Jurisprudenz. Würzburg, 1883. Berlin, 1919². (xi, 366 S.) Rev.: Sh. Jb. 56, 1920, S. 132–6, Rosenfeld; Bbl. 38, 1927, S. 200–204, M. Förster.

WILLIAM C. DEVECMON: *In re* Shakespeare's legal acquirements. Notes of an unbeliever therein. Shakespeare Soc. of New York, 1890. London, 1899. (viii, 52 pp.)

FRITZ FREUND: Shakespeare als Rechtsphilosoph. In: Sh. Jb. Jg. 28, 1893, S. 54–71.

J. CHURTON COLLINS: Was Shakespeare a lawyer? In the same writer's: Studies in Shakespeare. London, 1904.

EDW. J. WHITE: Commentaries on the law in Shakespeare with explanations of the legal terms used in the plays, poems, and sonnets, and a consideration on the criminal types presented. St. Louis, Mo., 1911, 1913². (xlviii, 524 pp.) Rev.: Sh. Jb. 50, 1914, S. 192, M. Förster.

GEORGE GREENWOOD: Shakespeare's law. London, 1920. (48 pp.)

K. GÖRRES: Öffentliches Recht bei Shakespeare.=Abhdl. v. Rechtsanwälten d. Kammergerichtsbezirks. Festschr. f. ERNST HEINITZ. Berlin, 1926, S. 68–123.

SIR DUNBAR PLUNKET BARTON: Links between Shakespeare and the law. With a foreword by JAMES MONTGOMERY BECK. London, 1929.

Cf. also the literature of the Shakespeare-Bacon Controversy (Castle 1897, Allen 1900, J. M. Robertson 1913), and works dealing with 'The Merchant of Venice' (Eberstadt, 1908, Niemeyer, 1912).

(8) SHAKESPEARE'S ATTITUDE TOWARDS NATURE AND SCIENCE

(a) NATURE AND SCIENCE IN GENERAL

H. W. SEAGER: Natural history in Shakespeare's time, being extracts illustrative of the subject as he knew it. London, 1896. (viii, 358 pp.)

EDMUND O. VON LIPPMANN: Naturwissenschaftliches aus Shakespeare. In: Zs. f. Naturwiss., Bd. 74, 6. Folge Bd. 12, 1901, S. 305 ff. Also published separately in Stuttgart, 1902, and in: Abhdl. und Vorträge z. Gesch. der Naturwiss., Leipzig, 1906.

EDWARD DOWDEN: Shakespeare as a man of science. In his Essays, modern and Elizabethan. London, 1910, pp. 282–307.

Shows that the views of Shakespeare and Bacon which coincide were commonly accepted views of the time.

P. ANSELL ROBIN: The old physiology in English literature. London, 1911. (vii, 184 pp.) Rev.: Sh. Jb. 48, 1912, S. 336, M. Förster.

GREGOR SARRAZIN: Shakespeare als Landmann. Festvortrag. In: Sh. Jb. Jg. 48, 1912, S. xii–xxx.

(b) ZOOLOGY

ROBERT PATTERSON: The natural history of the insects mentioned in Shakespeare's plays. London, 1841.

JAMES E. HARTING: The birds of Shakespeare, critically examined, explained, and illustrated. London, 1871. (xxiii, 321 pp.)

EMMA PHIPSON: The animal-lore of Shakespeare's time, including quadrupeds, birds, reptiles, fish and insects. London, 1883. (xvi, 476 pp.)

(c) BOTANY

SIDNEY BEISLEY: Shakspere's garden, or the plants and flowers named in his works described and defined. London, 1864. (xx, 172 pp.)

HENRY N. ELLACOMBE: The plant-lore and garden-craft of Shakespeare. Exeter [1878], London, 1884² (438 pp.). 1896.

ESTHER SINGLETON: The Shakespeare garden. London, 1923. (xxii, 360 pp.)

F. G. SAVAGE: The flora and folk-lore of Shakespeare. Cheltenham, 1923. (v, 420 pp.)

(d) MEDICINE

J. CH. BUCKNILL: The medical knowledge of Shakespeare. London, 1860. (viii, 292 pp.)

H. AUBERT: Shakespeare als Mediziner. Rostock, 1873.

REINHOLD SIGISMUND: Die medizinische Kenntnis Shakespeares (nach seinen Dramen historisch-kritisch bearbeitet). I, II, III. In: Sh. Jb. Jg. 16, 1881, S. 39–143; Jg. 17, 1882, S. 6–66; Jg. 18, 1883, S. 36–80.

W. KÜHNE: Venus, Amor und Bacchus in Shakespeares Dramen. Eine medizinisch-poetische Studie. Braunschweig, 1902. (74 S.) Rev.: Sh. Jb. 38, 1902, S. 254–5, W. Keller.

JULIUS HIRSCHBERG: Shakespeare-Anmerkungen eines Augenarztes. In: Sh. Jb. Jg. 56, 1920, S. 95–105.

H. SOMERVILLE: Madness in Shakespearian tragedy. London, 1929. (207 pp.)

(e) PHARMACY

A. CARTAZ: La toxicologie dans les drames de Shakespeare. Paris, 1911. Rev.: Sh. Jb. 52, 1916, S. 222, M. Förster.

HERMANN SCHELENZ: Shakespeare und sein Wissen auf den Gebieten der Arznei- und Volkskunde. Bd. 1. Leipzig & Hamburg, 1914. (vii, 328 S.) Rev.: Sh. Jb. 52, 1916, S. 217–25, M. Förster.

(9) SHAKESPEARE'S ATTITUDE TOWARDS ART

FRIEDRICH FÖRSTER: Shakespeare und die Tonkunst. In: Sh. Jb. Jg. 2, 1867, S. 155–83.
Discusses Shakespeare's musical taste and gifts.

E. W. NAYLOR: Shakespeare and music, with illustrations from the music of the 16th and 17th centuries. London, 1896. (238 pp.) Rev.: Sh. Jb. 36, 1900, S. 296–9, H. Hecht.

LOUIS CH. ELSON: Shakespeare in music, a collection of the chief musical allusions in the plays . . . London, 1901. (364 pp.) Detailed summary in Sh. Jb. 38, 1902, S. 364–5, No. 735.
Examination of the musical element in Shakespeare's works.

(Cf. also pp. 106–107)

HENRY GREEN: Shakespeare and the emblem writers. An exposition of their similarities of thought and expression, preceded by a view of emblem literature to 1616. London, 1870. (xvi, 572 pp.)

(10) SHAKESPEARE'S ATTITUDE TOWARDS EDUCATION
(Cf. also pp. 178–179)

JULIUS ZUPITZA: Shakespeare über Bildung, Schulen, Schüler und Schulmeister. Festvortrag. In: Sh. Jb. Jg. 18, 1883, S. 1–31.

SHAKESPEARES LATEINGRAMMATIK: Lilys Grammatica latina nach der ältesten bekannten Ausgabe von 1527 und der für Shakespeare in Betracht kommenden Ausgabe von 1566 (London, R. Wolfius). Neugedruckt von S. BLACH. In: Sh. Jb. Jg. 44, 1908, S. 65–117 u. Jg. 45, 1909, S. 51–100.

(11) SHAKESPEARE'S GEOGRAPHICAL KNOWLEDGE. HIS ALLEGED TRAVELS
(Cf. also pp. 180–181)

JOHN BRUCE: Who was 'Will, my Lord of Leicester's jesting player'? In: The Shakespeare Soc.'s Papers, i, 1844, pp. 88–95.

The author supposes that Shakespeare accompanied the Earl of Leicester to Holland as an actor.

KARL ELZE: Shakespeares mutmassliche Reisen. In: Sh. Jb. Jg. 8, 1873, S. 46–91.

GREGOR SARRAZIN: Shakespeare in Mantua? In: Sh. Jb. Jg. 29–30, 1894, S. 249–54.

Cf. also, by the same author, 'Shakespeares Lehrjahre', Weimar, 1897, Kap. 5.

FRANK M. BRISTOL: Shakespeare and America. Chicago, 1898.

Discusses those passages in Shakespeare's dramas which refer to the New World.

E. KOEPPEL: War Shakespeare in Italien? In: Sh. Jb. Jg. 35, 1899, S. 122–6.

THEODOR ELZE: Venezianische Skizzen zu Shakespeare. München, 1899. (vi, 162 S.)

MARY AUGUSTA SCOTT: Elizabethan translations from the Italian. The titles of such works now first collected and arranged, with annotations. In: PMLA., vol. 14, N.S. vol. 7, 1899, pp. 465–571.

Valuable bibliography of English translations of Italian travel-reports, historical and political works, and treatises on manners and customs.

GREGOR SARRAZIN: Neue italienische Skizzen zu Shakespeare. In: Sh. Jb. Jg. 36, 1900, S. 95–108.

HENRI LOGEMAN: Shakespeare te Helsingör. In: Mélanges PAUL FREDERICY. Bruxelles, 1904. (10 S.) Rev.: Sh. Jb. 41, 1905, S. 241, Sarrazin.

Refutes the supposition that Shakespeare visited Helsingör.

W. J. LAWRENCE: Was Shakespeare ever in Ireland? A conjectural study. In: Sh. Jb. Jg. 42, 1906, S. 65–75.

LACY COLLISON-MORLEY: Shakespeare in Italy. Stratford, 1916. (180 pp.) Rev.: MLR. 14, 1919, pp. 435–6, J. G. Robertson.

MORRIS P. TILLEY: Shakespeare and Italian geography. In: JEGPh., vol. 16, 1917, pp. 454–5.

ATTILIO NULLI: Shakespeare in Italia. Milano, 1918. (245 pp.) Rev.: MLR. 14, 1919, pp. 435–6, J. G. Robertson.

EDWARD H. SUGDEN: A topographical dictionary to the works of Shakespeare and his fellow dramatists. Manchester & London, 1925. (xix, 580 pp.)
Dictionary of the place-names occurring in the works of Shakespeare, the Elizabethan dramatists, and Milton.

(12) SHAKESPEARE AND SPORT

D. H. MADDEN: The Diary of Master William Silence. A study of Shakespeare and Elizabethan sport. London, 1897. (x, 386 pp.)

(13) SHAKESPEARE AND HERALDRY
(Cf. also p. 180)

ALFRED VON MAUNTZ: Heraldik in Diensten der Shakespeare-Forschung. Selbststudien. Berlin, 1903. (331 S.) Rev.: Sh. Jb. 39, 1903, S. 283–85, W. Keller; Bbl. 15, 1904, S. 113–20, Ph. Aronstein.

SAMUEL A. TANNENBAUM: The Shakspere coat-of-arms. New York, 1908. (20 pp.) Rev.: Sh. Jb. 45, 1909, S. 400, M. Förster.

A. H. NASON: Heralds and heraldry in Ben Jonson's plays, masques and entertainments. New York, 1907. (xviii, 164 pp.) Rev.: Bbl. 20, 1909, S. 169, K. Lincke.

(14) SHAKESPEARE AND WOMEN (Love, Marriage, Family)

A. FREIHERR VON LOËN: Shakespeare über die Liebe. Festvortrag. In: Sh. Jb. Jg. 19, 1884, S. 1–15.

RICHARD GOSCHE: Shakespeares Ideal der Gattin und Mutter. Festvortrag. In: Sh. Jb. Jg. 21, 1886, S. 1–14.

C. H. HERFORD: Shakespeare's treatment of love and marriage. In: Edda, vol. 6, 1916, S. 92–111. Also in Herford's Shakespeare's treatment of love and marriage and other essays. London (1921). (201 pp.) Rev.: Sh. Jb. 54, 1918, S. 151, Jantzen.

C. H. HERFORD: The normality of Shakespeare, illustrated in his treatment of love and marriage. London, 1920. (16 pp.)=The Engl. Assoc. Pamphl. No. 47.

MORTON LUCE: Love in Shakespeare. In: The nineteenth century and after, vol. 96, 1924, pp. 335–342.

LEVIN L. SCHÜCKING: Die Familie bei Shakespeare. In: E. St., Bd. 62, 1927, S. 187–226.

MARIE GOTHEIN: Die Frau im englischen Drama vor Shakespeare. In: Sh. Jb. Jg. 40, 1904, S. 1–50.

ALOIS BRANDL: Thomas Elyot's 'Verteidigung guter Frauen' (1545) und die Frauenfrage in England bis Shakespeare. Anhang: Thomas Elyot's 'Schutzmittel gegen den Tod' (1545). In: Sh. Jb. Jg. 51, 1915, S. 111–70.

IRMGARD RÖHRICHT: Massingers Idealbild der Frau in seinem Wesen und seiner Bedeutung. Diss. München, 1918. (121 S.)

IRMGARD VON INGERSLEBEN: Das elisabethanische Ideal der Ehefrau bei Overbury ⟨1613⟩. Cöthen, 1921. (108 S.)=Neue anglist. Arbeiten, hrsg. von Schücking und Deutschbein, No. 5. Rev.: Bbl. 34, 1923, S. 308-9, J. Caro.

LEVIN L. SCHÜCKING: Zu den Anfängen des Familienlebens in England 1200-1600. In: N. Spr. Jg. 32, 1924, S. 1-18.

LEVIN L. SCHÜCKING: Die Familie im Puritanismus. Studien über Familie und Literatur in England im 16., 17. und 18. Jhrh. Leipzig, 1929. (xii, 219 S.)

V. TEXT: TRANSMISSION AND EMENDATION

(1) PRINTING OF WORKS IN SHAKESPEAREAN TIMES

(a) PRINTING IN GENERAL AND THE TRANSMISSION OF SHAKESPEARE'S TEXT

WILLIAM BLADES: Shakspere and typography, being an attempt to show Shakspere's personal connection with and technical knowledge of the art of printing. London, 1872. (v, 67 pp.)

PHOEBE SHEAVYN: Writers and the publishing trade, circa 1600. In: Libr., N.S., vol. 7, 1906, pp. 337-65.

RONALD B. MCKERROW: Notes on bibliographical evidence for literary students and editors of English works of the 16th and 17th centuries. London, 1914. (102 pp.)=Repr. from Bibliogr. Soc. Trans., vol. 12, 1914. Rev.: Sh. Jb. 52, 1916, S. 210-13, M. Förster.

Deals with the practical side of English printing and with the printing of an Elizabethan text.

ALFRED W. POLLARD: Authors, players, and pirates in Shakespeare's day. In: Libr. 3rd ser., vol. 7, 1916, pp. 73-101.

ALFRED W. POLLARD: The manuscripts of Shakespeare's plays. In: Libr. 3rd ser., vol. 7, 1916, pp. 198-226.

H. ROBINSON SHIPHERD: Play publishing in Elizabethan times. In: PMLA., vol. 34, N.S. vol. 27, 1919, pp. 580-600.

A. W. POLLARD and J. DOVER WILSON: The 'stolne and surreptitious' Shakespearian texts. I. Why some of Shakespeare's plays were pirated. II. How some of Shakespeare's plays were pirated. In: TLS., Jan. 9 and 16, 1919, pp. 18 and 30.

Cf. also the following numbers under 'Correspondence'.

ALFRED W. POLLARD: Shakespeare's fight with the pirates, and the problems of the transmission of his text. Cambridge, 1920. (110 pp.)=Shakespeare problems, 1. Rev.: Sh. Jb. 59-60, 1924, S. 187-92, W. Keller; Dt. Vjschr. Jg. 6, 1928, S. 179-80, Schücking; Bbl. 35, 1924, S. 113-15, H. T. Price.

EVELYN M. ALBRIGHT: Notes on the status of literary property, 1500–1545. In: Mod. Philol., vol. 17, 1919, pp. 439–55.

WALTER W. GREG: The printing of the Beaumont and Fletcher folio of 1647. In: Bibliogr. Soc. Trans., N.S. ii, no. 2, 1921, pp. 109–15.

PERCY SIMPSON: The bibliographical study of Shakespeare. In: Oxf. Bibliogr. Soc. Proceed. and Papers, vol. i, part 1, 1922–3. O.U.P., 1923. (64 pp.) Rev.: Bbl. 35, 1924, S. 127–8, Flasdieck.
Description of the new bibliographical method of research.

E. K. CHAMBERS: The printing of plays. In his The Elizabethan stage, vol. iii, Oxford, 1923, pp. 157–200.
Expert summary.

H. DE GROOT: Een nieuwe methode in het Shakespeare-onderzoek. In: De Gids, 1924, S. 76–87.
Deals with the bibliographical method.

C. J. SISSON: Bibliographical aspects of some Stuart dramatic manuscripts. In: RESt., vol. 1, 1925, pp. 421–30.

WALTER W. GREG: Prompt copies, private transcripts, and the playhouse scrivener. In: Libr., 4th ser., vol. 6, 1925, pp. 148–56.

R. B. MCKERROW: Elizabethan printers and the composition of reprints. In: Libr., vol. 5, 1925, pp. 357–64.

EVELYN MAY ALBRIGHT: Dramatic publication in England, 1580–1640. New York, 1927. (442 pp.)=Mod. Lang. Ass. of America, Monograph Ser., II. Rev.: MLN. 42, 1927, pp. 547–51, A. Thaler; Arch. 152, 1927, S. 295–6; RESt. 4, 1928, pp. 91–100, Greg; Engl. Studies, 11, 1929, pp. 108–14, H. de Groot; MLR. 23, 1928, pp. 72–4, E. K. Chambers.
Contents: 1. Organization and control of dramatic companies. 2. Literary and dramatic censorship. 3. Authorship and ownership of plays as affecting publication. 4. Conditions affecting the time of publication. 5. Sources of play texts printed. 6. Printing and publishing conditions as affecting the state of the text.
With detailed bibliography.

PERCY SIMPSON: Proof-reading by English authors of the 16th and 17th centuries. In: Oxf. Bibliogr. Soc. Proc. and Papers, II, 1928, pp. 5–24.

(b) PRINTERS, PUBLISHERS, AND BOOKSELLERS

JOHN P. COLLIER: Book entries of the Stationers' Register relating to the drama and popular literature . . . to 1586. Shakespeare Soc., 1848–49. Continued to 1595 in: N. & Q., Ser. 2, xii and Ser. 3, i–iii.

A transcript of the Registers of the Stationers' Company, 1554–1640. Ed. by EDWARD ARBER. 5 vols. London, 1875–94. Continued in: A transcript of the Registers of the worshipful Company of Stationers, 1640–1708. Ed. by G. E. B. EYRE. 3 vols. 1913–14. [Roxburghe Club.]

SIR SIDNEY LEE: An Elizabethan bookseller. In: Bibliographica, 1, 1895, pp. 474–98.

ALFRED W. POLLARD: Woodcuts in English plays printed before 1660. In: Libr., N.S. vol. 1, 1900, pp. 71–88.

HENRY R. PLOMER: A short history of English printing, 1476–1898. London, 1900. Rev. ed. 1921.

BASTIAN A. P. VAN DAM and CORNELIUS STOFFEL: Chapters on English printing, prosody and pronunciation [1550–1700]. Heidelberg, 1902. (iii, 206 pp.)= Anglist. Forsch., hrsg. v. Hoops, H. 9. Rev.: Sh. Jb. 40, 1904, S. 243–49, W. W. Greg; Bbl. 16, 1905, S. 1–7, Luick.

HENRY R. PLOMER: Shakespeare's printers. In: The Bibliographer, 2, 1903, pp. 174–88 and 299–319.

LORENZ HAAS: Verleger und Drucker der Werke Shakespeares bis zum Jahre 1640. Diss. Erlangen, 1904. (iv. 53 S.)

E. G. DUFF: A century of the English book trade, 1457–1557.=Bibliogr. Soc., 1905.

HENRY R. PLOMER: The printers of Shakespeare's plays and poems. In: Libr., N.S., vol. 7, 1906, pp. 149–66.

E. GORDON DUFF: The printers, stationers, and bookbinders of Westminster and London from 1476 to 1535. Cambridge, 1906. Rev.: Libr., N.S., vol. 8, 1907, pp. 102–7.

HENRY R. PLOMER: A dictionary of the booksellers and printers . . . in England, Scotland, and Ireland, 1641–67.=Bibliogr. Soc. 1907. Continued for 1668–1725 in: Bibliogr. Soc. 1922.

K. SCHNEIDER: Die Drucker Shakespeares. In: Zs. f. Bücherfreunde, Jg. 11, 1907, S. 345 ff.

MAX J. WOLFF: Shakespeare im Buchhandel seiner Zeit. In: Sh. Jb. Jg. 44, 1908, S. 126–41.

HENRY R. PLOMER: Henry Bynneman, printer, 1566–83. In: Libr., N.S. vol. 9, 1908, pp. 225–44.

HENRY R. PLOMER: Henry Denham, printer. In: Libr., N.S. vol. 10, 1909, pp. 241–50.

HARRY G. ALDIS: The book-trade, 1557–1625. In: CHEL., vol. 4, 1909, chap. 18.
With bibliography.

RONALD B. MCKERROW: A dictionary of printers and booksellers in England, Scotland, and Ireland, and of foreign printers of English books, 1557–1640. London, 1910.=Bibliogr. Soc.

MAX J. WOLFF: Der englische Buchhandel zur Zeit Shakespeares. In: E. St., Bd. 42, 1910, S. 223–38. Rev.: Sh. Jb. 47, 1911, S. 284, Grabau.

ALFRED W. POLLARD: The regulation of the book trade in the 16th century. In: Libr., 3rd ser., vol. 7, 1916, pp. 18–43.

RONALD B. MCKERROW: Booksellers, printers, and the stationers' trade. In: Shakespeare's England, vol. ii. O.U.P., 1916, pp. 212–39.

HENRIK SCHÜCK: Shakespeare och bokhandeln. In his Shakespeare ok hans tid. Stockholm, 1916, S. 254–81.

ARTHUR W. REED: The regulation of the book trade before the proclamation of 1538.=Bibliogr. Soc. Trans. 15, 1917–19, pp. 157–84.

HARRY FARR: Notes on Shakespeare's printers and publishers, with special reference to the poems and Hamlet. In: Libr., 4th ser., vol. 3, 1923, pp. 225–60.

WALTER W. GREG: An Elizabethan printer and his copy. [RICHARD FIELD and a MS. of Harington's translation of 'Orlando Furioso']. In: Libr. 1923, pp. 102–18.

R. B. MCKERROW: Elizabethan printers and the composition of reprints. In: Libr., vol. 5, 1925, pp. 357–64.

WALTER W. GREG: The decrees and ordinances of the Stationers' Company, 1576–1602. In: Libr., vol. 8, 1928, pp. 395–425.

(c) ELIZABETHAN HANDWRITING

(Cf. Works on Shakespeare's Handwriting, p. 24, and on Sir Thomas More, pp. 277–278)

EDWARD MAUNDE THOMPSON: Autograph MSS. of A. Mundy. In: Bibliogr. Soc. Trans. 14, 1915–17, pp. 325–57.

EDWARD MAUNDE THOMPSON: Handwriting. In: Shakespeare's England, vol. i. O.U.P., 1917, pp. 284–310.

HILARY JENKINSON: Elizabethan handwritings. A preliminary sketch. In: Libr., 4th ser., vol. 3, 1922, pp. 1–34.

WALTER W. GREG: Autograph plays by Anthony Munday. In: MLR., vol. 8, 1923, pp. 89–90.

LEON KELLNER: Restoring Shakespeare. A critical analysis of the misreadings in Shakespeare's works. With facsimiles and numerous plates. Leipzig, 1925. (xvi, 216 S.)=Engl. Bibliothek, hrsg. von Max Förster, Bd. 4.
Contains short sketch of Elizabethan handwriting, pp. 18–30.

M. ST. CLARE BYRNE: Elizabethan handwriting for beginners. In: RESt., vol. 1, 1928, S. 198–209.
Elementary introduction.

English literary autographs, 1550–1650. Selected for reproduction and ed. by W. W. GREG in collaboration with J. P. Gilson, Hilary Jenkinson, R. B. McKerrow, A. W. Pollard. Part I: Dramatists. Part II: Poets. Oxford, 1925 and 1928.

HILARY JENKINSON: The later court hands in England from the 15th to the 17th century. Illustrated from the Common Paper of the Scriveners' Company of London, the English writing masters and the public records. C.U.P., 1927. (x, 200 pp.) Rev.: MLR. 23, 1928, pp. 352–3, Ch. Sisson.

R. B. MCKERROW: The capital letters in Elizabethan handwriting. In: RESt., vol. 3, 1927, pp. 28–36.

(d) ELIZABETHAN SHORTHAND

St. Paul's Epistle to Titus, 1586. Reprint of the shorthand letter appears in
MATTHIAS LEVY: William Shakespeare and Timothe Bright, London, 1910,
p. 60.

HENRIE SMITH: A fruitfull sermon upon part of the 5th chapter of the first
epistle of Saint Paul to the Thessalonians. Which sermon being taken by
characterie, is now republished with the authentic version by H. T. PRICE.
Halle, 1922. (xxxii, 41 pp.) Rev.: Sh. Jb. 59–60, 1924, S. 192–3, W. Keller;
MLR. 19, 1924, pp. 232–4, A. W. Pollard.
The original and the shorthand text of the sermon printed on opposite pages.

TIMOTHE BRIGHT: Characterie, an arte of shorte, swifte, and secrete writing
by character. L. I. Windet, 1588. Reprinted by J. HERBERT FORD, 1888.
Cf. HANS ROLOFF: Zu Fords Neudruck von Brights Stenographiesystem
'Characterie', 1588. In: Arch. 143, 1922, S. 47–51.

The divine prophesies of the *ten sibills* by JANE SEAGER, 1589. (Additional MS.
10037, Brit. Mus.)

MATTHIAS LEVY: Shakespeare and shorthand. London, 1884. (16 pp.)

CURT DEWISCHEIT: Shakespeare und die Stenographie. In: Sh. Jb. Jg. 34,
1898, S. 170–219.

A. SEEBERGER: Zur Entstehung der Quartausgabe des First Part of Jeronimo.
In: Arch. f. Stenogr. Jg. 1908, S. 236 ff.

MATTHIAS LEVY: William Shakespeare and Timothe Bright. London, 1910.

WILLIAM J. CARLTON: Timothe Bright, doctour of phisicke. London, 1911.

P. FRIEDRICH: Studien zur englischen Stenographie im Zeitalter Shakespeares.
Timothe Brights Characterie entwicklungsgeschichtlich und kritisch
betrachtet. Mit einem Anhang: Neue Gesichtspunkte für stenogr. Untersuchungen von Shakespeare-Quartos, dargelegt an der ersten Quarto der
'Merry Wives of Windsor' 1602. Diss. Leipzig, 1914. (94 S.) Rev.: Sh. Jb.
52, 1916, S. 206–10, M. Förster.

HEREWARD T. PRICE: The text of Henry V. Newcastle-under-Lyme, 1920.
(55 pp.)

WALTHER SORG: Ein Beitrag zur Geschichte der englischen Kurzschrift. In:
E. St. 57, 1922, S. 113 ff.

B. A. P. VAN DAM: The text of Shakespeare's Hamlet. London, 1924. (vii,
380 pp.)

(e) CENSORSHIP IN ELIZABETHAN TIMES

FRED. G. FLEAY: A chronicle history of the London stage, 1559–1642. London,
1890.

PHOEBE SHEAVYN: Writers and official censors under Elizabeth and James I.
In: Libr., N.S. vol. 8, 1907, pp. 134–63.

VIRGINIA C. GILDERSLEEVE: Government regulation of the Elizabethan drama. New York, 1908. (viii, 259 pp.)=Columbia Univ. Studies in English, Ser. II, vol. iv, no. 1. Rev.: Sh. Jb. 45, 1909, S. 326–7, M. J. Wolff; JEGPh. 9, 1910, pp. 121–33, J. W. Cunliffe.

C. M. G[ODDEN]: The stage censor, 1544–1907. An historical sketch. London, 1908. (128 pp.)

FRANK FOWELL and FRANK PALMER: Censorship in England. London, 1913.

(f) SOCIAL POSITION OF WRITERS

PHOEBE SHEAVYN: Patrons and professional writers under Elizabeth and James I. In: Libr., N.S. vol. 7, 1906, pp. 301–36.

PHOEBE SHEAVYN: The literary profession in the Elizabethan age. Manchester, 1909. (xi, 222 pp.)=Publ. of the Univ. of Manchester, Engl. Ser., no. 1. Rev.: Sh. Jb. 46, 1910, S. 285–6, A. Brandl; MLR. 6, 1911, pp. 118–21, O. L. Hatcher; Bbl. 22, 1911, S. 8–10, G. Binz.
Deals with the relations between writers, publishers, and the public.

WILHELM CREIZENACH: Beruf und Stellung der Theaterdichter. In his Geschichte des neueren Dramas. Bd. 4. Halle, 1909, S. 66–114.

D. NICHOL SMITH: Authors and patrons. In: Shakespeare's England. O.U.P., 1917. Vol. ii, pp. 182–211.

SAMUEL MOORE: General aspects of literary patronage in the Middle Ages. In: Libr. 3rd ser., vol. 4, 1913, pp. 369–92.

K. J. HOLZKNECHT: Literary patronage in the Middle Ages. Philadelphia, 1923. (258 pp.) Rev.: MLR. 20, 1925, pp. 478–9, G. G. Coulton; Bbl. 36, 1925, S. 102–7, E. Deckner.

A. BELJAME: Le public et les hommes de lettres en Angleterre au 18e siècle. Paris, 1881. (506 pp.)

A. S. COLLINS: Authorship in the days of Johnson. Being a study of the relation between author, patron, publisher and the public, 1726–1780. London, 1927. (278 pp.)

(2) OLDEST PRINTED TEXTS. FOLIOS AND QUARTOS
(a) BIBLIOGRAPHY OF OLDEST TEXTS IN GENERAL

WALTER W. GREG: Catalogue of the books presented by Edward Capell to the Library of Trinity College in Cambridge. Cambridge, 1904. (ix, 172 pp.) Rev.: Sh. Jb. 41, 1905, S. 223–4, W. Keller.

ROBERT PRÖLSS: Von den ältesten Drucken der Dramen Shakespeares und dem Einflusse, den die damaligen Londoner Theater und ihre Einrichtungen auf diese Dramen ausgeübt haben. Leipzig, 1905. (iv, 144 S.) Rev.: Sh. Jb. 41, 1905, S. 238–9, W. Keller; Bbl. 16, 1905, S. 302–7, Konr. Meier.

ALFRED W. POLLARD: Shakespeare folios and quartos. A study in the bibliography of Shakespeare's plays, 1594–1685. With 37 illustr. London, 1909. (vi, 176 pp.) Rev.: Sh. Jb. 46, 1910, S. 269–71, A. Brandl.
A very important work.

WALTER W. GREG: A descriptive catalogue of the early editions of the works of Shakespeare preserved in the library of Eton College. O.U.P., [1909]. (viii, 27 pp.) Rev.: Sh. Jb. 46, 1910, S. 306, M. Förster.

A catalogue of the Shakespeare exhibition held in the Bodleian Library to commemorate the death of Shakespeare, April 23, 1616. Oxford, 1916. (xvi, 99 pp.)

HENRIETTA C. BARTLETT: Catalogue of the exhibition of Shakespeareana held at the New York Public Library, April 2 to July 15, 1916, in commemoration of the tercentenary of Shakespeare's death. New York, 1917. Rev.: Libr. 3rd ser., vol. 8, 1917, pp. 183–6.

HENRIETTA C. BARTLETT: Mr. William Shakespeare. Original and early editions of his quartos and folios, his source books and those containing contemporary notices. New Haven & London, 1922. (xxviii, 217 pp.)

SIR ISRAEL GOLLANCZ: In commemoration of the First Folio Tercentenary. A resetting of the preliminary matter of the First Folio, with a catalogue of Shakespeareana exhibited in the Hall of the Worshipful Company of Stationers. London, 1923. (55 pp.)

Guide to the MSS. and printed books exhibited [by the British Museum] in celebration of the tercentenary of the First Folio Shakespeare. [Ed. by A. W. POLLARD.] London, 1923. (77 pp.)

Specimens of Shakespeareana in the Bodleian Library at Oxford. Oxford, 1927. (72 pp.)

ROBERT METCALF SMITH: The Shakespeare folios and the forgeries of Shakespeare's handwriting in the Lucy Packer Linderman Memorial Library of Lehigh University. With a list of original folios in American libraries. Lehigh Univ., Bethlehem, Penn. 1927. (47 pp.)=Lehigh Univ. Publ., vol. i, no. 2=The Institute of Research. Circular no. 7. Studies in the Humanities no. 1. Rev.: Bbl. 38, 1927, S. 319–21, G. Binz.

(b) THE FOUR FOLIOS

α. THE FIRST FOLIO

(aa) Reprints

Shakespeare, a reprint of his collected works as put forth in 1623. 3 vols. London, LIONEL BOOTH, 1864.
Careful reprint, but not a facsimile.

Shakespeare, the first collected edition of the dramatic works . . . A reproduction in exact facsimile of the famous First Folio, 1623, by photolithography under the superintendence of HOWARD STAUNTON. London, Day & Son, 1866.

The works of William Shakespeare in reduced facsimile from the famous First Folio Edition of 1623. With an introd. by J. O. HALLIWELL-PHILIPPS. London, Chatto & Windus, 1876.

Shakespeare's comedies, histories and tragedies, being a reproduction in facsimile of the First Folio Edition, 1623, from the Chatsworth copy in the possession of the Duke of Devonshire. With introd. and census of copies by SIDNEY LEE. Oxford, 1902. (xxxv, 908 pp.) Rev.: Sh. Jb. 39, 1903, S. 267–70, W. Bang.

Both introductions and the census, which has also been published separately, are extremely important.

Mr. William Shakespeare's comedies, histories, and tragedies faithfully reproduced in facsimile from the edition of 1623. London, Methuen, 1910.

Shakespeare facsimiles. Edited by J. DOVER WILSON, with introduction and a list of modern readings. London, 1929 seq.

Facsimile of the First Folio. Already published: Macb., Temp., Tw., Cor., As, Wint., Caes., Ant.

(bb) Studies

WALTER W. GREG: The bibliographical history of the First Folio. In: Libr., N.S. vol. 4, 1903, pp. 258–85.

Notes on Lee's introduction to the Oxford facsimile.

SIDNEY LEE: Notes and additions to the Census of copies of the Shakespeare First Folio. In: Libr. N.S. vol. 7, 1906, pp. 113–19.

Supplementing his census in the Oxford facsimile 1902. Cf. above.

GEORGE W. COLE: The First Folio of Shakespeare. A further word regarding the correct arrangement of its preliminary leaves. New York, [1910]. Rev.: Libr. 3rd ser., vol. 1, 1910, pp. 211–17.

WOLFGANG KELLER: Shakespeares literarisches Testament. In: E. St., Bd. 50, 1916, S. 1–16.

Attempts to prove that Shakespeare himself planned the collecting and publishing of his works.

WOLFGANG KELLER: Die Anordnung von Shakespeares Dramen in der ersten Folio-Ausgabe. In: Sh. Jb. Jg. 56, 1920, S. 90–4.

HANS HECHT: Shakespeares Testament und die Vorrede der Schauspieler zur ersten Folio. In: GRM. Jg. 10, 1922, S. 162–71.

Refers to Keller's thesis in E. St., vol. 50 (cf. above).

R. CROMPTON RHODES: Shakespeare's First Folio. A study. Oxford, 1923. (viii, 147 pp.) Rev.: TLS. June 21, 1923; MLR., vol. 18, 1923, pp. 485–6, E. K. Chambers.

ALFRED W. POLLARD: The foundations of Shakespeare's text. O.U.P., 1923. (18 pp.) Rev.: MLR. 18, 1923, pp. 484–5, E. K. Chambers.

HENRY GUPPY: A brief summary of the history of the First Folio edition of Shakespeare's dramas, 1623–1923. Manchester, 1923. (31 pp.)

Studies in the First Folio, written for the Shakespeare Association . . . by M. H. SPIELMANN, J. DOVER WILSON, SIR SIDNEY LEE, R. CROMPTON RHODES,

W. W. GREG, ALLARDYCE NICOLL. Introduction by SIR ISRAEL GOLLANCZ. O.U.P., 1924. (xxxiv, 182 pp.) Rev.: Bbl. 37, 1926, S. 103–15, E. Deckner.

CONTENTS: ISRAEL GOLLANCZ: General introduction, ix–xxxiv; M. H. SPIELMANN: Shakespeare's portraiture, 1–52; J. DOVER WILSON: The task of Heminge and Condell, 53–77; SIDNEY LEE: A survey of First Folios, 78–105; R. CROMPTON RHODES: The First Folio and the Elizabethan stage, 106–28; W. W. GREG: The First Folio and its publishers, 129–56; ALLARDYCE NICOLL: The editors of Shakespeare from First Folio to Malone, 157–78. Rev.: MLR. 20, 1925, pp. 470–3, F. S. Boas.

WOLFGANG KELLER: Shakespeare, Ben Jonson und die Folio von 1623. In: Sh. Jb. Jg. 59–60, N.F. Bd. 1, 1924, S. 123–9.

MAX FÖRSTER: Zum Jubiläum der Shakespeare-Folio. In: Zs. f. Bücherfreunde, N.F. xvi, 1924, S. 53–64, with 11 illustrations.

ELMER EDGAR STOLL: On the anniversary of the Folio. In Stoll's Shakespeare studies, New York, 1927, pp. 1–38.

E. E. WILLOUGHBY: A note on the pagination of the First Folio. In: MLN., vol. 44, 1929, pp. 373–4.

β. THE 2ND–4TH FOLIOS

WILLIAM SHAKESPEARE: Comedies, histories, and tragedies, faithfully reproduced in facsimile from the edition of 1632. London, Methuen, 1909.

C. ALPHONSO SMITH: The chief differences between the first and second folios of Shakespeare. In: E. St., Bd. 30, 1902, S. 1–20.

ROBERT METCALF SMITH: The variant issues of Shakespeare's second folio and Milton's first published English poem. A bibliographical problem. Bethlehem, Penn., 1928. (62 pp.)=Lehigh Univ. Publ., vol. ii, no. 3. The Institute of Research. Circular no. 14. Studies in the Humanities, No. 4. Rev.: Bbl. 39, 1928, S. 339–40, G. Binz.

WILLIAM SHAKESPEARE: Comedies, histories, and tragedies, faithfully reproduced in facsimile from the edition of 1664. London, Methuen, 1905.

WILLIAM SHAKESPEARE: Comedies, histories, and tragedies, faithfully reproduced from the edition of 1685. London, Methuen, 1904. (998 pp.)

(c) THE QUARTOS

Shakspere quarto facsimiles. Issued under the superintendence of F. J. FURNIVALL. 43 vols. London [1885]–91. Separate titles, e.g. Shakspere's Lov's labors lost, the first quarto, 1598, a facsimile in photo-lithography by WILLIAM GRIGGS. With foreword by F. J. FURNIVALL. London, n.d.

FREDERICK G. FLEAY: Tabular view of the quarto editions of Shakespeare's works, 1593–1630. In: New Shakespeare Soc. Trans. P. 1, 40–50. London, 1874.

ALBRECHT WAGNER: Eine Sammlung von Shakespeares Quartos in Deutschland. In: Anglia, Bd. 25, 1902, S. 518–32.

H. B. WHEATLEY: Post-Restoration quartos of Shakespeare's plays. In: Libr. 3rd ser., vol. 4, 1913, pp. 237–69.

HENRIETTA BARTLETT and ALFRED W. POLLARD: A census of Shakespeare's plays in quarto, 1594–1709. New Haven, 1916. (xii, 153 pp.)

Supplement: THE QUESTION OF THE QUARTO EDITIONS OF 1619 ('PAVIER'S COLLECTION')

WALTER W. GREG: On certain false dates in Shakespearian quartos. In: Libr., N.S. vol. 9, 1908, pp. 113–31 and 381–409.

WILLIAM JAGGARD: False dates in Shakespearian quartos. In: Libr. N.S. vol. 10, 1909, pp. 208–11.

WILLIAM J. NEIDIG: The Shakespeare quartos of 1619. In: Mod. Phil., vol. 8, 1910, pp. 145–64.

A. H. HUTH and A. W. POLLARD: On the supposed false dates in certain Shakespeare quartos. In: Libr. 3rd ser., vol. 1, 1910, pp. 36–53.

(3) LATER EDITIONS WITH CRITICAL TEXT REVISION

(a) GENERAL LITERATURE

WILLIAM S. BRASSINGTON: Handlist of collective editions of Shakespeare's works published before the year 1800. Stratford-upon-Avon, 1898. (8 pp.)

JANE SHERZER: American editions of Shakespeare (1753–1866). In: PMLA., vol. 22, N.S. vol. 15, 1907, pp. 633–96.

H. B. WHEATLEY: Shakespeare's editors from 1623 to the 20th century.= Bibliogr. Soc. Trans. xiv, 1915–17, pp. 145–75.

ALLARDYCE NICOLL: The editors of Shakespeare from First Folio to Malone. In: Studies in the First Folio. London, 1924. pp. 157–78.

(b) EDITIONS

1709–10. The works of W. Shakespear. Revised and corrected, with an account of the life and writings of the author by NICHOLAS ROWE. 7 vols. London, 1709–10. 1714^2 (in 9 vols.).
Substantially a reprint of F 4. With biography.

1723–5. The works of Shakespear. Collated and corrected by MR. POPE. 7 vols. London, 1723–5. Later editions 1728, 1735, 1768.
Essentially a reprint of Rowe's edition.

Cf. also: HANS SCHMIDT: Die Shakespeare-Ausgabe von Pope. Diss. Giessen, 1912. (114 S.) Rev.: Sh. Jb. 49, 1913, S. 177, H. Weyhe.

1733. The works of Shakespeare. Collated with the oldest copies, and corrected. With notes, explanatory and critical, by MR. L. THEOBALD. 7 vols. London, 1733. Later editions 1740, 1762, 1772, 1773.
Theobald takes over many textual improvements from F 1.

Cf. also: WENDEL MERTZ: Die Shakespeare-Ausgabe von Theobald (1733). Diss. Giessen, 1925. (55 S.) Also in: Giessener Beitr. z. Erforsch. d. Sprache und Kultur Englands und Nordamerikas, hrsg. von W. Horn, Bd. 2, 1925, S. 193–248. Rev.: Z. f. e. U. 27, 1928, S. 228, Jantzen.

THOMAS R. LOUNSBURY: The first editors of Shakespeare (Pope and Theobald). The story of the first Shakespearian controversy and of the earliest attempt at establishing a critical text of Shakespeare. London, 1906. (xxii, 579 pp.) Rev.: Sh. Jb. 43, 276; MLR. 2, 1907, p. 265, A. R. Waller.

1743–4. The works of Shakespear. In 6 vols. Carefully revised and corrected by SIR THOMAS HANMER. 6 vols. Oxford, 1743–4, 1770–1[2].
Contains many new emendations.

1747. The works of Shakespear in eight volumes. The genuine text, collated . . ., corrected and emended . . . by MR. POPE and MR. WARBURTON. 8 vols. London, 1747.

Cf. OTTO GANS: Die Shakespeare-Ausgabe von Warburton [1747]. Diss. Giessen, 1922. (39 S.) Also in Giessener Beiträge, 1922.

1765. The plays of William Shakespeare, in eight volumes. With the corrections and illustrations of various commentators, to which are added notes by SAMUEL JOHNSON. 8 vols. London, 1765, 1768[2]. Cf. the editions of Steevens (1773), Malone (1790), Boswell (1821).
Johnson bases his edition on Warburton's text, but adds new readings and emendations.

1766. Twenty of the plays of Shakespeare, being the whole number printed in quarto during his life-time, or before the Restoration. Published from the originals by GEORGE STEEVENS. 4 vols. London, 1766.

1768. Mr. William Shakespeare his comedies, histories, and tragedies, . . . re-published in ten volumes [by EDWARD CAPELL]. 10 vols. London, 1768.
Based on careful collation of the Folios and Quartos.

1773. The plays of William Shakespeare. In ten volumes. With the corrections and illustrations of various commentators; to which are added notes by SAMUEL JOHNSON and GEORGE STEEVENS. With an appendix. 10 vols. London, 1773. The second edition, revised and augmented [by I. REED]. 10 vols. London, 1778. Supplement to the edition of Shakespeare's plays published in 1778 by S. JOHNSON and G. STEEVENS. 2 vols. London, 1780, 1785[3], 1793[4].

1790. The plays and poems of William Shakespeare, in ten volumes. Collated verbatim with the most authentick copies . . . with notes by E. MALONE. 10 vols. London, 1790.

1803. The plays of William Shakspear . . . With the corrections and illustrations of various commentators, to which are added notes by SAMUEL JOHNSON and GEORGE STEEVENS. The 5th edition [i.e. of Johnson and Steevens], revised and augmented by I. REED, with a glossarial index. 21 vols. London, 1803.= *The First Variorum Edition.*
This edition contains in foot-notes all the emendations and text-interpretations up to the year of publication.

1813. The plays of William Shakspeare ... with the corrections and illustrations of various commentators, to which are added notes by SAMUEL JOHNSON and GEORGE STEEVENS. Revised and augmented by I. REED. The 6th edition [i.e. of Johnson and Steevens]. 21 vols. London, 1813.=*The 2nd Variorum Edition.*

1821. The plays and poems of William Shakspeare, with the corrections and illustrations of various commentators, comprehending a life of the poet, and an enlarged history of the stage by the late EDMOND MALONE, with a new glossarial index [ed. by J. BOSWELL]. 21 vols. London, 1821.= *The 3rd Variorum Edition.*

1826. The dramatic works of William Shakespeare. With notes, original and selected, by SAMUEL WELLER SINGER, and a life of the poet by C. SYMMONS. 10 vols. London, 1826.

From point of view of textual criticism of little value.

1842. The pictorial edition of the works of Shakspere, ed. by CHARLES KNIGHT. 8 vols. London [1839]-42.

1842-4. The works of William Shakespeare. The text formed from an entirely new collation of the old editions. With the various readings, notes, a life of the poet, and a history of the early English stage. By J. PAYNE COLLIER. In 8 vols. London, 1842-4. Later editions 1858, 1878.

1847. Shakespeare's plays, with his life, critical introductions and notes, original and selected. Edited by G. C. VERPLANCK. 3 vols. New York, 1847.

1853-65. The works of William Shakespeare. The text formed from a new collation of the early editions . . . By J. O. HALLIWELL. 16 vols. London, 1853-65.

1854. Shakspeares Werke, hrsg. und erklärt von NICOLAUS DELIUS. 2 Bde. Elberfeld, 1854, 1864[2], 1872[3], 1876[4], 1882[5]. Important review: Neue Jbb. der Philologie und Pädagogik, Bd. 72, 1855, S. 57 ff., 107 ff., 159 ff., Tycho Mommsen.

Best commentated German edition of the collected works.

1857. The works of Shakespeare. The text revised by ALEXANDER DYCE. 6 vols. London, 1857. Second ed. (with glossary) in 9 vols. 1864-7. 5th ed. (10 vols.) 1886.

Based on above: The works of William Shakespeare. From the text of Alex. Dyce's 2nd ed. 7 vols. Leipzig, Tauchnitz 1868. Also: Shakespeare's complete works in one volume. From the text of A. Dyce's second edition. Leipzig, Tauchnitz, 1916. (viii, 3360 S.) Rev.: Sh. Jb. 52, 1916, S. 202-3, M. Förster.

1858-60. The works of Shakespeare. Ed. by HOWARD STAUNTON. 3 vols. London, 1858-60.

1860. Shakespeare's works, edited, with a scrupulous revision of the text, by MARY COWDEN CLARKE. New York, 1860.

1863–6. The works of William Shakespeare. Ed. by W. G. CLARK, J. GLOVER and W. A. WRIGHT. In 9 vols. Cambridge, 1863–6, 1891–3^2=*The Cambridge Edition*.

The edition is based on a renewed comparison of the Folios, Quartos, and the subsequent critical editions. The various readings are given in foot-notes. The text itself is fairly conservative.

Cf. ARNOLD SCHRÖER: Zur Neuausgabe der 'Cambridge Edition'. In: Sh. Jb. Jg. 31, 1895, S. 354–9.

1864. The works of William Shakespeare. Ed. by WILLIAM G. CLARK and WILLIAM A. WRIGHT. London, 1864 (and subsequent editions). (viii, 1079 pp.) =*The Globe Edition*.

This edition has the same text as the Cambridge Edition and is usually quoted.

1865. The works of William Shakespeare. Ed. by RICHARD GRANT WHITE. 12 vols. Boston, 1865.

1871 seq. A new variorum edition of the works of Shakespeare, ed. by HORACE HOWARD FURNESS and HORACE HOWARD FURNESS, JR. Philadelphia, 1871 seq. The following plays have appeared: John, Cymb., Rom., Haml., Lear, Oth., Macb., Merch., Ant., Caes., As, Temp., Mids., Wint., Ado, Tw., R. III, L.L.L., Cor.

The text is, on the whole, that of the First Folio. In addition the editors give the variant readings and reprint extensively from the existing Shakespeare literature. Any expression of personal opinions is reserved.

Cf. LAWRENCE MASON: The Furness Variorum. In: JEGPh., vol. 18, 1919, pp. 346–59.

1877. *The Leopold Shakespeare*. The poet's works, in chronological order, from the text of Delius. With an introduction by F. J. FURNIVALL. London, 1877 (and subsequent editions).

1880–91. The works of William Shakspere. Edited with critical notes and introductory notices by M. WAGNER and L. PROESCHOLDT. 12 vols. Hamburg, 1880–91.

1881. The complete works of William Shakespeare. With a life of the poet, explanatory foot-notes, critical notes, and a glossarial index. By HENRY N. HUDSON. 20 vols. Boston, Mass., 1881.=*The Harvard Edition*.

With very independent text.

1883. William Shakespeare's comedies, histories, tragedies and poems. The text newly edited with notes and glossary by RICHARD GRANT WHITE. 3 vols. Boston, 1883.=*The Riverside Shakespeare*.

1886–1906. *The Bankside Shakespeare*, edited by APPLETON MORGAN. 22 vols. New York Shakespeare Soc., 1886–1906.

The Quartos and the First Folio printed side by side.

1894. The works of William Shakespeare, edited by H. STAUNTON. 6 vols. London, 1894.

1894–1922. The works of William Shakespeare. Ed. by ISRAEL GOLLANCZ. 40 vols. London, 1894–1922.=*The Temple Shakespeare*.

1899 seq. *The Arden Shakespeare.* General editors: W. J. CRAIG, 1899–1906, R. H. CASE, 1909–24.

Very good annotated edition with detailed literary introductions. The editors of the various works are as follows: All's by W. O. BRIGSTOCKE; Ant. by R. H. CASE; As by J. W. HOLME; Err., Macb. and Mids. by HENRY CUNINGHAM; Cor. by W. J. CRAIG and R. H. CASE; Cymb., Haml. and Rom. by EDW. DOWDEN; Caes. by MICHAEL MACMILLAN; 1 H. IV by R. P. COWL and A. E. MORGAN; 2 H. IV by R. P. COWL; H. V by H. A. EVANS; 1, 2, 3 H. VI by H. C. HART and C. K. POOLER; H. VIII, Merch., Sonn. and Poems by C. K. POOLER; John and R. II by IVOR B. JOHN; R. III by A. HAMILTON THOMPSON; L.L.L., Wiv., Meas. and Oth. by H. C. HART; Lear by W. J. CRAIG; Ado by GRACE R. TRENERY; Per., Tim. and Troil. by K. DEIGHTON; Shr. and Gent. by R. WARWICK BOND; Temp. and Tw. by MORTON LUCE; Tit. by H. B. BAILDON; Wint. by F. W. MOORMAN.

1899–1900. The works of Shakespeare, ed. with introductions and notes by C. H. HERFORD. In 10 vols. London, 1899–1900.=*The Eversley Edition.*

Good introductions with fine appreciation of Shakespeare's art and explanatory notes.

1903–8. The complete works of William Shakespeare. Reprinted from the First Folio, ed. by CHARLOTTE PORTER and H. A. CLARKE. With an introduction by JOHN CH. COLLINS. 13 vols. London, 1903–8.=*The Pembroke Edition.* Rev.: MLR. 2, 1907, pp. 358–60, G. G. Smith.

1903–12. William Shakespeare: First Folio Edition. Ed. with notes, introduction, glossary, list of variorum readings, and selected criticism, by CHARLOTTE PORTER and HELEN A. CLARKE. 40 vols. New York, 1903–12.= *The American First Folio Edition.*

Reprint of First Folio in the original orthography; with good introductions, valuable commentary, variant readings, and reprints of aesthetic criticism. Small 12mo volumes.

1904. *The Oxford Shakespeare.* The complete works of Shakespeare, ed. with a glossary by W. J. CRAIG. Oxford, 1904. (viii, 1264 pp.).

The text is substantially that of the First Folio in modern spelling, and takes into account the variant readings of the Quartos and of later editors. A counterpart of the Globe Edition.

1904 seq. *The Old Spelling Shakespeare.* Being the works of Shakespeare in the spelling of the best quarto and folio texts, ed. by F. J. FURNIVALL and W. G. BOSWELL-STONE. London, 1904 seq.

A critical text in the original spelling with modern punctuation. Short introductions.

1906. The complete dramatic and poetic works of William Shakespeare. Ed. from the text of the early quartos and the First Folio by WILLIAM ALLAN NEILSON. Boston & New York, 1906. (xxii, 1237 pp.)=*The Cambridge Edition of the Poets.*

American edition in one volume with independent text.

1911–13. *The Tudor Shakespeare.* Ed. by WILLIAM ALLAN NEILSON and ASHLEY HORACE THORNDIKE. In 40 vols. New York & London, 1911–13.

The text is the same as in the Neilson edition of 1906. With literary introductions, explanatory notes, textual variants, and a glossary.

1917 seq. *The Yale Shakespeare.* Ed. by WILBUR L. CROSS and TUCKER BROOKE. New Haven & O.U.P., 1917 seq.

The editors of the various works are as follows: Temp. by CH. B. TINKER; Gent. by

K. YOUNG; Wiv. by G. VAN SANTVOORD; Ado, 1, 2, 3 H. VI, and Cor. by TUCKER BROOKE; L.L.L. by W. L. CROSS and TUCKER BROOKE; Mids. and Rom. by W. H. DURHAM; Merch. and Lear by W. L. PHELPS; As, Haml. and R. III by JACK R. CRAWFORD; Shr. by HENRY TEN EICK PERRY; Tw. by G. H. NETTLETON; Wint. by F. E. PIERCE; R. II by L. M. BUELL; 1, 2 H. IV and Cymb. by S. B. HEMINGWAY; H. V and Err. by ROBERT D. FRENCH; Tim. and John by STANLEY T. WILLIAMS; Caes. and Oth. by L. MASON; Macb. by C. M. LEWIS; Ant. by HENRY S. CANBY; Sonn. by E. B. REED; Meas. by W. H. DURHAM; Tit. by A. M. WITHERSPOON; H. VIII by JOHN M. BERDAN and TUCKER BROOKE; All's by ARTHUR E. CASE; Per. by ALFRED R. BELLINGER; Troil. by BURTON PARADISE; Ven. and the other poems by ALBERT FEUILLERAT.

Uniform with above: TUCKER BROOKE: Shakespeare of Stratford. A hand-book for students. Rev.: JEGPh. 19, 1920, pp. 426–30, H. E. Wood-bridge.

1921 seq. The works of Shakespeare. Ed. by SIR ARTHUR QUILLER-COUCH and JOHN DOVER WILSON. C.U.P. 1921 seq.= *The New Shakespeare.* Rev.: MLR. 17, 1922, pp. 174–91, W. W. Greg; 19, 1924, pp. 108–11; 20, 1925, pp. 340–5, and 22, 1927, pp. 220–4, E. K. Chambers.

Independent text, new rhetorical punctuation. Important edition. The following vols. have appeared:

(1) Temp. 1921	(5) Err. 1922	(9) Merch. 1926
(2) Gent. 1921	(5) Ado 1923	(10) As 1926
(3) Wiv. 1921	(7) L.L.L. 1923	(11) Shr. 1928
(4) Meas. 1922	(8) Mids. 1924	(12) All's 1929

(4) TEXTUAL CRITICISM

In addition to the later editions with critical text interpretation already mentioned the following works should be consulted:

LEWIS THEOBALD: Shakespeare restored, or a specimen of the many errors as well committed as unemended by Mr. Pope in his late edition of this poet. Designed to restore the true reading of Shakespeare in all the editions ever yet printed. London, 1726. (vi, 194 pp.)

JOHN UPTON: Critical observations on Shakespeare. London, 1746. (iv, 362 pp.)

THOMAS EDWARDS: A supplement to Mr. Warburton's edition of Shakespeare. London, 1748. (62 pp.)

ZACHARY GREY: Critical, historical, and explanatory notes on Shakespeare, with emendations of the text and metre. 2 vols. London, 1754.

BENJAMIN HEATH: Revisal of Shakespeare's text. London, 1765. (xiv, 574 pp.)

WILLIAM KENRICK: Review of Dr. Johnson's new edition of Shakespeare, in which the ignorance or inattention of that editor is exposed . . . London, 1765. (xvi, 134 pp.)

THOMAS TYRWHITT: Observations and conjectures upon some passages of Shakespeare. Oxford, 1766. (54 pp.)

JOSEPH RITSON: Remarks, critical and illustrative . . . on the last edition of Shakespeare [i.e. 2nd ed. of Johnson and Steevens, 1778]. London, 1783. (viii, 240 pp.)

J. M. MASON: Comments on the plays of Beaumont and Fletcher. With an appendix containing some further observations on Shakespeare, extended to the late editions of Malone and Steevens. London, 1797–1798.

J. M. MASON: Comments on the several editions of Shakespeare's plays, extended to those of Malone and Steevens. Dublin, 1807. (xvi, 608 pp.)

FRANCIS DOUCE: Illustrations of Shakespeare and of ancient manners, with dissertations on the clowns and fools of Shakespeare . . . 2 vols. London, 1807, 1839².

ALEXANDER DYCE: Remarks on J. P. Collier's and C. Knight's editions of Shakespeare. London, 1844.

J. PAYNE COLLIER: Notes and emendations to the text of Shakespeare's plays, from early manuscript corrections in a copy of the folio 1632. London, 1852, 1853². (xxvi, 528 pp.)
This work of the notorious forger called forth a flood of hostile criticism.

NICOLAUS DELIUS: Alte handschriftliche Emendationen zum Shakspere gewürdigt. Bonn, 1853.

CHARLES KNIGHT: Old lamps, or new? A plea for the original editions of the text of Shakspere. London, 1853.

F. A. LEO: Beiträge und Verbesserungen zu Shakespeares Dramen nach handschriftlichen Änderungen in einem von J. Payne Collier aufgefundenen Exemplare der Folio-Ausgabe von 1632. Berlin, 1853. (xxvi, 341 S.)

RICHARD GRANT WHITE: Shakespeare's scholar. Being historical and critical studies of his text, characters, and commentators, with an examination of Mr. Collier's folio of 1632. New York, 1854. (xliv, 504 pp.)

WILLIAM SIDNEY WALKER: A critical examination of the text of Shakespeare, with remarks on his language and that of his contemporaries, together with notes on his plays and poems. Edited by W. N. LETTSOM. 3 vols. London, 1860.

N. E. S. A. HAMILTON: An inquiry into the genuineness of the manuscript-corrections of Mr. J. Payne Collier's annotated Shakspere Folio 1632. London, 1860. (iv, 156 pp.)

F. A. LEO: Die neue englische Text-Kritik des Shakespeare. In: Sh. Jb. Jg. 1, 1865, S. 189–219.

ROBERT CARTWRIGHT: New readings in Shakespeare, or proposed emendations of the text. London, 1866.

C. M. INGLEBY: The still lion. An essay towards the restoration of Shakespeare's text. In: Sh. Jb. Jg. 2, 1867, S. 196–243. Enlarged under the title: Shakespeare hermeneutics, or the still lion. Being an essay towards the restoration of Shakespeare's text. London, 1875. (viii, 168 pp.)

ALEXANDER SCHMIDT: Zur Shakespeareschen Textkritik. Ein Sendschreiben an den Herausgeber. In: Sh. Jb. Jg. 3, 1868, S. 341–69.

P. A. DANIEL: Notes and conjectural emendations of certain doubtful passages in Shakespeare's plays. London, 1870. (94 pp.)

HENRY H. VAUGHAN: New readings and new renderings of Shakespeare's tragedies. 3 vols. London, 1878–86.

K. ELZE: Noten und Konjekturen zu Mucedorus, Locrine, Edward III, The Taming of the Shrew, 2 King Henry IV. In: Sh. Jb. Jg. 13, 1878, S. 45–91.

WILHELM WAGNER: Verbesserungsvorschläge zu Shakespeare. In: Sh. Jb. Jg. 14, 1879, S. 285–303.

ED. TIESSEN: Beiträge zur Feststellung und Erklärung des Shakespeare-Textes. In: E. St., Bd. 2, 1879, S. 185–204 und S. 440–75; Bd. 3, 1880, S. 15–42.
Contributions to textual criticism based on the edition of Delius.

F. A. LEO: Besprechung über Verbesserungsvorschläge zu Shakespeare (s. Jg. 14, 285 ff.). In: Sh. Jb. Jg. 15, 1880, S. 164–72.
Review of Wagner's essay (1879).

K. ELZE: Exegetisch-kritische Marginalien. In: Sh. Jb. Jg. 16, 1881, S. 228–53.

F. A. LEO: Emendationen. In: Sh. Jb. Jg. 19, 1884, S. 265–70.

F. A. LEO: Verzeichnis noch zu erklärender oder zu emendierender Textlesarten in Shakespeares Dramen. In: Sh. Jb. Jg. 20, 1885, S. 149–71.

ALEXANDER SCHMIDT: Zur Shakespeareschen Textkritik. In his: Gesammelte Abhandlungen, Berlin, 1889, S. 313–42.

ROBERT SPRENGER: Bemerkungen zu Dramen Shakespeares. Progr. Northeim, 1891.

F. A. LEO: Robert Sprengers Bemerkungen zu Shakespeares Dramen. In: Sh. Jb. Jg. 27, 1892, S. 217–24.

ERNEST WALDER: Shakespearean criticism, textual and literary, from Dryden to the end of the 18th century. Bradford, 1895. (136 pp.)

P. VAN DAM and C. STOFFEL: William Shakespeare, prosody and text. An essay in criticism, being an introduction to a better editing and a more adequate appreciation of the works of the Elizabethan poets. Leyden, 1900. (437 pp.) Rev.: Sh. Jb. 38, 1902, S. 242–5, G. Sarrazin; Bbl. 13, 1902, S. 322–5, Rud. Fischer.

W. BANG: Bemerkungen zum Text von Shakespeare und Marlowe. In: Sh. Jb. Jg. 39, 1903, S. 202–21.

HERMANN CONRAD: Schwierigkeiten der Shakespeare-Übersetzung. Erläuterung zweifelhafter und bisher mangelhaft übersetzter Textstellen. Stuttgart, 1903, 1906². Rev.: Z. f. e. U., Bd. 5, 1906, S. 268 ff., Kaluza.

THOMAS R. LOUNSBURY: The text of Shakespeare, its history from the publication of the quartos and folios down to and including the publication of the editions of Pope and Theobald. New York, 1906. (xxii, 579 pp.)

ARNOLD SCHRÖER: Neuere und neuste Shakespeare-Ausgaben und die Kritik des Textes. In: GRM. Jg. 1, 1909, S. 119–32.

ERNEST WALDER: The text of Shakespeare. In: CHEL., vol. 5, 1910, pp. 259–82.
With bibliography.

CHARLES D. STEWART: Some textual difficulties in Shakespeare. New Haven, 1914. (ix, 251 pp.) Rev.: MLR. 11, 1916, pp. 98–100, G. C. Moore Smith.

ALFRED W. POLLARD: The foundations of Shakespeare's text. In: Brit. Acad. Proceed., vol. 11, 1923. (18 pp.)

LEON KELLNER: Restoring Shakespeare. A critical analysis of the misreadings in Shakespeare's works. With facsimiles and numerous plates. Leipzig, 1925. (xvi, 216 pp.)=Englische Bibliothek, hrsg. v. M. Förster, Bd. 4. Rev.: RESt., vol. 1, 1928, pp. 463–78, W. W. Greg; N. Spr. 36, 1928, S. 530–3, W. Fischer; JEGPh. 25, 1926, pp. 578–85, J. W. Draper; Bbl. 37, 1926, S. 166–72, E. Ekwall; Engl. Studies 7, pp. 150–4, van Dam; Arch. 151, 1926, S. 116–18, K. Brunner.

B. A. P. VAN DAM: Textual criticism of Shakespeare's plays. In: Engl. Studies, vol. 7, 1925, pp. 97–115.
Criticism of Dover Wilson's method of interpretation of the text in The New Shakespeare.

W. W. GREG: Principles of emendation in Shakespeare. O.U.P., 1928. (72 pp.) =Annual Shakespeare Lecture of the Brit. Acad. 1928.=Brit. Acad. Proceed., vol. 14. Rev.: Sh. Jb. 65, 1929, S. 192–3, W. Keller.

For Textual Criticism compare also the many valuable individual contributions in *Notes and Queries*.

VI. SHAKESPEARE'S SOURCES, LITERARY INFLUENCES AND CULTURAL RELATIONS

(1) GENERAL

(a) COLLECTED SOURCES OF SHAKESPEARE'S WORKS

[CHARLOTTE LENNOX]: Shakespear illustrated, or, the novels and histories on which the plays of Shakespear are founded, collected and translated from the original authors. With critical remarks. By the author of the Female Quixote. 3 vols. London, 1753–4. (xiv, 292; 274 and 308 pp.)

K. SIMROCK: Die Quellen des Shakespeare in Novellen, Märchen und Sagen. Bonn, 1831, 1870².

J. P. COLLIER: Shakespeare's library. A collection of the romances, novels, poems and histories, used by Shakespeare as the foundation of his dramas. Now first collected and printed. 2 vols. London [1843], 1850².

COLLIER-HAZLITT: Shakespeare's library. A collection of the plays, romances, novels, poems, and histories employed by Shakespeare in the composition of his works. Ed. by J. P. COLLIER and W. CAREW HAZLITT. 6 vols. 2nd ed. London, 1875.

The Shakespeare Classics. General editor SIR I. GOLLANCZ. O.U.P., 1907 seq.

Lodge's 'Rosalynde': Being the Original of Shakespeare's 'As You Like It'. Edited by W. W. GREG. 1907.

Greene's 'Pandosto', or 'Dorastus and Fawnia': Being the Original of Shakespeare's 'Winter's Tale'. Newly edited by P. G. THOMAS. 1907.

Brooke's 'Romeus and Juliet': Being the Original of Shakespeare's 'Romeo and Juliet'. Newly edited by J. J. MUNRO. 1908.

'The Taming of a Shrew': Being the original of Shakespeare's 'Taming of the Shrew'. Edited by F. S. BOAS. 1908.

The Sources and Analogues of 'A Midsummer-Night's Dream'. Compiled by FRANK SIDGWICK. 1908.

Shakespeare's Plutarch: Edited by C. F. TUCKER BROOKE. Vol. i: containing The Main Sources of Julius Caesar. 1909.

Shakespeare's Plutarch: Edited by C. F. TUCKER BROOKE. Vol. ii: containing The Main Sources of Antony and Cleopatra and of Coriolanus. 1909.

The Chronicle History of King Leir: The Original of Shakespeare's 'King Lear'. Edited by SIDNEY LEE. 1909.

The Menaechmi: The Original of Shakespeare's 'Comedy of Errors'. The Latin Text together with the Elizabethan Translation. Edited by W. H. D. ROUSE. 1912.

Rich's 'Apolonius & Silla': An Original of Shakespeare's 'Twelfth Night Edited by MORTON LUCE. 1912.

(b) GENERAL STUDIES

ASHLEY HORACE THORNDIKE: Shakespeare as a debtor. New York, 1916.

HENRIETTA C. BARTLETT: Mr. William Shakespeare: original and early editions of his quartos and folios, his source books and those containing contemporary notices. New Haven, 1922. (xxviii, 217 pp.)

FELIX E. SCHELLING: Foreign influences in Elizabethan plays. London, 1923. (xii, 160 pp.) Rev.: TLS., Aug. 30, 1923.

WALTER F. SCHIRMER: Antike, Renaissance und Puritanismus. Eine Studie zur englischen Literaturgeschichte des 16. und 17. Jhrh. München, 1924. (ix, 233 S.)

LAURIE MAGNUS: English literature in its foreign relations, 1300–1800. London, 1927. Containing: III. Shakespeare, pp. 47–86.

(c) SHAKESPEARE'S READING AND BOOK-KNOWLEDGE

RICHARD FARMER: Essay on the learning of Shakespeare. Cambridge, 1767. (vi, 50 pp.); 1767² (viii, 98 pp.); 1789³, &c.

H. R. D. ANDERS: Shakespeare's books. A dissertation on Shakespeare's reading and the immediate sources of his works. Berlin, 1904. (xx, 316 pp.)= Schriften d. Dt. Sh.-Ges., Bd. I. Rev.: Sh. Jb. 40, 1904, S. 262–4, Bang.

Cf.: E. KOEPPEL: Randglossen zu dem Anders'schen Werk über Shakespeares Belesenheit. In: Arch., Bd. 113, 1904, S. 49–55.

G. G. GREENWOOD: Is there a Shakespeare problem? London, 1916. (xxi, 613 pp.) Containing a chapter: The learning of Shakespeare, pp. 111–67.

Supplement: THE THOUGHT AND LEARNING OF SHAKESPEARE'S TIMES

HANS HEIDRICH: *John Davies of Hereford* (1565?–1618) und sein Bild von Shakespeares Umgebung. Leipzig, 1924. (vi, 124 S.)=Palaestra, 143. Chapter II: Die Belesenheit. Rev.: RESt., vol. 1, 1925, pp. 242–4, McKerrow; E. St. 59, 1925, S. 294–5, M. J. Wolff.

WILLY NUMERATZKI: *Michael Draytons* Belesenheit und literarische Kritik. Diss. Berlin, 1915. (90 S.) Rev.: Sh. Jb. 51, 1915, S. 273, Creizenach; Bbl. 26, 1915, S. 368–9, B. Fehr.

Gabriel Harvey's Marginalia. Collected and ed. by G. C. MOORE SMITH. Stratford-upon-Avon, 1913. (xvi, 327 pp.)
The marginal notes give a good impression of Harvey's learning.

PAUL BIRCK: Literarische Anspielungen in den Werken *Ben Jonsons*. Diss. Strassburg, 1908. Rev.: Sh. Jb. 45, 1909, S. 278, Brie.

Ben Jonson. Ed. by C. H. HERFORD and PERCY SIMPSON. Vol. i. Oxford, 1925. Chap. IV: Books in Jonson's library, pp. 250–71.

John Lyly: The complete works, ed. by R. WARWICK BOND. 3 vols. Oxford, 1902.
The introduction deals with Lyly's learning.

M. ST. CLARE BYRNE: *Anthony Munday* and his books. In: Bibliogr. Soc. Trans., N.S. I, no. 4, 1921, pp. 225–56. Also in: Libr. 4th ser., vol. 1, 1921, pp. 225–56.

Thomas Nash: The works, ed. by RONALD MCKERROW. 5 vols. London, 1904–8.
Introduction deals with Nash as a scholar.

J. RÜHFEL: Die Belesenheit von Thomas Nash. Diss. München, 1911. (48 S.)

WILHELM RIEDNER: *Spensers* Belesenheit. 1. Teil: Die Bibel und das klassische Altertum. Leipzig, 1908. (x, 131 S.)=Münch. Beitr. z. rom. und engl. Philol., hrsg. von Breymann und Schick, H. 38. Rev. Sh. Jb. 44, 1908, S. 389, M. Förster.

(*d*) WORKS ON XVITH-CENTURY TRANSLATIONS IN GENERAL

THOMAS WARTON: The history of English poetry from the 11th to the 17th century. London, 1778. Containing: Translators, sect. 57–60, pp. 866–943. Good survey.

CHARLES WHIBLEY: Translators. In: CHEL., vol. 4, 1909, pp. 1–25.
In the extensive bibliography the translations of the XVIth century are noted.

W. J. HARRIS: The first printed translations into English of the great foreign classics, 1909.

O. L. HATCHER: Aims and methods of Elizabethan translators. In: ESt., Bd. 44, 1912, S. 174–92.

Shakespeare's England. Vol. i, 1917: Chap. IX, pp. 251–83=Scholarship. (1) Chroniclers and historians, pp. 251–6; (2) Classical scholars, pp. 256–9; (3) Translators, pp. 259–81.
With bibliography.

Tudor translations. Edited by CHARLES WHIBLEY. London, Constable & Co.:

The Conspiracy of Catiline and the War of Jugurtha. Written by SALLUST. Translated by THOMAS HEYWOOD, 1608. With an Introduction by CHARLES WHIBLEY.

The Rogue: or the Life of Guzman de Alfarache. Written in Spanish by MATHEO ALEMAN, and done into English by JAMES MABBE, 1623. With an Introduction by JAMES FITZMAURICE-KELLY. 4 vols.

The Famous Hystory of Herodotus. Translated into English by B. R., 1584. With an Introduction by LEONARD WHIBLEY.

The Civile Conversation of M. Steeven Guazzo: The first three books translated by GEORGE PETTIE, 1581, the fourth by BARTHOLOMEW YOUNG, 1586. With an Introduction by SIR EDWARD SULLIVAN. 2 vols.

SENECA His Tenne Tragedies: Translated into English. Edited by THOMAS NEWTON, 1581. With an Introduction by T. S. ELIOT. 2 vols.

Joyfull Newes out of the Newe-Founde Worlde. Written in Spanish by NICHOLAS MONARDES, Physician of Seville, and Englished by JOHN FRAMPTON, Merchant, 1577. With an Introduction by STEPHEN GASELEE. 2 vols.

(2) SHAKESPEARE AND CLASSICAL LITERATURE

(a) GENERAL TREATISES

PAUL STAPFER: Shakespeare et l'antiquité. 2 vols. Paris, 1879–80. Nouv. éd. 1884. I. Drames et poèmes antiques, 1884. II. Les tragédies romaines, 1883. Translated by EMILY J. CAREY: Shakespeare and classical antiquity. London, 1880. (x, 484 pp.)

RUDOLF GUTERMANN: Shakespeare und die Antike. Progr. Heilbronn, 1900. (28 S.) Rev.: Sh. Jb. 38, 1902, S. 255, W. Keller; Litbl. 1907, Sp. 13 ff., O. Glöde.

J. CHURTON COLLINS: Shakespeare as a classical scholar. In his Studies in Shakespeare. London, 1904. (336 pp.)

W. BANG und H. DE VOCHT: Klassiker und Humanisten als Quelle älterer Dramatiker. In: E. St., Bd. 36, 1906, S. 385–93.

WILLIAM THEOBALD: The classical element in the Shakespeare plays. [Ed. by R. M. THEOBALD.] London, 1909. (408 pp.) Rev.: Sh. Jb. 46, 1910, S. 312–13, M. Förster.

(b) ENGLISH TRANSLATIONS OF THE ANCIENT CLASSICS IN THE XVITH CENTURY

CHARLES WHIBLEY: Translators. In: CHEL., vol. 4, 1909. Cf. the bibliography, pp. 435–41.

HENRIETTA R. PALMER: List of English editions and translations of Greek and Latin classics printed before 1641. In: Bibliogr. Soc. London, 1911. (xxxii, 119 pp.)

F. M. K. FOSTER: English translations from the Greek. A bibliographical survey. =Columbia Univ. Stud. in Engl. and Compar. Lit. 1918.

O. L. JIRICZEK: Specimens of Tudor translations from the classics. With a glossary. Heidelberg, 1923. (200 pp.)=German. Bibl., hrsg. v. Streitberg, I, 3. Reihe, Bd. 6. Rev.: Sh. Jb. 59–60, 1924, S. 196–7, W. Keller; Bbl. 34, 1923, S. 360–2, Liljegren.

Examples of various translations of the same passages together with the Latin and Greek originals. With synopsis of the variant readings and a good glossary.

CAREY H. CONLY: The first English translators of the classics. New Haven & O.U.P., 1927. (158 pp.). Rev.: Bbl. 39, 1928, S. 191–3, Liljegren; JEGPh. 28, 1929, pp. 288–90, P. Aitken; MLR. 22, 1927, pp. 460–1, G. D. Willcock.

Deals with the translators during the period 1550–72.

(c) INFLUENCE OF INDIVIDUAL LATIN CLASSICAL AUTHORS

Latin Quotations: K. A. F. DORRINCK: Die lateinischen Zitate in den Dramen der wichtigsten Vorgänger Shakespeares. Diss. Strassburg, 1907. (viii, 61 S.) Rev.: Sh. Jb. 45, 1909, S. 270–1, Brie; Bbl. 19, 1908, S. 144–5, K. Lincke.

FRANZ KETTLER: Lateinische Zitate in den Dramen namhafter Zeitgenossen Shakespeares. Diss. Strassburg, 1909. (xvi, 120 S.)

Apuleius: The Golden Asse of Lucius Apuleius, translated out of Latin by WILLIAM ADLINGTON. With an introduction by E. B. OSBORN. London, 1923. Rev.: Sh. Jb. 62, 1926, S. 172–3, W. Keller.

A. HOFFMANN: Das Psyche-Märchen des Apuleius in der englischen Literatur. Diss. Strassburg, 1908. (ix, 111 S.)

Cicero. ANNA B. MODERSOHN: Cicero im englischen Geistesleben des 16. Jahrhunderts. In: Arch. 149, 1925, S. 33–51 and 219–45. Rev.: Sh. Jb. 63, 1927, S. 229–30, Beckmann.

Horace. OTTO L. JIRICZEK: Der elisabethanische Horaz. In: Sh. Jb. Jg. 47, 1911, S. 42–68.

Livy. AUGUST KOCH: Die schottische Livius-Übersetzung des John Bellenden (1533). Diss. Königsberg, 1915. (134 S.) Rev.: Sh. Jb. 52, 1916, S. 265, M. Förster.

Ovid: The heroycall epistles of the learned poet PUBLIUS OVIDIUS NASO. Translated into English verse by GEORGE TURBERVILE [1567]. Ed. by FREDERICK BOAS. London, 1928. (349 pp.)

F. A. LEO: Shakespeares Ovid in der Bodleian Library zu Oxford. In: Sh. Jb. Jg. 16, 1881, S. 367–75.

Shakespeare's Ovid, being Arthur Golding's translation of the Metamorphoses. Ed. by W. H. D. ROUSE. London, 1904.

W. CREIZENACH: Shakespeare und Ovid. In: Sh. Jb. Jg. 41, 1905, S. 211.

LEO RICK: Ovids Metamorphosen in der englischen Renaissance. Diss. Münster, 1915. (xii, 64 S.) Rev.: Sh. Jb. Jg. 52, 1916, S. 264–5, M. Förster.

EDMUND WITZ: Die englischen Ovid-Übersetzungen des 16. Jahrhunderts. Diss. Strassburg, 1915. (viii, 59 S.) Rev.: Sh. Jb. Jg. 52, 1916, S. 264, M. Förster.

LEO RICK: Shakespeare und Ovid. In: Sh. Jb. Jg. 55, 1919, S. 35–53.

Plautus. W. CLAUS: Über die Menechmen des Plautus und ihre Nachbildung, besonders durch Shakespeare. Progr. Stettin, 1861. (48 S.)

K. VON REINHARDSTOETTNER: Spätere Bearbeitungen plautinischer Lustspiele. Leipzig, 1886.

ADAM E. A. KARL ROEDER: Menechmi und Amphitruo im englischen Drama bis zur Restauration, 1661. Diss. Leipzig, 1904. (84 S.)

CORNELIA C. COULTER: The Plautine tradition in Shakespeare. In: JEGPh., vol. 19, 1920, pp. 66–83.

HELEN W. COLE: The influence of Plautus and Terence upon the Stonyhurst Pageants. In: MLN., vol. 38, 1923, pp. 393–9.

Seneca. J. W. CUNLIFFE: The influence of Seneca on Elizabethan tragedy. London, 1893. (iv, 155 pp.)

J. M. MANLEY: The influence of the tragedies of Seneca upon early English drama. 1907.

E. JOCKERS: Die englischen Seneca-Übersetzer des 16. Jhrh. Diss. Strassburg, 1909. (vii, 143 S.) Rev.: Bbl. 21, 1910, S. 167, Kratz.

EVELYN M. SPEARING: The Elizabethan 'Tenne Tragedies of Seneca'. In: MLR., vol. 4, 1909, pp. 437–61. Printed in extended form as The Elizabethan translations of Seneca's tragedies. Cambridge, 1912. (x, 78 pp.) Rev.: Sh. Jb. Jg. 49, 1913, S. 255–6, M. Förster; Bbl. 24, 1913, S. 242–3, Ph. Aronstein.

An examination of the style of the translations.

JOHN STUDLEY's translations of Seneca's Agamemnon and Medea, ed. from the octavos of 1566 by E. M. SPEARING=Mat. z. Kunde d. ält. engl. Dramas, Bd. 38, 1913.

The poetical works of SIR WILLIAM ALEXANDER. Ed. by L. E. KASTNER and H. B. CHARLTON. Vol. i. Manchester, 1921. (ccxx, 482 pp.)

In the exhaustive introduction the influence of Seneca on Elizabethan literature is discussed.

F. L. LUCAS: Seneca and Elizabethan tragedy. C.U.P., 1922. (136 pp.) Rev.: JEGPh. 22, 1923, pp. 581–2, A. S. Pease; MLR. 18, 1923, pp. 110–11, H. B. Charlton.

M. ST. CLARE BYRNE: An early translation of Seneca. In: Libr. 4th ser., vol. 4, 1924, pp. 277–85.

Deals with the translations of Seneca's moral treatises.

SENECA his tenne tragedies, translated into English, ed. by THOMAS NEWTON anno 1581. With an introd. by T. S. ELIOT. 2 vols. London, 1927. (liv, 232 and 258 pp.)=The Tudor Translations. Rev.: Engl. Studies, vol. 10, 1928, pp. 79–87, M. Praz.

With good introduction concerning the influence of Seneca on the Elizabethan drama.

T. S. ELIOT: Shakespeare and the stoicism of Seneca. London, 1927. (17 pp.) =The Shakespeare Assoc. Rev.: Bbl. 39, 1928, S. 108–9, A. Eichler; Lit. Zbl. 1928, Sp. 450, Frieser; E. St. 10, 1928, S. 79–87, M. Praz; Sh. Jb. 65, 1929, S. 190–1, W. Keller.

An examination of the stoic attitude of Shakespeare's characters.

Terence. HARDIN CRAIG: Terentius Christianus and the Stonyhurst Pageants. In: Philolog. Quart. 1923.

HELEN W. COLE: The influence of Plautus and Terence upon the Stonyhurst Pageants. In: MLN., vol. 38, 1923, pp. 393–9.

Cf. also HAROLD WALTER LAWTON: Térence en France au 16ᵉ siècle. Paris, 1927.

(d) INFLUENCE OF THE GREEK CLASSICAL AUTHORS

α. GENERAL TREATISES

L. M. WATT: Attic and Elizabethan tragedy. London, 1908. (x, 356 pp.)

SAMUEL LEE WOLFF: The Greek romances in Elizabethan prose fiction. New York, 1912. (ix, 529 pp.)=Columbia Univ. Stud. in comparative lit. Rev.: Sh. Jb. 49, 1913, S. 264, M. Förster.

Treats the influence of the late Greek novel (Heliodorus' Aethiopica, Longus' Daphnis and Chloe, Achilles Tatius' Clitophon and Leukippe) on the Elizabethan. With detailed bibliography.

ELISABETH WOLFFHARDT: Shakespeare und das Griechentum. Diss. Berlin, 1919 (Weimar, 1920). (54 S.) Rev.: Sh. Jb. 57, 1921, S. 96–7, W. Keller.

F. L. SCHOELL: L'hellénisme français en Angleterre à la fin de la Renaissance. In: Rev. de litt. comp., 1925, pp. 193–238.

β. INDIVIDUAL GREEK AUTHORS

Aristophanes. LEONHARD RECHNER: Aristophanes in England. Eine literarhistorische Untersuchung. Diss. München, 1914. (164 S.) Rev.: Sh. Jb. 52, 1916, S. 251–2, M. Förster.

Batrachomyomachia. FRIEDRICH WILD: Die Batrachomyomachia in England. Wien und Leipzig, 1918.=Wiener Beitr. z. engl. Phil. Bd. 48. Rev.: Sh. Jb. 55, 1919, S. 177–8, W. Keller.

Euripides. THEODOR VATKE: Shakespeare und Euripides. Eine Parallele. In: Sh. Jb. Jg. 4, 1869, S. 62–93.

Plato and Platonism. JOHN SMITH HARRISON: Platonism in English poetry of the 16th and 17th centuries. New York & London, 1903. (x, 235 pp.) Rev.: Sh. Jb. 40, 1904, S. 253–4, A. Brandl.

KURT SCHROEDER: Platonismus in der englischen Renaissance vor und bei Lyly. Diss. Berlin, 1907. (76 S.)

EMIL WOLFF: Francis Bacons Verhältnis zu Platon. Diss. München, 1908. Rev.: Archiv 122, 1909, S. 450, A. Brandl.

KURT SCHROEDER: Platonismus in der englischen Renaissance vor und bei Thomas Eliot, nebst Neudruck von Eliots 'Disputacion Platonike', 1533. Berlin, 1920. (153 und 106 S.)=Palaestra 83. Rev.: Sh. Jb. 57, 1921, S. 105, W. Keller; Arch. 143, 1922, S. 285–6; Bbl. 32, 1921, S. 56–7, H. Schöffler.

FREDERICK J. POWICKE: The Cambridge Platonists. A study. London, 1926. (x, 219 pp.)

Plutarch. SHAKESPEARE'S PLUTARCH, being a selection from the lives in North's Plutarch, which illustrate Shakespeare's plays. Ed. with a preface, notes, index of names, and glossarial index by W. W. SKEAT. London, 1875.

F. A. LEO: Four chapters of North's Plutarch, containing the lives of C. Marcius Coriolanus, Julius Caesar, M. Antonius and M. Brutus, as sources to Shakespeare's tragedies: Coriolanus, Julius Caesar, Antony and Cleopatra, and partly to Hamlet and Timon of Athens. Photolithographed in the size of the original edition of 1595. London, 1878.

REINHOLD SIGISMUND: Übereinstimmendes zwischen Shakespeare und Plutarch. In: Sh. Jb. Jg. 18, 1883, S. 156–82.

Shakespeare's Plutarch, ed. by C. F. TUCKER BROOKE. Vol. i: Containing the main sources of Julius Caesar. Vol. ii: Containing the main sources of Antony and Cleopatra and of Coriolanus. London, 1909. (xxiv, 211 and xix, 230 pp.)=The Shakespeare Library. Rev.: Sh. Jb. 46, 1910, S. 308–10, M. Förster; MLR. 5, 1910, pp. 520–1, G. C. Moore Smith.

M. W. MACCALLUM: Shakespeare's Roman plays and their background. London, 1910. (xv, 666 pp.)

RUDOLF HIRZEL: Plutarch. Leipzig, 1912. (211 S.)=Das Erbe der Alten. Schriften über Wesen und Wirkung der Antike, H. 4. Rev.: Sh. Jb. 49, 1913, S. 254, M. Förster.

Sophocles. ADOLF SCHÖLL: Shakespeare und Sophokles. In: Sh. Jb. Jg. 1, 1865, S. 127–37.

Theocritus. O. L. JIRICZEK: Die erste englische Theokrit-Übersetzung. In: Sh. Jb. Jg. 55, 1919, S. 30–4.

(e) CLASSICAL MYTHOLOGY

NICOLAUS DELIUS: Klassische Reminiszenzen in Shakespeares Dramen. In: Sh. Jb. Jg. 18, 1883, S. 81–103.

Points out allusions to mythology and legends in Shakespeare's dramas.

ROBERT KILBURN ROOT: Classical mythology in Shakespeare. New York, 1903. (134 pp.)=Yale Stud. in English, vol. 19. Rev.: Sh. Jb. 40, 1904, S. 264–5, Erskine.

DOUGLAS BUSH: Notes on Shakespeare's classical mythology. In: Phil. Quart., vol. 6, 1927, pp. 295–302.

KARL FREY: Die klassische Götter- und Heldensage in den Dramen von Marlowe, Lyly, Kyd, Greene und Peele. Diss. Strassburg, 1909. (89 S.)

HEINRICH SARTORIUS: Die klassische Götter- und Heldensage in den Dramen Beaumonts und Fletchers, Chapmans, Ben Jonsons und Massingers. Diss. Strassburg, 1912. (153 S.) Rev.: Sh. Jb. Jg. 49, 1913, S. 176, Weyhe; Bbl. 24, 1913, S. 305–6, Ph. Aronstein.

(3) INFLUENCE OF CONTEMPORARY CONTINENTAL LITERATURE

(a) GENERAL

W. BANG und H. DE VOCHT: Klassiker und Humanisten als Quelle älterer Dramatiker. In: E. St., Bd. 36, 1906, S. 385–93.

VALD. VEDEL: Shakespeare und die Renaissance. In: GRM. Jg. 3, 1911, S. 633–48.

MAX DEUTSCHBEIN: Shakespeare und die Renaissance. In: N. Spr., Bd. 23, 1916, S. 9–21.

FRANK L. SCHOELL: Études sur l'humanisme continental en Angleterre à la fin de la Renaissance. Paris, 1926. (vii, 268 pp.)=Bibl. de la Revue de litt. comp., t. 29. Rev.: Bbl. 39, 1928, S. 217–20, H. Schöffler; English Studies, 4, 1927, pp. 158–60, M. Praz; Litteris, 4, 1927, S. 142–54, Ferguson; Arch. 153, 1928, S. 305; Litbl. 49, 1928, Sp. 111–13, W. Schirmer; E. St. 64, 1929, S. 124–5, M. J. Wolff.

Examination of the influence of continental humanism on England, in particular on Chapman, whose knowledge of classical antiquity is derived not from the original texts but from the writings of the humanists.

(b) INFLUENCE OF ITALIAN LITERATURE

(α) GENERAL

J. R. MURRAY: The influence of Italian upon English literature during the 16th and 17th centuries. Cambridge, 1886.

MARY AUGUSTA SCOTT: Elizabethan translations from the Italian. The titles of such works now first collected and arranged, with annotations. In: PMLA., vol. 10, N.S. vol. 3, 1895, pp. 249–93: I. Romances. Vol. 11, N.S. vol. 4, 1896, pp. 377–484: II. Translations of poetry, plays, and metrical romances. Vol. 13, N.S. vol. 6, 1898, pp. 42–153.: III. Miscellanea. (a) Religion and theology, pp. 45–88; (b) science and the arts, pp. 88–122; (c) grammars and dictionaries, pp. 122–40; (d) proverbs, pp. 140–6. Vol. 14, N.S. vol. 7, 1899, pp. 465–571: IV. Miscellanea. (a) Voyages and discovery, pp. 469–85; (b) history and politics, pp. 485–524; (c) manners and morals, pp. 524–64.

L. FRÄNKEL: Romanisch- insbesondere italienisch-englische Wechselbe-
ziehungen im 16, 17. und 18. Jhrh. In: Krit. Jb. über d. Fortschr. d. roman.
Philol., Bd. 8, 1904, S. II, 189–215, 1896–1902; Bd. 12, 1909–10, S. II,
405–75, und Bd. 13, 1911–12, S. 603–8.

LEWIS EINSTEIN: The Italian Renaissance in England. Studies. New York,
1902. (xvii, 420 pp.) Rev.: JEGPh., 5, 1903–5, pp. 95–101, Mary A. Scott;
Bbl. 15, 1904, S. 200–1, G. Noll.
Deals with the cultural and sociological conditions. With extensive bibliography.

MARY A. SCOTT: Elizabethan translations from the Italian. Boston, 1916.
(lxxxi, 558 pp.)

T. F. CRANE: Italian social customs of the 16th century and their influence on
the literatures of Europe. New Haven, 1920=Cornell Studies, vol. 5.

(β) ITALIAN NOVEL AND DRAMA

WILHELM KÖNIG: Über die Entlehnungen Shakespeares, insbesondere aus
Rabelais und einigen italienischen Dramatikern. In: Sh. Jb. Jg. 9, 1874,
S. 195–232.

EMIL KOEPPEL: Studien zur Geschichte der italienischen Novelle in der
englischen Literatur des 16. Jahrh. Strassburg, 1892. (100 S.)=Quellen
und Forschungen, 70.
Examination of the English romance collections based on Italian models.

MARY A. SCOTT: Elizabethan translations from the Italian. The titles of such
works now first collected and arranged, with annotations. In: PMLA.,
vol. 10, N.S. vol. 3, 1895, pp. 249–93: I. Romances; vol. 11, N.S. vol. 4,
1896, pp. 377–484: II. Translations of poetry, plays, and metrical romances.

LEVIN L. SCHÜCKING: Studien über die stofflichen Beziehungen der englischen
Komödie zur italienischen bis Lilly. Halle, 1901. (190 S.)=Stud. z. engl.
Phil., hrsg. v. Morsbach, H. 9. Rev.: Sh. Jb. Jg. 38, 1902, S. 276–8, W. Bang.

A. OTT: Die italienische Novelle im englischen Drama von 1600 bis zur
Restauration. Diss. Zürich, 1904. (123 S.)

J. W. CUNLIFFE: The influence of Italian on early Elizabethan drama. In:
Mod. Phil., vol. 4, 1906, pp. 597–604. Rev.: Sh. Jb. Jg. 44, 1908, S. 278,
C. Grabau.

R. WARWICK BOND: Early plays from the Italian. Ed. with essay, introductions
and notes. Oxford, 1911. (cxviii, 332 pp.) Rev.: Sh. Jb. Jg. 47, 1911,
S. 322–3, L. L. Schücking.
Reprints of Gascoigne's Supposes, of Buggbears and Misogonus; with good introduction, notes, and glossary.

Shakespeares italienische Novellen. Hrsg. von PAUL SCHUBRING. Berlin, 1920.
(313 S.) Rev.: Lit. Echo, 24, 1921, S. 373–4.

PIERO RÉBORA: L'Italia nel dramma inglese (1558–1642). Milano & London,
1925. (319 pp.)
Deals with the influence of the Italian on the English drama.

VIOLET M. JEFFERY: John Lyly and the Italian Renaissance. Paris, 1928. (vii, 149 pp.)=Bibl. de la Revue de litt. comparée, t. 53. Rev.: Rev. de litt. comparée, vol. 9, 1929, pp. 775–6, É. Legouis; Engl. Studies 12, 1930, pp. 40–1.

(γ) INDIVIDUAL ITALIAN AUTHORS

Ariosto. JAKOB SCHÖMBS: Ariosts Orlando Furioso in der englischen Literatur des Zeitalters der Elisabeth. Diss. Strassburg, 1898. (107 S.) Rev.: Sh. Jb. 35, 1899, S. 348, A. Brandl.

Bruno. WILHELM KÖNIG: Shakespeare und Giordano Bruno. In: Sh. Jb. Jg. 11, 1876, S. 97–139.

ROBERT BEYERSDORFF: Giordano Bruno und Shakespeare. In: Sh. Jb. Jg. 26, 1891, S. 258–324. Also in: Progr. Oldenburg, 1899. (46 S.)

[ANON.]: Giordano Bruno in England. In: Quart. Rev., vol. 196, 1902, pp. 483–508.
Review of seven works dealing with G. Bruno and his influence.

RONALD B. LEVINSON: Spenser and Bruno. In: PMLA., vol. 43, 1928, pp. 675–81.

Dante. WILHELM KÖNIG: Shakespeare und Dante. In: Sh. Jb. Jg. 7, 1872, S. 170–213.

E. KOEPPEL: Dante in der englischen Literatur des 16. Jhrh. In: Zs. f. vgl. Lit. gesch., Bd. 3, 1890, S. 449–51.

PAGET TOYNBEE: Dante in English literature. London, 1909.

Machiavelli. EDWARD MEYER: Machiavelli and the Elizabethan drama. Diss. Heidelberg, 1897. (34 S.). Enlarged in: Lit. histor. Forsch., hrsg. v. Schick und von Waldberg. I, 1897. (xii, 180 S.) Rev.: Bbl. 8, 1898, S. 355–6, R. Fischer. Cf.: ADOLF HAUFFEN: Zu Machiavelli in England. In: Sh. Jb. 35, 1899, S. 274–6.

E. A. GREENLAW: The influence of Machiavelli on Spenser. In: Mod. Phil., vol. 7, 1909, pp. 187–202.

AD. GERBER: Niccolò Machiavelli. Die Handschriften, Ausgaben und Übersetzungen seiner Werke im 16. und 17. Jhrh. Eine kritisch-biblio-graphische Studie. Gotha, 1912.

NADJA KEMPNER: Raleghs staatstheoretische Schriften. Die Einführung des Machiavellismus in England. Leipzig, 1928. (138 S.)=Beitr. z. engl. Phil., hrsg. v. M. Förster, H. 7. Rev.: Engl. Studies, 11, 1929, pp. 114–16, M. Praz; E. St. 64, 1929, S. 126, M. J. Wolff; Sh. Jb. 65, 1929, S. 204–5, W. Keller.

MARIO PRAZ: Machiavelli and the Elizabethans. O.U.P., 1928. (52 pp.)= Annual Italian Lecture, Brit. Acad., vol. 13, 1928. Rev.: Revue anglo-améric. 6, 1929, pp. 358–9, A. Brulé; Sh. Jb. 65, 1929, S. 203–4, W. Keller.

HANS KEPPLER: Das Problem des Konflikts zwischen Politik und Moral bei Machiavelli. Diss. München, 1928. (84 S.)

FRIEDRICH MEINECKE: Die Idee der Staatsraison in der neueren Geschichte. Berlin, 1924, 1925².

Pescetti. GREGOR SARRAZIN: Shakespeare und Orlando Pescetti. In: E. St., Bd. 46, 1912–13, S. 347–54.

Petrarch. P. BORGHESI: Petrarch and his influence on English literature. Bologna, 1905. (136 pp.)

Tasso. EMIL KOEPPEL: Die englischen Tasso-Übersetzungen des 16. Jhrh. In: Anglia, Bd. 11, 1899, S. 11–38; Bd. 12, 1890, S. 103–42; Bd. 13, 1891, S. 42–71.

(δ) ITALIAN CONDUCT BOOKS AND THE ENGLISH IDEAL OF A GENTLEMAN

MARY AUGUSTA SCOTT: The Book of the Courtyer. In: PMLA., vol. 16, N.S. vol. 9, 1901, pp. 475–502.

ALBERT WESSELSKI: Der Hofmann des Grafen Baldesar Castiglione. München und Leipzig, 1907.

GIOVANNI DELLA CASA: Galateo of manners and behaviours. A Renaissance courtesy book. With an introduction by J. E. SPINGARN. Boston, 1914. (1230 pp.)=The Humanist's Library, VIII. Rev.: Sh. Jb. 52, 1916, S. 197–8, A. Brandl.

ALBERT EICHLER: Der Gentleman in der englischen Literatur. In: Zs. f. d. österr. Gymnasium, Bd. 69, 1920, S. 257–98 und 540–65.

ALBERT EICHLER: Shakespeares Begriff des Gentleman. In: GRM., Jg. 9, 1921, S. 358–70.

E. N. S. THOMPSON: Literary bypaths of the Renaissance. New Haven & London, 1924. (vi, 189 pp.)
Deals among other things with books of courtesy.

RUTH KELSO: Sixteenth century definitions of the gentleman in England. In: JEGPh., vol. 24, 1925, pp. 370–82.

M. STEEVEN GUAZZO: The civile conversation: the first 3 books transl. by GEORGE PETTIE, anno 1581, and the 4th by BARTH. YOUNG, anno 1586. With an introd. by SIR EDWARD SULLIVAN. 2 vols. New York & London, 1925. (xcii, 249 and 216 pp.)

BALDASSARE CASTIGLIONE: The book of the courtier, done into English by SIR THOMAS HOBY, 1561. London, 1928. (xviii, 324 pp.)=Everyman's Library.

RUTH KELSO: The doctrine of the English gentleman in the 16th Century. Univ. of Illinois Press, 1929. (288 pp.)=Univ. of Illinois Stud. in Lang. and Lit.

(c) INFLUENCE OF FRENCH LITERATURE

(α) GENERAL

M. MAIBERGER: Studien über den Einfluss Frankreichs auf die elisabethanische Literatur. Diss. München, 1903. (54 S.)

ALFRED H. UPHAM: The French influence in English literature from the accession of Elizabeth to the Restoration. New York, 1908. (ix, 560 pp.) Rev.:

Dt. Litztg. 29, 1908, Sp. 3177 ff., E. Koeppel; Arch. 121, 1908, S. 476–7, A. Brandl; Bbl. 20, 1909, S. 234–40, G. Becker.

SIDNEY LEE: The French Renaissance in England. An account of the literary relations of England and France in the 16th century. Oxford, 1910. (xxiv, 494 pp.) Rev.: Sh. Jb. 47, 1911, S. 309–10, A. Brandl; MLR. 6, 1911, pp. 246–53, L. E. Kastner; Bbl. 22, 1911, S. 193–7, E. Koeppel.

Cf. also: HEINRICH MORF: Geschichte der französischen Literatur im Zeitalter der Renaissance. Strassburg, 1914. (viii, 268 S.) = Grundr. d. roman. Philol.
Best general comprehensive account.

(β) INDIVIDUAL FRENCH AUTHORS

Froissart. ROBERT METCALF SMITH: Froissart and the English chronicle play. New York, Col. Univ. Pr. 1915 = Columbia Univ. Stud. in comparative lit. Rev.: Sh. Jb. 55, 1919, S. 169–70, W. Keller.

Garnier. ALEXANDER M. WITHERSPOON: The influence of Robert Garnier on Elizabethan drama. Diss. Yale Univ., New Haven, 1924. (vi, 197 pp.) = Yale Stud. in English, 65. Rev.: Litbl. 50, 1929, Sp. 185–6, W. Fischer.

Hardy. H. CARRINGTON LANCASTER: Alexandre Hardy and Shakespeare. In: The Alfred Todd Memorial Volumes. 2 vols. The Columbia Univ. Press.
Announced, but not yet published.

Montaigne. JACOB FEIS: Shakespeare and Montaigne. An endeavour to explain the tendency of 'Hamlet' from allusions in contemporary works. London, 1884. (viii, 210 pp.)

Montaigne: The essays, done into English by JOHN FLORIO, published by DAVID NUTT. London, 1892 = The Tudor Translations.

JOHN M. ROBERTSON: Montaigne and Shakespeare. London, 1897. (169 pp.) New edition entitled: Montaigne and Shakespeare, and other essays on cognate questions. London, 1909. (vii, 358 pp.) Rev.: Sh. Jb. 35, 1899, S. 313–14, A. Brandl; Sh. Jb. 46, 1910, S. 272–3, A. Brandl; MLR. 5, 1910, pp. 361–70, R. W. Bond.

ELIZABETH R. HOOKER: The relation of Shakespeare to Montaigne. In: PMLA., vol. 17, N.S. vol. 10, 1902, pp. 312–66.

F. DIECKOW: John Florios englische Übersetzung der Essais Montaignes und Lord Bacons, Ben Jonsons und Robert Burtons Verhältnis zu Montaigne. Diss. Strassburg, 1903. (117 S.) Rev.: Bbl. 15, 1904, S. 236–8, Ph. Aronstein.

J. CHURTON COLLINS: Shakespeare and Montaigne. In his Studies in Shakespeare. London, 1904.

The essayes of Michael Lord of Montaigne, translated by JOHN FLORIO. 3 vols. Oxford, 1904 & 1906. (429, 605 and 440 pp.) = The World's Classics.
Cheap reprint.

PIERRE VILLEY: Montaigne and Shakespeare, a book of homage to Shakespeare, 1916.

Denies Montaigne's influence.

PIERRE VILLEY: Montaigne et les poètes dramatiques anglais du temps de Shakespeare. In: Revue d'hist. litt. de la France, vol. 24, 1917, pp. 357–93.

CLARA LONGWORTH-CHAMBRUN: Giovanni Florio. Paris, 1921.

GEORGE C. TAYLOR: Shakespeare's debt to Montaigne. O.U.P., 1925. (vi, 66 pp.) Rev.: JEGPh. 26, 1927, pp. 134–5, R. A. Law.

Assumes strong influence.

PAUL HENSEL: Montaigne und die Antike. In: Vorträge d. Bibl. Warburg, hrsg. von F. Saxl. Vorträge 1925–6, Leipzig, 1928, S. 67–94. Rev.: Arch. 154, 1928, S. 130–1.

Rabelais. WILHELM KÖNIG: Über die Entlehnungen Shakespeares, insbesondere aus Rabelais und einigen italienischen Dramatikern. In: Sh. Jb. Jg. 9, 1874, S. 195–232.

(d) INFLUENCE OF SPANISH LITERATURE

(α) GENERAL

ALBERT R. FREY: William Shakespeare and alleged Spanish prototypes. In: New York Shakespeare Soc. Papers, 1886.

A. L. STIEFEL: Die Nachahmung spanischer Komödien in England unter den ersten Stuarts.=Roman. Forsch. 5. 1890.

L. BAHLSEN: Spanische Quellen der dramatischen Literatur besonders Englands zu Shakespeares Zeit. In: Zs. f. vgl. Lit. gesch., N.F. 6, 1893, S. 151 ff.

JOHN G. UNDERHILL: Spanish literature in the England of the Tudors. Diss. Columbia Univ., New York, 1899. (x, 438 pp.) Rev.: JEGPh. 5, 1903–5, pp. 564–69, H. R. Lang.

M. HUME: Some Spanish influences in Elizabethan literature. London, 1909= Trans. Royal Soc. of Lit., 2nd ser., vol. xxix, pp. 1 seq.

RUDOLF GROSSMANN: Spanien und das elisabethanische Drama. Hamburg, 1920. (138 S.)=Hamb. Univ., Abhdl. aus d. Gebiet d. Auslandskunde. Bd. 4, Reihe B, Bd. 3. Rev.: Sh. Jb. 57, 1921, S. 107–8, W. Keller; Litbl. 44, 1923, Sp. 351–4; Bbl. 35, 1924, S. 115–19, W. Fischer.

H. THOMAS: Shakespeare and Spain. O.U.P., 1922. (32 pp.)

(β) INDIVIDUAL SPANISH AUTHORS

Cervantes. G. BECKER: Die Aufnahme des Don Quijote in die englische Literatur. (1605–1770). Diss. Berlin, 1902 (30 S.)

Guevara. JOSÉ MARIA GALVEZ: Guevara in England, nebst Neudruck von Lord Berners' 'Golden Boke of Marcus Aurelius' (1535)=Palaestra, 109. Rev.: Sh. Jb. 56, 1920, S. 130–1, W. Keller.

Lope de Vega. ARTURO FARINELLI: Grillparzer und Lope de Vega. Berlin, 1894.

Shakespeare's relation to Lope de Vega is also discussed.

Montemayor. T. P. HARRISON, JR.: Shakespeare and Montemayor's Diana. In: Univ. of Texas Bull. Stud. in English, 1926, pp. 72–120.

(e) INFLUENCE OF GERMAN LITERATURE

(a) GENERAL

CHARLES H. HERFORD: Studies in the literary relations of England and Germany in the 16th century. Cambridge, 1886. (xxx, 426 pp.)

GILBERT WATERHOUSE: The literary relations of England and Germany in the 17th century. Cambridge, 1914. (vii, 190 pp.) Rev.: Sh. Jb. 51, 1915, S. 273–4, W. Creizenach.

The history of the drama is not included in this account. With extensive bibliography.

(β) INDIVIDUAL GERMAN AUTHORS

Ayrer. Ayrer: Dramen. Hrsg. von A. VON KELLER. 5 Bde. Stuttgart, 1865= Bibl. d. Lit. Vereins in Stuttgart, Bd. 76–80.

K. LÜTZELBERGER: Das deutsche Schauspiel und Jakob Ayrer und sein Verhältnis zu Shakespeare. In: Album d. lit. Ver. in Nürnberg, 1867.

J. G. ROBERTSON: Zur Kritik Jakob Ayrers. Mit besonderer Rücksicht auf sein Verhältnis zu Hans Sachs und den englischen Komödianten. Diss. Leipzig, 1892. (70 S.)

WILLIBALD WODICK: Jakob Ayrers Dramen in ihrem Verhältnis zur einheimischen Literatur und zum Schauspiel der englischen Komödianten. (1. Teil.) Diss. Breslau, 1912. (43 S.) Enlarged: Halle, 1912. (xii, 112 S.) Rev.: Sh. Jb. 49, 1913, S. 233–4, M. Förster.

GUSTAV HEINRICH: Ayrer und Shakespeare. In: Magyar Shakespeare-Târ. Bd. 8, 1916. Rev.: Sh. Jb. 54, 1918, S. 157–8, A. Weber.

Contains critical survey of recent research.

(4) INFLUENCE OF CONTEMPORARY ENGLISH NON-DRAMATIC LITERATURE

E. HERMANN: Shakespeare und Spenser. In his Drei Shakespeare-Studien. Erlangen (1879).

D. BALLMANN: Chaucers Einfluss auf das englische Drama im Zeitalter der Königin Elisabeth und der beiden ersten Stuart-Könige. Diss. Strassburg, 1901. (85 S.)

WILLIAM HENRY SCHOFIELD: Chivalry in English literature. Chaucer, Malory, Spenser and Shakespeare. Cambridge, Harv. Univ. Pr. 1912. (x, 294 pp.)= Harvard Stud. in comp. lit., vol. II. Rev.: Sh. Jb. 50, 1914, S. 191–2, M. Förster.

WILLARD FARNHAM: The 'Mirror for Magistrates' and Elizabethan tragedy. In: JEGPh., vol. 25, 1926, pp. 66–78.

W. G. BOSWELL-STONE: Shakespeare's Holinshed. The chronicle and the historical plays compared. London, 1896, 1907². (xxii, 532 pp.) Rev.: Sh. Jb. 44, 1908, S. 361, M. Förster; Bbl. 8, 1898, S. 1–4, L. T. Smith.
Reprint of all passages which Shakespeare used.

RICHARD HAKLUYT: The principal navigations, voyages, traffiques and discoveries of the English nation, made by sea or overland to the remote and farthest distant quarters of the earth at any time within the compasse of these 1600 years. With an introduction by JOHN MASEFIELD. In 8 vols. London, 1927.

A. AND J. NICHOL: Holinshed's chronicles as used in Shakespeare's plays. London, 1927. (233 pp.)=Everyman's Library.

D. T. STARNES: Shakespeare and Elyot's Governour. In: Stud. in English, Univ. of Texas. No. 7, 1927, pp. 112–32.

(5) INFLUENCE OF CONTEMPORARY ENGLISH DRAMATISTS

KATHARINE H. GATCH: Shakespeare's allusions to the older drama. In: Philol. Quart., vol. 7, 1928, pp. 27–44.

Beaumont and Fletcher. ASHLEY H. THORNDIKE: The influence of Beaumont and Fletcher on Shakespeare. Worcester, Mass., 1901. (vii, 176 pp.) Rev.: Sh. Jb. 40, 1904, S. 289–90, Schelling; Arch. 106, 1901, S. 473; JEGPh. 4, 1902, pp. 239–47, M. W. Sampson; Bbl. 14, 1903, S. 100–5, G. Sarrazin.
A valuable study.

Chapman. FRIEDR. BODENSTEDT: Chapman in seinem Verhältnis zu Shakespeare. In: Sh. Jb. Jg. 1, 1865, S. 300–36.

J. M. ROBERTSON: Shakespeare and Chapman. A thesis of Chapman's authorship of 'A Lover's Complaint' and his origination of 'Timon of Athens', with indication of further problems. London, 1917. (302 pp.) Rev.: MLR. 13, 1918, pp. 244–50, H. D. Sykes.

Greene. JOSEPH L. TYNAN: The influence of Greene on Shakespeare's early romance. In: PMLA., vol. 27, N.S. vol. 20, 1912, pp. 246–64.

Jonson. PHILIPP ARONSTEIN: Shakespeare and Ben Jonson. In: E. St., Bd. 34, 1904, S. 193–211.
Deals with the mutual relations.

EMIL KOEPPEL: Ben Jonson und Shakespeare. In: Sh. Jb. Jg. 42, 1906, S. 203–8.

EMIL KOEPPEL: Ben Jonsons Wirkung auf zeitgenössische Dramatiker, und andere Studien zur inneren Geschichte des englischen Dramas. Heidelberg, 1906. (v, 238 S.)=Anglist. Forsch., 20. Rev.: Bbl. 17, 1906, S. 228–31, Ph. Aronstein.

P. BIRCK: Literarische Anspielungen in den Werken Ben Jonsons. Diss. Strassburg, 1908. (xi, 121 S.)

MINA KERR: Influence of Ben Jonson on English comedy (1598–1642). New York, 1912. (132 pp.) Rev.: Sh. Jb. 49, 1913, S. 258, M. Förster.

PERCY ALLEN: Shakespeare, Jonson and Wilkins as borrowers. A study in Elizabethan dramatic origins and imitations. With an introduction by R. P. COWL. London, 1928. (xix, 236 pp.) Rev.: TLS., April 5, 1928, p. 255.

Lilly. C. C. HENSE: John Lilly und Shakespeare. I: Lilly und Shakespeare in ihrem Verhältnis zum klassischen Altertum. II: [Without special subtitle]. In: Sh. Jb. Jg. 7, 1872, S. 238–300; Jg. 8, 1873, S. 224–79.

JOHN GOODLET: Shakespeare's debt to John Lilly. In: E. St., Bd. 5, 1882, S. 356–63.

Marlowe. TYCHO MOMMSEN: Marlowe and Shakespeare. Progr. Eisenach, 1854.

H. ULRICI: Christopher Marlowe und Shakespeares Verhältnis zu ihm. In: Sh. Jb. Jg. 1, 1865, S. 57–85.

ARTHUR W. VERITY: The influence of Christopher Marlowe on Shakespeare's earlier style. Cambridge, 1886.

E. HÜBENER: Der Einfluss von Marlowes Tamburlaine auf die zeitgenössischen und folgenden Dramatiker. Diss. Halle, 1901. (74 S.) Rev.: Sh. Jb. 40, 1904, S. 256–7, R. Fischer.

ADOLF GEISSLER: Der Einfluss der Tamburlaine-Rolle bis zum Untergang des Elisabeth-Theaters. Diss. Berlin, 1925. (44 S.)

ALFRED STERN: Shakespeare und Marlowe. In: Arch., Jg. 84, Bd. 156, 1929, S. 195–202.

Marston. FRIEDRICH RADEBRECHT: Shakespeares Abhängigkeit von John Marston. Cöthen, 1918. (78 S.)=Neue anglist. Arb., hrsg. von L. L. Schücking und Deutschbein, H. 3. Rev.: Sh. Jb. 55, 1919, S. 152–4, W. Keller; MLR. 17, 1922, pp. 301–3, H. B. Charlton; Bbl. 30, 1919, S. 95–8, Ph. Aronstein.

Middleton. H. JUNG: Das Verhältnis Thomas Middletons zu Shakespeare. Diss. München, 1903. (51 S.) Enlarged in: Münchener Beitr., H. 29. Leipzig, 1904. (viii, 99 S.) Rev.: Sh. Jb. 40, 1904, S. 278–9, W. Bang; Bbl. 15, 1904, S. 101–5, E. Koeppel.

Rowley. A. ZAUNER: Shakespeare und Rowley. Progr. Sternberg, 1896. (40 S.)

Tourneur. LEVIN L. SCHÜCKING: Eine Anleihe Shakespeares bei Tourneur. In: E. St. 50, 1916, S. 80–105.

E. SCHÄFER: Shakespeare und das domestic drama. In: GRM., Bd. 13, 1925, S. 202–86.

(6) INFLUENCE OF FOLK-TALES, JEST-BOOKS, EMBLEM-BOOKS, ETC.

K. SIMROCK: Die Quellen des Shakspeare in Novellen, Märchen und Sagen, mit sagengeschichtlichen Nachweisungen. Bonn, 1831, 1870². (2 Teile: vii, 372 und iv, 346 S.)

W. CAREW HAZLITT: Shakespeare's jest books. Reprints of the early and rare jest books supposed to have been used by Shakespeare. 3 vols. London, 1864.

HENRY GREEN: Shakespeare and the emblem writers. An exposition of their similarities of thought and expression, preceded by a view of emblem-literature down to 1616. London, 1870. (xvi, 572 pp.)

W. C. HAZLITT: Fairy tales, legends, and romances illustrating Shakespeare and other early English writers. London, 1875.

THOMAS DYER: Folk-lore of Shakespeare. London, 1883.

FRIEDRICH BRIE: Die englischen Ausgaben des Eulenspiegel und ihre Stellung in der Geschichte des Volksbuches. Diss. Breslau, 1902. (68 S.) Rev.: JEGPh. 6, 1906–7, pp. 146–8, C. H. Herford.

FRIEDRICH BRIE: Eulenspiegel in England. Berlin, 1903. (vii, 151 S.)= Palaestra, 27. Rev.: Sh. Jb. 41, 1905, S. 225–6, W. Keller; Bbl. 15, 1904, S. 276–8, A. Andrae.

E. RÜHL: Grobianus in England. Nebst Neudruck der ersten Übersetzung 'The Schoole of Slovenrie' (1605) und erster Herausgabe des Schwankes Grobiana's Nuptials (c. 1640) aus MS. 30 Bodl. Oxf. Kapitel III–V. Diss. Berlin, 1904. (34 S.) Enlarged in: Palaestra, 38. Berlin, 1904. (lxxxii, 191 S.) Rev.: Bbl. 16, 1905, S. 51–3, A. Andrae.

FRANK WADLEIGH CHANDLER: The literature of roguery. 2 vols. London, 1907. (viii, 584 pp.) Rev.: Sh. Jb. 45, 1909, S. 422–4, M. Förster; Bbl. 19, 1908, S. 228–31, A. Andrae.
Deals with the tales of rogues.

H. DE VOCHT: De invloed van Erasmus op de engelsche tooneelliteratuur der 16ᵉ en 17ᵉ eeuwen. Eerste deel: Shakespeare jest-books.—Lyly. Gent, 1908. (xvi, 287 S.) Rev.: Sh. Jb. 45, 1909, S. 372–4, F. Brie.

A. L. STIEFEL: 'Mery tales, wittie questions, and quicke answeres.' In: Anglia, 31, 1908, S. 453–520.

ERNST SCHULZ: Die englischen Schwankbücher bis herab zu 'Dobson's Drie Bobs' (1607). Berlin, 1912. (xi, 226 S.)=Palaestra, 117. Rev.: Sh. Jb. 49, 1913, S. 264–5, M. Förster; Bbl. 23, 1912, S. 399–402, A. Andrae.

FRIEDRICH BRIE: Shakespeare und die Impresa-Kunst seiner Zeit. In: Sh. Jb. Jg. 50, 1914, S. 9–30.

RONALD S. CRANE: The vogue of Guy of Warwick from the close of the middle ages to the romantic revival. In: PMLA., vol. 30, 1915, pp. 125–94.

E. N. S. THOMPSON: Literary bypaths of the Renaissance. New Haven & O.U.P., 1924. (vi, 189 pp.)

On character books, emblem-books, books of courtesy, &c.

AURELIUS POMPEN: The English versions of the 'Ship of Fools'. A contribution to the history of the early French Renaissance in England. London, 1925. (xiv, 345 pp.). Rev.: Arch. 1927, S. 241-4, F. Liebermann; Litteris 2, S. 257-60, Liljegren; Rev. anglo-amér. 3, pp. 140-51, É. Legouis.

(7) INFLUENCE OF THE BIBLE

(Cf. Section IV, 3, pp. 35-36)

VII. THE ART OF SHAKESPEARE

PART I. SHAKESPEARE'S LANGUAGE, VOCABULARY, PROSODY AND STYLE

(1) SHAKESPEARE'S LANGUAGE AND VOCABULARY

Bibliography. ARTHUR G. KENNEDY: A bibliography of writings on the English language from the beginning of printing to the end of 1922. Cambridge & New Haven, 1927. (xvii, 517 pp.)

(*a*) SHAKESPEARE'S LANGUAGE IN GENERAL AND THE LANGUAGE OF HIS TIMES

WILLIAM SIDNEY WALKER: A critical examination of the text of Shakespeare, with remarks on his language and that of his contemporaries, together with notes on his plays and poems. 3 vols. London, 1860.

E. A. ABBOTT: A Shakespearian grammar. London, 1869 and later editions. (xxiv, 511 pp.)

F. HOELPER: Die englische Schriftsprache in Tottel's 'Miscellany' (1557) und in Tottel's Ausgabe von Brooke's 'Romeus and Juliet', 1562. Diss. Strassburg, 1894. (65 S.)

WILHELM FRANZ: Shakespeare-Grammatik. Halle a. S. 1898-1900, 1909[2]. (xii, 427 S.) Heidelberg, 1924[3]. (xxxiv, 640 S.) Rev.: E. St. 29, S. 81-106, Stoffel; Dt. Litztg. 20, 1889, Sp. 629-30; Sh. Jb. 35, 1899, S. 316-20, K. Luick; Sh. Jb. 38, 1902, S. 248-9, K. Luick; MLR. 20, 1925, pp. 345-7, J. H. G. Grattan; Bbl. 10, 1900, S. 49-57 und 12, 1901, S. 76-80, E. Wülfing.

The best comprehensive work.

K. SCHAU: Sprache und Grammatik der Dramen Marlowes. Diss. Leipzig, 1901. (102 S.)

WILHELM FRANZ: Die Grundzüge der Sprache Shakespeares. Berlin, 1902. (viii, 227 S.) Rev.: Dt. Litztg. 23, 1902, Sp. 2783-6, M. Förster; Sh. Jb. 39, 1903, S. 270-2, H. Spies; Bbl. 16, 1905, S. 129-45, Wilh. Horn.

A sketch of Shakespearian grammar, omitting examples.

Neudrucke frühneuenglischer Grammatiken, hrsg. von RUDOLF BROTANEK. 8 Bde. Halle, 1905–13:

1. George Mason's Grammaire angloise. Nach den Drucken von 1622 und 1633 herausgegeben von RUDOLF BROTANEK. 1905. (xlii, 117 S.)
2. Dr. John Jones's practical Phonography (1701). Edited by EILERT EKWALL. 1907. (cccv, 201 S.)
3. Simon Daine's Orthoepia Anglicana (1640) herausgegeben von M. RÖSLER und R. BROTANEK. Mit einer Einleitung und Darstellung des Lautbestandes ... der Orthoepia von R. BROTANEK. 1908. (lxxxviii, 113 S.)
4, 1. Charles Butler's English Grammar (1634) herausgegeben von A. EICHLER. 1910. (xix, 12. 134 S.)
4, 2. A. Eichler: Schriftbild und Lautwert in Charles Butler's English Grammar (1633, 1634) und Feminin 'Monarchi' (1634). 1913. (viii, 134 S.)
5. Coopers Grammatica Linguae Anglicanae (1685), herausgegeben von JOHN D. JONES. 1911. (231 S.)
6. The Writing Scholar's Companion (1695), edited by EILERT EKWALL. 1911. (xxii, 134 S.)
7. J. B. Gen. Ca., Le Maistre d'Escole Anglois (1580). Herausgegeben von THEO SPIRA. 1912. (vii, 83 S.)
8. Thomas Smith, De recta et emendata linguae Anglicae scriptione dialogus (1568). Herausgegeben von OTTO DEIBEL. 1913. (viii, 63, iii S., 44 Bl. und xxii S.)

WILHELM FRANZ: Orthographie, Lautgebung und Wortbildung in den Werken Shakespeares mit Ausspracheproben. Heidelberg, 1905. (vi, 125 S.) Rev.: Sh. Jb. 42, 1906, S. 248–54, R. Brotanek; MLR. 1, 1906, p. 342, A. Mawer.

FR. HELMECKE: Die Technik der Sprache in den Tragödien John Marston's. Diss. Halle, 1907. (148 S.)

P. CRUSIUS: Eine Untersuchung der Sprache John Webster's. Diss. Halle, 1908. (217 S.)

FRIEDRICH KLUGE: Über die Sprache Shakespeares. Vortrag. In: Bunte Blätter. Kulturgeschichtl. Vorträge und Aufsätze v. Fr. Kluge. Freiburg i. Br. 1908. S. 175–93. Rev.: Sh. Jb. 45, 1909, S. 404, M. Förster.

W. PREIN: Puristische Strömungen im 16. Jhrh. Ein Beitrag zur englischen Sprachgeschichte. Progr. Wanne und Eickel, 1909. (59 S.)

EILERT EKWALL: Historische neuenglische Laut- und Formenlehre. Berlin & Leipzig, 1914. (150 S.)= Göschen Slg. Rev.: Sh. Jb. 52, 1916, S. 241, M. Förster.

MORRIS P. TILLEY: Some evidence in Shakespeare of contemporary effort to refine the language of the day. In: PMLA., vol. 31, N.S. vol. 24, 1916, pp. 65–78.

HENRY BRADLEY: Shakespeare's English. In: Shakespeare's England. O.U.P., 1917. Vol. II, pp. 539–74.

HENRY CECIL WYLD: A history of modern colloquial English. London, 1920, 1921². (xvi, 416 pp.) Chap. IV: The English of Henry VIII and Queen Elizabeth, pp. 99–147.

GEORG BORCHARDT: Schreibung, Aussprache und Formenbau im Tagebuch des Richard Cocks (1615–1622). Diss. Giessen, 1925. (30 S.)

OTTO JESPERSEN: Shakespeare and the language of poetry. In his Growth and structure of the English language. Leipzig, 1926⁵. Chap. IX. (23 pp.)

(b) PHONOLOGY, PRONUNCIATION, AND ORTHOGRAPHY

JOHN B. NOYES and CH. S. PEIRCE: Shakespearian pronunciation. In: North Amer. Rev., Boston, 1864, pp. 342–69.

ALEXANDER J. ELLIS: On early English pronunciation with especial reference to Shakespere and Chaucer. 5 vols. London, 1867–89=Early Engl. Text Soc. Extra ser. nos. 2, 7, 14, 23 and 56.

EDUARD MÜLLER: Shakespeares Aussprache. Nach Alexander J. Ellis. In: Sh. Jb. Jg. 8, 1873, S. 92–137.

AUG. LUMMERT: Die Orthographie der ersten Folioausgabe der Shakespeareschen Dramen. Diss. Berlin, 1883. (30 S.) Rev.: Sh. Jb. 35, 1899, S. 320, K. Luick; Litbl. 5, Sp. 390, A. Brandl.

E. BRUGGER: Zur lautlichen Entwicklung der englischen Schriftsprache im Anfang des 16. Jhrh. 1. Teil: Quantitätsverhältnisse. Diss. Zürich, 1893. (84 S.)

ALEXANDER GILL: Logonomia anglica, nach der Ausgabe von 1621 diplomatisch herausgegeben von Otto L. Jiriczek. Strassburg, 1903. (lxix, 288 S.)= Quellen und Forsch., Bd. 90. Rev.: Bbl. 15, 1904, S. 230–3, W. Franz.

E. RUDOLF: Die englische Orthographie von Caxton bis Shakespeare. Diss. Marburg, 1904. (49 S.)

GRACE F. SWEARINGEN: English orthography. In: MLN., vol. 20, 1905, pp. 212–14.

WILHELM VIËTOR: Shakespeare's pronunciation. Vol. I: A Shakespeare phonology. With a rime-index to the poems as a pronouncing vocabulary. Vol. II: A Shakespeare reader in the old spelling and with a phonetic transcription. Marburg, 1906. (xvi, 290 and xii, 179 pp.) Rev.: Sh. Jb. 43, 1907, S. 263–9, R. Brotanek; MLR. 2, 1907, pp. 74–7, F. J. Curtis; Bbl. 18, 1907, S. 258–61, E. Kruisinga.

E. HAUCK: Systematische Lautlehre Bullokars [1580]. (Vokalismus.) Diss. Marburg, 1906. (104 S.) Rev.: Bbl. 18, 1907, S. 226–9, E. Kruisinga.

L. DIEHL: Englische Schreibung und Aussprache im Zeitalter Shakespeares, nach Briefen und Tagebüchern. Diss. Giessen, 1906. (72 S.) Rev.: Bbl. 18, 1907, S. 226–9, E. Kruisinga.

OTTO JESPERSEN: John Hart's pronunciation of English (1569 and 1570). Heidelberg, 1907. (123 pp.)=Anglist. Forsch., hrsg. v. Hoops, H. 22. Rev.: Sh. Jb. 45, 1909, S. 402–3, M. Förster; Bbl. 19, 1908, S. 169–75, A. Eichler.

F. SCHNAAR: Die englische Orthographie seit Shakespeare. Mit Berücksichtigung der Grossschreibung und Interpunktion. Diss. Marburg, 1907. (106 S.)

OTTO JESPERSEN: A modern English grammar on historical principles. Part I. Sounds and spellings. Heidelberg, 1909. (xi, 485 pp.)=German. Bibl. i. 9. Rev.: Sh. Jb. 46, 1910, S. 320, M. Förster.

ROBERT BACH: Die Schreibung in den englischen Theaterurkunden aus dem Zeitalter der Königin Elisabeth. Diss. Giessen, 1911. (87 S. und 14 Tab.)

THEO SPIRA: Die englische Lautentwicklung nach französischen Grammatiker-Zeugnissen. Strassburg, 1912. (xi, 278 S.)=Quellen und Forsch., H. 115. Rev.: Sh. Jb. 50, 1914, S. 221, M. Förster.

OTTO DEIBEL: Thomas Smith, De recta et emendata linguae Anglicae scriptione dialogus (1568). Diss. Giessen, 1912. (71 S.) Rev.: Sh. Jb. 50, 1914, S. 221, M. Förster.
Examination of the theories of pronunciation of the Cambridge professor, Th. Smith (1513–77).

R. E. ZACHRISSON: Pronunciation of English vowels, 1400–1700. Göteborg, 1913. (xiv, 232 pp.) Rev.: Sh. Jb. 50, 1914, S. 221, M. Förster.

R. E. ZACHRISSON: Shakespeares uttal. Uppsala, 1914. (43 S.)=Studier i modern språkvetenskap v, 2. Detailed and important review: Sh. Jb. 51, 1915, S 254–8, M. Förster.
Determination of the phonetic values of the vowels.

WALTER BENDIX: Englische Lautlehre nach Nares. Diss. Giessen, 1921. (74 S.)

ALFRED W. POLLARD: Elizabethan spelling as a literary and bibliographical clue. In: Libr., 4th ser., vol. 4, 1923, pp. 1–8.

M. ST. CLARE BYRNE: Anthony Munday's spelling as a literary clue. In: Libr., 4th ser., vol. 4, 1923, pp. 9–23.

EDUARD SIEVERS in: Shakespeares Anteil am King Lear. In: Anglica. Festschr. für Alois Brandl. Bd. 2. Leipzig, 1925=Palaestra 148.
An examination of Shakespeare's pronunciation according to the phono-analytical method.

R. E. ZACHRISSON: The English pronunciation at Shakespeare's time as taught by William Bullokar. With word-lists from all his works. Uppsala, Leipzig (1927). (xiii, 243 pp.) = Skrifter utgivna av K. Humanistika Vetenskap. Samfundet i Uppsala, 22, 6. Rev.: Bbl. 39, 1928, S. 153–66, K. Luick; Arch. 53, 1928, S. 266–7, A. Brandl; E. St. 63, 1929, S. 406–8, W. Franz.

WILHELM MARSCHALL: Shakespeares Orthographie. In: Anglia, Bd. 51, 1927, S. 307–22.

(c) ACCIDENCE

P. BRONISCH: Das neutrale Possessivpronomen bei Shakespeare. Diss. Greifswald, 1878. (53 S.)

K. POLLERT: Über die 3. Person pluralis auf s in Shakespeare. Diss. Marburg, 1881. (59 S.)

STATIUS SPEKKER: Über die Kongruenz des Subjekts und des Prädikats in der Sprache Shakespeares. Diss. Jena, 1881. (55 S.)

C. ALPHONSO SMITH: Shakespeare's present indicative s-endings with plural subjects. A study in the grammar of the First Folio. In: PMLA., vol. 11, N.S. vol. 4, 1896, pp. 363–76. Rev.: Bbl. 7, 1897, S. 342–4, E. Wülfing.

W. VON STADEN: Entwicklung der Präsens Indikativ-Endungen im Englischen unter besonderer Berücksichtigung der 3. Person Singular von ungefähr 1500 bis auf Shakespere. Diss. Rostock, 1903. (109 S.) Rev.: Bbl. 15, 1904, S. 225–30, W. Franz.

KURT BÖHM: Spensers Verbalflexion. Diss. Berlin, 1909. (ii, 59 S.) Rev.: Sh. Jb. 46, 1910, S. 191–2, Fr. Brie.

JACOB KNECHT: Die Kongruenz zwischen Subjekt und Prädikat und die 3. Person Pluralis Praesentis auf -s im elisabethanischen Englisch. Heidelberg, 1911. (xiv, 152 S.)=Anglist. Forsch., hrsg. von Hoops, H. 33. Rev.: Sh. Jb. 48, 1912, S. 327–8, Max Förster; Arch. 127, 1911, S. 475, A. Brandl; Dt. Litztg. 1912, Sp. 232–3, A. Schröer.

FRIEDRICH STROHEKER: Doppelformen und Rhythmus bei Marlowe und Kyd. Diss. Heidelberg, 1913. (xii, 105 S.) Rev.: Sh. Jb. 50, 1914, S. 235, M. Förster; Bbl. 25, 1914, S. 135–7, E. Björkman.

K. KNEILE: Die Formenlehre bei John Lyly. Diss. Tübingen, 1914. (xii, 89 S.)

OTTO ZIESENIS: Der Einfluss des Rhythmus auf Silbenmessung, Wortbildung, Formenlehre und Syntax bei Lyly, Greene und Peele. Diss. Kiel, 1915. (118 S.) Rev.: Sh. Jb. 52, 1916, S. 261–2, M. Förster.
Grammatical doublets depending on the rhythm.

WILLARD E. FARNHAM: Colloquial contractions in Beaumont, Fletcher, Massinger, and Shakespeare as a test of authorship. In: PMLA., vol. 31, N.S. vol. 24, 1916, pp. 326–58.

(d) SYNTAX

H. BAHRS: Die Anakoluthe bei Shakespeare. Diss. Jena, 1878. (44 S.)

G. STERN: Über das persönliche Geschlecht unpersönlicher Substantiva bei Shakespeare. Diss. Leipzig und Progr. Dresden, 1881. (63 S.)

LEON KELLNER: Zur Syntax des englischen Verbums mit besonderer Berücksichtigung Shakespeares. Wien, 1885. (vii, 103 S.)

R. UTECH: Über Wortstellungen bei Shakespeare. Diss. Halle, 1892. (30 S.)

M. LIENING: Die Personifikation unpersönlicher Hauptwörter bei den Vorläufern Shakespeares (Lyly, Kyd, Marlowe, Peele und Greene). Ein Beitrag zur Grammatik und Poetik der elisabethanischen Zeit. Diss. München, 1904. (viii, 107 S.)

RICHARD VOGT: Das Adjektiv bei Christopher Marlowe. Diss. Berlin, 1908. (68 S.) Rev.: Sh. Jb. 45, 1909, S. 271, Fr. Brie.

E. SCHOLZ: Der absolute Infinitiv bei Shakespeare. Diss. Berlin, 1908. (72 S.) Rev.: Sh. Jb. 45, 1909, S. 275–6, Fr. Brie.

H. ENGEL: Spensers Relativsatz. Diss. Berlin, 1908. (82 S.)

FRITZ HOFFMANN: Das Partizipium bei Spenser mit Berücksichtigung Chaucers und Shakespeares. Diss. Berlin, 1909. (vi, 48 S.) Rev.: Sh. Jb. 46, 1910, S. 191, Fr. Brie.

H. DRUVE: Der absolute Infinitiv in den Dramen der Vorgänger Shakespeares. Diss. Kiel, 1910. (98 S.) Rev.: Bbl. 25, 1914, S. 75–6, B. Fehr.

VICTOR SCHULZ: Das persönliche Geschlecht unpersönlicher Substantiva (mit Einschluss der Tiernamen) bei Spenser. Diss. Kiel, 1913. (viii, 114 S.) Rev.: Sh. Jb. 51, 1915, S. 259, M. Förster.

E. REINICKE: Der Gebrauch des bestimmten Artikels in der englischen Prosa des 16. Jhrh. Diss. Halle, 1915. (163 S.)

HILDEGARD HARZ: Die Umschreibung mit do in Shakespeares Prosa. Cöthen, 1918. (vii, 142 S.)=Neue anglist. Arb., hrsg. v. Schücking und Deutschbein, H. 2. Rev.: Bbl. 30, 1919, S. 228–32, E. Ekwall.

W. FRANZ: Grammatisches zu Shakespeare. In: E. St., Bd. 54, 1920, S. 132–8. I. Zur Interpunktion der Shakespeare-Folio von 1623. II. Der Satztypus: The book sells well.

A. FRANK: Das Kausativum bei Shakespeare. MS. Diss. Marburg, 1925. (xiii, 215 S.)

WALTER GEBHARDT: Die progressive Form bei Shakespeare. Diss. Marburg, 1927. (72 S.)

ERNST STANDKE: Studien zum Gebrauch des Plurals bei Shakespeare. Diss. Marburg, 1927. (89 S.) Rev.: Litbl. 1928, Sp. 470.

(e) PUNCTUATION

O. GLÖDE: Die englische Interpunktionslehre. In: E. St., Bd. 19, 1894, S. 206–45. I. Die Entwicklung der englischen Interpunktions- und Lesezeichen bis zur Erfindung der Buchdruckerkunst. II. Form und Anwendung der Interpunktionszeichen von der Zeit der Erfindung der Buchdruckerkunst bis auf die Gegenwart.

PERCY SIMPSON: Shakespearian punctuation. Oxford, 1911. (107 S.) Rev.: Sh. Jb. 48, 1912, S. 302–3, M. Förster; Bbl. 23, 1912, S. 110–11, E. Dick; MLN. 27, 1912, pp. 199–200; E. St. 45, 1912, S. 80–1, W. Franz.
Supposes a system of rhythmic punctuation.

W. FRANZ: Grammatisches zu Shakespeare. In: E. St., Bd. 54, 1920, S. 132–8. I. Zur Interpunktion der Shakespeare-Folio von 1623.

ALFRED W. POLLARD: Shakespeare's fight with the pirates and the problems of the transmission of his text. C.U.P., 1917, 1920^2. (xxviii, 110 pp.)
Supports the theory of the rhythmic principle of punctuation.

Times Literary Supplement, 1921 and 1922. Concerning punctuation cf. controversial correspondence of WILLIAM POEL and BERNARD SHAW against A. W. POLLARD and DOVER WILSON: 1921, pp. 91, 107, 127, 178, 196, 211, 228, 244, 259. 1922, pp. 459, 476.

E. SULLIVAN: Punctuation in Shakespeare. In: Nineteenth Century, 1921, pp. 995–1006.

The works of Shakespeare. Ed. by SIR ARTHUR QUILLER-COUCH and JOHN DOVER WILSON. I. The Tempest. C.U.P., 1921.

Wilson here defends the theory of dramatic punctuation and indicates it by means of special signs.

PERCY SIMPSON: The bibliographical study of Shakespeare. In: Oxf. Bibliogr. Soc., vol. i, pt. i, 1923, pp. 19–49.

Defends his own view of Elizabethan punctuation as opposed to that of Sidney Lee.

RAYMOND M. ALDEN: The punctuation of Shakespeare's printers. In: PMLA., vol. 39, 1924, pp. 557–80. Rev.: Sh. Jb. 63, 1927, S. 222, Beckmann.

Considers Simpson's theory as not proven.

CHARLES C. FRIES: Shakespearian punctuation. In: Studies in Shakespeare, Milton and Donne. New York, 1925, pp. 65–86. Rev.: E. St. 63, 1928, S. 116–17, A. Eichler; JEGPh. 27, 1928, p. 93, Northup.

Supposes a logical-syntactical system of punctuation.

HILARY JENKINSON: Notes on the study of English punctuation of the 16th century. In: RESt., vol. 2, 1926, pp. 152–8.

Studies the punctuation in documents, letters, etc.

J. ISAACS: A note on Shakespeare's dramatic punctuation. In: RESt., vol. 2, 1926, pp. 461–3.

Points out that at the time of the Restoration nothing was known of rhythmic punctuation.

(f) THE VOCABULARY OF SHAKESPEARE AND HIS CONTEMPORARIES

(a) VOCABULARY IN GENERAL

GIOVANNI FLORIO: A worlde of wordes, or dictionarie in Italian and English. London, 1598.

RANDLE COTGRAVE: A dictionarie of the French and English tongues. 2 parts. London, 1611.

––––––––

JOH. SCHÜMANN: See und Seefahrt, nebst dem metaphorischen Gebrauch dieser Begriffe in Shakespeares Dramen. I. Progr. Leipzig, 1876. (40 S.)

FRIEDR. KLUGE: Über die Sprache Shakespeares. Festvortrag. In: Sh. Jb. Jg. 28, 1893, S. 1–15.

Shakespeare as a creative spirit in the language.

EILERT EKWALL: Shakspere's vocabulary. Its etymological elements. I. Uppsala Univ. Årsskrift, 1903. (xix, 99 S.) Rev.: E. St. 34, 1904, S. 269–70, W. Franz; Bbl. 15, 1904, S. 120–2, W. Franz.

H. LOEWE: Shakespeare-Studien: 100 Stellen weidmännisch erklärt und übersetzt. Progr. Zerbst, 1904. (iii, 32 S.)

W. FRANZ: Die Wortbildung bei Shakespeare. In: E. St., Bd. 35, 1905, S. 34–85.

M. PRIESS: Die Bedeutungen des abstrakten substantivierten Adjektivs und des entsprechenden Substantivs bei Shakespeare. Diss. Göttingen, 1906. (57 S.)

J. L. MOORE: Die theoretische Stellungnahme der englischen Schriftsteller zur Fremdwörterfrage während der Tudor-Stuart-Zeit. (Teildruck: Kap. VI). Diss. Göttingen, 1909. (38 S.)

W. B. WHALL: Shakespeare's sea terms explained. Bristol, 1910. (111 pp.) Rev.: Sh. Jb. 47, 1911, S. 348–9, M. Förster.

CHARLES BASTIDE: La France et les Français dans le théâtre de Shakespeare. In: Edda. Bd. 6, 1916, S. 112–23.
Collection of French words and phrases in Shakespeare's works.

H. HENSE: Shakespeares seetechnische Ausdrücke. Diss. Münster, 1920.

ALBERT EICHLER: 'Master' als Höflichkeitswort in Shakespeares Dramen. In: E. St., Bd. 60, 1925–26, S. 134–9.

GEORGE GORDON: Shakespeare's English. Oxford, 1928. (22 pp.)=Soc. for Pure Engl. Tract no. 29. Rev.: Bbl. 40, 1929, S. 111–12, A. Eichler.
About new word-formations.

(β) ENGLISH DIALECTS

JAMES ORCHARD HALLIWELL: A dictionary of archaic and provincial words, obsolete phrases, proverbs, and ancient customs, from the 14th century. 2 vols. London, 1855³. (xxxvi, 960 pp.)

R. W. HUNTLEY: A glossary of the Cotswold Gloucestershire dialect, illustrated by examples from ancient authors. London, 1869.

E. PANNING: Dialektisches Englisch in elisabethanischen Dramen. Diss. Halle, 1884. (53 S.)

G. F. NORTHALL: A Warwickshire word-book comprising obsolescent and dialect words, colloquialisms, &c., gathered from oral relation, and collated with accordant works. London, 1896. (xx, 279 pp.)=Engl. Dialect Soc., vol. 31, part ii.

JOSEPH WRIGHT: English Dialect Dictionary. 6 vols. London, 1898–1905.
Chief standard work on English dialect forms.

APPLETON MORGAN: A study in Warwickshire dialect, with a glossary and notes touching the Edward the Sixth grammar schools and the Elizabethan pronunciation. New York Shakespeare Soc. Papers, No. 10, 1900⁴. (xv, 485 pp.)

JOSEPH WRIGHT: The English dialect grammar. Oxford, 1905. (xxiv, 696 pp.)

EDUARD ECKHARDT: Die Dialekt- und Ausländertypen des älteren englischen Dramas. 2 Teile. Louvain, 1910, 1911. (xv, 163 und xxxi, 189 S.)=Mat. z. Kunde d. ält. engl. Dramas. Bd. 27 und 32.

O. L. JIRICZEK: Ein elisabethanisches Dialektgedicht. [i.e. THOMAS HOWELL: Jacke showes his qualities and great good will to Jone.] In: Sh. Jb. Jg. 55, 1919, S. 54–8.
Reprint, with introduction.

MAX FÖRSTER: Die kymrischen Einlagen bei Shakespeare. In: GRM., Jg. 12, 1924, S. 349–64.

(γ) PROPER NAMES

ERNST ERLER: Die Namengebung bei Shakespeare. Diss. Jena, 1913. (23 S.) Enlarged in: Anglist. Arbeiten, hrsg. von Schücking, H. 2. Heidelberg, 1913. (v, 144 S.) Rev.: Sh. Jb. 50, 1914, S. 194–8, M. Förster.

F. G. STOKES: A dictionary of the characters and proper names in the works of Shakespeare. London, 1924. (xvi, 360 pp.) Rev.: MLR. 20, p. 108, G. C. Moore Smith.

ARTHUR E. BAKER: A Shakespeare dictionary. Taunton, n.d. Up to the present the following plays have appeared: 1. Caes. 2. As. 3. Macb. 4. Temp. 5. Haml. 6. Lear. 7. John. 8. Merch. 9. R. II. 10. 1 H. IV. 11. 2 H. IV.
A dictionary arranged for the individual plays and explaining in particular the proper names.

WILHELM OELRICH: Die Personennamen in elisabethanischen Dramen Englands. Diss. Kiel, 1911. (108 S.) Rev.: Sh. Jb. 52, 1916, S. 253–7, M. Förster.

HANS DETLEFSEN: Die Namengebung in den Dramen der Vorgänger Shakespeares. Diss. Kiel, 1914. (ix, 60 S.) Rev.: Sh. Jb. 52, 1916, S. 257–60, M. Förster.

OTTO HINZE: Studien zu Ben Jonson's Namengebung in seinen Dramen. Diss. Leipzig, 1918. (84 S.) Rev.: Sh. Jb. 56, 1920, S. 130, W. Keller.

RESI GIELEN: Untersuchungen zur Namengebung bei Beaumont, Fletcher und Massinger. Diss. Münster, 1929. (82 S.)

(δ) DICTIONARIES AND GLOSSARIES

ROBERT NARES: A glossary, or, collection of words, phrases, names, and allusions to customs, proverbs, etc. which have been thought to require illustration, in the works of English authors, particularly Shakespeare and his contemporaries. London, 1822. (viii, 585 pp.) A new edition, with considerable additions both of words and examples by JAMES O. HALLIWELL and THOMAS WRIGHT. 2 vols. London, 1859. (476 and 981 pp.) Cf. A book of words [i.e. Nares' Glossary]. In: TLS., June 1, 1922=(Leading article).

ALEXANDER SCHMIDT: Shakespeare-Lexicon. Vollständiger englischer Sprachschatz mit allen Wörtern, Wendungen und Satzbildungen in den Werken des Dichters. Berlin, 1874–5, 1886². 3. Aufl., durchges. und erweit. von GREGOR SARRAZIN. 2 Bde. Berlin, 1902. (xiii, 1484 S.) Rev.: Sh. Jb. 39, 1903, S. 272–3, W. Bang; Bbl. 14, 1903, S. 97–9, F. Holthausen.
The text remains almost unaltered, but Sarrazin has added a supplement.

ALEXANDER DYCE: A glossary to the works of William Shakespeare. Revised by HAROLD LITTLEDALE. London, 1902. (xii, 570 pp.) Rev.: Sh. Jb. 39, 1903, S. 273-4, W. Keller; Lit. Zbl. 54, 1903, Sp. 221 f.

New edition of the glossary to A. Dyce's large edition of Shakespeare. Contains only those expressions which require explanatory notes.

JOHN FOSTER: A Shakespeare word-book. Being a glossary of archaic forms and varied usages of words employed by Shakespeare. London [1908]. (xi, 735 pp.) Rev.: Sh. Jb. 45, 1909, S. 403-4, M. Förster.

MARIAN EDWARDES: A pocket lexicon and concordance to the works of Shakespeare. London, 1909. (viii, 274 pp.) Rev.: Sh. Jb. 46, 1910, S. 320-1, M. Förster.

Supplementary volume in the 'Temple Shakespeare' edition. Very comprehensive.

RICHARD J. CUNLIFFE: A new Shakespearean dictionary. London, 1910. (xi, 342 pp.) Rev.: Sh. Jb. 47, 1911, S. 347-8, M. Förster; Dt. Litztg. 32, 1911, Sp. 1577-9, W. Franz.

A useful shorter dictionary of obsolete expressions.

C. T. ONIONS: A Shakespeare glossary. Oxford, 1911. (xii, 259 pp.) Rev.: Sh. Jb. 48, 1912, S. 325-7, M. Förster; Arch. 127, 1911, S. 479; MLR. 7, 1912, pp. 559-61, G. C. Macaulay; Bbl. 23, 1912, S. 354-9, Max Born.

Explanations of the more difficult words.

WALTER W. SKEAT: A glossary of Tudor and Stuart words, especially from the dramatists. Ed. with additions by A. L. MAYHEW. Oxford, 1914. (xix, 461 pp.) Rev.: Sh. Jb. 50, 1914, S. 221-2, M. Förster; Bbl. 26, 1915, S. 98-9, A. Eichler.

LEON KELLNER: Shakespeare-Wörterbuch. Leipzig, 1922. (viii, 358 S.)=Engl. Bibliothek, hrsg. von M. Förster, Bd. 1. Rev.: Sh. Jb. 58, 1922, S. 137, W. Keller; MLR. 18, 1923, p. 213, W. W. Greg; Bbl. 37, 1926, S. 33-6, E. Deckner.

A careful work.

(ε) CONCORDANCES

MARY COWDEN CLARKE: The complete concordance to Shakspere, being a verbal index to all the passages in the dramatic works of the poet. New and revised edition. London, 1870. (viii, 860 pp.)

JOHN BARTLETT: A new and complete concordance or verbal index to words, phrases, and passages in the dramatic works of Shakespeare, with a supplement concordance to the poems. London, 1906. (1910 pp.)

CHARLES CRAWFORD: A concordance to the works of THOMAS KYD. Louvain, 1906-10. (v, 690 pp.)=Mat. z. Kunde des ält. engl. Dramas. Bd. 15. Rev.: Sh. Jb. 47, 1911, S. 348, M. Förster.

CHARLES CRAWFORD: The Marlowe concordance. 1. Teil. Louvain, 1911. (xx, 200 S.) 2. Teil 1912. (S. 201-360)=Mat. z. Kunde d. älteren engl. Dramas. Bd. 34.

(ζ) DICTIONARIES OF QUOTATIONS

WILLIAM DODD: The beauties of Shakespear, regularly selected from each play. With a general index, digesting them under proper heads. 2 vols. London, 1752. (xxii, 264 and 258 pp.)

G. SOMERS BELLAMY: The new Shaksperian dictionary of quotations. London, 1875. (xxv, 272 pp.)

F. A. LEO: Geflügelte Worte und volkstümlich gewordene Aussprüche aus Shakespeares dramatischen Werken. In: Sh. Jb. Jg. 27, 1892, S. 4–107. Nachtrag: S. 311–14.

(2) SHAKESPEARE'S PROSODY

(a) GENERAL WORKS ON ENGLISH PROSODY

J. SCHIPPER: Englische Metrik. 1. Teil: Altenglische Metrik. 2. Teil: Neuenglische Metrik. Bonn, 1881, 1888. (1061 S.)

J. SCHIPPER: Grundriss der englischen Metrik. Wien & Leipzig, 1895= Wiener Beitr., Bd. 2.

J. A. SYMONDS: Blank verse. London, 1895.

JOSEPH B. MAYOR: Chapters on English metre. Cambridge, 1901².

R. B. MCKERROW: The use of so-called classical metres in Elizabethan verse, I. II. In: Mod. Lang. Quart., vol. 4, 1901, pp. 172–80 and vol. 5, 1902, pp. 6–13. Rev.: Sh. Jb. 39, 1903, S. 325–6, Dibelius.

GEORGE SAINTSBURY: Prosody from Chaucer to Spenser. In: CHEL., vol. 3. Cambridge, 1909, pp. 273–88.

GEORGE SAINTSBURY: History of English prosody. 3 vols. London, 1906, 1923.

MAX KALUZA: Englische Metrik in historischer Entwicklung. Berlin, 1909. (xvi, 384 S.)

GEORGE SAINTSBURY: Historical manual of English prosody. London, 1910. (xvii, 347 pp.) Rev.: Sh. Jb. 48, 1912, S. 328–9, M. Förster.

(b) SHAKESPEARE'S PROSODY

WILLIAM SIDNEY WALKER: On Shakespeare's versification. London, 1854. (xxiv, 296 pp.)

CHARLES BATHURST: Remarks on the difference in Shakespeare's versification in different periods of his life and on the like points of difference in poetry generally. London, 1857. (218 pp.)

F. G. FLEAY: On metrical tests as applied to dramatic poetry. In: The New Shakspere Soc. Trans. Ser. I, vol. i, pt. 1, 2, 1874. Part I: Shakspere, pp. 1–40. Part II: Beaumont, Fletcher, and Massinger, pp. 41–84.

JOHN K. INGRAM: On the weak endings of Shakespeare. With some account of the history of the verse-tests in general. In: The New Shakspere Soc. Trans., 1874, pp. 442 ff.

K. SEITZ: Die Alliteration im Neuenglischen vor und bei Shakespeare. Progr. Marne, 1875.

F. S. PULLING: The speech-ending test applied to twenty of Shakspere's plays. In: The New Shaksp. Soc. Trans., 1877–9, pp. 457 seq.

W. HERTZBERG: Metrisches, Grammatisches, Chronologisches zu Shakespeares Dramen. In: Sh. Jb. 13, 1878, S. 248–66.

J. HARRISON, J. GOODLET, and R. BOYLE: Report of the Tests Committee of the St. Petersburg Shakespeare Circle (28. 2. 1880). In: E. St., Bd. 3, 1880, S. 473–504.

ARNOLD SCHRÖER: Über die Anfänge des Blankverses in England. In: Anglia, Bd. 4, 1881, S. 1–72.

GOSWIN KÖNIG: Der Vers in Shakespeares Dramen. Strassburg, 1888= Quellen und Forsch., 61.

HERMANN KRUMM: Die Verwendung des Reims in dem Blankverse des englischen Dramas zur Zeit Shakespeares, 1561–1616. I. Teil: Der Reim in dem fünffüssigen Jambus des vor-Shakespeareschen Dramas. Leipzig, 1889.

JULIUS HEUSER: Der Coupletreim in Shakespeares Dramen. Diss. Marburg, 1893. (96 S.). Also in: Sh. Jb. Jg. 28, 1893, S. 177–272 und Jg. 29–30, 1894, S. 235–45.

HERMANN CONRAD: Metrische Untersuchungen zur Feststellung der Abfassungszeit von Shakespeares Dramen (mit 4 metrischen Tabellen). In: Sh. Jb. Jg. 31, 1895, S. 318–54.

P. VAN DAM and C. STOFFEL: William Shakespeare, prosody and text. An essay in criticism, being an introduction to a better editing and a more adequate appreciation of the works of the Elizabethan poets. Leyden, 1900. (vii, 437 pp.) Rev.: Sh. Jb. 38, 1902, S. 242–5, G. Sarrazin; Dt. Litztg. 22, 1901, Sp. 667–71, W. Franz; Bbl. 13, 1902, S. 322–5, Rud. Fischer.

F. LITTSCHWAGER: Alexandriner in den Dramen Shakespeares. I. Teil: Scheinbare Alexandriner. Diss. Königsberg, 1912. (47 S.)

M. A. BAYFIELD: A study of Shakespeare's versification, with an inquiry into the trustworthiness of the early texts. An examination of the 1616 folio of Ben Jonson's works and appendices, including a revised text of Antony and Cleopatra. C.U.P., 1920. (xii, 521 pp.) Rev.: Bbl. 34, 1923, S. 325–38, M. Förster.

B. A. P. VAN DAM: The text of Shakespeare's Hamlet. London, 1924. Chap. VI and VII, pp. 191–252.

SIR GEORGE YOUNG: Shakespeare as a metrist. In: An English prosody on inductive lines. Cambridge, 1928, pp. 155–217.

(c) PROSODY OF SHAKESPEARE'S CONTEMPORARIES

JAKOB SCHIPPER: De versu Marlovii. Diss. Bonn, 1867. (43 S.)

R. BOYLE: Beaumont, Fletcher and Massinger. In: E. St., Bd. 5, 1882, S. 74–96; Bd. 7, 1884, S. 66–87; Bd. 8, 1885, S. 39–61; Bd. 9, 1886, S. 209–39; Bd. 10, 1887, S. 383–411.

W. VON SCHOLTEN: Metrische Untersuchungen zu John Marstons Trauerspielen. Diss. Halle, 1886. (55 S.)

WILH. WILKE: Metrische Untersuchungen zu Ben Jonson. Diss. Halle, 1888. (70 S.)

WILH. WILKE: Anwendung der rhyme-test und double-ending-test auf Ben Jonson's Dramen. In: Anglia, Bd. 10, 1888, S. 512–21.

EDUARD HANNEMANN: Metrische Untersuchungen zu John Ford. Diss. Halle, 1888. (62 S.)

E. PENNER: Metrische Untersuchungen zu George Peele. Diss. Halle, 1890. (40 S.) Also in: Arch. Jg. 44, Bd. 85, 1890, S. 269–308.

C. KNAUT: Über die Metrik Robert Greenes. Diss. Halle, 1890. (63 S.)

E. ELSTE: Der Blankvers in den Dramen George Chapmans. Diss. Halle, 1892. (62 S.)

O. SCHULZ: Über den Blankvers in den Dramen Thomas Middletons. Diss. Halle, 1892. (48 S.)

A. DOLESCHAL: Der Versbau in Thomas Kyds Dramen. Ein Beitrag zur Geschichte der englischen Metrik. Progr. Steyr, 1892. (23 S.)

P. KUPKA: Über den dramatischen Vers Thomas Dekkers. Diss. Halle, 1893. (37 S.)

M. MEINERS: Metrische Untersuchungen über den Dramatiker John Webster. Diss. Halle, 1893. (40 S.)

V. SPENCER: Alliteration in Spenser's poetry, discussed and compared with the alliteration as employed by Drayton and Daniel. Diss. Zürich, 1900. (144 pp.)

WILHELM CREIZENACH: Verskunst und Stil. In his Geschichte des neueren Dramas. Bd. 4. Halle, 1909, S. 358–400.

K. WIEHL: Thomas Kyd und sein Vers. Ein Beitrag zur Geschichte des englischen Dramas. (Hauptteil 1). Diss. München, 1910. (vi, 58 S.)

TUCKER BROOKE: Marlowe's versification and style. In: Stud. in Philol., vol. 19, 1922, pp. 186–205.

(3) SHAKESPEARE'S LITERARY STYLE

(a) GENERAL WORKS ON SHAKESPEARE'S STYLE

BENNO TSCHISCHWITZ: De ornantibus epithetis in Shakespeareï operibus. Halle, 1871.

OTTO LUDWIG: Shakespeare-Studien. Aus dem Nachlass hrsg. von M. Heydrich. Leipzig, 1872, 1901².

WILLIAM SPALDING: A letter on Shakspere's authorship of 'The Two Noble Kinsmen', and on the characteristics of Shakespere's style, and the secret of his supremacy. Edinburgh, 1833. Reprint in: New Shaksp. Soc. 1876 (with a life of the author, by John Hill Burton).
The standard work on the characteristic forms of Shakespeare's style.

NICOLAUS DELIUS: Die epischen Elemente in Shakespeares Dramen. Vortrag. In: Sh. Jb. Jg. 12, 1877, S. 1–13. Nachtrag: S. 14–28.

CHARLES and MARY COWDEN CLARKE: The Shakespeare key, unlocking the treasures of his style, elucidating the peculiarities of his construction, and displaying the beauties of his expression. London, 1879. (xi, 810 pp.)
Comprehensive collection of the elements of Shakespeare's style, arranged alphabetically.

ARTHUR W. VERITY: The influence of Christopher Marlowe on Shakespeare's earlier style. Cambridge, 1886.

H. HOFFMANN: Über die Beteuerungen in Shakespeares Dramen. Diss. Halle, 1894. (52 S.)

W. TOLL: Über die Beteuerungen in Ben Jonsons Werken. Diss. Halle, 1909. (74 S.)

HEINRICH MEYN: Beteuerungen und Verwünschungen bei Marlowe, Kyd, Lyly, Greene und Peele. Diss. Kiel, 1914. (92 S.) Rev.: Sh. Jb. 51, 1915, S. 271, Creizenach.

GREGOR SARRAZIN: William Shakespeares Lehrjahre. Weimar, 1897. (xii, 232 S.) Rev.: Bbl. 10, 1900, S. 117–19, R. Fischer.

GREGOR SARRAZIN: Aus Shakespeares Meisterwerkstatt. Stilgeschichtliche Studien. Berlin, 1906. (vii, 226 S.) Rev.: Sh. Jb. 43, 1907, S. 246–57, E. Koeppel; Bbl. 21, 1910, S. 4–7, Gust. Binz.
Critical examination of Shakespeare's works from the point of view of style.

WILLIAM LOWES RUSHTON: Shakespeare and 'The arte of English poesie' [Puttenham]. Liverpool, 1909. (167 pp.) Rev.: Sh. Jb. 45, 1909, S. 396, M. Förster.
Expresses the view that Shakespeare consciously borrowed his figures of speech from Puttenham's work.

HERMANN BARTH: Das Epitheton in den Dramen des jungen Shakespeare und seiner Vorgänger. (Teildr.) Diss. Göttingen, 1913. (vii, 34 S.) Printed in extended form in: Stud. z. engl. Philol., hrsg. v. Morsbach, 52, 1914. (xi, 203 S.) Rev.: E. St. 50, S. 146–7, W. Franz; Bbl. 27, 1916, S. 4–9, A. Eichler.

HERMANN CONRAD: Anfängerstil und Jugendstil Shakespeares. In: Preuss. Jbb. Bd. 156, 1914, S. 442–91.

META CORSSEN: Kleists und Shakespeares dramatische Sprache. Diss. Berlin, 1919. (74 S.) Rev.: Sh. Jb. 57, 1921, S. 104–5, W. Keller.

DONALD LEMEN CLARK: Rhetoric and poetry in the Renaissance . A study of rhetorical terms in English Renaissance literary criticism. New York, 1922. (x, 166 pp.)=Columbia Univ. Stud. in Engl. and Comp. Lit.

WILHELM MICHELS: Barockstil bei Shakespeare und Calderón. Diss. Frankfurt, 1928. (89 S.) Also published in Revue hispanique, 1929.

O. MICHAEL: Der Stil in Thomas Kyds Originaldramen. Diss. Berlin, 1905. (120 S.)

WILHELM CREIZENACH: Verskunst und Stil. In his Geschichte des neueren Dramas, Bd. 4, Halle, 1909, S. 358–400.

E. LANDSBERG: Der Stil in George Peeles sicheren und zweifelhaften dramatischen Werken. Diss. Breslau, 1910. (vi, 135 S.)

A. HETTLER: Roger Ascham, sein Stil und seine Beziehung zur Antike. Ein Beitrag zur Entwicklung der englischen Sprache unter dem Einfluss des Humanismus. Diss. Freiburg i. B., 1915. (100 S.)

TUCKER BROOKE: Marlowe's versification and style. In: Stud. in Phil., vol. 19, 1922, pp. 186–205.

E. H. C. OLIPHANT: The plays of Beaumont and Fletcher. An attempt to determine their respective shares and the shares of others. New Haven & London (1928). (xviii, 553 pp.) Rev.: Bbl. 40, 1929, S. 101–4, H. T. Price; Mod. Phil. 26, 1929, pp. 355–7, B. Maxwell.
Good analysis of the style of Beaumont and Fletcher and other collaborating dramatists.

(b) SIMILE AND METAPHOR

JOH. SCHÜMANN: See und Seefahrt, nebst dem metaphorischen Gebrauch dieser Begriffe in Shakespeares Dramen. I. Progr. Leipzig, 1876. (40 S.)

H. VON OE: Bilder aus dem Jägerleben. In: Sh. Jb. Jg. 29–30, 1894, S. 192–209.

FRED. J. CARPENTER: Metaphor and simile in the minor Elizabethan drama. Diss. Chicago, 1895.

H. VON OE: Bilder aus dem Schlaf- und Traumleben. In: Sh. Jb. Jg. 33, 1897, S. 231–52.

HEINRICH LOEWE: Shakespeare und die Weidmannskunst. In: Sh. Jb. Jg. 40, 1904, S. 51–68.

HERMANN VOIGT: Gleichnisse und Metaphern in Shakespeares Dramen und in seinen Quellenschriften. Diss. Strassburg, 1908. (116 S.) Rev.: Sh. Jb. 45, 1909, S. 274, Fr. Brie; Bbl. 20, 1909, S. 173–4, Ph. Aronstein.

WALTER HÜBNER: Der Vergleich bei Shakespeare. Diss. Berlin, 1908. (149 S.) Rev.: Sh. Jb. 45, 1909, S. 273–4, Fr. Brie; Bbl. 20, 1909, S. 174–5, Ph. Aronstein.

ERICH SCHULZE: Das Hendiadyoin und Hendiatrion in Shakespeares dramatischen Werken. Diss. Halle, 1908. (56 S.) Rev.: Sh. Jb. 45, 1909, S. 276,
Fr. Brie.

WILHELM HEISE: Die Gleichnisse in Edmund Spensers Faerie Queene und
ihre Vorbilder. Diss. Strassburg, 1902. (xii, 181 S.) Rev.: Sh. Jb. 39,
1903, S. 322–3, W. Drechsler.

F. G. HUBBARD: Repetition and parallelism in the earlier Elizabethan drama.
In: PMLA., vol. 20, N.S. vol. 13, 1905, pp. 360–79.

FEDERICO OLIVERO: A study on the metaphor in Dante. In: Giornale
dantesco, vol. 28, 1925.
With frequent references to Shakespeare.

HERMANN PONGS: Das Bild in der Dichtung. I. Bd.: Versuch einer Mor-
phologie der metaphorischen Formen. Marburg, 1927. (xx, 513 S.)

ELIZABETH HOLMES: Aspects of Elizabethan imagery. Oxford, 1929. (x,
134 pp.) Rev.: TLS., March 6, 1930, p. 184; Engl. Studies, ii. 1929,
pp. 227–31, M. Praz.

(c) SHAKESPEARE'S PROSE AND EUPHUISM

(a) SHAKESPEARE'S PROSE IN GENERAL

NICOLAUS DELIUS: Die Prosa in Shakespeares Dramen. In: Sh. Jb. Jg. 5, 1870,
S. 227–73.
Shakespeare's prose divided into three groups or grades according to the social
position of the speaker.

H. SHARPE: The prose in Shakespeare's plays, the rules for its use, and the
assistance that it gives in understanding the plays. In: The New Sh. Soc.
Trans. 24, 1885.
Continues on lines of Delius.

VINCENT F. JANSSEN: Shakespeare-Studien. I: Die Prosa in Shakespeares
Dramen. Diss. Giessen, 1897. (105 S.) Rev.: Litbl. 20, 1899, Sp. 72,
L. Proescholdt; Bbl. 9, 1899, S. 4–6, Ph. Wagner; Dt. Litztg. 21, 1900, Sp.
1893–4, W. Keller.

EDUARD NORDEN: Die antike Kunstprosa vom 6. Jahrhundert v. Chr. bis in
die Zeit der Renaissance. Leipzig, 1898.
Important work.

GERTRUD BORDUKAT: Die Abgrenzung zwischen Vers und Prosa in den Dramen
Shakespeares. Diss. Königsberg, 1918. (119 S.) Rev.: Sh. Jb. 56, 1920,
S. 128–9, W. Keller; Bbl. 34, 1923, S. 306–8, H. Mutschmann.

MARY MUNCASTER: The use of prose in Elizabethan drama. A summary sketch.
In: MLR., vol. 14, 1919, pp. 10–15.

MORRIS WILLIAM CROLL: Attic prose in the 17th century. In: Stud. in Phil.,
vol. 18, 1921, pp. 79–128.

R. L. MÉGROZ: Shakespeare as a letter writer and artist in prose. A disquisition, two anthologies, and a ramble. London (1928). (223 pp.) Rev.: TLS., March 15, 1928, p. 185.

MORRIS W. CROLL: The baroque style in prose. In: Studies in English philology. A miscellany in honor of Frederick Klaeber. Minneapolis, 1929, pp. 427–56.

(β) EUPHUISM

The complete works of John Lyly. Ed. by R. WARWICK BOND. 3 vols. Oxford, 1902.
With valuable notes on euphuism.

JOHN LYLY: Euphues, the anatomy of wit; Euphues and his England. Ed. by MORRIS W. CROLL and HARRY CLEMONS. London, 1916. (lxiv, 473 pp.) Rev.: Sh. Jb. 54, 1918, S. 113–14, Grabau.
Important introduction by Croll.

———

WILLIAM L. RUSHTON: Shakespeare's euphuisms. London, 1871. (viii, 108 pp.)

FR. LANDMANN: Der Euphuismus, sein Wesen, seine Quelle, seine Geschichte. Giessen, 1881. Also in English, entitled: Shakespeare and euphuism. In: Trans. New Sh. Soc., 1880–2, pp. 241–76. Rev.: E. St. 5, 1882, S. 409 ff., Breymann; E. St. 6, 1883, S. 94–111, Eduard Schwan.

C. G. CHILD: John Lyly and euphuism. Erlangen & Leipzig, 1894.

MAURITS BASSE: Stijlaffectatie bij Shakespeare, vooral uit het oogpunt van het euphuisme. Gand, 1895. (216 S.) Rev.: E. St. 23, 1896, S. 95, L. Fränkel.

L. WENDELSTEIN: Beitrag zur Vorgeschichte des Euphuismus. Diss. Halle, 1902. (89 S.)

LORENZ MORSBACH: Shakespeare und der Euphuismus. In: Abhdl. Ges. d. Wiss. Göttingen, phil.-hist. Kl., 1908, H. 6, S. 660–9. Rev.: Sh. Jb. 46, 1910, S. 210–11, Grabau.

ALBERT FEUILLERAT: John Lyly. Contribution à l'histoire de la renaissance en Angleterre. C.U.P., 1910. (xii, 661 pp.) Rev.: Sh. Jb. 47, 1911, S. 311–13, A. Brandl; MLR. 6, 1911, pp. 103–14, John D. Wilson; Bbl. 23, 1912, S. 114–19, G. Binz; MLN. 27, 1912, pp. 147–52, C. R. Baskervill.
Important for the sources of euphuism.

M. LAMPEL: Der Stil in Lylys Lustspielen. Diss. Bern, 1913. (90 S.)

G. KLINGER: Euphuistische Elemente in Shakespeares Prosa. MS. Diss. Breslau, 1922.

VIOLET M. JEFFERY: John Lyly and the Italian Renaissance. Paris, 1929. (vii, 147 pp.)

(d) PROVERBS, MAXIMS, RIDDLES, PUNS, ETC

(a) PROVERBS AND MAXIMS

(aa) Collections

R. TAVERNER: Proverbes or adagies with newe addicions, gathered out of the Chiliades of ERASMUS, 1539.

JOHN HEYWOOD: A dialogue containing . . . all the proverbs in the English tongue. London, 1562.
Incorporates five collections in the form of instructive dialogue.

J. SANDFORD: Garden of pleasure, [or, as in the 2nd edition] Houres of recreation, 1573. Translated from L. Guicciardini's Hore di ricreatione.

JOHN FLORIO his firste fruites. London, 1578.

JOHN FLORIO'S second frutes. London, 1591.

THOMAS DRAXE: Bibliotheca scholastica instructissima, or, a treasurie of ancient adagies and sententious proverbs, 1633.—Cf. Das elisabethanische Sprichwort nach Thomas Draxe's Treasurie of ancient adagies (1616), hrsg. von Max Förster. In: Anglia, Bd. 42, N. F. Bd. 30, 1918, S. 361–424.
Reprint of an edition of 1616 in the Breslau Municipal Library.

JOHN RAY: A compleat collection of English proverbs. London, 1670, 1678[2], 1742[3], 1798[4] (considerably enlarged and improved), 1813[5] (by J. B.).

THOMAS FULLER: Gnomologia. Adages and proverbs with sentences and witty sayings, ancient and modern, foreign and British, 1732.

HENRY G. BOHN: A handbook of proverbs, comprising an entire republication of Ray's collection of English proverbs . . . London, 1855 and later editions.

W. CAREW HAZLITT: English proverbs and proverbial phrases, collected from the most authentic sources . . . London, 1869, 1882[2].
Based on the works of Ray and Bohn.

IDA und OTTO VON DÜRINGSFELD: Sprichwörter der germanischen und romanischen Sprachen, vergleichend zusammengestellt. 2 Bde. Leipzig, 1872–5. (xii, 522 und viii, 638 S.) 1890[2].

A. OTTO: Die Sprichwörter der Römer. Leipzig, 1890. (481 S.)

VINCENT STUCKEY LEAN: Collectanea. Collections of proverbs (English and foreign), folk-lore, and superstitions, also compilations towards dictionaries of proverbial phrases and words, old and disused. 4 vols. Bristol, 1902–4.

Shakespeare proverbs, ed. by M. C. CLARKE and W. J. ROLFE. London, 1908.

W. W. SKEAT: Early English proverbs, chiefly of the 13th and 14th centuries. O.U.P., 1910. (xxiv, 148 pp.)

(bb) Treatises

JULIUS THÜMMEL: Über die Sentenz im Drama, namentlich bei Shakespeare, Goethe und Schiller. Vortrag. In: Sh. Jb. Jg. 14, 1879, S. 97–114.

M. C. WAHL: Die englische Parömiographie vor Shakespeare. I. Abt.: Die sprichwörtlichen Sammlungen. Erfurt, 1879. II. Abt.: Fundorte für die zerstreuten Sprichwörter. Erfurt, 1880.

M. C. WAHL: Parömiologische Spenden zur Shakespeare-Literatur, 1880.

M. C. WAHL: Das parömiologische Sprachgut bei Shakespeare. I–IV. Erfurt, 1884. Leipzig, 1885–7.

M. C. WAHL: Das parömiologische Sprachgut bei Shakespeare. In: Sh. Jb. Jg. 22, 1887, S. 45–130 und Jg. 23, 1888, S. 21–98.

A. GASPARY: Allgemeine Aussprüche in den Dramen Philip Massingers. Diss. Marburg, 1890. (37 S.)

H. DE VOCHT: De invloed van Erasmus op de engelsche tooneel-literatuur der 16^e en 17^e eeuwen. 1. deel: Shakespeare jest-books.—Lyly. Gent, 1908. (xvi, 287 S.) Rev.: Sh. Jb. 45, 1909, S. 372–4, Fr. Brie; E. St. 41, 1909, S. 138–40, H. Swaen.

LUDWIG MARX: Die Sentenz in den Dramen Shakespeares. Diss. Giessen, 1915. (94 S.) Rev.: Sh. Jb. 52, 1916, S. 229–30, M. Förster.

WALTER FRIESER: Das Sprichwort in den dramatischen Werken John Lylys. MS. Diss. Leipzig, 1920.

R. JENTE: The proverbs of Shakespeare with early and contemporary parallels. Washington, 1926=Repr. from: Wash. Univ. Stud., Humanistic Series, vol. xiii, no. 2, 1926, pp. 391–444. Rev.: Bbl. 38, 1927, S. 198–9, Liljegren.

MORRIS PALMER TILLEY: Elizabethan proverb lore in Lyly's 'Euphues' and in Pettie's 'Petite Pallace', with parallels from Shakespeare. New York, 1926. (x, 461 pp.)=Univ. of Michigan Publ., Lang. and Lit., vol. ii. Rev.: MLN. 42, 1927, pp. 484–6, R. Jente; RESt. 4, 1928, pp. 354–5, B. E. C. Davis; Arch. 152, 1927, S. 295; Bbl. 38, 1927, S. 198–9, Liljegren; N. Spr. 37, 1929, S. 604, W. Fischer.

(β) RIDDLES

Shakespeares 'Book of merry riddles' und die andern Rätselbücher seiner Zeit. Hrsg. von ALOIS BRANDL. In: Sh. Jb. Jg. 42, 1906, S. 1–64.

ALOIS BRANDL: Noch eine Rätselsammlung der Shakespeare-Zeit. In: Sh. Jb. Jg. 45, 1909, S. 139–45.

ROSE CORDS: Wit's Academy, eine Sammlung von Scherzfragen, zugeschrieben Ben Jonson, 1656. In: Sh. Jb. Jg. 53, 1917, S. 49–68.
Reprint from Arch. Bodl. B. ii. 84, with introduction.

(γ) POSIES

HEINRICH SPIES: Posies. Ein Beitrag zur englischen Volkskunde. In: Festschr. z. 16. Neuphilologentag in Bremen, 1914, S. 45–69.

ANNA H. METGER: Posies. Diss. Greifswald, 1921. (40 S.) Rev.: Sh. Jb. 57, 1921, S. 110, W. Keller; Arch. 144, 1922, S. 117–18, F. Liebermann.

(δ) PUNS

LEOPOLD WURTH: Das Wortspiel bei Shakespeare. Progr. Wien, 1894. (36 S.) Reprinted in enlarged form in: Wiener Beitr. z. engl. Phil., hrsg. v. J. Schipper. Bd. 1, 1895. (xiv, 255 S.) Rev.: Bbl. 7, 1897, S. 140–4, J. Hoops.

PAUL NELLE: Das Wortspiel im englischen Drama des 16. Jhrh. vor Shakespeare. Diss. Halle, 1900. (53 S.) Rev.: Sh. Jb. 38, 1902, S. 278–80. L. Wurth.

GREGOR SARRAZIN: Wortechos bei Shakespeare. I. II. In: Sh. Jb. Jg. 33, 1897, S. 120–65 und Jg. 34, 1898, S. 119–69.

VIII. THE ART OF SHAKESPEARE
PART II. SHAKESPEARE'S DRAMATIC ART
(1) SHAKESPEARE'S CREATIVE FACULTIES

WILHELM DILTHEY: Das Erlebnis und die Dichtung. Leipzig, 1922[8]. Cf. essay: Goethe und die dichterische Phantasie, pp. 202–17.

CHRISTIAN JANENTZKY: Shakespeares Weltbild, das Tragische und Hamlet. In: Die Ernte. Franz Muncker zu seinem 70. Geb. Halle, 1925, S. 241–63.

MAX J. WOLFF: Shakespeares Form. In: GRM. Jg. 13, 1925, S. 382–90.

The author attempts to trace the connexion between the poet's frame of mind and the atmosphere and internal form of the play.

WALTHER LINDEN: Zum Aufbau des Shakespeareschen Erlebnisses. In: Sh. Jb. Jg. 64, N.F. Bd. 5, 1928, S. 43–62.

———

HEINRICH LILIENFEIN: Shakespeares dichterische Phantasie. Festvortrag. In: Sh. Jb. Jg. 59–60, N.F. Bd. 1, 1924, S. 19–40.

HENRY W. WELLS: Poetic imagery, illustrated from Elizabethan literature. Studies in English and comparative literature. New York & London, 1924. (231 pp.)

———

KARL GROOS und ILSE NETTO: Psychologisch-statistische Untersuchungen über die visuellen Sinneseindrücke in Shakespeares lyrischen und epischen Dichtungen. In: E. St., Bd. 43, 1910, S. 27–51.

MEINRAD HABERL: Die Entwicklung des optischen und akustischen Sinnes bei Shakespeare. Diss. München, 1913. (70 S.) Rev.: Sh. Jb. 50, 1914, S. 192–3, M. Förster; Bbl. 26, 1915, S. 298–9, B. Fehr.

LUDWIG SOHR: Die visuellen Sinneseindrücke und akustischen Phänomene in Spensers poetischen Werken. MS. Diss. München, 1921.

———

ALFRED HOYER: Eine historisch-genetische Analyse der Begriffe nature und fortune bei Shakespeare bis zum Abschluss der Hamlet-Periode. Diss. Halle, 1913. (viii, 82 S.)

M. FRANCIOSA: Il sentimento della giustizia nell' opera di Shakespeare. Milano, 1927. (121 pp.)

(2) SHAKESPEARE'S DRAMATIC TECHNIQUE

(a) GENERAL TREATISES ON SHAKESPEARE'S DRAMATIC TECHNIQUE

(α) TECHNIQUE OF THE DRAMA IN GENERAL

GUSTAV FREYTAG: Die Technik des Dramas. Leipzig, 1863, 1908[11].

W. T. PRICE: Technique of the drama. London, 1897.

ELISABETH WOODBRIDGE: The drama, its laws and its technique. Boston & London, 1898. (xvi, 181 S.) Rev.: Sh. Jb. 35, 1899, pp. 295–7, A. H. Tolman.

HEINRICH FRIEDEMANN: Das Formproblem des Dramas. Diss. Erlangen, 1911. (95 S.)

WILLIAM ARCHER: Play-making. A manual of craftsmanship. London, 1912. (x, 322 pp.)

GEORGE PIERCE BAKER: Dramatic technique. Boston & New York, 1919. (viii, 531 pp.) Rev.: Sh. Jb. 57, 1921, S. 115–17, R. Fischer.

ERNST HIRT: Das Formgesetz der epischen, dramatischen und lyrischen Dichtung. Leipzig & Berlin, 1923. (227 S.)

EMIL ERMATINGER: Die Kunstform des Dramas. Leipzig, 1925.

HALLIAM BOSWORTH: The technique in dramatic art. New York, 1926. (xviii, 438 pp.)

OSKAR WALZEL: Gehalt und Gestalt im Kunstwerk des Dichters. Berlin (1923) (409 S.)=Handbuch d. Lit. wiss.

(β) SHAKESPEARE'S TECHNIQUE IN GENERAL

HERM. ULRICI: Über Shakespeares dramatische Kunst und sein Verhältnis zu Calderon und Goethe. Halle, 1839. 2nd edition entitled: Shakespeares dramatische Kunst. Geschichte und Charakteristik des Shakespeareschen Dramas. Leipzig, 1847, 1868–9[3], 1874[4]. English translation: Shakespeare's dramatic art. 2 vols. London, 1876.

GUSTAV RÜMELIN: Shakespeare-Studien. Stuttgart, 1866, 1873[2].

OTTO LUDWIG: Shakespeare-Studien. Aus dem Nachlass hrsg. von M. Heydrich. Leipzig, 1872, 1901[2] (Halle).

HERMANN ULRICI: Über Shakespeares Fehler und Mängel. Vortrag. In: Sh. Jb. Jg. 3, 1868, S. 1–19.

EDWARD E. DOWDEN: Shakespeare, a critical study of his mind and art. London, 1875, 1876[2], and later editions.

RICHARD G. MOULTON: Shakespeare as a dramatic artist. A popular illustration of the principles of scientific criticism. Oxford, 1885, 1906[3]. (xiv, 443 pp.) Rev.: Bbl. 5, 1895, S. 329–30, L. Proescholdt.

L. A. SHERMAN: Shakespeare's first principles of art. In: PMLA., vol. 10, N.S. vol. 3, 1895, pp. 97–109.

WILHELM WETZ: Shakespeare vom Standpunkte der vergleichenden Literaturgeschichte. Hamburg, 1897.
Contrasts Shakespeare's individual art with that of Corneille.

FRIEDRICH THEODOR VISCHER: Shakespeare-Vorträge. I–VI. Stuttgart & Berlin, 1899–1905.

WALTER BORMANN: Shakespeares szenische Technik und dramatische Kunst. In: Sh. Jb. Jg. 37, 1901, S. 181–208.

RICHARD M. MEYER: Otto Ludwigs Shakespearestudium. In: Sh. Jb. Jg. 37, 1901, S. 59–84.

WILLIAM H. FLEMING: Shakespeare's plots. A study in dramatic construction. New York, 1902. (467 pp.)

A. C. BRADLEY: Shakespearean tragedy. Lectures on Hamlet, Othello, King Lear, Macbeth. London, 1904. (498 pp.)

GEORGE PIERCE BAKER: The development of Shakespeare as a dramatist. New York, 1907. (x, 329 pp. and 30 illust.) Rev.: Sh. Jb. 44, 1908, S. 325–7, W. Keller; JEGPh. 9, 1910, pp. 141–5, A. H. Thorndike.

L. L. SCHÜCKING: Shakespeare als Volksdramatiker. In: Internat. Mschr. f. Wiss. und Techn. Jg. 6, 1912, Sp. 1513–34.

BRANDER MATTHEWS: Shakspere as a playwright. New York & London, 1913.

E. HERNRIED: Weltanschauung und Kunstform von Shakespeares Drama. In: Zs. f. Ästh. und allgem. Kunstwiss., Bd. 9, 1914, S. 519 ff.

MAX DEUTSCHBEIN: Shakespeare und die Renaissance. In: N. Spr., Bd. 23, 1916, S. 9–21.

OSKAR WALZEL: Shakespeares dramatische Baukunst. In: Sh. Jb. Jg. 52, 1916, S. 3–35. Cf. important review by MAX J. WOLFF: Shakespeare als Künstler des Barocks. In: Internat. Mschr. f. Wiss., Kunst und Technik, Jg. 11, 1917, S. 995–1020.
Walzel characterizes Shakespeare's art as free, atectonic style and contrasts it with the severe, architectonic style of the classical writers.

SIR ARTHUR QUILLER-COUCH: Shakespeare's workmanship. London, 1918, 1924, 1927.

RICHARD KOPPEL: Das Primitive in Shakespeares Dramatik und die irreführenden Angaben und Einteilungen in den modernen Ausgaben seiner Werke. Berlin, 1918=Neue Folge der Shakespeare-Studien. Rev.: Bbl. 30, 1919, S. 153–8, W. Keller.

ROMAN DYBOSKI: Rise and fall in Shakespeare's dramatic art. O.U.P., 1923. (29 pp.)=The Sh. Assoc. Pamphl. no. 9. Rev.: TLS., Sept. 13, 1923.

HELENE RICHTER: [Shakespeare], der Formkünstler. In the same writer's Shakespeare der Mensch. Leipzig, 1923, S. 72–110. Rev.: Dt. Vjschr. 6, 1928, S. 188–90, L. L. Schücking; Sh. Jb. 59–60, 1924, S. 176–8, W. Keller; Bbl. 35, 1924, S. 102–12, B. Fehr.
CONTENTS: (a) Symmetrie und Asymmetrie, S. 80–4; (b) Das Gesetz der Einheiten,

S. 84–8; (c) Typus und Individualität, S. 88–94; (d) Ruhe und Bewegung, S. 94–6; (e) Konkretheit und Symbolik, S. 96–8; (f) Verschmelzung von Stimmungsgegensätzen, S. 98–100; (g) Idealschönheit und Naturschönheit, S. 100–2; (h) Schlichtheit und Prunk, S. 102–3; (i) Form und Phantasie, S. 103–10.

H. GRANVILLE-BARKER: From 'Henry V' to 'Hamlet'. O.U.P., 1925. (29 pp.)= The Brit. Acad. annual Shakespeare lecture. Rev.: Sh. Jb. 61, 1925, S. 131, W. Keller.

PAUL FENYVES: Studien zur dramatischen Technik in Shakespeares Tragödien. (Der Weg vom 'Höhepunkt' bis zur 'Katastrophe'.) Extract in: Jb. d. philos. Fak. d. dt. Univ. Prag, 1924–5, 2. Jg. Prag, 1926, S. 71–4.

EDUARD ECKHARDT: Gehört Shakespeare zur Renaissance oder zum Barock. In: Festschr. f. Friedr. Kluge. Tübingen, 1926.

ELMER EDGAR STOLL: Shakespeare studies, historical and comparative in method. New York, 1927. (xi, 502 pp.) Rev.: Dt. Vjschr. f. Lit. wiss. und Geistesgesch. Jg. 6, 1928, S. 192–7, L. L. Schücking.

JOSEF SCHICK: Shakespeares Genie. In: Sh. Jb. Jg. 63, 1927, S. 54–74.

The author shows the genius of Shakespeare in his choice of material, in plot construction, in character depiction, in the language and rhythm of his verse, &c.

C. M. HAINES: The development of Shakespeare's stagecraft. In: The Sh. Assoc., 1925–6. London, 1927, pp. 35–61.

(γ) TECHNIQUE OF SHAKESPEARE'S CONTEMPORARIES

RUDOLF FISCHER: Zur Kunstentwicklung der englischen Tragödie von ihren ersten Anfängen bis zu Shakespeare. Strassburg, 1893. (xiii, 192 S.)

HARRIOTT ELY FANSLER: The evolution of technic in Elizabethan tragedy. Chicago & New York (1914). (283 pp.) Rev.: MLR. 10, 1915, pp. 382–3, O. L. Hatcher; Bbl. 28, 1917, S. 353–61, B. Fehr.

V. VEDEL: Den digteriske barockstil omkring aar 1600. In: Edda, Jg. 2, 1914, S. 17–40.

KARL WEINER: Die Verwendung des Parallelismus als Kunstmittel im engl. Drama vor Shakespeare. Diss. Giessen, 1916. Rev.: Bbl. 29, 1918, S. 327–8, L. Kellner.

W. J. LAWRENCE: The mechanics of Elizabethan play-writing. In: Athenaeum, April 30, 1920. _____

ESTHER C. DUNN: *Ben Jonson's* art. Elizabethan life and literature as reflected therein. Smith College, Northampton, Mass., 1925. (xviii, 159 pp.) Rev.: MLN. 42, 1927, pp. 543–5, Briggs.

GEORGE P. BAKER: Dramatic technique in *Marlowe*. In: Essays and Studies by members of the Engl. Assoc., vol. 4, 1913, pp. 172–82.

H. REUSS: *Massingers* dramatische Technik. MS. Diss. München, 1920.

WILBUR DWIGHT DUNKEL: The dramatic technique of *Thomas Middleton* in his comedies of London life. Diss. Chicago, 1925. (126 pp.) Rev.: JEGPh. 26, 1927, pp. 601–2, Baldwin.

(b) VARIOUS ASPECTS OF SHAKESPEARE'S DRAMATIC TECHNIQUE

(a) DEPENDENCE OF THE DRAMATIC FORM ON EXTERNAL INFLUENCES

(aa) *On Theatrical Conditions*

RUDOLF GENÉE: Über die szenischen Formen Shakespeares in ihrem Verhältnis zur Bühne seiner Zeit. In: Sh. Jb. Jg. 26, 1891, S. 131–49.

WILHELM OECHELHÄUSER: Zur Szenierungsfrage. In: Sh. Jb. Jg. 27, 1892, S. 108–14.

EDWARD EVERETT HALE, JR.: The influence of theatrical conditions on Shakespeare. In: Mod. Phil., vol. 1, 1903–4, pp. 171–92.

ROBERT PRÖLSS: Von den ältesten Drucken der Dramen Shakespeares und dem Einflusse, den die damaligen Londoner Theater und ihre Einrichtungen auf diese Dramen ausgeübt haben. Leipzig, 1905. (iv, 141 S.) Rev.: Sh. Jb. 41, 1905, S. 238–9, W. Keller; Bbl. 16, 1905, S. 302–7, Konr. Meier.

GEORGE F. REYNOLDS: Some principles of Elizabethan staging. I, II. Chicago, 1905.
Deals with the influence of theatrical conditions on the form of the drama.

JOHANNES E. SCHMIDT: Shakespeares Dramen und sein Schauspielerberuf. Berlin, 1914. (258 S.) Rev.: Sh. Jb. 50, 1914, S. 190, M. Förster; MLR. 10, 1915, pp. 228–31, O. L. Hatcher.

G. B. HARRISON: Shakespeare's actors. In: The Sh. Assoc. 1925–6. London, 1927. pp. 62–87.
Deals with the influence of the actors on the form of the drama.

G. H. COWLING: Shakespeare and the Elizabethan stage. In: The Sh. Assoc. 1925–6. London, 1927. pp. 157–85.

WALTHER MÜLLER: Der schauspielerische Stil im Passionsspiel des Mittelalters. Leipzig, 1927. (140 S.)=Form und Geist. I. Rev.: Litbl. 49, 1928, Sp. 336–8, R. Alewyn.
Deals with conditions in Germany.

(bb) *On Public Taste*

GEORGE PIERCE BAKER: The development of Shakespeare as a dramatist. New York, 1907. (x, 329 pp.) Rev.: Sh. Jb. 44, 1908, S. 325–7, W. Keller.
Emphasizes very strongly the influence of the public.

A. C. BRADLEY: Shakespeare's theatre and audience. In: Oxford lectures on poetry. London, 1909, pp. 361–93.

CHARLES J. SISSON: Le goût public et le théâtre élisabéthain jusqu' à la mort de Shakespeare. Dijon, 1922. (196 pp.)

ROBERT BRIDGES: The influence of the audience on Shakespeare's drama. O.U.P., 1927. (x, 29 pp.)=Collected Essays I. Rev.: Litbl. 1928, Sp. 235.

(cc) On Customs of the Printing and Publishing Trades

EVELYN MAY ALBRIGHT: Dramatic publication in England, 1580–1640. A study of conditions affecting content and form of drama. New York, 1927. (vi, 442 pp.) Rev.: JEGPh. 27, 1928, pp. 285–8, Campbell; MLN. 42, 1927, pp. 547–51, A. Thaler; TLS. Apr. 28, 1927, p. 291.
With detailed bibliography.

(dd) Political Propaganda and the Drama

RICHARD SIMPSON: On the political use of the stage in Shakespeare's time. In: Trans. New Sh. Soc., Ser. 1, pt. 2, 1874, pp. 371–95.

MADELEINE H. DODDS: Early political plays. In: Libr., 3rd ser., vol. 4, 1913, pp. 393–408.

THORNTON S. GRAVES: The political use of the stage during the reign of James I. In: Anglia. Bd. 38, 1914, S. 137–56.

(β) PLAY CONSTRUCTION OF SHAKESPEARE AND THE ELIZABETHAN DRAMATISTS

ERNST ZIEL: Über die dramatische Exposition. Ein Beitrag zur Technik des Dramas. Diss. Rostock, 1869. (55 S.)

GUSTAV RÜMELIN: Shakespeares Eigentümlichkeiten in der Charakteristik der Personen und in der Motivierung der dramatischen Handlung. In Rümelin's Shakespeare-Studien. Stuttgart, 1874², S. 59 seq.

C. C. HENSE: Polymythie in dramatischen Dichtungen Shakespeares. In: Sh. Jb. Jg. 11, 1876, S. 245–73.
Deals with the parallel actions.

P. A. DANIEL: Time analysis of the plots of Shakespeare's plays. In: Trans. New Sh. Soc. 1877–9.

WILHELM KÖNIG: Über die bei Shakespeare vorkommenden Wiederholungen. In: Sh. Jb. Jg. 13, 1878, S. 111–36.

CHARLES and MARY COWDEN CLARKE: Dramatic time. In the same authors' The Shakespeare key, unlocking the treasures of his style. London, 1879. pp. 105–283.

KARL LUICK: Zur Geschichte des englischen Dramas im 16. Jhrh. In: Forsch. zur neueren Lit. gesch. Festgabe f. Richard Heinzel. Weimar, 1898, S. 131–87. Rev.: Sh. Jb. 35, 1899, S. 297–9, W. Keller.

J. EBNER: Beitrag zu einer Geschichte der dramatischen Einheiten in Italien. Erlangen & Leipzig, 1898. (176 S.)=Münch. Beitr. z. roman. und engl. Philol., hrsg. v. Breymann und Schick, H. 15. Rev.: Sh. Jb. 36, 1900, S. 310–11, E. Wechssler.
The author deals with the theory and practice of the Italian drama in the XVIth century.

HEINRICH BULTHAUPT: Raum und Zeit bei Shakespeare und Schiller. Festvortrag. In: Sh. Jb. Jg. 36, 1900, S. xvi–xlii.

G. H. SANDER: Das Moment der letzten Spannung in der englischen Tragödie bis zu Shakespeare. Berlin, 1902. (67 S.) Rev.: Sh. Jb. 39, 1903, S. 307–10, Ed. Eckhardt; Bbl. 14, 1903, S. 99–100, R. Ackermann.

B. KIEHL: Wiederkehrende Begebenheiten und Verhältnisse in Shakespeares Dramen. Ein Beitrag zur Shakespeare-Psychologie. Diss. Berlin, 1904. (89 S.)

LOUIS SIEGMUND FRIEDLAND: Dramatic unities in England. In: JEGPh., vol. 10, 1911, pp. 56–89, 280–99, 453–67. Rev.: Bbl. 23, 1912, S. 274–5, Ph. Aronstein.

MABEL BULAND: The presentation of time in the Elizabethan drama. New York, 1912. (iv, 354 pp.)=Yale Studies in English, No. 44. Rev.: Sh. Jb. 49, 1913, S. 236–7, M. Förster.
Contains time analyses of about seventy-five plays.

ERNST AUGUST LÜDEMANN: Shakespeares Verwendung von gleichartigem und gegensetzlichem Parallelismus bei Figuren, Situationen, Motiven und Hand-lungen. Diss. Bonn, 1912. (70 S.) Printed in enlarged form in: Bonner Stud. z. engl. Philol., hrsg. v. K. D. Bülbring, H. 7, 1913. (vi, 185 S.) Rev.: Sh. Jb. 50, 1914, S. 193–4, M. Förster; Bbl. 25, 1914, S. 104–6, Ph. Aronstein; Arch. 131, S. 251, A. Brandl.

JOSEPH GUTMANN: Die dramatischen Einheiten bei Ben Jonson. Diss. Mün-chen, 1913. (103 S.) Rev.: Sh. Jb. 50, 1914, S. 240–1, M. Förster.

LEVIN L. SCHÜCKING: Die Handlungsbegründung. In his Die Charakter-probleme bei Shakespeare. Leipzig, 1919, 1927², S. 206–51.

ALFRED LANGE: Die Einführung der Personen in Shakespeares Römerdramen. MS. Diss. Leipzig, 1920.

RICHARD KÜHNEMUND: Die Rolle des Zufalls in Shakespeares Meistertragödien. Halle, 1923. (47 S.)=Stud. z. engl. Philol., hrsg. v. Morsbach, H. 67. Rev.: Sh. Jb. 59–60, 1924, S. 183–4, W. Keller.

GERTRUDE BUSCH: Die Ausblicke in den Historien und Tragödien Shakespeares. Ein Beitrag zur Untersuchung der dramatischen Technik des Dichters. MS. Diss. Prag. Extract in: Jb. d. philos. Fak. d. dt. Univ. in Prag, 1924.

ALWIN THALER: Shakspere and the unhappy happy ending. In: PMLA., vol. 42, 1927, pp. 736–61.

(γ) ACT AND SCENE DIVISION

JAMES SPEDDING: On the division of the acts in Lear, Much Ado, and Twelfth Night. In: The New Sh. Soc.'s Trans. 1877–9, pp. 11–26.

OSKAR WALZEL: Aufzugsgrenzen in den Dramen Shakespeares. In: Edda, Bd. 6, 1916, S. 164–84. Rev.: Sh. Jb. 54, 1918, S. 152–3, Jantzen.

MARK HUNTER: Act and scene division in the plays of Shakespeare. In: RESt., vol. 2, 1926, pp. 295–310. Rev.: Sh. Jb. 63, 1927, S. 222, Beckmann.
Assumes that Shakespeare worked according to the five-act scheme and divided the acts into scenes. Author asserts that 70 per cent. of 200 Elizabethan plays show act-division.

J. DOVER WILSON: Act- and scene-divisions in the plays of Shakespeare. A rejoinder to Sir Mark Hunter. In: RESt., vol. 3, 1927, pp. 385–97. Rev.: Sh. Jb. 64, 1928, S. 211, Beckmann; Arch. 183, 1928, S. 306.

Wilson contests the assertion that Shakespeare used the five-act scheme.

WALTER W. GREG: Act-divisions in Shakespeare. In: RESt., vol. 4, 1928, pp. 152–8. Rev.: Sh. Jb. 64, 1928, S. 211, Beckmann.

Only 20 per cent. of the plays performed by adult troupes in public theatres show act-division.

EDWIN ELIOTT WILLOUGHBY: The heading actus primus, scaena prima, in the First Folio. In: RESt., vol. 4, 1928, pp. 323–6.

(δ) SCENE TECHNIQUE

RICHARD KOPPEL: Szenen-Einteilungen und Ortsangaben in den Shakespeare-schen Dramen. In: Sh. Jb. Jg. 9, 1874, S. 269–94.

WALTER BORMANN: Shakespeares szenische Technik und dramatische Kunst. In: Sh. Jb. Jg. 37, 1901, S. 181–208.

ALOIS BRANDL: Zur Szenenführung bei Shakespeare.=Sitzber. Preuss. Akad. d. Wiss. H. 37, 1906, S. 630–45. Rev.: Sh. Jb. Jg. 43, 1907, S. 317–18, C. Grabau.

Distinguishes three types of scene: (i) scenes producing atmosphere; (ii) scenes in which important determinations are arrived at, and (iii) informative or expositional scenes.

LEVIN L. SCHÜCKING: Primitive Kunstmittel und moderne Interpretation. Ein Beitrag zur Shakespeare-Forschung. In: GRM., Bd. 4, 1912, S. 321–39.

RICHARD KOPPEL: Das Primitive in Shakespeares Dramatik und die irre-führenden Angaben und Einteilungen in den modernen Ausgaben seiner Werke. Berlin, 1918. (144 S.)=Neue Folge der Shakespeare-Studien. Rev.: Bbl. 30, 1919, S. 153–8, W. Keller; Sh. Jb. 55, 1919, S. 184–5, R. Fischer.

W. SCHLEGEL: Zur Szenenführung bei Marlowe. MS. Diss. Leipzig, 1926. (176 S.)

AUGUST C. MAHR: Dramatische Situationsbilder und -bildtypen, eine Studie zur Kunstgeschichte des Dramas. California, 1928. (96 S.)=Stanford Univ. Publ., Lang. and Lit., vol. 4.

(ε) DEPICTION OF MILIEU AND INTERPRETATION OF NATURE

C. PHILIPS: Lokalfärbung in Shakespeares Dramen. I, II. Progr. Köln, 1887, 1888. (32 und 31 S.)

FREDERIC W. MOORMAN: The interpretation of nature in English poetry from Beowulf to Shakespeare. Strassburg, 1905. (244 pp.)=Quellen und For-schungen, H. 95. Rev.: Sh. Jb. 42, 1906, S. 231–3, W. Keller; MLR. 2, 1907, pp. 179–81, C. H. Herford.

ERICH HARTMANN: Naturschilderung und Natursymbolik bei Shakespeare. Diss. Leipzig, 1908. (viii, 158 S.)

EDMUND VOIGT: Gegenstände und Verwendung der Naturschilderungen Shakespeares. Diss. Leipzig, 1908. (ii, 118 S.) Enlarged in: Anglistische Forschungen, hrsg. v. Hoops, H. 26.

EDMUND VOIGT: Shakespeares Naturschilderungen. Heidelberg, 1909. (viii, 146 S.)=Anglist. Forsch., hrsg. v. Hoops, H. 28. Rev.: Sh. Jb. 46, 1910, S. 312, M. Förster; Bbl. 21, 1910, S. 113, G. Becker.

BRINUS KÖHLER: Die Schilderung des Milieus in Shakespeares Hamlet, Macbeth und King Lear. Diss. Göttingen, 1911. (viii, 59 S.) Enlarged in: Stud. z. engl. Philol., hrsg. v. Morsbach 46, 1912. (xi, 65 S.) Rev.: Sh. Jb. 48, 1912, S. 285–90, L. L. Schücking.

MARIE LUISE GOTHEIN: Der lebendige Schauplatz in Shakespeares Dramen. In: Edda, Bd. 6, 1916, S. 124–57. Rev.: Sh. Jb. 54, 1918, S. 151–2, Jantzen. Action of plays symbolized in the scenery.

E. BERNDT: Dame nature in der englischen Literatur bis herab zu Shakespeare. Diss. Berlin, 1922. (viii, 107 S.)

DAVID W. RANNIE: Scenery in Shakespeare's plays and other studies. Oxford, 1926. (370 pp.) Rev.: Neue Jbb. f. Wiss. und Jugendbildung. Jg. 3, 1927, S. 745, Hübner.

(ζ) USE OF MUSIC, SONGS, ACROBATICS AND DANCES

NICOLAUS DELIUS: Einlagen und Zutaten in Shakespeares Dramen. In: Sh. Jb. Jg. 21, 1886, S. 18–42.

REINHOLD SIGISMUND: Die Musik in Shakespeares Dramen. In: Sh. Jb. Jg. 19, 1884, S. 86–112.

LUDWIG FRÄNKEL: Shakespeare und das Tagelied. Ein Beitrag zur vergleichenden Literaturgeschichte der germanischen Völker. Hannover, 1893. Rev.: Bbl. 5, 1895, S. 6–7, L. Proescholdt.

EDWARD EDWARDS: A book of Shakespeare's songs. With musical settings by various composers. New York, 1903. (100 pp.)

W. J. LAWRENCE: Music in the Elizabethan theatre. In: Sh. Jb. Jg. 44, 1908, S. 36–50.

[ANON.]: Early Elizabethan stage music. In: The Musical Antiquary, May 1909.

EDWARD W. NAYLOR: Music and Shakespeare. In: The Musical Antiquary, April 1910.

Shakespeare music (music of the period). Ed. by EDWARD W. NAYLOR. London [1912]. (xvii, 66 pp.) Rev.: Sh. Jb. 49, 1913, S. 241–3, M. Förster.

G. H. COWLING: Music on the Shakespearian stage. Cambridge, 1913. (vii, 116 pp.) Rev.: Sh. Jb. 49, 1913, S. 243–4, M. Förster; JEGPh. 14, 1915, pp. 617–20, J. Q. Adams.

RICHMOND NOBLE: Shakespeare's use of song, with the text of the principal songs. O.U.P., 1923. (160 pp.)

FREDERICK BRIDGE: 'O Mistress Mine.' Shakespearean music in the plays and early operas. London, 1923. (xiii, 93 pp.)

RICHMOND NOBLE: Shakespeare's songs and stage. In: The Sh. Assoc. 1925–6. London, 1927, pp. 120–33.

JOHN ROB. MOORE: The songs of the public theaters in the time of Shakespeare. In: JEGPh., vol. 28, 1929, pp. 166–202.

TUCKER BROOKE: The Shakespeare songs. Being a complete collection of the songs written by or attributed to William Shakespeare. With an introduction by Walter de la Mare. London, 1929. (xxxii, 168 pp.)

HANS GEORG MEYER-BALL: Die Instrumentalmusik in Beaumont und Fletchers Dramen. Ein Beitrag zur Kenntnis der Bühnenmusik im elisabethanischen Drama. Diss. Leipzig, 1916. (93 S.) Rev.: Sh. Jb. 55, 1919, S. 175, W. Keller.

EDWARD BLISS REED: Songs from the British drama. New Haven & O.U.P., 1925. (398 pp.)

LOUIS B. WRIGHT: Extraneous song in Elizabethan drama after the advent of Shakespeare. In: Stud. in Philol., vol. 24, 1927, pp. 261–74.

———

OLA ELIZABETH WINSLOW: Low comedy as a structural element in English drama from the beginnings to 1642. Diss. Chicago, 1926. (xii, 186 pp.) Rev.: RESt. 3, 1927, pp. 485–6, A. Nicoll.

LOUIS B. WRIGHT: Juggling tricks and conjury on the English stage before 1642. In: Mod. Phil., vol. 24, 1927, pp. 269–84.

LOUIS B. WRIGHT: Variety show clownery on the Pre-Restoration stage. In: Anglia, Bd. 52, 1928, S. 51–68.

LOUIS B. WRIGHT: Vaudeville dancing and acrobatics in Elizabethan plays. In: E. St., Bd. 63, 1928, S. 59–76.

BEATRICE OLSON: The morris dance in drama before 1640. In: Quart. Journ. of the Univ. of North Dakota, vol. 10, 1920, pp. 422–35.

(θ) TYPICAL SCENES—MOBS, GHOSTS, MADNESS, ETC.

F. A. LEO: Shakespeare, das Volk und die Narren. Festvortrag. In: Sh. Jb. Jg. 15, 1880, S. 1–17.

WILHELM OECHELHÄUSER: Die Zechbrüder und Trunkenen in Shakespeares Dramen. In: Sh. Jb. Jg. 16, 1881, S. 25–83.

J. CORBIN: The Elizabethan Hamlet. A study of the sources, and of Shakespeare's environment, to show that the mad scenes had a comic aspect now ignored. London, 1895. Rev.: Bbl. 6, 1896, S. 296–9, Rud. Fischer.

HANS SCHWAB: Das Schauspiel im Schauspiel zur Zeit Shaksperes. Wien & Leipzig, 1896. (viii, 67 S.)=Wiener Beitr. z. engl. Philol., hrsg. v. J. Schipper, Bd. 5. Rev.: Bbl. 8, 1898, S. 65–71, R. Fischer.

LEOPOLD WURTH: Dramaturgische Bemerkungen zu den Geisterszenen in Shaksperes Tragödien. In: Beitr. z. neueren Philol., Jakob Schipper z. 19. Juli 1902. Wien & Leipzig, 1902. Rev.: Sh. Jb. 40, 1904, S. 239, L. Richter.

E. SCHULZ: Das Verkleidungsmotiv bei Shakespeare. Mit Untersuchung der Quellen. Diss. Halle, 1904. (59 S.)

ROBERT PETSCH: Die Volksszenen in Shakespeares Dramen. In: Frankf. Ztg. v. 19. Sept. 1905. Rev.: Sh. Jb. 42, 1906, S. 315–16.

ROBERT OEHME: Die Volksszenen bei Shakespeare und seinen Vorgängern. Diss. Berlin, 1908. (vi, 102 S.) Rev.: Sh. Jb. 45, 1909, S. 271–2, Fr. Brie.

THEODOR VETTER: Shakespeare und das Volk. Festvortrag. In: Sh. Jb., Bd. 46, 1910, S. xiv–xxxii.

BERTHOLD BLAESE: Die Stimmungsszenen in Shakespeares Tragödien. Diss. Greifswald, 1910. (111 S.) Rev.: Sh. Jb. 48, 1912, S. 205–7, Weyhe; Bbl. 22, 1911, S. 326–8, Ph. Aronstein.

W. GROSCH: Bote und Botenbericht im engl. Drama bis Shakespeare. Diss. Giessen, 1911. (126 S.) Rev.: Sh. Jb. 48, 1912, S. 204–5, Weyhe.

W. BERGHÄUSER: Die Darstellung des Wahnsinns im engl. Drama bis zum Ende des 18. Jhrh. Diss. Giessen, 1914. (94 S.)

EDGAR ALLISON PEERS: Elizabethan drama and its mad folk. Cambridge, 1914. (iv, 189 pp.)=The Harniss Prize Essay for 1913. Rev.: Sh. Jb. 51, 1915, S. 268–9, W. Creizenach.

VICTOR O. FREEBURG: Disguise plots in Elizabethan drama. New York, 1915. (x, 241 pp.)=Columbia Univ. Stud. in English and comparative literature. Rev.: Bbl. 27, 1916, S. 304–14, A. Eichler.

ALBERT EICHLER: Zur Technik der Lauschszene bei Shakespeare. In: E. St., Bd. 50, 1916, S. 17–50. Rev.: Sh. Jb. 53, 1917, S. 206, C. Grabau.

J. F. A. PYRE: Shakespeare's pathos. In: Shakespeare Stud. by members of the department of English of the Univ. of Wisconsin, 1916, pp. 36–77. Rev.: Z. f. e. U. 16, 1917, S. 185–6, Jantzen.
Deals with the 'moving' scenes in Shakespeare's plays.

ÉMILE LEGOUIS: The Bacchic element in Shakespeare's plays. London, 1926. (20 pp.) Rev.: E. St. 62, 1928, S. 438–9, A. Eichler; Sh. Jb. 64, 1928, S. 212, Beckmann; Bbl. 38, 1927, S. 247–8, A. Eichler.
Scenes representing drinking-bouts and orgies.

O. STEINHERTZ: Die Szene hinter der Bühne in den Tragödien und Historien Shakespeares. MS. Diss. Prag. Extract in: Jb. d. philos. Fak. d. dt. Univ. in Prag, 1924–5. Prag, 1926, S. 74–8.

F. S. BOAS: The play within the play. In: The Shakespeare Assoc. 1925–6. London, 1927, pp. 134–56.

(ι) DEFINITE MOTIVES—FRIENDSHIP, SUICIDE, DREAMS, ETC.

NICOLAUS DELIUS: Die *Freundschaft* in Shakespeares Dramen. In: Sh. Jb. Jg. 19, 1884, S. 19–41.

HANS KLIEM: Sentimentale Freundschaft in der Shakespeare-Epoche. Diss. Jena, 1915. (62 S.) Rev.: Sh. Jb. 51, 1915, S. 260–1, M. Förster.

HELEN GRIERSON: Friendship in Shakespeare's plays. In: Contemp. Rev., Nov. 1921, pp. 665–76.

LOUIS B. WRIGHT: The male-friendship cult in Thomas Heywood's plays. In: MLN., vol. 42, 1927, pp. 510–14.

GERTRUD JAHRMANN: Das *Gebet* in Shakespeares Tragödien. In: Arch., Bd. 141, 1921, S. 41–58.

R. BROTANEK: Shakespeare über den *Krieg*. Festvortrag. In: Sh. Jb. Jg. 52, 1916, S. xvi–xlviii.

JAMES HOLLY HANFORD: *Suicide* in the plays of Shakespeare. In: PMLA., vol. 27, N.S. vol. 20, 1912, pp. 380–97.

FRITZ EISINGER: Das Problem des Selbstmords in der Literatur der engl. Renaissance. Diss. Freiburg, 1925. (viii, 119 S.) Rev.: Bbl. 39, 1928, S. 364–5, Liljegren.

HUGO DAFFNER: Der Selbstmord bei Shakespeare. In: Sh. Jb., Bd. 64, N.F. Bd. 5, 1928, S. 90–131.

E. NAUJOCKS: Gestaltung und Auffassung des *Todes* bei Shakespeare und seinen englischen Vorgängern im 16. Jhrh. Diss. Berlin, 1916. (vi, 49 S.)

M. ARNOLD: Die Verwendung des *Traummotivs* in der englischen Dichtung von Chaucer bis auf Shakespeare. Diss. Kiel, 1912. (xv, 71 S.)

JÜRGEN STRUVE: Das Traummotiv im englischen Drama des 17. Jhrh. Diss. Kiel, 1913. (xiv, 104 S.) Rev.: Sh. Jb. 51, 1915, S. 270, W. Creizenach.

(κ) MONOLOGUE, DIALOGUE, AND CHORUS

(aa) *Monologue*

NICOLAUS DELIUS: Über den Monolog in Shakespeares Dramen. Festvortrag. In: Sh. Jb. Jg. 16, 1881, S. 1–21.

E. KILIAN: Der Shakespearesche Monolog und seine Spielweise. In: Sh. Jb. Jg. 39, 1903, S. xiv–xlii.

OTTO SOEHRING: Zur Technik des Monologs in Shakespeares Tragödien. In: Z. f. e. U., Bd. 10, 1911, S. 97–122.

MORRIS LE ROY ARNOLD: The soliloquies of Shakespeare. A study in technic. New York, 1911. (x, 177 pp.)=Columbia Univ. Stud. in English. Rev.: Sh. Jb. 48, 1912, S. 311–12, M. Förster; Bbl. 23, 1912, S. 321, Ph. Aronstein.

HERMANN POEPPERLING: Studien über den Monolog in den Dramen Shakespeares. Diss. Giessen, 1912. (141 S.) Rev.: Sh. Jb. 49, 1913, S. 173, Weyhe.

ELMER E. STOLL: Hamlet and Iago. In: Anniversary papers by colleagues and pupils of G. L. KITTREDGE. Boston, 1913.

Defends the view that the monologues of Hamlet and Iago contain only objective truth.

BERNHARD LOTT: Der Monolog im englischen Drama vor Shakespeare. Diss. Greifswald, 1909. (114 S.) Rev.: Sh. Jb. 46, 1910, S. 190–1, Fr. Brie; Bbl. 21, 1910, S. 110–11, G. Becker.

(*bb*) *Dialogue*

G. KRAMER: Über Stichomythie und Gleichklang in den Dramen Shakespeares. Diss. Kiel, 1889. (69 S.)

GEORG PLOCH: Über den Dialog in den Dramen Shakespeares und seiner Vorläufer. In: Giessener Beitr. z. Erforsch. d. Sprache und Kultur Englands und Nordam., hrsg. von W. Horn, Bd. ii, 2, 1925, S. 129–92. Rev.: Z. f. e. U. 27, 1928, S. 227–8, Jantzen.

JULIUS HALLER: Die Technik des Dialogs im mittelalterlichen Drama Englands. Diss. Giessen, 1916. (xv, 157 S.) Rev.: Sh. Jb. 55, 1919, S. 167, W. Keller.

For 'Dialogue' cf. also Italian Conduct-books, p. 72.

(*cc*) *Chorus*

KURT REINECKE: Der Chor in den wichtigsten Tragödien der engl. Renaissance-Literatur. Diss. Leipzig, 1916. (95 S.) Rev.: Sh. Jb. 55, 1919, S. 168, W. Keller.

HEINRICH RAUSCH: Der 'Chorus' im englischen Drama bis 1642. Giessen, 1922. (52 S.)

LORENZ MORSBACH: Shakespeares Prologe, Epiloge und Chorus-Reden. Eine kritische Untersuchung. Berlin, 1929. (80 S.)=Nachr. Ges. Wiss. Gött., philos.-hist. Kl. Jg. 78, 1928, H. 3. Rev.: Bbl. 40, 1929, S. 112–14, A. Eichler; N. Spr. 38, 1930, S. 161–5, R. Petsch.

(λ) PROLOGUE AND EPILOGUE

FERDINAND LÜDERS: Prolog und Epilog bei Shakespeare. In: Sh. Jb. Jg. 5, 1870, S. 274–91.

LORENZ MORSBACH: Shakespeares Prologe, Epiloge und Chorus-Reden. Cf. above.

OTTO SPAAR: Prolog und Epilog im mittelalterlichen englischen Drama. Diss. Giessen, 1913. (81 S.) Rev.: Sh. Jb. 51, 1915, S. 270, W. Creizenach.

FRIEDRICH FRENZEL: Die Prologe der Tragödien Senecas. Diss. Leipzig, 1914. (105 S.) Rev.: Sh. Jb. 55, 1919, S. 185–6, Sonnenburg.

(μ) ACTION AND CHARACTER

LEVIN L. SCHÜCKING: Charakter und Handlung. In his Die Charakter-probleme bei Shakespeare. Leipzig, 1919, 1927[2], S. 109–205.

JULIA GRACE WALES: Character and action in Shakespeare. A consideration of some sceptical views. In: Univ. of Wisconsin Stud. in Lang. and Lit., vol. 18, 1923, pp. 118–45.

KARL YOUNG: Samuel Johnson on Shakespeare, one aspect.=Stud. by members of the department of English, ser. 3. Univ. of Wisconsin Stud. No. 18, 1924. (226 pp.)
Deals with the problem of the inconsistency existing between action and character.

ELMER EDGAR STOLL: The characterization. In Stoll's Shakespeare studies. New York, 1927, pp. 90–146.

Cf. also:

OTTO LUDWIG: Shakespeare-Studien.

B. TEN BRINK: Shakespere.

H. VON FRIESEN: Briefe über Shaksperes Hamlet and Shakspere-Studien.

(v) ART OF CHARACTER DEPICTION

(aa) Problems of Character in General

GUSTAV RÜMELIN: Shakespeares Eigentümlichkeiten in der Charakteristik der Personen und in der Motivierung der dramatischen Handlung. In his Shakespeare-Studien, 1874², S. 59–71.

LEVIN L. SCHÜCKING: Die Charakterprobleme bei Shakespeare. Eine Einführung in das Verständnis des Dramatikers. Leipzig, 1919, 1927². (xvi, 286 S.) English translation: Character problems in Shakespeare's plays. Transl. by W. H. Peters. New York & London, 1922. (269 pp.) Rev.: E. St. 63, 1929, S. 269–72, L. Kellner; Bbl. 39, 1928, S. 89–94, Ph. Aronstein; N. Spr. 37, 1929, S. 337–42, Hel. Richter; Litteris, Jg. 3, 1926, S. 16–28, A. Feuillerat; MLR. 16, 1921, pp. 78–87, H. V. Routh.

Cf.: GERDA STAHR: Zur Methodik der Shakespeare-Interpretation. Aus Anlass von Schückings Charakterproblemen. Diss. Rostock, 1925. (38 S.) Rev.: Sh. Jb. 63, 1927, S. 199–200, W. Keller.

ELMER EDGAR STOLL: Shakespeare studies, historical and comparative in method. New York, 1927. (xi, 502 pp.) Rev.: Bbl. 38, 1927, S. 305–12, L. L. Schücking; TLS., Sept. 1, 1927, p. 589.

(bb) Particular Problems of Character

WILHELM VERSHOFEN: Charakterisierung durch Mithandelnde in Shakespeares Dramen. Bonn, 1905. (157 S.)=Bonner Beitr. z. Anglistik, H. 20.

ARTHUR BORCHERS: Der Charakterkontrast in den Dramen Shakespeares bis Henry IV. 1. Teil. Diss. Halle, 1912. (96 S.) Rev.: Sh. Jb. 49, 1913, S. 174, Weyhe.

LEVIN L. SCHÜCKING: Primitive Kunstmittel und moderne Interpretation. In: GRM. Jg. 4, 1912, S. 321–39. Rev.: Sh. Jb. 52, 1916, S. 213, M. Förster.
Deals with reflex and direct self-characterization.

E. H. WRIGHT: Reality and inconsistency in Shakespeare's characters. In: Shakesperian studies. Columbia Univ. Pr., 1916.
Shakespeare's characters cannot be reduced to a simple formula.

LISBETH NICLAS: Der Charakterkontrast in Shakespeares Tragödien. Diss. Halle, 1917. (144 S.)

(cc) Individual Characters

WILLIAM RICHARDSON: Essays on some of Shakespeare's dramatic characters. To which is added an Essay on the faults of Shakespeare. 5th ed. London, 1797. (viii, 401 pp.)
Characters discussed include: Macb., Haml., Jacques, Imogen, Rich. III, Falst., Lear, Timon.

WILLIAM HAZLITT: Characters of Shakespeare's plays, 1817. Cheap edition, with an introd. by SIR ARTHUR QUILLER-COUCH. O.U.P., 1917. (xl, 288 pp.)= The World's Classics, No. 205.

CHARLES C. CLARKE: Shakespeare-characters, chiefly those subordinate. London, 1863. (viii, 522 pp.)

JOHANNES MEISSNER: Über die innere Einheit in Shakespeares Stücken. In: Sh. Jb. Jg. 7, 1872, S. 82–123.
Studies of the characters of the individual plays.

HENRY N. HUDSON: Shakespeare, his life, art and characters. 2 vols. Boston, 1872, 1895[4].
Chiefly analyses of characters.

J. THÜMMEL: Vorträge über Shakespeares Charaktere. 2 Bde. Halle, 1881.

WILHELM WETZ: Die Menschen in Shakespeares Dramen.=Shakespeare vom Standpunkte der vergleichenden Literaturgeschichte. Bd. 1. Worms, 1890. (579 S.) [Vol. 2 not published.]

ALFRED KLAAR: Shakespeares Charaktere und ihre Darstellung. Festvortrag. In: Sh. Jb. Jg. 49, 1913, S. xi–xxxiv.

H. SOMERVILLE: Madness in Shakespearian tragedy. London, 1929. (207 pp.)
Deals with the mental defects of the chief characters in the tragedies.

EVANGELINE M. O'CONNOR: An index to the works of Shakespere. London, 1887. (vi, 419 pp.)

FRANCIS GRIFFIN STOKES: A dictionary of the characters and proper names in the works of Shakespeare, with notes on the sources and dates of the plays and poems. London (1924). (xv, 350 pp. and appendices.)

(dd) Character Types

(aa) Artisan and Professional Types

JULIUS THÜMMEL: Über Shakespeares Geistlichkeit. In: Sh. Jb. Jg. 16, 1881, S. 349–66.

H. DEICHERT: Der Lehrer und der Geistliche im elisabethanischen Drama. Diss. Halle, 1906. (81 S.)

RICHARD RÖHMER: Priestergestalten im englischen Drama bis zu Shakespeare. Einleitung: Die ausserdramatische Literatur bis zu Chaucer. Abschn. I: Der Geistliche im Drama vor der Reformation. 1. Kap.: Die Mysterien. 2. Kap.: Die Mirakelspiele. 3. Kap.: Die Moralitäten. Diss. Berlin, 1909. (xii, 50 S.) Rev.: Sh. Jb. 46, 1910, S. 194, Fr. Brie.

H. BORMANN: Der Jurist im Drama der elisabethanischen Zeit. Diss. Halle, 1906. (41 S.)

JULIUS THÜMMEL: Der Miles gloriosus bei Shakespeare. Vortrag. In: Sh. Jb. Jg. 13, 1878, S. 1–12.

H. GRAF: Der Miles gloriosus im englischen Drama bis zur Zeit des Bürgerkrieges. Diss. Rostock, 1892. (58 S.) Rev.: Bbl. 4, 1894, S. 131–3.

GERTRUD GOETZE: Der Londoner Lehrling im literarischen Kulturbild der elisabethanischen Zeit. Diss. Jena, 1918. (xii, 74 S.) Rev.: Bbl. 29, 1918, S. 321–5, Ph. Aronstein.

CHARLES W. CAMP: The artisan in Elizabethan literature. New York, Columbia Univ. Pr., 1924. (170 pp.) Rev.: Bbl. 35, S. 357, Liljegren; JEGPh. 24, pp. 453–6, Boyer.

(ββ) Female Characters

ANNA B. JAMESON: Shakespeare's heroines. Characteristics of women, moral, poetical, and historical. 2 vols. London, 1832, 1833[2], 1836[3], &c. German translation: Shakespeares Frauengestalten. Übers. von LEVIN SCHÜCKING. Bielefeld, 1840.

HEINRICH HEINE: Shakespeares Mädchen und Frauen. In: Sämtliche Werke, Bd. 5, 1839.

FRIEDRICH BODENSTEDT: Shakespeares Frauencharaktere. Berlin, 1874, 1887[4]. (xix, 380 S.)

HELENA FAUCIT MARTIN: On some of Shakespeare's female characters. London, 1885. German translation: Über einige von Shakespeares Frauencharakteren, Übers. von KARL LENTZNER. In: Sh. Jb. Jg. 17, 1882, S. 230–51.

JULIUS BAHNSEN: Charakterzüge aus Shakespeares Frauenwelt. In the same author's Wie ich wurde, was ich ward. Aus d. Nachlass hrsg. von RUDOLF LOUIS. München, 1905, S. 184–230. Rev.: Sh. Jb. 41, 1905, S. 262–3, E. Kilian.

ALEXANDER VON GLEICHEN-RUSSWURM: Shakespeares Frauengestalten. Nürnberg, 1909. (310 S.) Rev.: Sh. Jb. 46, 1910, S. 277–8, M. Gothein.

FRANK HARRIS: The women of Shakespeare. New York, 1912.

AGNES M. MACKENZIE: The women in Shakespeare's plays. A critical study from the dramatic and the psychological points of view and in relation to the development of Shakespeare's art. London, 1924. (xiv, 474 pp.) Rev.: Sh. Jb. 62, 1926, S. 223. _____

THEODOR VATKE: Das weibliche Schönheitsideal in der älteren englischen Dichtung, besonders bei Shakespeare. In: Sh. Jb. Jg. 22, 1887, S. 164–71.

GRACE LATHAM: Einige von Shakespeares Kammerfrauen. In: Sh. Jb. Jg. 25, 1890, S. 77–112. Rosalinde, Celia und Helena. op. cit. Jg. 26, 1891, S. 43–77. Julia, Silvia, Hero und Viola. op. cit. Jg. 28, 1893, S. 20–53.

ORTGIES SIEFKEN: Das geduldige Weib in der englischen Literatur bis auf Shakespeare. 1. Teil: Der Konstanzetypus. Diss. Leipzig, 1903. (77 S.)

ORTGIES SIEFKEN: Der Konstanze-Griseldistypus in der englischen Literatur bis auf Shakespeare. Progr. Rathenow, 1903. (110 S.)

H. DIESTEL: Die schuldlos verdächtigte Frau im elisabethanischen Drama. Diss. Rostock, 1909. (53 S.)

G. A. JACOBI: Die Frauengestalten der Beaumont-Fletcherschen Dramen. Diss. Halle, 1909. (99 S.)

HENRY D. GRAY: The evolution of Shakespeare's heroine. In: JEGPh., vol. 12, 1913, pp. 122–37.

(γγ) Ghosts

F. W. MOORMAN: Shakespeare's ghosts. In: MLR., vol. 1, 1905–6, pp. 192–201.

F. W. MOORMAN: The Pre-Shakspearian ghost. In: MLR., vol. 1, 1905–6, pp. 85–95.

HANS ANKENBRAND: Die Figur des Geistes im Drama der englischen Renaissance. Leipzig, 1906. (46 S.)=Münch. Beitr. z. roman. und engl. Philol., hrsg. von Breymann und Schick, H. 35. Rev.: Sh. Jb. 43, 1907, S. 240, Fuller; Bbl. 17, 1906, S. 335–6, Konr. Meier.

ELMER EDGAR STOLL: The objectivity of the ghosts in Shakespeare. In: PMLA., vol. 22, N.S. vol. 15, 1907, pp. 201–33.
The ghosts are not hallucinations.

ELMER EDGAR STOLL: The ghosts. In his Shakespeare studies. New York, 1927, pp. 187–254.

(δδ) Children and Old Men

JULIUS THÜMMEL: Shakespeares Kindergestalten. Vortrag. In: Sh. Jb. Jg. 10, 1875, S. 1–21.

A. TETZLAFF: Die Kindergestalten bei den englischen Dramatikern vor Shakespeare und bei Shakespeare selbst. Diss. Halle, 1898. (72 S.)

W. BAETKE: Kindergestalten bei den Zeitgenossen und Nachfolgern Shakespeares. Diss. Halle, 1908. (108 S.)

JULIUS THÜMMEL: Shakespeares Greise. In: Sh. Jb. Jg. 18, 1883, S. 127–55.

(εε) The Melancholy Type

LEVIN L. SCHÜCKING: Shakespeares Melancholie. In: Preuss. Jbb. 128, 1907, S. 383–403.

GUSTAV ARTHUR BIEBER: Der Melancholikertypus Shakespeares und sein Ursprung. Diss. Jena, 1913. (33 S.) Enlarged in Anglist. Arbeiten, hrsg. von L. L. Schücking, H. 3. (92 S.) Rev.: Sh. Jb. 52, 1916, S. 213–15, M. Förster; Bbl. 25, 1914, S. 262–4, Ph. Aronstein.

(ζζ) Fools, Clowns and the Devil

FRANCIS DOUCE: On the clowns and fools of Shakespeare. In his Illustrations of Shakespeare. London, 1807. Vol. 2, pp. 297–332.

JOHN CH. BUCKNILL: The mad folk of Shakespeare. Psychological essays. London, 1867. (xvi, 334 pp.)

JULIUS THÜMMEL: Über Shakespeares Narren. In: Sh. Jb. Jg. 9, 1874, S. 87–106.

JULIUS THÜMMEL: Über Shakespeares Clowns. In: Sh. Jb. Jg. 11, 1876, S. 78–96.

F. A. LEO: Shakespeare, das Volk und die Narren. Festvortrag. In: Sh. Jb. Jg. 15, 1880, S. 1–17.

L. W. CUSHMAN: Die Figuren des Teufels und des Vice in dem ernsten englischen Drama bis auf Shakespeare. Diss. Göttingen, 1900. (56 S.) Enlarged and published under the title: The Devil and the Vice in the English dramatic literature before Shakespeare. Halle, 1900. (xv, 148 pp.)=Stud. z. engl. Philol., hrsg. v. Morsbach, H. 6. Rev.: Sh. Jb. 38, 1902, S. 272–6, Churchill; Bbl. 13, 1902, S. 321–2, Rud. Fischer.

EDUARD ECKHARDT: Die lustige Person im älteren englischen Drama (bis 1642). Berlin, 1902. (xxxii, 478 S.)=Palaestra 17. Rev.: Sh. Jb. 39, 1903, S. 313–16, W. Keller; Bbl. 19, 1908, S. 375–6, R. Ackermann.

S. DAVEY: Fools, jesters, and comic characters in Shakespeare. In: Trans. Royal Soc. of Lit. 2nd ser., vol. 23, 1902, pp. 129–90.

VICTOR SCHOLDERER: The development of Shakespeare's fools. In: Libr., N.S. vol. 10, 1909, pp. 201–7.

OLIVE MARY BUSBY: Studies in the development of the fool in the Elizabethan drama. O.U.P., 1923. (87 pp.) Rev.: MLR. 19, 1924, pp. 230–2, W. W. Greg.

FREDERIC WARDE: The fools of Shakespeare. Los Angeles, 1923.

C. J. HASLINGHUIS: De duivel in het drama der middeleeuwen. Leiden, 1927. With extensive bibliography.

WALTER GAEDICK: Der weise Narr in der englischen Literatur von Erasmus bis Shakespeare. Diss. Berlin, 1928. (iii, 55 S.) Rev.: Sh. Jb. 64, 1928, S. 196, W. Keller; N. Spr. 37, 1929, S. 251–2, Rob. Petsch; E. St. 64, 1929, S. 126–8, E. Eckhardt.

J. W. RUDWIN: Der Teufel in den deutschen geistlichen Spielen des Mittelalters und der Reformationszeit. Ein Beitrag zur Literatur-, Kultur- und Kirchengeschichte Deutschlands. (106 S.)=Hesperia No. 6.

(ηη) National Types

EDUARD ECKHARDT: Die Dialekt- und Ausländertypen des älteren englischen Dramas. 2 Teile. Louvain, 1910, 1911. (xv, 163 und xxxi, 189 S.)=Mat. z. Kunde d. ält. engl. Dramas, Bd. 27, 32. Rev.: Sh. Jb. 47, 1911, S. 366–7, M. Förster.

A. E. HUGHES: Shakespeare and his Welsh characters. O.U.P., 1918. (34 pp.)
=The Sh. Assoc. Pamphl. No. 2.

FRED JAMES HARRIES: Shakespeare and the Welsh. London, 1919. Rev.:
JEGPh. 20, 1921, pp. 410–12, John J. Parry.

W. J. LAWRENCE: Welsh portraiture in Elizabethan drama. In: TLS., Nov. 9,
1922.

CHARLES BASTIDE: La France et les Français dans le théâtre de Shakespeare.
In: Edda, Bd. 6, 1916, S. 112–23. Rev.: Sh. Jb. 54, 1918, S. 151, Jantzen.

WILHELM MEYER: Der Wandel des jüdischen Typus in der englischen Literatur.
Diss. Marburg, 1912. (xi, 88 S.)

GERALD FRIEDLANDER: Shakespeare and the Jew. With an introduction by
Maurice Moscovitch. London & New York, 1921. (viii, 79 pp.)

L. J. CARDOZO: The contemporary Jew in the Elizabethan drama. Amsterdam,
1925. (xii, 335 pp.)

H. MICHELSON: The Jew in early English literature. Diss. Amsterdam, 1926.
(xii, 175 pp.)

DAVID STRUMPF: Die Juden in der mittelalterlichen Mysterien-, Mirakel-
und Moralitätendichtung Frankreichs. Diss. Heidelberg, 1919. (41 S.)

(θθ) Social Types

V. KNAUER: Die Könige Shakespeares. Wien, 1863.

HUGO VON HOFMANNSTHAL: Shakespeares Könige und grosse Herren. Festvortrag. In: Sh. Jb. Jg. 41, 1905, S. x–xxvii.

J. C. STOBART: Shakespeare's monarchs. London, 1926. (255 pp.) Rev.: TLS.,
Febr. 25, 1926, p. 143.

JULIUS THÜMMEL: Shakespeares Helden. In: Sh. Jb. Jg. 20, 1885, S. 85–118.

FREDERICK TUPPER, JR.: The Shakesperean mob. In: PMLA., vol. 27, N.S.
vol. 20, 1912, pp. 486–523.
For the Gentleman, cf. p. 72.
Cf. also: Shakespeare's Attitude to the Social Classes, p. 39.

(ι) Criminal Types

J. KOHLER: Verbrechertypen in Shakespeares Dramen. Berlin (1903). (108 S.)
Rev.: Sh. Jb. 40, 1904, S. 268–70, R. Petsch.
From a legal point of view.

AUGUST GOLL: Forbrydertyper hos Shakespeare. Seks foredrag. Kjøbenhavn
og Kristiania 1907. (184 S.) German translation: Verbrecher bei Shakespeare.
Mit Vorw. von E. von Liszt. Stuttgart [1908]. (vi, 212 S.) English translation: Criminal types in Shakespeare. Authorized translation from the Danish
by Mrs. Charles Weekes. London [1909]. (271 pp.)
From the point of view of modern criminal psychology.

ERICH WULFFEN: Shakespeares grosse Verbrecher. Richard III., Macbeth, Othello. Berlin, 1911. (292 S.) Rev.: Sh. Jb. 48, 1912, S. 278–80, R. Fischer. Pathological studies.

ELMER EDGAR STOLL: Criminals in Shakespeare and in science. In: Mod. Phil., vol. 10, 1912–13, pp. 55–80.

JAKOB BLASS: Die Entwicklung der Figur des gedungenen Mörders im älteren englischen Drama bis Shakespeare. Diss. Giessen, 1913. (77 S.) Rev.: Sh. Jb. 51, 1915, S. 270–1, W. Creizenach.

CLARENCE V. BOYER: The villain as hero in Elizabethan drama. London, 1914. (xii, 264 pp.)

ELMER EDGAR STOLL: The criminals. In his Shakespeare studies. New York, 1927, pp. 337–402.

(κκ) Various Types

JULIUS THÜMMEL: Der Liebhaber bei Shakespeare. In: Sh. Jb. Jg. 19, 1884, S. 42–85.

W. THOMANN: Der eifersüchtige Ehemann im Drama der elisabethanischen Zeit. Diss. Halle, 1908. (104 S.)

ARTHUR B. STONEX: The usurer in the Elizabethan drama. In: PMLA., vol. 31, N.S. vol. 24, 1916, pp. 190–210. Rev.: Sh. Jb. 53, 1917, S. 191, C. Grabau.

WALTER REINICKE: Der Wucherer im älteren englischen Drama. Diss. Halle, 1907.

(3) THE TRAGIC AND THE COMIC

JOHANNES VOLKELT: Ästhetik des Tragischen. München, 1897, 1906², 1917³. (552 S.) Rev.: Sh. Jb. 54, 1918, S. 144–5, Schücking.

CHRISTIAN JANENTZKY: Shakespeares Weltbild, das Tragische und Hamlet. Halle, 1925=Die Ernte. Franz Muncker z. 70. Geb., S. 241–63.

FRANZ LEDERER: Die Ironie in den Tragödien Shakespeares. Diss. Berlin, 1907. (84 S.) Rev.: Sh. Jb. 45, 1909, S. 272–3, Fr. Brie; Bbl. 20, 1909, S. 116–18, R. Hauschild.

KÄTHE ECKLEBEN: Die tragische Ironie bei Shakespeare. Diss. Halle, 1912. (43 S.) Rev.: Sh. Jb. 49, 1913, S. 173, Weyhe.

ADOLF HÜDEPOHL: Die tragische Ironie in der englischen Tragödie und Historie vor Shakespeare. Diss. Halle, 1915. (xvii, 156 S.) Rev.: Sh. Jb. 52, 1916, S. 260–1, M. Förster.

HERMANN ULRICI: Über Shakespeares Humor. Vortrag. In: Sh. Jb. Jg. 6, 1871, S. 1–12.

JOHN WEISS: Wit, humour, and Shakespeare. 12 essays. Boston, 1876. (iv, 428 pp.)

JOS. EHRLICH: Der Humor Shakespeares. Wien, 1878.

EDUARD ECKHARDT: Die Komik in Shakespeares Trauerspielen. In: Zs. f. d. dt. Unt. Jg. 21, 1907, S. 737–52. Rev.: Sh. Jb. 44, 1908, S. 298.

HELENE RICHTER: Der Humor bei Shakespeare. In: Sh. Jb. Jg. 45, 1909, S. 1–50.

MAX J. WOLFF: Das Komische bei Shakespeare. In: E. St. Bd. 46, 1912–13, S. 206–27.

RAYMOND M. ALDEN: The use of comic material in the tragedy of Shakespeare and his contemporaries. In: JEGPh., vol. 13, 1914, pp. 281–98.

HERMANN JOSEF GÖTZ: Die komischen Bestandteile von Shakespeares Tragödien in der literarischen Kritik Englands. Diss. Giessen, 1917. (139 S.) Rev.: Sh. Jb. 55, 1919, S. 165–6, W. Keller; Bbl. 29, 1918, S. 97–9, L. Kellner. Survey of critical opinion.

WILHELM HORN: Das Komische in Shakespeares Tragödien und die Maler Reynolds und Hogarth. In: Arch. Jg. 72, Bd. 137, 1918, S. 159–91.

JOHN B. MOORE: The comic and the realistic in English drama. Univ. of Chicago Pr., 1925. (viii, 231 pp.)

ELMER EDGAR STOLL: The comic method. In his Shakespeare studies. New York, 1927, pp. 147–86.
Cf. also Shakespeare's Fools, p. 115.

(4) SYMBOLISM: ALLUSIONS TO PLACES AND TO CONTEMPORARY PERSONS AND EVENTS

A. LINDNER: Bemerkungen über symbolische Kunst im Drama, mit besonderer Berücksichtigung Shakespeares. In: Sh. Jb. Jg. 2, 1867, S. 184–95.

GEORGE RUSSELL FRENCH: Shakspeareana genealogica. Pt. I: Identification of the dramatis personae in Shakspeare's historical plays, from King John to King Henry VIII. Notes on characters in Macbeth and Hamlet. Persons and places, belonging to Warwickshire, alluded to in several plays. Pt. II: The Shakespeare and Arden families, and their connections, with tables of descent. London & Cambridge, 1869. (xiv, 590 pp.)

JULIUS THÜMMEL: Allegorisches und Tendenziöses in Shakespeares Dramen. In: Sh. Jb. Jg. 21, 1886, S. 43–68.

GREGOR SARRAZIN: William Shakespeares Lehrjahre. 1897, and the same author's Aus Shakespeares Meisterwerkstatt. Berlin, 1906. (vii, 226 S.)
Sarrazin assumes that Shakespeare's dramatis personae to a great extent reveal intentional portraiture.

WALTER DEMPEWOLF: Shakespeares angebliche Modelle. Diss. Jena, 1914. (90 S.) Rev.: Sh. Jb. 51, 1915, S. 259–60, M. Förster.
A survey of the subject.

LEVIN L. SCHÜCKING: Symbolische Charaktere. In his Die Charakterprobleme bei Shakespeare. Leipzig, 1919, 1927², S. 252–83.

PERCY ALLEN: Shakespeare and Chapman as topical dramatists. Being a further study of Elizabethan dramatic origins and imitations. London, 1929. (280 pp.) Rev.: TLS., March 21, 1929, p. 229.

IX. SHAKESPEARE'S STAGE AND THE PRODUCTION OF HIS PLAYS

(1) THE THEATRE

(a) HISTORY OF THE ELIZABETHAN THEATRE

(α) SOURCES

(aa) *The Revels at Court*

PETER CUNNINGHAM: Extracts from the accounts of the Revels at Court, in the reigns of Queen Elizabeth and King James I. With introd. and notes. London, printed for the Shakespeare Soc., 1842. (li, 228 pp.)

JAMES O. HALLIWELL-PHILLIPS: A collection of ancient documents respecting the office of the Master of the Revels, and other papers relating to the early English theatre, from the original manuscripts formerly in the Haslewood Collection. London, 1870.

ALBERT FEUILLERAT: Documents relating to the Office of the Revels in the time of Queen Elizabeth. Louvain, 1908. (xvii, 513 pp.)=Mat. z. Kunde des ält. engl. Dramas, hrsg. von W. Bang, Bd. 21. Rev.: Sh. Jb. 44, 1908, S. 364, M. Förster; MLR. 5, 1910, pp. 510–15, F. S. Boas; Bbl. 19, 1908, S. 193–9, R. Brotanek.
Careful and complete edition of the Losely MSS. with many additions and a very complete index.

ALBERT FEUILLERAT: Documents relating to the Revels at Court in the time of King Edward VI and Queen Mary [The Loseley MSS.]. Ed. with notes and indexes. Louvain, 1914. (xv, 340 pp.)=Mat. z. Kunde des ält. engl. Dramas, hrsg. von W. Bang, Bd. 44.

JOSEPH QUINCY ADAMS: The dramatic records of Sir Henry Herbert, Master of the Revels, 1623–73. New Haven, 1917. (xiii, 155 pp.)=Cornell Stud. in English III. Rev.: Sh. Jb. 57, 1921, S. 105–7, W. Keller.
An attempt to reconstruct the missing office-book of Sir Henry Herbert from the quotations of Malone and Chalmers.

(bb) *Philip Henslowe*

JOHN P. COLLIER: The diary of Philip Henslowe, from 1591 to 1609. Printed from the original MS. preserved at Dulwich College. London, Sh. Soc. 1845. (xxxiv, 290 pp.)

WALTER W. GREG: Henslowe's Diary. Pt. I: Text. Pt. II: Commentary. London, 1904 and 1908. (li, 240 and 400 pp.) Rev.: Sh. Jb. 41, 1905, S. 222–3, und 45, 1909, S. 338–42, A. Brandl; GRM. 1, 1909, S. 201–4, W. Bang; MLR. 4, 1909, pp. 407–13, E. K. Chambers.

WALTER W. GREG: Henslowe Papers, being documents supplementary to Henslowe's Diary. London, 1907. (187 pp.) Rev.: Sh. Jb. 44, 1908, S. 352–3, A. Brandl.
A collection of supplementary documents concerning the history of the theatre.

Cf. T. W. BALDWIN: Posting Henslowe's accounts. In: JEGPh., vol. 26, 1927, pp. 42–90. Rev.: Sh. Jb. 63, 1927, S. 228–9, Beckmann.

An examination of Henslowe's statements.

(cc) *Master of Rolls*

Calendar of State Papers, foreign, Elizabeth. Vols. 1–7, ed. by J. STEVENSON; vols. 8–11, ed. by A. J. CROSBY. London, 1863–80.

Calendar of State Papers, foreign and domestic, Henry VIII. Vols. 1–4, ed. by J. S. BREWER; vols. 5–15, ed. by J. GAIRDNER. London, 1880–96.

Calendar of State Papers, Elizabeth. 2 vols., ed. by M. A. S. HUME. London, 1892–5.

(dd) *The Lord Chamberlain's Accounts*

WILLIAM KELLY: Notices illustrative of the drama and other popular amusements, chiefly in the 16th and 17th centuries . . . Extracted from the Chamberlain's Accounts and other MSS. of the Borough of Leicester. London, 1865. (viii, 310 pp.)

(ee) *The Privy Council*

J. R. DASENT: Acts of the Privy Council of England. New series, 1542–1604. 32 vols. London, 1890–1907.

CHARLOTTE C. STOPES: Dramatic records from the Privy Council Register. James I and Charles I. In: Sh. Jb. Jg. 48, 1912, S. 103–15.

(ff) *The Malone Society Collections.* Oxford, 1907 et seq.

Cf. pp. 7–9

(gg) *Registers of the Stationers' Company*

A transcript of the registers of the Company of Stationers of London, 1554–1640. Ed. by EDWARD ARBER. 5 vols. London, 1875–94.

(β) GENERAL TREATISES

EDMOND MALONE: Historical account of the rise and progress of the English stage and of the economy and usages of the ancient theatres in England, 1790.

Reprinted from Malone's edition of Shakespeare 1790; also contained in the Third Variorum Edition. Vol. 3, 1821. Full of useful material for the study of the Elizabethan theatre.

CHARLES DIBDIN: Complete history of the English stage. 5 vols. London [1795].

GEORGE CHALMERS: An account of the rise and progress of the English stage. In: An apology for the believers in the Shakspeare Papers . . . London, 1797. (iv, 628 pp.) Enlarged under the title: A supplemental apology for the believers in the Shakspeare Papers. London, 1799. (viii, 656 pp.)

J. PAYNE COLLIER: The history of English dramatic poetry to the time of Shakespeare, and annals of the stage to the Restoration. 3 vols. London, 1831. (xxxvi, 454; vi, 488, and vi, 508 pp.)

Very extensive, but not always quite reliable.

JOHN GENEST: Some account of the English stage, from 1660 to 1830. 10 vols. Bath, 1832.

Full of valuable information.

The Shakespeare Society's Publications [ed. by J. P. COLLIER]. 19 vols. London, 1841–53. For list of titles cf. WILLIAM JAGGARD: Shakespeare bibliography. Stratford-upon-Avon, 1911, pp. 606–7.

NICOLAUS DELIUS: Über das englische Theaterwesen zu Shaksperes Zeit. Bremen, 1859.

M. RAPP: Studien über das englische Theater. Tübingen, 1862.

W. C. HAZLITT: The English drama and stage under the Tudor and Stuart princes, 1543–1664. Illustrated by a series of documents, treatises and poems. Printed for the Roxburghe Library, 1869.

The New Shakespeare Society's Publications and Transactions. London, 1874–92. For list of publications and transactions cf. WILLIAM JAGGARD: Shakespeare bibliography. Stratford-upon-Avon, 1911, pp. 228–31.

J. J. JUSSERAND: Le théâtre en Angleterre depuis la conquête jusqu'aux prédécesseurs immédiats de Shakespeare, 1878–81.

HENRY B. BAKER: The London stage. Its history and traditions, 1576–1888. 2 vols. 1889. Later editions under the title: History of the London stage and its famous players, 1576–1903. 1904.

FREDERICK G. FLEAY: A chronicle history of the London stage, 1559–1642. London, 1890.

HAROLD CHILD: The Elizabethan theatre. In: CHEL., vol. 6, 1910, pp. 241–78.

With bibliography.

WILLIAM J. LAWRENCE: The Elizabethan playhouse and other studies. Stratford-upon-Avon, 1912. (xv, 265 pp.) 2nd ser. 1913. (xiii, 261 pp.) Rev.: JEGPh. 13, 1914, pp. 356–61, J. Q. Adams, Jr.

Valuable essays on various aspects of the Elizabethan theatre (Lord's Room, title and locality boards, stage curtain, theatre programmes, play-bills, system of admission, &c.).

WILLIAM ARCHER and W. J. LAWRENCE: The playhouse. In: Shakespeare's England, 1917. Vol. ii, pp. 283–310.

MAURICE JONAS: Shakespeare and the stage. With a complete list of theatrical terms used by Shakespeare in his plays and poems, arranged in alphabetical order, and explanatory notes. London, 1918. (406 pp.) Rev.: Bbl. 30, 1919, S. 98–102, B. Fehr.

E. K. CHAMBERS: The Elizabethan stage. 4 vols. Oxford, 1923. (xli, 388; 557; 518, and 467 pp.) Contents: I. The court; II. The control of the stage; III. The companies; IV. The playhouses; V. Plays and playwrights. Rev.: Litteris, vol. 3, 1926, S. 209–17, L. L. Schücking; Libr., 4th ser., vol. 4, 1924, pp. 332–6, A. W. Pollard; MLR. 19, 1924, pp. 474–6, A. Nicoll; Litbl. 46, S. 360–3, Flasdieck.

Comprehensive survey of knowledge of the Elizabethan theatre, with full bibliographical references to sources and treatises. With numerous appendices.

E. K. CHAMBERS: The mediaeval stage. 2 vols. Oxford, 1903. (xlii, 419 and v, 480 pp.) Rev.: Sh. Jb. 40, 1904, S. 254–6, Brotanek; Bbl. 17, 1906, S. 353–61, G. Sarrazin.

Standard work on the medieval English theatre, with extensive bibliography. Collection of all evidence concerning dramatic performances and a full list of all medieval English plays still extant.

FREDERICK S. BOAS: Shakespeare and the universities. Oxford, 1923. (viii, 272 pp.) Rev.: MLR. 18, 1923, pp. 487–90, G. C. Moore Smith.

The university stage and its productions.

PHILIPP ARONSTEIN: Das englische Renaissancetheater. In: N. Spr. Bd. 33, 1925, S. 265–80.

P. BARDI: Teatro Shakespeariano. Bari, 1926. (viii, 282 pp.)

ALLARDYCE NICOLL: The development of the theatre. A study of theatrical art from the beginnings to the present day. London, 1927. (247 pp.) Rev.: E. St. 63, 1928, S. 95–8, Fr. Brie.

Comprehensive account of the development of the European and in particular of the English stage.

WILLIAM J. LAWRENCE: Pre-Restoration stage studies. Cambridge, Harv. Univ. Pr., 1927. (viii, 435 pp.)

Contains valuable essays on various aspects of the Elizabethan stage: e.g. Practice of doubling, stage jig, stage traps, composite plays, stage realism, complex-disguise plays, stage properties, dramatic collaboration, prompt-books, &c.

(γ) PURITAN ATTACK UPON STAGE

ELBERT N. S. THOMPSON: The controversy between the Puritans and the stage. New York, 1903. (275 pp.)=Yale Stud. in Engl. 20. Contents: I. The Puritan attack on the stage; II. The dramatists' reply to the Puritans. Rev.: Bbl. 15, 1904, S. 267–70, Ph. Aronstein; MLR. 1, 1906, pp. 143–5, W. W. Greg.

With good bibliography.

J. DOVER WILSON: The Puritan attack upon the stage. In: CHEL., vol. 6, 1910, pp. 373–409.

With bibliography.

MORRIS P. TILLEY: Shakespeare and the Puritan's 'Pensive regard for the well-bestowal of time'. In: JEGPh., vol. 17, 1918, pp. 546–64.

(b) THE COURT AND THE STAGE

In addition to the general works on the history of the theatre (cf. pp. 120–122) the following works should be consulted:

ELIZ. NICHOLS: The progresses and public processions of Queen Elizabeth. 3 vols. London, 1788–1807, 1823².

JAMES NICHOLS: The progresses, processions, and magnificent festivities of King James I. 4 vols. London, 1828.

F. W. FAIRHOLT: History of Lord Mayors' pageants. London, 1843.=Percy Soc. Publ., vol. 10.

EDMUND K. CHAMBERS: Court performances before Queen Elizabeth. In: MLR., vol. 2, 1906, pp. 1–13.

EDMUND K. CHAMBERS: Notes on the history of the Revels Office under the Tudors. London, 1906. (80 pp.) Rev.: Bbl. 18, 1907, S. 355–6, Ph. Aronstein.

E. PERCY: The Privy Council under the Tudors. 1907.

VIRGINIA C. GILDERSLEEVE: Government regulation of the Elizabethan drama. New York, 1908. (vii, 259 pp.) Contents: I. National regulation; II. The Master of the Revels; III. The nature of the censorship; IV. Local regulations in London, 1543–92; V. Local regulations in London, 1592–1642; VI. The Puritan victory. Rev.: Bbl. 20, 1909, S. 171–3, Ph. Aronstein.

EDMUND K. CHAMBERS: Court performances under James I. In: MLR., vol. 4, 1909, pp. 153–66.

ANNA A. HELMHOLTZ-PHELAN: The staging of the court drama to 1595. In: PMLA., vol. 24, N.S. vol. 17, 1909, pp. 185–206.

ALBERT FEUILLERAT: Le bureau des menus-plaisirs et la mise en scène à la cour d'Élisabeth. Louvain, 1910. (88 pp.) Rev.: Sh. Jb. 47, 1911, S. 351–3, M. Förster; Bbl. 23, 1912, S. 41–4, G. Binz.

C. HORNEMANN: Das Privy Council von England zur Zeit der Königin Elisabeth. Hannover, 1912. (vi, 160 S.)

THORNTON S. GRAVES: The court and the London theatres during the reign of Queen Elizabeth. Menasha, Wis., 1913.

ROBERT WITHINGTON: English pageantry, an historical outline. 2 vols. Cambridge, Harv. Univ. Pr., & London, 1918 and 1920. (xx, 258 and vi, 435 pp.)

E. K. CHAMBERS: The court. In the same author's The Elizabethan stage. Oxford, 1923, vol. i, pp. 1–388.

E. R. ADAIR: The sources for the history of the Council in the 16th and 17th centuries. London, 1924. (vi, 96 pp.)

MARY SUSAN STEELE: Plays and masques at court during the reigns of Elizabeth, James, and Charles. New Haven & London, 1926. (xvi, 300 pp.)=Cornell Stud. in English. Rev.: JEGPh. 27, 1928, pp. 141–2, Hillebrand.
A catalogue of court performances.

(c) PUBLIC AND PRIVATE THEATRES

(α) PLAN AND SITUATION

FAIRMAN ORDISH: Early London theatres in the Fields. London, 1894. (xii, 298 pp.)

GUSTAV BINZ: Londoner Theater und Schauspiele im Jahre 1599. In: Anglia Bd. 22, 1899, S. 456–64.
A reprint of extracts from Thomas Platter's diary (1599).

ASHLEY H. THORNDIKE: Shakespeare's theater. With illustrations. New York, 1916. (xiv, 472 pp.) Rev.: MLR. 11, 1916, pp. 467–74, W. J. Lawrence.
With bibliography.

JOSEPH QUINCY ADAMS: Shakespearean playhouses. A history of English theatres from the beginnings to the Restoration. Boston (1917). (xiv, 473 pp. and illustr.) Rev.: JEGPh. 17, 1918, pp. 473–6, W. J. Lawrence.
History of the various playhouses. With extensive bibliography.

E. K. CHAMBERS: The playhouses. In the same author's The Elizabethan stage. Oxford, 1923. Vol. ii, pp. 353–557.

———

ALBERT FEUILLERAT: The origin of Shakespeare's *Blackfriars* theatre. Recent discovery of documents. In: Sh. Jb. Jg. 48, 1912, S. 81–102.

CHARLES WILLIAM WALLACE: The evolution of the English drama up to Shakespeare, with a history of the first Blackfriars theatre. Berlin, 1912. (xxi, 246 pp.)=Schriften d. Dt. Shakespeare-Ges., Bd. 4. Rev.: Bbl. 24, 1913, S. 97–104, Ph. Aronstein.
Deals chiefly with the foundation of the first Blackfriars Theatre.

ALBERT FEUILLERAT: Blackfriars records.=Malone Soc. Coll. II, 1, 1913. (136 pp.)

WILLIAM ARCHER: The *Fortune* theatre, 1600. In: Sh. Jb. Jg. 44, 1908, S. 159–66.

CHARLES W. WALLACE: Advance sheets from Shakespeare, the *Globe*, and Blackfriars. Stratford-upon-Avon, 1909. (16 pp.) Reprinted in part in: Sh. Jb. 46, 1910, S. 235–9.
According to Wallace the Globe Theatre stood on the north side of Park Street.

W. MARTIN: The site of the Globe playhouse of Shakespeare. London, 1910. Special reprint from: Surrey Archaeolog. Collect., vol. xxiii, 149 seq.
Places the Globe Theatre on the south side of Park Street.

W. W. BRAINES: The site of the Globe playhouse, Southwark. London, 1921. (112 pp.)
According to Braines on the south side of Park Street.

GEORGE HUBBARD: On the site of the Globe playhouse of Shakespeare, lying to the north of Maiden Lane, Bankside, Southwark. New York & C.U.P., 1923. (viii, 47 pp.)

JOS. QUINCY ADAMS: The housekeepers of the Globe. In: Mod. Philol., vol. 17, 1919, pp. 1–8.

CHARLES W. WALLACE: The *Swan* theatre and the Earl of Pembroke's servants. In: E. St. Bd. 43, 1911, S. 340–95.

J. S. GRAVES: A note on the Swan theatre. In: Mod. Phil., vol. 9, 1912, pp. 431–4.

W. W. BRAINES: Holywell Priory and the site of the *Theatre*, Shoreditch. London, 1915.=Indications of houses of historical interest in London, issued by the London County Council, part 43.

JAMES GREENSTREET: The *White Friars* theatre in the time of Shakespeare. In: New Sh. Soc. Publ., ser. 1, 1888, pp. 269–85.

(β) STAGING AND STAGE MACHINERY

NICOLAUS DELIUS: Die Bühnenweisungen in den alten Shakespeare-Ausgaben. In: Sh. Jb. Jg. 8, 1873, S. 171–201.

KARL THEODOR GAEDERTZ: Zur Kenntnis der altenglischen Bühne, nebst andern Beiträgen zur Shakespeare-Literatur. Bremen, 1888. (79 S.)

H. BARTON BAKER: The London stage, its history and traditions from 1576 to 1888. 2 vols. London, 1889. (xv, 296 and 323 pp.)

Shakespeares dramatische Werke. Übers. von AUG. WILH. VON SCHLEGEL und LUDWIG TIECK. Hrsg. von ALOIS BRANDL. 10 Bde. Leipzig, Bibliogr. Institut. [1897–9.]

In the introduction to vol. i, Brandl gives a description of Shakespeare's stage.

CECIL BRODMEIER: Die Shakespeare-Bühne nach den alten Bühnenanweisungen. Diss. Jena, 1902. (115 S.) Also: Weimar, 1904. (115 S.) Rev.: Sh. Jb. 40, 1904, S. 275–7, C. Grabau.

Confirms Brandl's account.

W. BANG: Zur Bühne Shakespeares. In: Sh. Jb. Jg. 40, 1904, S. 223–5.

WOLFGANG KELLER: Nochmals zur Bühne Shakespeares. In: Sh. Jb. Jg. 40, 1904, S. 225–7.

P. MÖNKEMEYER: Prolegomena zu einer Darstellung der englischen Volksbühne zur Elisabeth- und Stuart-Zeit nach den alten Bühnenanweisungen. Diss. Göttingen, 1905. (94 S.)

GEORGE F. REYNOLDS: Some principles of Elizabethan staging. Pts. I, II. Diss. Chicago, 1905. (34 and 29 pp.) Also in: Mod. Philol. vol. 2, 1905, pp. 581–614.

CARL HERMANN KAULFUSS-DIESCH: Die Inszenierung des deutschen Dramas an der Wende des 16. und 17. Jhrh. Ein Beitr. zur älteren deutschen Bühnengeschichte. Leipzig, 1905. (viii, 236 S.)=Probefahrten, hrsg. von A. Köster, Bd. 7. Rev.: Sh. Jb. 42, 1906, S. 276–7, Joh. Bolte; MLR. 4, 1909, pp. 531–7, M. B. Evans; Bbl. 20, 1909, S. 241–2, Konr. Meier.

WILLIAM J. LAWRENCE: The situation of the Lord's Room. In: E. St. Bd. 39, 1906, S. 402.

GEORGE F. REYNOLDS: 'Trees' on the stage of Shakespeare. In: Mod. Phil. vol. 5, 1907, pp. 153–68.

Raises the question: was there any 'wood scenery'?

CHARLOTTE C. STOPES: Elizabethan stage scenery. In: Fortnightly Rev., June 1907, pp. 1107–17.

RICHARD WEGENER: Die Bühneneinrichtung des Shakespeareschen Theaters nach den zeitgenössischen Dramen. [Preisgekrönt von der Dt. Sh.-Ges.] Halle, 1907. (iv, 164 S.) Rev.: Sh. Jb. 44, 1908, S. 327–9, W. Keller; Litbl. 1908, Sp. 60–1, R. Ackermann.

Cf. also: WILLIAM ARCHER: Deutsche Studien über die Bühne im Zeitalter der Elisabeth. In: Frankf. Ztg. 1908, No. 324.

A review of the works of Mönkemeyer, Brodmeier, and Wegener.

WILLIAM ARCHER: The Elizabethan stage. In: The Quart. Rev. 1908, pp. 442–71.

VICTOR E. ALBRIGHT: The Shakespearian stage. New York, 1909. (xii, 194 pp.) Rev.: Sh. Jb. 46, 1910, S. 291–2, A. Brandl; Bbl. 21, 1910, S. 105–9, G. Binz.

A. R. SKEMP: Some characteristics of the English stage before the Restoration. In: Sh. Jb. Jg. 45, 1909, S. 101–25.

WILLIAM J. LAWRENCE: Title and locality boards on the Pre-Restoration stage. In: Sh. Jb. Jg. 45, 1909, S. 146–70.

Cf. HERMANN CONRAD: Bemerkungen zu W. J. Lawrence' Aufsatz: 'Title and locality boards'. In: Sh. Jb. Jg. 46, 1910, S. 106–13.

B. NEUENDORFF: Die englische Volksbühne im Zeitalter Shakespeares nach den Bühnenanweisungen. Berlin, 1910. (230 S.)=Literarhist. Forsch., hrsg. von Schick und Waldberg, 43. Rev.: Archiv 126, S. 239 ff., A. Brandl; Sh. Jb. 47, 1911, S. 306–8, W. Keller; Bbl. 22, 1911, S. 324–6, Ph. Aronstein.
Assumes that scenery was not used on the Shakespearian stage.

ALBERT EICHLER: Die frühneuenglische Volksbühne. I. II. In: GRM. Jg. 3, 1911, S. 461–75 und 542–57. Rev.: Sh. Jg. 48, 1912, S. 252–3, C. Grabau.
Comprehensive essay giving a survey of the sources of our knowledge of stage conditions and of all previous works on the subject.

WILLIAM J. LAWRENCE: The evolution and influence of the Elizabethan playhouse. In: Sh. Jb. Jg. 47, 1911, S. 18–41.

LEO PILCH: Shakespeare als Regisseur. In: Z. f. e. U., Bd. 10, 1911, S. 385–406.
Attempts to show that Shakespeare indicates in his text the scenery to be used.

SIEGFRIED MAUERMANN: Die Bühnenanweisungen im deutschen Drama bis 1700. Berlin, 1911. (xxix, 248 S.)=Palaestra 102. Rev.: Sh. Jb. 48, 1912, S. 330–1, M. Förster.

GEORGE F. REYNOLDS: What we know of the Elizabethan stage. In: Mod. Phil., vol. 9, 1911–12, pp. 47–82. Rev.: Sh. Jb. 48, 1912, S. 253–4, C. Grabau; Dt. Litztg. 1912, Sp. 298–9, A. Eichler.
A general survey.

WILLIAM J. LAWRENCE: The Elizabethan playhouse and other studies. Stratford-upon-Avon, 1912, 1913. Rev.: Sh. Jb. 50, 1914, S. 172–3, A. Brandl.
For list of contents cf. p. 121.

WILLIAM J. LAWRENCE: Light and darkness in the Elizabethan theatre. In: E. St. Bd. 45, 1912, S. 181–200.
On stage illumination in the Elizabethan theatre.

WILLIAM J. LAWRENCE: Windows on the Pre-Restoration stage. In: Anglia Bd. 36, 1912, S. 450–78.

THORNTON SHIRLEY GRAVES: The court and the London theatres during the reign of Queen Elizabeth. Diss. Chicago. Menasha, Wis., 1913. (93 pp.) Rev.: Sh. Jb. 52, 1916, S. 198–9, A. Brandl.
Assumes that the popular playhouse stage was well equipped and decorated.

A. KÖSTER: Die Einrichtung der Bühne zu Shakespeares Zeit. Festvortrag. [Not given in full.] In: Sh. Jb. Jg. 50, 1914, S. xxvii–xxx.

T. S. GRAVES: The origin of the custom of sitting on the stage. In: JEGPh., vol. 13, 1914, pp. 104–9.

T. S. GRAVES: Night scenes in the Elizabethan theatres. In: E. St. Bd. 47, 1914, S. 63–71.

WILLIAM J. LAWRENCE: Night performances in the Elizabethan theatres. A reply to Dr. T. S. Graves. In: E. St. Bd. 48, 1915, S. 213–30.

WILLIAM J. LAWRENCE: The Elizabethan stage throne. In: Texas Rev., Jan. 1918.

R. CROMPTON RHODES: The stagery of Shakspere. Birmingham, 1922. (xi, 102 pp.) Rev.: MLR. 18, 1923, pp. 485–6, E. K. Chambers.

LILY B. CAMPBELL: Scenes and machines on the English stage during the Renaissance. A classical revival. C.U.P., 1923. (x, 302 pp.)

WILLIAM J. LAWRENCE: Bells on the Elizabethan stage. In: Fortnightly Rev., July, 1924.

WILLIAM J. LAWRENCE: Pre-Restoration stage studies. Cambridge, Harv. Univ. Pr., 1927. (viii, 435 pp.) Rev.: MLN. 43, 1928, pp. 119–20, L. B. Wright; TLS., Dec. 8, 1927.

WILLIAM J. LAWRENCE: The physical conditions of the Elizabethan public playhouse. Cambridge, Harv. Univ. Pr., & O.U.P., 1927. (viii, 129 pp.) Rev.: Sh. Jb. 63, 1927, S. 204–5, W. Keller; MLN. 43, 1928, pp. 118–20, L. B. Wright; TLS., Dec. 8, 1927, p. 927; JEGPh. 28, 1929, pp. 433–7, J. Q. Adams.

LOUIS B. WRIGHT: Elizabethan sea drama and its staging. In: Anglia. Bd. 51, 1927, S. 104–18.

(2) THE ACTORS AND THEIR ART

(a) CHILD-ACTORS

A. ALBRECHT: Das englische Kindertheater. Diss. Halle, 1883. (56 S.)

H. MAAS: Die Kindertruppen, ein Kapitel aus der Geschichte der englischen Theatergesellschaften in dem Zeitraum von 1559–1642. Diss. Göttingen, 1901. (28 S. und 1 Tab.)

CHARLES W. WALLACE: The Children of the Chapel at Blackfriars, 1597–1603. Introductory to the Children of the Revels, their origin, course and influences. A history based upon original records, documents and plays, being a contribution to the knowledge of the stage and drama of Shakespeare's time. Lincoln, Nebraska, 1908. (xvi, 207 pp.) Rev.: Sh. Jb. 45, 1909, S. 323–6, A. Brandl; MLR. 5, 1910, pp. 224–7, E. K. Chambers.

CHARLOTTE C. STOPES: William Hunnis and the Revels of the Chapel Royal. A study of his period and the influences which affected Shakespeare.

Louvain, 1910. (xiv, 360 pp.)=Mat. z. Kunde des ält. engl. Dramas, Bd. 29. Rev.: Libr., 3rd ser., vol. 2, 1911, pp. 217–19.

A study of the life and influence of this Master of the Chapel Royal.

JOHN MATTHEWS MANLY: The Children of the Chapel Royal and their masters. In: CHEL., vol. 6, 1910, pp. 279–92.

With bibliography.

HAROLD N. HILLEBRAND: The early history of the Chapel Royal. In: Mod. Phil., vol. 18, 1920, pp. 233–68.

HAROLD N. HILLEBRAND: The Children of the King's Revels at Whitefriars. In: JEGPh., vol. 21, 1922, pp. 318–34.

HAROLD N. HILLEBRAND: The child-actors. A chapter in Elizabethan stage history. Urbana, 1926. (355 pp.)=Univ. of Illinois Stud. in lang. and lit. XI, 1, 2. Rev.: Sh. Jb. 63, 1927, S. 206–7, W. Keller; Arch. 152, 1927, S. 295; RESt. 3, 1927, pp. 482–4, R. E. Brettle; E. St. 63, 1928, S. 101–7, E. Eckhardt; MLN. 48, 1928, pp. 199–201, G. F. Reynolds; JEGPh. 27, 1928, pp. 434–7, T. Brooke; MLR. 23, 1928, pp. 76–7, W. W. Greg; Mod. Phil. 24, 1927, pp. 498–9, Baskervill.

Detailed account of the child-actors and their influence on the dramatic literature of the time.

PHILIPP ARONSTEIN: Die englischen Knabentheater und ihr Drama. In: N. Spr. Bd. 35, 1927, S. 427–39.

(b) DRAMATIC COMPANIES

JAMES GREENSTREET: Documents relating to the players at the Red Bull, Clerkenwell, and the Cockpit in Drury Lane in the time of James I. In: New Sh. Soc. 1880–5.

JAMES O. HALLIWELL-PHILLIPS: Visits of Shakespeare's company of actors to the provincial cities and towns of England. Brighton, 1887.

JOHN T. MURRAY: English dramatic companies in the towns outside of London, 1550–1600. In: Mod. Phil., vol. 2, 1905, pp. 539–59.

HERMANN MAAS: Äussere Geschichte der englischen Theatertruppen in dem Zeitraum von 1559–1642. Louvain, 1907. (x, 283 S.)=Mat. z. Kunde des älteren engl. Dramas, Bd. 19. Rev.: Sh. Jb. 44, 1908, S. 365, M. Förster; Dt. Litztg. 1908, Sp. 1713 ff., A. Eichler.

A comprehensive account of the results of previous research.

JOHN TUCKER MURRAY: English dramatic companies, 1558–1642. Vol. I: London companies. Vol. II: Provincial companies. London, 1910. (xvi, 370 and xii, 434 pp.) Rev.: Sh. Jb. 47, 1911, S. 350–1, M. Förster.

History of the various troupes and accounts of their performances.

CHARLES WILLIAM WALLACE: The Swan theatre and the Earl of Pembroke's servants. In: E. St. Bd. 43, 1910–11, S. 340–95.

ALWIN THALER: The Elizabethan dramatic companies. In: PMLA., vol. 35, N.S. vol. 28, 1920, pp. 123–59.

E. K. CHAMBERS: The companies. In the same author's: The Elizabethan stage. Oxford, 1923.

A detailed account with sources and bibliography.

(c) ENGLISH PLAYERS ON THE CONTINENT

(a) COLLECTIONS OF THEIR PLAYS AND GENERAL TREATISES

For bibliography cf. K. GOEDEKES Grundriss zur Geschichte der deutschen Dichtung, 10 Bde. Dresden, 1884–1913[2].

ALBERT COHN: Shakespeare in Germany in the 16th and 17th centuries. An account of English actors in Germany and the Netherlands and of the plays performed by them during the same period. London, 1865. (cxxxviii, 422 pp.)

JULIUS TITTMANN: Die Schauspiele der englischen Komödianten in Deutschland. Leipzig, 1880. (lxii, 248 S.)=Deutsche Dichter des 16. Jhrh., hrsg. von K. Goedeke und J. Tittmann, Bd. 13.

WILHELM CREIZENACH: Die Schauspiele der englischen Komödianten. Berlin & Stuttgart [1889]=Kürschners Dt. National-Literatur, Bd. 23. Rev.: Zs. f. vgl. Lit. Gesch. N. F. Bd. 3, 1890, S. 146 ff., M. Koch.

The introduction contains a detailed and authoritative account of the English Players. Five German stage-versions of the following plays are reprinted in the text: Titus Andronicus, Was ihr wollt, Hamlet, Tragikomödie (Rosalina), Die Tragödie vom unzeitigen Vorwitz.

EMIL HERZ: Englische Schauspieler und englisches Schauspiel zur Zeit Shakespeares in Deutschland. (1. Teil.) Diss. Bonn, 1901. (64 S.) Printed in full in: Theatergeschichtl. Forsch., hrsg. v. B. Litzmann, No. 18. Hamburg & Leipzig, 1903. (x, 144 S.) Rev.: Sh. Jb. 40, 1904, S. 281–3, A. Hauffen; Dt. Litztg. 1904, A. v. Weilen; Zs. f. dt. Phil. Bd. 36, Witkowski.

An account of the wanderings of the English Players and their repertoire.

JOHANNES BOLTE: Die Singspiele der englischen Komödianten und ihrer Nachfolger in Deutschland, Holland und Skandinavien. Hamburg & Leipzig, 1893. (vii, 194 S.)=Theatergeschichtl. Forsch., hrsg. von B. Litzmann, VII.

Description and collection of plays.

JOHANNES BOLTE: Das Danziger Theater im 16. und 17. Jhrh. Hamburg & Leipzig, 1895=Theatergeschichtl. Forsch., hrsg. von B. Litzmann, No. 12.

W. J. LAWRENCE: Shakespeare and the Italian comedians. In: TLS., Nov. 11, 1920.

ALWIN THALER: The travelling players in Shakespeare's England. In: Mod. Phil., vol. 17, 1920, pp. 489–514.

ALWIN THALER: Strolling players and provincial drama after Shakspere. In: PMLA., vol. 37, 1922, pp. 243–80.

GUSTAF FREDÉN: A propos du théâtre anglais en Allemagne. L'auteur inconnu des 'Comédies et tragédies anglaises' de 1620. In: Rev. de litt. comp., vol. 8, 1928, pp. 420–32.

S

(β) SPECIAL ESSAYS ON VISITS TO VARIOUS CITIES AND COUNTRIES

JOHANNES MEISSNER: Die englischen Komödianten in Österreich. In: Sh. Jb. Jg. 19, 1884, S. 113–54.

KARL TRAUTMANN: Englische Komödianten in Nürnberg bis zum Schlusse des 30jährigen Krieges (1593–1648). Ein englischen Springer am Hofe zu Turin (1665). Eine Augsburger Lear-Aufführung (1665). Engl. Komödianten in Stuttgart (1600, 1609, 1613–14) und Tübingen (1597). Engl. Komödianten in Ulm 1602. In: Arch. f. Lit. gesch. Bd. 14 und 15, 1886–7.

ALBERT COHN: Englische Komödianten in Köln (1592–1656). In: Sh. Jb. Jg. 21, 1886, S. 245–76.

ALBERT COHN: König Lear 1692 und Titus Andronicus 1699 in Breslau aufgeführt. In: Sh. Jb. Jg. 23, 1888.

JOHANNES BOLTE: Englische Komödianten in Dänemark und Schweden. In: Sh. Jb. Jg. 23, 1888, S. 99–106.

C. F. MEYER: Englische Komödianten am Hofe des Herzogs Philipp Julius v. Pommern-Wolgast. In: Sh. Jb. Jg. 38, 1902, S. 196–211.

ALOIS BRANDL: Englische Komödianten in Frankfurt. In: Sh. Jb. Jg. 40, 1904, S. 229–30.

FRANCES A. YATES: English actors in Paris during the lifetime of Shakespeare. In: RESt., vol. 1, 1925, pp. 392–403.

(d) INDIVIDUAL ACTORS

J. PAYNE COLLIER: Memoirs of the principal actors in the plays of Shakespeare. In: Sh. Soc. Publ. 1846.

E. K. CHAMBERS: Actors. In the same writer's: The Elizabethan stage, vol. 2, 1923, pp. 295–350.
Deals with the well-known actors in alphabetical order.

ALLISON GAW: Actors' names in basic Shakespearean texts, with special reference to Romeo and Juliet and Much Ado. In: PMLA., vol. 40, 1925, pp. 530–50.

EDMUND K. CHAMBERS: Elizabethan stage gleanings. In: RESt., vol. 1, 1925, pp. 75–8 and 182–6.

EDWIN NUNGEZER: A dictionary of actors and of other persons associated with the public representation of plays in England before 1642. New Haven, 1929. (vi, 438 pp.) = Cornell Stud. in English, xiii. Rev.: MLN. 45, 1930, pp. 331–3, G. E. Bentley; RESt. 6, 1930, pp. 359–60, W. W. Greg.

G. E. BENTLEY: New actors of the Elizabethan period. In: MLN., vol. 44, 1929, pp. 368–72. ————

J. PAYNE COLLIER: Memoirs of Edward *Alleyn*, founder of Dulwich College, including some new particulars respecting Shakespeare, Ben Jonson, Massinger, Marston, Dekker, etc. London, 1841. (219 pp.)

J. PAYNE COLLIER: A collection of original documents illustrative of the life and times of Edward Alleyn and of the early English stage and drama. 2 vols. =Sh. Soc. Publ., vol. 18. London, 1843.

WILLIAM YOUNG: The history of Dulwich College. With a life of Edward Alleyn. 2 vols. Edinburgh, 1889.

W. W. GREY: Edward Alleyn. In: The Shakespeare Assoc. 1925–6. London, 1927, pp. 1–34. Rev.: Sh. Jb. 64, 1928, S. 194, W. Keller.

AUSTIN K. GRAY: Robert *Armine*, the foole. In: PMLA., vol. 42, 1927, pp. 673–85.

CHARLOTTE C. STOPES: *Burbage* and Shakespeare's stage. London, 1913. (xvi, 272 pp.) Rev.: Sh. Jb. 50, 1914, S. 212, M. Förster; MLN. 29, 1914, pp. 6–11, W. Nicholson.
Biographical notes concerning James and Richard Burbage.

ALLISON GAW: John *Sincklo* as one of Shakespeare's actors. In: Anglia Bd. 49, 1926, S. 289–303.

J. O. HALLIWELL: *Tarlton's* jests and news out of purgatory. With notes and some account of the life of Tarlton. London, Sh. Soc., 1844. (xlviii, 136 pp.)

(e) ANIMALS AS ACTORS ON THE ELIZABETHAN STAGE

T. S. GRAVES: The ass as actor. In: South Atlantic Quart., vol. 15, 1916, pp. 175–82.

W. STRUNK, JR.: The Elizabethan showman's ape. In: MLN., vol. 32, 1917, pp. 215–21.

T. S. GRAVES: The Elizabethan trained ape. In: MLN., vol. 35, 1920, pp. 248–9.

LOUIS B. WRIGHT: Animal actors on the English stage before 1642. In: PMLA., vol. 42, 1927, pp. 656–69.

(f) INTERNAL ORGANIZATION OF THE ELIZABETHAN THEATRE (RELATIONS OF ACTORS, MANAGERS, AND AUDIENCES)

SAMUEL H. WANDELL: The law of the theatre. A treatise on the legal relations of actors, managers, and audiences. New York, 1891.

HERMANN MAAS: Äussere Geschichte der englischen Theatertruppen in dem Zeitraum von 1559–1642. Louvain, 1907. (x, 283 S.)=Mat. z. Kunde des ält. engl. Dramas, Bd. 19. Rev.: Sh. Jb. 44, 1908, S. 365, M. Förster; Dt. Litztg. 1908, Sp. 1713 ff., A. Eichler.
The third essay discusses the business and financial aspects of the theatre and its organization.

CHARLES W. WALLACE: Discussions of the Globe and Blackfriars systems of finance. In: TLS., Oct. 2 and 9, 1909.

PHILIPP ARONSTEIN: Die Organisation des englischen Schauspiels im Zeitalter Shakespeares. I. II. In: GRM. Jg. 2, 1910, S. 165–75 und 216–31. Rev.: Sh. Jb. 47, 1911, S. 281, C. Grabau.

ALWIN THALER: Finance and business management of the Elizabethan theatre. MS. Diss. Harv. Univ., 1918.

ALWIN THALER: The 'free-list' and theatre tickets in Shakespeare's time and after. In: MLR., vol. 15, 1920, pp. 124–36.

ALWIN THALER: Shakspere to Sheridan. A book about the theatre of yesterday and to-day. Cambridge, Mass., & London, 1922. (xviii, 339 pp.)

Describes the internal conditions of the theatre from Shakespeare up to the end of the XVIIIth century. The author gives in an appendix a list of prices of admission up to 1642.

ALWIN THALER: Minor actors and employees in the Elizabethan theater. In: Mod. Phil., vol. 20, 1922, pp. 49–60.

KARL J. HOLZKNECHT: Theatrical billposting in the age of Elizabeth. In: Philol. Quart., Oct. 1923, pp. 267–81.

THORNTON S. GRAVES: Women on the Pre-Restoration stage. In: Stud. in Philol., vol. 22, 1925, pp. 184–97.

THOMAS W. BALDWIN: The organization and personnel of the Shakespearean Company. Princeton Univ. Pr. & London, 1927. (xii, 464 pp.) Rev.: Sh. Jb. 64, 1928, S. 191–3, W. Keller; TLS., Dec. 15, 1927, p. 954; JEGPh. 27, 1928, pp. 558–65, T. M. Parrott.

A comprehensive survey.

F. P. WILSON: Ralph Crane, scrivener to the King's Players. In: Libr., 1927.

(g) THE ART OF THE ACTOR IN THE TIME OF SHAKESPEARE

(a) GENERAL

GEORGE HENRY LEWES: On actors and the art of acting. Leipzig, 1875.

KARL ELZE: Eine Aufführung im Globus-Theater. Vortrag. In: Sh. Jb. Jg. 14, 1879, S. 1–20.

PERCY SIMPSON: Actors and acting. In: Shakespeare's England, 1917. Vol. ii, pp. 240–82.

GEORGE F. REYNOLDS: What we know of the Elizabethan stage. In: Mod. Phil., vol. 9, 1911–12, pp. 47–82. Rev.: Sh. Jb. 48, 1912, S. 253–4, C. Grabau; Dt. Litztg. 1912, Sp. 298–9, A. Eichler.

Deals with the principles of stage-management.

GEORG HERM. REESE: Studien und Beiträge zur Geschichte der engl. Schauspielkunst im Zeitalter Shakespeares. Diss. Jena, 1911. (36 S.)

Study of the costume of stage-types.

ELISABETH WINNINGHOFF: Das Theaterkostüm bei Shakespeare. Diss. Münster, 1928. (85 S.) Rev.: Sh. Jb. 65, 1929, S. 193–4, W. Keller.

GEORG HARTMANN: Die Gesten bei Shakespeare als Ausdruck von Gemütsbewegungen. MS. Diss. Leipzig, 1921–2. Published under the title: Die

Bühnengesten in Shakespeares Dramen als Ausdruck von Gemütsbewegungen. Ein Beitrag zur Geschichte der Schauspieltechnik im elisabethanischen Zeitalter. In: Sh. Jb. Jg. 59–60, N.F. Bd. 1, 1924, S. 41–61.

———

NICOLAUS DELIUS: Die Bühnenweisungen in den alten Shakespeare-Ausgaben.
In: Sh. Jb. Jg. 8, 1873, S. 171–201.

A collection of the stage directions in the Quartos and Folios.

(β) 'ACT TIME'; ACT AND SCENE DIVISIONS; INTERVALS AND HOW FILLED

THORNTON SHIRLEY GRAVES: The 'act time' in Elizabethan theatres. In: Stud.
in Phil., vol. 12, 1915, pp. 103–4. Rev.: Sh. Jb. 52, 1916, S. 200–2, A. Brandl;
MLR. 11, 1916, pp. 96–8, W. J. Lawrence.

J. DOVER WILSON: Introduction to 'The Tempest' in the New Cambridge
Shakespeare, 1921.

Wilson assumes that there were no intervals between scenes and acts.

R. CROMPTON RHODES: The stagery of Shakespeare. Birmingham, 1922. (xi,
102 pp.)

MARK HUNTER: Act- and scene-division in the plays of Shakespeare. In: RESt.,
vol. 2, 1926, pp. 295–310.

Attempts to disprove Wilson's view.

JOHN DOVER WILSON: Act- and scene-divisions in the plays of Shakespeare.
A rejoinder to Sir Mark Hunter. In: RESt., vol. 3, 1927, pp. 385–97.

W. J. LAWRENCE: Act-intervals in early Shakespearean performances. In:
RESt., vol. 4, 1928, pp. 78–9.

Lawrence assumes that there were intervals.

W. W. GREG: Act-divisions in Shakespeare. In: RESt., vol. 4, 1928, pp. 152–8.

J. DOVER WILSON: 'They sleepe all the act'. In: RESt., vol. 4, 1928, pp. 191–3.

For Inter-act music cf. pp. 106–107.

(γ) COMMEDIA DELL' ARTE

(aa) *The Italian Improvised Comedy*

WINIFRED SMITH: The commedia dell' arte. A study in Italian popular comedy.
New York, 1912. (xv, 290 pp.)=Columbia Univ. Stud. in English and
compar. lit. Cf. Chap. IV: The commedia dell' arte in Elizabethan and
Jacobean England, pp. 170–99. Rev.: Sh. Jb. 49, 1913, S. 252–3, M. Förster;
JEGPh. 13, 1914, pp. 368–70, V. L. Parsons; MLR. 8, 1913, pp. 563–6,
C. Foligno; Bbl. 25, 1914, S. 36–8, A. Feuillerat.

ENZO PETRACCONE: La commedia dell' arte. Storia, tecnica, scenari. Napoli,
1927. (viii, 458 pp.) Rev.: Lit. Zbl. 1928, Sp. 897, H. Schneider.

CONSTANT MIC: La commedia dell' arte. Paris, 1927. Rev.: MLN. 43, 1928,
pp. 489–90, Winifred Smith.

Good account with full bibliography.

PIERRE LOUIS DUCHARTRE: The Italian comedy. The improvisation, scenarios, lives, attributes, portraits, and masks of the illustrious characters of the commedia dell' arte. Authorized translation from the French by RANDOLPH T. WEAVER. London, 1929. (336 pp.)

(bb) *Shakespeare and the Improvised Comedy*

MAX J. WOLFF: Shakespeare und die Commedia dell' arte. In: Sh. Jb. Jg. 46, 1910, S. 1–20.

S. T. GRAVES: Some aspects of extemporal acting. In: Stud. in Phil., vol. 19, 1922, pp. 429–56.

LOUIS B. WRIGHT: Will Kemp and the commedia dell' arte. In: MLN., vol. 41, 1926, pp. 516–20.

G. S. GARGANO: La commedia dell' arte e l'antico teatro inglese. In: Marzocco, 1928.

WILHELM MARSCHALL: Das 'Sir Thomas Moore'-Manuskript und die englische Commedia dell' arte. In: Anglia Bd. 52, 1928, S. 193–241.

In agreement with Collier's views, Marschall regards the theatrical plots as plans of improvised plays.

WILHELM MARSCHALL: Die neun Dichter des Hamlet. Heidelberg (1928). (75 S.)

Regards Hamlet as commedia dell' arte and attempts to analyse the style of the nine improvisors.

KATHLEEN M. LEA: Sir Aston Cokayne and the commedia dell' arte. In: MLR., vol. 23, 1928, pp. 47–51.

(δ) DRAMATIC PLOTS (STAGE ABRIDGEMENTS)

W. W. GREG: Henslowe Papers, being documents supplementary to Henslowe's Diary. London, 1907. Appendix II: Dramatic plots.

W. W. GREG: 'Bad' quartos outside Shakespeare. 'Alcazar' and 'Orlando'. In: Libr., 3rd ser., vol. 10, 1919, pp. 193–222.

W. W. GREG: Two Elizabethan stage abridgements, the Battle of Alcazar and Orlando Furioso. An essay in critical bibliography. O.U.P., 1923. (vii, 366 pp.) Rev.: Libr. iv, 1923, pp. 242–8, E. K. Chambers; JEGPh. 23, 1924, pp. 605–9, J. Q. Adams.

W. W. GREG: The evidence of theatrical plots for the history of the Elizabethan stage. In: RESt., vol. 1, 1925, pp. 257–74.

B. A. P. VAN DAM: Alleyn's player's part of Greene's Orlando Furioso, and the text of the Q of 1594. In: Engl. Studies, vol. 11, 1929, pp. 182–203.

(ε) THE DOUBLING OF ROLES AND NUMBER OF ACTORS

W. STREIT: The Life and Death of Thomas Lord Cromwell. Eine literar-historische Untersuchung. Diss. Jena, 1904. (64 S.)

Proves that the 45 characters of the drama can be played by 10 actors.

K. GLATHE: Die Schauspielerzahl in Shakespeares Historien. MS. Diss. Leipzig, 1924.

J. KLEMENZ: Rollenkumulation in Shakespeares Tragödien. MS. Diss. Leipzig, 1925.

JULIA ENGELEN: Die Schauspieler-Ökonomie in Shakespeares Dramen. Diss. Münster, 1926. (97 S.) Also in: Sh. Jb. Jg. 62, 1926, S. 44–97 und Jg. 63, 1927, S. 75–158.

WILLIAM J. LAWRENCE: The practice of doubling and its influence on early dramaturgy. In his Pre-Restoration stage studies. Harv. Univ. Pr., 1927, pp. 43–78.

THOMAS W. BALDWIN: The organization and personnel of the Shakespearean Company. Princeton Univ. Press & London, 1927. (xii, 464 pp.)

MARIA SACK: Darstellerzahl und Rollenverteilung bei Shakespeare. Leipzig, 1928. (76 S.)=Beitr. z. engl. Phil., hrsg. von M. Förster, H. 8. Rev.: Bbl. 40, 1929, S. 114–15, H. Richter.

X. LITERARY TASTE IN SHAKESPEARE'S TIME

(1) THEORETICAL WORKS OF THE ENGLISH RENAISSANCE PERIOD

(a) SOURCES

G. GREGORY SMITH: Elizabethan critical essays. With an introduction. 2 vols. Oxford, 1904. (xcii, 431 and iv, 509 pp.)

CONTENTS:
Vol. I: ROGER ASCHAM: Of imitation. From The Scholemaster, Book II. 1570. pp. 1–45.

RICHARD WILLES: From: Poematum Liber. 1573. Footnote, pp. 46–7.

GEORGE GASCOIGNE: Certayne notes of instruction. 1575. pp. 46–57.

GEORGE WHETSTONE: The dedication to Promos and Cassandra. 1578. pp. 58–60.

THOMAS LODGE: Defence of poetry. 1579. pp. 61–86. Contains: Bibliographical list of pamphlets for and against the stage.

SPENSER-HARVEY correspondence. 1579–80. pp. 87–126.

E. K.: Epistle dedicatory to The Shepheards Calender. 1579. pp. 127–34.

RICHARD STANYHURST: From the dedication and preface to the translation of the Aeneid. 1582. pp. 135–47.

SIR PHILIP SIDNEY: An apologie for poetrie. c. 1583 (printed 1595). pp. 148–207.

KING JAMES VI: Ane schort treatise conteining some reulis and cautelis to be obseruit and eschewit in Scottis poesie. 1584. pp. 208–25.

WILLIAM WEBBE: A discourse of English poetry. 1586. pp. 226–302.

ABRAHAM FRAUNCE: From The Arcadian rhetorike. 1588. pp. 303–6.

THOMAS NASH: I. Preface to Greene's Menaphon. 1589. pp. 307–20. II. From The anatomie of absurditie, 1589. pp. 321–37.

Appendix: From: E. Hoby's translation of Coignet's Politique discourses. 1586. pp. 339–44.

Vol. II: GEORGE PUTTENHAM: The arte of English poesie. 1589. pp. 1–193.

SIR JOHN HARINGTON: A preface, or rather a briefe apologie of poetrie, prefixed to the translation of Orlando Furioso. 1591. pp. 194–222.

THOMAS NASH: Preface to Sidney's Astrophel and Stella. 1591. pp. 223–8.

GABRIEL HARVEY: From: Foure letters. 1592. pp. 229–38.

THOMAS NASH: From: Strange newes, or foure letters confuted. 1592. pp. 239–44.

GABRIEL HARVEY: I. From: Pierce's supererogation. 1593. pp. 245–82. II. From: A new letter of notable contents. 1593. pp. 282–4.

RICHARD CAREW: The excellency of the English tongue. ?1595–6. pp. 285–94.

GEORGE CHAPMAN: I. Preface to Seaven bookes of the Iliades of Homere. 1598. pp. 295–7. II. Dedication, &c. of Achilles Shield. 1598. pp. 297–307.

FRANCIS MERES: From: Palladis Tamia. 1598. pp. 308–24.

WILLIAM VAUGHAN: From: The golden grove. 1600. pp. 325–6.

THOMAS CAMPION: Observations in the art of English poesie. 1602. pp. 327–55.

SAMUEL DANIEL: A defence of ryme. ?1603. pp. 356–84.

Appendix:

I. Ben Jonson: I and II. From: Every man in his humour. pp. 387–90. III. From: Every man out of his humour. pp. 390–3. IV. From: The poetaster. pp. 393–7.

II. The returne from Parnassus, 1601. Part II, I (ii). pp. 398–403.

(b) TREATISES ON THE ELIZABETHAN CRITICS

H. BERLI: GABRIEL *Harvey*, der Dichterfreund und Kritiker. Diss. Zürich, 1913. (151 S.)

PHIL. ARONSTEIN: BEN *Jonson's* Theorie des Lustspieles. In: Anglia Bd. 17, 1895, S. 466–85.

H. REINSCH: Ben Jonson's Poetik und seine Beziehungen zu Horaz. Leipzig & München, 1899. (x, 130 S.)=Münch. Beitr. z. roman. und engl. Philol., hrsg. v. Breymann und J. Schick, H. 16. Rev.: Litbl. 21, 1900, Sp. 12–14, O. Glöde; Bbl. 11, 1900, S. 159–61, R. Fischer.

HELMUTH GROSSMANN: Ben Jonson als Kritiker. Diss. Jena, 1898. (33 S.)

J. J. JUSSERAND: Ben Jonson's views on Shakespeare's art. In his The school for ambassadors, and other essays. London, 1924. (359 pp.) No. 8.

WILLIAM L. RUSHTON: Shakespeare and 'The arte of English poesie'. [*Puttenham*]. Liverpool, 1909. (167 pp.) Rev.: Sh. Jb. 45, 1909, S. 396, M. Förster.

IDA LANGTON: Materials for a study of *Spenser's* theory of fine art. Ithaca, N.Y., 1911. (vii and lxiii and 118 pp.) Rev.: Sh. Jb. 49, 1913, S. 220–1, L. L. Schücking.

(2) GENERAL WORKS ON ENGLISH RENAISSANCE CRITICISM

KARL BORINSKI: Die Poetik der Renaissance und die Anfänge der literarischen Kritik in Deutschland. Berlin, 1886.

JOEL ELIAS SPINGARN: A history of literary criticism in the Renaissance. New York, 1899, 1908². Rev.: Bbl. 16, 1905, S. 353–9, K. D. Bülbring.
With bibliography.

KARL VOSSLER: Poetische Theorien in der italienischen Frührenaissance. Berlin, 1900. = Lit.histor. Forsch., hrsg. von Schick und von Waldberg. H. 12.

GEORGE SAINTSBURY: A history of criticism and literary taste in Europe from the earliest times to the present day. 3 vols. London, 1900–4.

HAROLD S. SYMMES: Les débuts de la critique dramatique en Angleterre jusqu'à la mort de Shakespeare. Diss. Paris, 1903. (xiv, 276 pp.) Rev.: Sh. Jb. 40, 1904, S. 252–3, A. Brandl; JEGPh. 5, 1903–5, pp. 186–9, E. N. S. Thompson.
With very extensive bibliography.

DAVID KLEIN: Literary criticism from the Elizabethan dramatists, repertory and synthesis, with an introductory note by J. E. SPINGARN. New York, 1910. (xviii, 257 pp.) Rev.: Sh. Jb. 48, 1912, S. 293–4, L. L. Schücking; MLR. 7, 1912, pp. 251–2, J. W. H. Atkins.

GEORGE SAINTSBURY: A history of English criticism. London, 1911, 1925. (xii, 551 pp.)

OTTO DIEDE: Der Streit der Alten und Modernen in der englischen Literaturgeschichte des 16. und 17. Jahrhunderts. Diss. Greifswald, 1912. (139 S.) Rev.: Bbl. 23, 1912, S. 319–21, Ph. Aronstein.
A short history of literary criticism up to 1700.

KARL BORINSKI: Die Antike in Poetik und Kunsttheorie. Leipzig, 1914. (xv, 324 S.)=Das Erbe der Antike, Bd. I, H. 9. Rev.: Sh. Jb. 51, 1915, S. 248–50, A. Brandl.
CONTENTS: I. Mittelalter; II. Frührenaissance; III. Hochrenaissance und Barock; IV. Poetik der Renaissance.

B. WILLEY: Tendencies in Renaissance literary theory. 1922.

DONALD L. CLARK: Rhetoric and poetry in the Renaissance. A study of rhetorical terms in English Renaissance literary criticism. New York, 1922. (x, 166 pp.)=Columbia Univ. Studies in English and Comparative Literature.

PAUL KAUFMAN: Heralds of original genius. In: Essays in memory of Barrett Wendell. Cambridge, Mass., 1926.

HANS THÜME: Beiträge zur Geschichte des Geniebegriffs in England. Halle, 1927. (ix, 102 S.)=Stud. z. engl. Philol., hrsg. von L. Morsbach und H. Hecht, H. 71. Rev.: JEGPh. 28, 1929, pp. 314–16, E. C. Knowlton.
Includes: 'Die elisabethanischen Kritiker (Produktivität und Phantasie des poetischen Schaffens): Lodge, Chapman, König Jacob, Harvey, Puttenham, Shakespeare.'

(3) THE ELIZABETHAN THEATRE PUBLIC; POPULAR TASTE AND THE LITERARY TASTE OF THE PERIOD IN GENERAL

GUSTAV RÜMELIN: Für wen dichtete Shakespeare? In his Shakespeare-Studien. Stuttgart, 1874², S. 34–59.

THEODOR VATKE: Das Theater und das Londoner Publikum in Shakespeares Zeit. In: Sh. Jb. Jg. 21, 1886, S. 227–44.

J. NAUMANN: Die Geschmacksrichtungen im englischen Drama bis zur Schliessung der Theater durch die Puritaner nach Theorie und Praxis der Dichter charakterisiert. Diss. Rostock, 1900. (75 S.)

HAROLD BAYLEY: The Shakespeare symphony. An introduction to the ethics of the Elizabethan drama. London, 1906, 1908². (ix, 393 pp.) Rev.: Sh. Jb. 45, 1909, S. 395–6, M. Förster.
Points out common features in the ideas of the Elizabethan dramatists.

GEORGE PIERCE BAKER: The development of Shakespeare as a dramatist. New York, 1907. (x, 329 pp.) Rev.: Sh. Jb. 44, 1908, S. 325–7, W. Keller.
The author defends the view that Shakespeare allowed himself to be guided by public taste.

SIDNEY LEE: Shakespeare and the Elizabethan playgoer. In his Shakespeare and the modern stage. London, 1907, pp. 25–48.

LEVIN L. SCHÜCKING: Shakespeare im literarischen Urteil seiner Zeit. Heidelberg, 1908. (viii, 196 S.) Rev.: Sh. Jb. 45, 1909, S. 354–5, R. Fischer; Bbl. 20, 1909, S. 97–102, Ph. Aronstein.

W. J. COURTHOPE: A history of English poetry. Vol. 4: Development and decline of the poetic drama; influence of the court and the people. London, 1911. (xxix, 476 pp.)

CHARLES J. SISSON: Le goût public et le théâtre élisabéthain jusqu' à la mort de Shakespeare. Dijon, 1922. (196 pp.) Rev.: Bbl. 35, 1924, S. 16–20, B. Fehr.

G. B. HARRISON: Books and readers, 1591–94. In: Libr., N.S. vol. 8, 1927, pp. 273–302.
An attempt to determine public taste from the books entered in the Stationers' Register, 1591–94.

ROBERT BRIDGES: The influence of the audience on Shakespeare's drama. O.U.P., 1927. (29 pp.)=Collected Essays I. Rev.: Sh. Jb. 64, 1928, S. 193–4, W. Keller; Bbl. 39, 1928, S. 263–5, H. T. Price.

M. ST. CLARE BYRNE: Shakespeare's audience. In: The Shakespeare Assoc., 1925–6. London, 1927. pp. 186–216.

XI. AESTHETIC CRITICISM OF SHAKESPEARE
(1) XVIITH AND XVIIITH CENTURY CRITICISM
(*a*) SOURCES

D. NICHOL SMITH: Eighteenth century essays on Shakespeare. Glasgow, 1903. (lxiii, 358 pp.) Reprints of the following essays:

ROWE: Some account of the life, &c., of Mr. William Shakespear (1709), pp. 1–23; DENNIS: On the genius and writings of Shakespeare (1711), pp. 24–46; Prefaces to the editions of POPE (1725), pp. 47–62; THEOBALD (1733), pp. 61–91; HANMER (1744), pp. 92–5; WARBURTON (1747), pp. 96–111; JOHNSON (1765), pp. 112–61; FARMER: Essay on the learning of Shakespeare (1767), pp. 162–215; MORGANN: Essay on the dramatic character of Sir John Falstaff (1777), pp. 216–303.

BEVERLY WARNER: Famous introductions to Shakespeare's plays by the notable editors of the 18th century. Ed. with a critical introduction, biographical and explanatory notes. New York, 1906. (xxxiv, 268 pp.) Rev.: Sh. Jb. 43, 1907, S. 277–9, W. Keller.

Warner includes later editors not to be found in Nichol Smith's collection (cf. above), and gives the introductions of Steevens 1766, Capell 1768, Reed 1785, and Malone 1790.

D. NICHOL SMITH: Shakespearean Criticism (Heminge and Condell to Carlyle). With an introduction. 1916. (xxxii, 416 pp.)=The World's Classics 212.

CONTENTS: HEMINGE and CONDELL, Preface to the first collection of Shakespeare's Plays; BEN JONSON, To the memory of my beloved, the Author, De Shakespeare Nostrati; MILTON, On Shakespeare; I.M.S., On Worthy Master Shakespeare and his Poems; FULLER, William Shakespeare; MARGARET CAVENDISH, DUCHESS OF NEWCASTLE, letter cxxiii; DRYDEN, from Of Dramatick Poesie, from various Prefaces and Prologues; PHILLIPS, from Theatrum Poetarum; ROWE, from Some Account of the Life of Mr. William Shakespear; ADDISON and STEELE, from The Spectator; POPE, from the Preface to Shakespeare's Works 1725, from the Epistle to Augustus; GRAY, from a letter to Richard West, from the Progress of Poesy; J. WARTON, from the Adventurer; LORD KAMES, from Elements of Criticism; LORD LYTTLETON, from Dialogues of the Dead; SAMUEL JOHNSON, from the Prologue at the opening of Drury Lane Theatre, the Dedication to Shakespear Illustrated, the Edition of Shakespear's Works 1765; WHATELEY, from Remarks on some of the Characters of Shakespeare; RICHARDSON, from the introduction to A Philosophical Analysis and Illustration of some of Shakespear's Remarkable Characters; MORGANN, from An Essay on the Dramatic Character of Sir John Falstaff; LAMB, On the Tragedies of Shakespeare; COLERIDGE, from Biographia Literaria, the Lectures, and Table Talk; HAZLITT, from Characters of Shakespear's Plays, Lectures on the English Poets, and Lectures on the Dramatic Literature of the Age of Elizabeth; JEFFREY, from review of Hazlitt's Characters of Shakespear's Plays; DE QUINCEY, On the Knocking at the Gate in Macbeth, from the article on Shakespeare in the Encyclopaedia Britannica; LANDOR, from Imaginary Conversations; CARLYLE, The Hero as Poet.

(b) TREATISES

CHARLES KNIGHT: A history of opinion on the writings of Shakspere. In his Pictorial edition of the works of Shakspere. Suppl. vol. London, 1866², pp. 331–400.

A history of Shakespearian criticism from Jonson to Coleridge.

ERNEST WALDEN: Shakespearean criticism, textual and literary, from Dryden to the end of the 18th century. Bradford, 1895. (136 pp.)=Harness prize essay.

PAUL HAMELIUS: Die Kritik in der englischen Literatur des 17. und 18. Jahrhunderts. Leipzig, 1897. Rev.: Bbl. 10, 1899, S. 121–3.

THOMAS R. LOUNSBURY: Shakespeare as a dramatic artist, with an account of his reputation at various periods. New York & London, 1901. (xix, 449 pp.) Rev.: Sh. Jb. 38, 1902, S. 245–7, A. Brandl; Bbl. 14, 1903, S. 106–9, v. Westenholz.

A history of English Shakespearian criticism in the XVIIth and XVIIIth centuries. With bibliography.

OTTO WENDT: Steeles literarische Kritik über Shakespeare im Tatler und Spectator. Diss. Rostock, 1901. (43 S.) Rev.: Zs. f. vgl. Lit.gesch., 1903, S. 175.

THOMAS R. LOUNSBURY: Shakespeare and Voltaire. New York, 1902. (x, 463 pp.)=Shakespearean Wars II. Rev.: Sh. Jb. 41, 1905, S. 259–60, Wechssler; JEGPh. 5, 1903–5, pp. 561–4, Ch. Bastide.

ALOIS BRANDL: Edward Young, On original composition. Ein Beitrag zur Geschichte der Shakespeare-Kritik des 18. Jahrhunderts. In: Sh. Jb. Jg. 39, 1903, S. 1–42.

H. A. EVANS: A Shakespearian controversy of the 18th century. In: Anglia Bd. 28, 1905, S. 457–76.

J. ADLER: Zur Shakespeare-Kritik des 18. Jahrhunderts. (Die Shakespeare-Kritik im Gentleman's Magazine). Diss. Königsberg, 1906. (74 S.)

THOMAS R. LOUNSBURY: The text of Shakespeare, its history from the publication of the quartos and folios down to and including the publication of the editions of Pope and Theobald. New York, 1906. (xxii, 579 pp.) Rev.: Sh. Jb. 43, 1907, S. 276–7, Dibelius.

Deals with Pope's literary feuds (1725–33).

MARIE JOACHIMI-DEGE: Deutsche Shakespeare-Probleme im 18. Jahrhundert. Diss. Bern, 1907. (iv, 98 S.) Printed in considerably enlarged form under the title: Deutsche Shakespeare-Probleme im 18. Jahrhundert und im Zeitalter der Romantik. Leipzig, 1907. (296 S.)=Unters. z. neueren Sprach- und Literaturgesch., hrsg. von Walzel, H. 12.

SIDNEY LEE: Pepys and Shakespeare. In his Shakespeare and the modern stage. London, 1907, pp. 82–110.

JOHNSON on Shakespeare. Essays and notes, set forth with an introduction by WALTER RALEIGH. London, 1908. (xxxii, 206 pp.) Rev.: Sh. Jb. 45, 1909, S. 394–5, M. Förster.

CHARLES F. JOHNSON: Shakespeare and his critics. Boston & New York, 1909. (xi, 386 pp.) Rev.: Sh. Jb. 46, 1910, S. 284–5, L. L. Schücking.

A. BÖHTLINGK: Shakespeare und unsere Klassiker. 3 Bde. Leipzig, 1909–10. 1. Bd: Shakespeare und Lessing. 2. Bd: Shakespeare und Goethe. 3. Bd.: Schiller und Shakespeare.

EDWARD DOWDEN: Some old Shakespearians. In his Essays, modern and Elizabethan. London, 1910, pp. 213–33.
Deals chiefly with I. Reed, Farmer, and Steevens.

FRIEDRICH GUNDOLF: Shakespeare und der deutsche Geist. Berlin, 1911, 1914². (359 S.). 1922⁶.
An important work.

PETRUS MAINZER: Die schöne Literatur Englands und die literarische Kritik in einigen der kleineren englischen Zeitschriften des 18. Jahrhunderts. Diss. Strassburg, 1911. (137 S.) Rev.: Bbl. 26, 1915, S. 138–40, B. Fehr.

JOSHUA H. NEUMANN: Shakespearean criticism in the Tatler and the Spectator. In: PMLA., vol. 39, 1924, pp. 612–23.

ALBERT H. TOLMAN: The early history of Shakespeare's reputation. In his Falstaff and other Shakespearean topics. New York & London, 1925. (xii, 270 pp.)

THOMAS M. RAYSOR: The study of Shakespeare's characters in the 18th century. In: MLN., vol. 42, 1927, pp. 495–500.

CAMILLE LOOTEN: La première controverse internationale sur Shakespeare entre l'Abbé Le Blanc et W. Guthrie, 1745—1747–1758.=Mémoires et travaux publ. par des professeurs des facultés cathol. de Lille, fasc. 32, 1927. (48 pp.) Rev.: Revue anglo-amér. 5, 1928, p. 361, F. L. Schoell.

D. NICHOL SMITH: Shakespeare in the 18th century. O.U.P., 1928. (viii, 92 pp.) Rev.: Bbl. 40, 1929, S. 99–101, H. T. Price.

R. W. BABCOCK: William Richardson's criticism of Shakespeare. In: JEGPh., vol. 28, 1929, pp. 117–36.
Deals with W. Richardson: A philosophical analysis and illustration of some of Shakespeare's remarkable characters [including Hamlet, Macbeth, Jaques, and Imogen]. London, 1774.

R. W. BABCOCK: A preliminary bibliography of 18th century criticism of Shakespeare. In: Stud. in Philol., Extra series, no. 1, 1929, pp. 58–76.

R. W. BABCOCK: A secondary bibliography of Shakespeare criticism in the 18th century. In: Stud. in Philol., Extra series, no. 1, 1929, pp. 77–98.

(2) XIXTH CENTURY CRITICISM
(a) CRITICAL WORKS

A. W. SCHLEGEL: Vorlesungen über dramatische Kunst und Literatur. 1809–11.

WILLIAM HAZLITT: Characters of Shakespeare's plays. London, 1817. (xxiv, 352 pp.) and later editions. New ed. by WILLIAM CAREW HAZLITT. London, 1873. (xx, 248 pp.)

NATHAN DRAKE: Shakspeare and his times, including the biography of the poet; criticisms on his genius and writings; a new chronology of his plays; a disquisition on the object of his sonnets; and a history of the manners, customs, and amusements, superstitions, poetry, and elegant literature of his age. In 2 vols. London, 1817. (xii, 735 and v, 677 pp.)

Ludwig Tieck. HENRY LÜDEKE: Das Buch über Shakespeare. Handschriftliche Aufzeichnungen von Ludwig Tieck. Aus seinem Nachlass herausgegeben. Halle, 1920. (524 S.)=Neudrucke dt. Lit.werke des 18. und 19. Jhrh., hrsg. von Leitzmann und W. Oehlke, No. 1. Rev.: Sh. Jb. 57, 1921, S. 103–4, W. Keller.
An edition of Tieck's literary fragments.

HENRY LÜDEKE: Ludwig Tieck und das alte englische Theater. Frankfurt a. M., 1922.

O. WEISSERT: Ludwig Tieck als Kritiker des Dramas und Theaters. Diss. München, 1928. (75 S.)

Hegel. MARIA SALDITT: Hegels Shakespeare-Interpretation. Berlin, 1927. (vi, 46 S.)=Philos. Forsch., hrsg. von K. Jaspers, H. 5.

F. GUIZOT: De Shakespeare et de la poésie dramatique. Paris, 1822.

HERMANN ULRICI: Über Shakespeares dramatische Kunst und sein Verhältnis zu Calderon und Goethe. Halle, 1839. Second edition entitled: Shakspeares dramatische Kunst. Geschichte und Charakteristik des Shakspeareschen Dramas. Teil 1–3. Leipzig, 1847, 1874[3]. (viii, 429; xii, 546 und vii, 235 S.)

SAMUEL TAYLOR COLERIDGE: Notes and lectures upon Shakespeare and some of the old poets and dramatists, with other literary remains. Ed. by SARA COLERIDGE. 2 vols. London, 1849. Reprinted in Everyman's Library, the New Universal Library, and Bohn's Library.

COLERIDGE'S literary criticism, ed. by J. W. MACKAIL. London, 1908. (xx, 226 pp.) Rev.: Bbl. 20, 1909, S. 44–6.
Shakespeare is dealt with on pp. 166–247.

Cf. also: ENRICO PIZZO: S. T. Coleridge als Kritiker. In: Anglia Bd. 40, N.F. Bd. 28, 1916, S. 201–55.

G. G. GERVINUS: Shakespeare. 4 Teile. Leipzig, 1849–50. 1862[3] in 2 vols. (xii, 601 und 586 S.) 1872[4] in 2 vols. with supplementary notes by RUDOLF GENÉE.

Cf. also: HERM. VON FRIESEN: Das Buch Shakespeare von Gervinus, ein Wort über dasselbe. Leipzig, 1869. (iv, 98 S.)

FRANÇOIS GUIZOT: Shakspeare et son temps. Étude littéraire. Paris, 1852. (v, 428 pp.) Engl. translation: Shakespeare and his times, with notices of his principal dramas. London, 1852.

FRIEDRICH KREYSSIG: Vorlesungen über Shakespeare, seine Zeit und seine Werke. 3 Bde. Berlin, 1858–60, 1874[2] in 2 vols. (viii, 495 und iv, 530 S.) 1887[3] in 2 vols.

A. MÉZIÈRES: Shakespeare, ses œuvres et ses critiques. Paris, 1860.

VICTOR HUGO: William Shakespeare. Paris, 1864. Reprinted in the Nelson Edition and in the New Universal Library.

C. HEBLER: Aufsätze über Shakespeare. Bern, 1865. 2nd enlarged edition: Bern, 1874. (xii, 294 S.)

GUSTAV RÜMELIN: Shakespeare-Studien. Stuttgart, 1866, 1874^2. (xiv, 315 S.)
  Cf.: FRIEDRICH THEODOR VISCHER: Die realistische Shakespeare-Kritik Hamlet. In: Sh. Jb. Jg. 2, 1867, S. 132–54.

  KARL ELZE: Der Shakespeare-Dilettantismus. Eine Antikritik. In: Sh. Jb. Jg. 9, 1874, S. 233–68.
  An answer to the attacks of the so-called Realists (Rümelin and Benedix).

CHARLES KNIGHT: Studies of Shakespeare . . . containing a history of opinion on the writings of Shakespeare, with the chronology of his plays. London, 1851. (300 pp.) 1868^2. (560 pp.)

OTTO LUDWIG: Shakespeare-Studien. Aus dem Nachlass des Dichters hrsg. von MORITZ HEYDRICH. Leipzig, 1872, 1874^2. (cxv, 541 S.) = Nachlassschriften Otto Ludwigs, hrsg. von Moritz Heydrich, Bd. 2. Rev.: Bbl 13, 1902, S. 11–13, v. Westenholz.

  Cf. LÉON MIS: Les 'Études sur Shakespeare' d'Otto Ludwig, exposées dans un ordre méthodique et précédées d'une introduction littéraire. Lille, 1922. (109 pp.) 1928^2. (200 pp.)

R. BENEDIX: Die Shakespearomanie. Zur Abwehr. Stuttgart, 1873.

HERMANN VON FRIESEN: Shakspere-Studien. Bd. 1: Altengland und William Shakspere. Wien, 1874. Bd. 2: William Shaksperes Dramen vom Beginn seiner Laufbahn bis 1601. Wien, 1875. Bd. 3: William Shaksperes Dramen von 1601 bis zum Schlusse seiner Laufbahn. Wien, 1876. (x, 454; 393 und vi, 549 S.)

EDWARD DOWDEN: Shakspere. A critical study of his mind and art. London, 1875. (xii, 430 pp.) New ed. with an introduction and a brief bibliography by W. D. HOWE. New York, 1918. (xxiii, 386 S.) German translation: Shakspere, sein Entwicklungsgang in seinen Werken. Übers. von W. WAGNER. Heilbronn, 1879.

KARL ELZE: Abhandlungen zu Shakespeare. Halle, 1877. (425 S.)

ALGERNON CHARLES SWINBURNE: A study of Shakespeare. London, 1880. (viii, 310 pp.)

WILHELM OECHELHÄUSER: Einführungen in Shakespeares Bühnendramen und Charakteristik sämtlicher Rollen. 2 Bde. Minden, 1885^2. (xiii, 384 und 414 S.)

RICHARD GRANT WHITE: Studies in Shakespeare. Boston, 1885.

FREDERICK G. FLEAY: Chronicle history of the life and work of William Shakespeare, player, poet, and playmaker. London, 1886. (viii, 364 pp.)

NICOLAUS DELIUS: Abhandlungen zu Shakespeare. 2 Teile. Berlin, 1889.

BERNHARD ten BRINK: Shakspere. Fünf Vorlesungen aus dem Nachlass. Strassburg, 1893, 1894². (vii, 160 S.) English translation: Five lectures on Shakespeare. Translated by J. Franklin. London, 1895. (248 pp.)

GEORG BRANDES: William Shakespeare. München, 1896. 2. Aufl. Leipzig & München, 1898. (1006 S.). Rev.: Sh. Jb. 37, 1901, S. 246–7, W. Keller.

FRIEDRICH THEODOR VISCHER: Shakespeare Vorträge. I–VI. Berlin & Stuttgart, 1899–1905. Rev.: Bbl. 11, 1900, S. 155–9 und 15, 1904, S. 341–3, Rud. Fischer.

MAX J. WOLFF: William Shakespeare. Studien und Aufsätze. Leipzig, 1903. Rev.: Sh. Jb. 40, 1904, S. 261–2, Dibelius.

J. CHURTON COLLINS: Studies in Shakespeare. London, 1904. (xv, 380 pp.)

RUDOLPH GENÉE: William Shakespeare in seinem Werden und Wesen. Berlin, 1905. (xii, 472 S.) Rev.: Sh. Jb. 42, 1906, S. 241–4, Westenholz.

STOPFORD A. BROOKE: On ten plays of Shakespeare. London, 1905, 1920². (311 pp.) Ten more plays of Shakespeare. London, 1913, 1920². (313 pp.) Rev.: Sh. Jb. 42, 1906, S. 246, A. Brandl; 50, 1914, S. 198–9, M. Förster.

LEO N. TOLSTOI: Shakespeare. Eine kritische Studie. Übers. von M. Enckhausen. Hannover, 1906. (148 S.) Rev.: Sh. Jb. 43, 1907, S. 245–6, A. Brandl.

MAX J. WOLFF: Shakespeare, der Dichter und sein Werk. 2 Bde. München, 1907, 1926⁶.

BRANDER MATTHEWS: Shakespeare as a playwright. London, 1913. (xiii, 399 pp.) Rev.: Sh. Jb. 50, 1914, S. 187–90, M. Förster.

GEORGES PELLISSIER: Shakespeare et la superstition shakespearéenne. Paris, 1914. (305 S.) Rev.: Sh. Jb. 52, 1916, S. 232, M. Förster.

Bernard Shaw.—JOSEF CARO: Bernard Shaw und Shakespeare. In: N. Spr. Bd. 22, 1914, S. 433–48 und 509–25.
An account of Shaw's Shakespearian criticism.

WILHELM REHBACH: Shaw's 'Besser als Shakespeare'. In: Sh. Jb. Jg. 52, 1916, S. 84–139.
CONTENTS: I. Shaw als Kritiker über Shakespeare. II. Shaw als Gestalter gegen Shakespeare.

Shaksperean Studies. By members of the department of English and comparative literature in Columbia University. Ed. by BRANDER MATTHEWS and ASHLEY H. THORNDIKE. New York, Columbia Univ. Pr., 1916. (452 pp.) Rev.: Sh. Jb. 56, 1920, S. 117–19, W. Keller.

EDWARD B. KOSTER: William Shakespeare gedenkboek 1616–1916. 's-Gravenhage, 1916. (174 S.) Rev.: Z. f. e. U. 17, 1918, S. 24–5, Jantzen.

A book of homage to Shakespeare. Ed. by ISRAEL GOLLANCZ. O.U.P., 1916. (xxx, 557 pp.) Rev.: Sh. Jb. 54, 1918, S. 148, Jantzen.

G. L. KITTREDGE: Shakspere. An address. Harv. Univ. Pr. & O.U.P., 1916. (54 pp.) Rev.: Sh. Jb. 57, 1921, S. 117–18, F. Schönemann.

ARTHUR QUILLER-COUCH: Shakespeare's workmanship. London, 1918. (368 pp.)

BENEDETTO CROCE: Ariosto, Shakespeare e Corneille. Bari, 1920. (286 pp., Shakespeare dealt with on pp. 75–218.) English translation by DOUGLAS AINSLIE. London, 1921.

Cf.: J. M. ROBERTSON: Croce as Shakespearean critic. London, 1922. (32 pp.)

GUSTAV LANDAUER: Shakespeare dargestellt in Vorträgen. 2 Bde. Frankfurt a. M., 1920. (vii, 352 und 395 S.) Rev.: Sh. Jb. 57, 1921, S. 94–5, W. Keller; Dt. Vjschr. 6, 1928, S. 185, L. L. Schücking.

ROMAIN ROLLAND: Die Wahrheit in dem Werke Shakespeares. (Aus dem Französ. übers. v. Hannah Szász). Berlin, 1920. (51 S.)

FAGUS: Essai sur Shakespeare. Amiens, 1923. (225 pp.)

JOHN MASEFIELD: Shakespeare and spiritual life. O.U.P., 1924. (32 pp.)= Romanes Lecture.

ALBERT H. TOLMAN: Falstaff and other Shakespearean topics. London, 1925. (xii, 270 pp.) Rev.: Sh. Jb. 61, 1925, S. 130–1, W. Keller.

E. K. CHAMBERS: Shakespeare, a survey. London, 1925. (x, 325 pp.) Rev.: Sh. Jb. 61, 1925, S. 130, W. Keller.

JULIUS BAB: Shakespeare. Wesen und Werk. Stuttgart (1925). (326 S.) Rev.: Dt. Vjschr. 6, 1928, S. 186–8, L. L. Schücking.

FELIX E. SCHELLING: Shakespeare and 'demi-science'. Papers on Elizabethan topics. Philadelphia & London, O.U.P., 1927. (221 pp.) Rev.: Sh. Jb. 64, 1928, S. 195–6, W. Keller.
Containing various essays.

HARLEY GRANVILLE-BARKER: Prefaces to Shakespeare. First series. London, 1927. (xl, 231 pp.) Second series. London, 1930. (xii, 345 pp.)

ROMAN DYBOSKI: William Shakespeare. Krakau, 1927. (352 S.)

ELMER EDGAR STOLL: Shakespeare studies, historical and comparative in method. New York, 1927. (xi, 502 pp.) Rev.: MLN. 43, 1928, pp. 135–8, G. C. Taylor; Sh. Jb. 63, 1927, S. 200–1, W. Keller.
CONTENTS: (1) On the anniversary of the Folio (1–38). (2) Literature and life (39–89). (3) The characterization (90–146). (4) The comic method (147–86). (5) The ghosts (187–254). (6) Shylock (255–336). (7) The criminals (337–402). (8) Falstaff (403–90).

ALLARDYCE NICOLL: Studies in Shakespeare. New York, 1928. (168 pp.)= Hogarth Lectures, No. 3. Rev.: MLN. 44, 1929, pp. 57–8, H. M. Ayres.

W. J. LAWRENCE: Shakespeare's workshop. Oxford, 1928. (161 pp.)
A collection of essays.

FRIEDRICH GUNDOLF: Shakespeare. Sein Wesen und Werk. 2 Bde. Berlin, 1928 und 1929. (467 und 453 S.) Rev.: Sh. Jb. 65, 1929, S. 189–90, W. Keller.
Gundolf analyses the individual dramas in chronological order and attempts thereby to trace Shakespeare's inner development.

(b) TREATISES DEALING WITH THE SHAKESPEARE CRITICISM OF THE XIXTH CENTURY

ARNOLD SCHRÖER: Prinzipien der Shakspere-Kritik. In: Beiträge z. neueren Philol. Jakob Schipper z. 19. Juli 1902. Wien & Leipzig, 1902. (29 S.) Rev.: Sh. Jb. 40, 1904, S. 238–9, Leop. Richter; Bbl. 14, 1903, S. 112–13, R. Ackermann.

RENÉ DOUMIC: Shakespeare et la critique française. In: Rev. des deux mondes, vol. 74, 1904, pp. 923–34.

ELMER EDGAR STOLL: Anachronism in Shakespeare criticism. In: Mod. Phil., vol. 7, 1910, pp. 557–75. Rev.: Sh. Jb. 47, 1911, S. 263–4, Grabau.

C. H. HERFORD: The German contribution to Shakespeare. In: A book of homage to Shakespeare. Ed. by Israel Gollancz. O.U.P., 1916. Rev.: Sh. Jb. 55, 1919, S. 181, A. Schröer.

EDMUND K. CHAMBERS: The disintegration of Shakespeare. O.U.P., 1924. (22 pp.)=The Brit. Acad. annual Shakespeare lecture, 1924. Rev.: MLR. 21, 1926, pp. 86–9, A. E. Morgan.

C. M. HAINES: Shakespeare in France, criticism, Voltaire to Victor Hugo. Oxford, 1925. Rev.: MLN. 42, 1927, pp. 541–2, Briggs.

SAMUEL ASA SMALL: The return to Shakespeare. The historical realists. Johns Hopkins Univ. Pr., 1927. (134 pp.)

EDWIN GREENLAW: Recent trends in Shakespeare criticism. In: The Sh. Assoc. Bull., vol. 2, 1927, No. 3, pp. 3–7.

EDMUND K. CHAMBERS: The unrest in Shakespearean studies. In: Nineteenth Cent. 1927, pp. 255–66.

ÉMILE LEGOUIS: La réaction contre la critique romantique de Shakespeare. In: Essays and Studies, vol. 13, 1928, pp. 74–87.

Supplement: SHORT INTRODUCTIONS TO THE STUDY OF SHAKESPEARE

FRED. G. FLEAY: Shakespeare manual. London, 1876, 1878.

FRED. G. FLEAY: Introduction to the Shakespearian study. London, 1877.

EDWARD DOWDEN: Shakespeare. London, 1877 and later editions.=Green's Literature Primers. German translation by Paul Tausig. Leipzig, Max Hesses Volksbücherei, Heft 245–7.

CHARLOTTE PORTER and HELEN A. CLARKE: Shakespeare study programmes. In: Poet-Lore. Boston, vol. 1, 1887 seq.

CYRIL RANSOME: Short studies of Shakespeare's plots. London, 1890, 1898⁴. (xii, 299 pp.) Rev.: Sh. Jb. 36, 1900, S. 301–2, R. Fischer.

WILLIAM H. FLEMING: How to study Shakespeare. 4 vols. New York, 1898–1904.

HIRAM CORSON: Introduction to the study of Shakespeare. Boston, 1899. (342 pp.)

MORTON LUCE: A handbook to the works of William Shakespeare. London, 1906. (463 pp.) Rev.: Sh. Jb. 43, 1907, S. 260–1, A. Brandl.

F. W. MOORMAN: An introduction to Shakespeare. Leipzig & Berlin, 1906. (82 S.)=Teubner's School Texts. Rev.: Sh. Jb. 43, 1907, A. Brandl.

ERNST SIEPER: Shakespeare und seine Zeit. Leipzig, 1907, 1913².=Aus Natur und Geisteswelt, Bd. 185. Rev.: Sh. Jb. 44, 1908, S. 234–5, R. Fischer.

F. J. FURNIVALL and JOHN MUNRO: Shakespeare, life and work. London, 1908. (279 pp.)=The Century Shakespeare. Rev.: Sh. Jb. 45, 1909, S. 397–8, M. Förster.

ALBERT H. TOLMAN: Questions on Shakespeare. Parts I, II. Chicago, 1910. (xv, 215 and x, 355 pp.)
With good bibliography.

H. N. MacCRACKEN, F. E. PIERCE, and W. H. DURHAM: An introduction to Shakespeare. New York, 1910. (viii, 222 pp.) Rev.: Sh. Jb. 47, 1911, S. 338, M. Förster.

DARRELL FIGGIS: Shakespeare, a study. London, 1911. (345 pp.) Rev.: Sh. Jb. 48, 1912, S. 275–6, W. Keller.

C. H. HERFORD: Shakespeare. London [1912]. (94 pp.)=The People's Books. Rev.: Sh. Jb. 48, 1912, S. 309, M. Förster.

WILLIAM A. NEILSON and ASHLEY H. THORNDIKE: The facts about Shakespeare. New York & London, 1913. (273 pp.)=The Tudor Shakespeare. Rev.: Sh. Jb. 50, 1914, S. 187, M. Förster.
With systematically arranged bibliography.

E. A. G. LAMBORN and G. B. HARRISON: Shakespeare, the man and his stage. O.U.P., 1923. (112 pp.)=The World's Manuals, No. 24.

RAYMOND M. ALDEN: A Shakespeare handbook. New York, 1925. (xvi, 240 pp.) Rev.: JEGPh. 22, 1923, pp. 294–8.

GEORGE H. COWLING: A preface to Shakespeare. London, 1925. (viii, 164 pp.) Rev.: RESt. 1925, pp. 359–61, A. W. Pollard; Arch. 149, 1925, S. 115–16, Brandl.

G. H. CRUMP: A guide to the study of Shakespeare's plays. London, 1925. (203 pp.)

TUCKER BROOKE: Shakespeare of Stratford. A handbook for students. O.U.P., 1926. (177 pp.)=The Yale Shakespeare. Rev.: Sh. Jb. 63, 1927, S. 199, W. Keller.

F. S. BOAS: An introduction to the reading of Shakespeare. O.U.P., 1927. (112 pp.)=The World's Manuals, vol. 43. Rev.: Bbl. 40, 1929, S. 107–11, E. Deckner; Sh. Jb. 63, 1927, S. 202, W. Keller.

XII. SHAKESPEARE'S INFLUENCE THROUGH THE CENTURIES

(1) SHAKESPEARE'S INFLUENCE IN ENGLAND

(a) GENERAL

WILHELM OECHELHÄUSER: Die Würdigung Shakespeares in England und Deutschland. In: Sh. Jb. Jg. 20, 1885, S. 54–68.

O. GLÖDE: Shakespeare in der englischen Literatur des 17. und 18. Jahrhunderts. Progr. Doberan, 1902. (20 S.)

EMIL KOEPPEL: Studien über Shakespeares Wirkung auf zeitgenössische Dramatiker. Louvain & Leipzig, 1905. (xi, 103 S.)=Mat. z. Kunde d. ält. engl. Dramas, hrsg. von W. Bang, Bd. 9.

HELENE RICHTER: Die Wiederbelebung Shakespeares und der Volkspoesie. In her Geschichte der englischen Romantik. Bd. 1, Teil 1. Halle a. S. 1911, S. 79–159.

J. J. JUSSERAND: What to expect of Shakespeare. London [1911]. (24 pp.)= The Brit. Acad. First annual Shakespeare lecture. Rev.: Sh. Jb. 48, 1912, S. 307–8, M. Förster.

D. NICHOL SMITH: Shakespeare in the 18th century. Oxford, 1928. (viii, 92 pp.) Rev.: Bbl. 40, 1929, S. 99–101, H. T. Price; MLN. 44, 1929, pp. 270–1, H. Spencer; Sh. Jb. 64, 1928, S. 201–2, W. Keller.

BERNHARD FEHR: Das Shakespeare-Erlebnis in der englischen Romantik. In: Sh. Jb. Jg. 65, 1929, S. 8–22.

(b) LITERARY ALLUSIONS TO SHAKESPEARE

INGLEBY—SMITH—FURNIVALL—MUNRO: The Shakspere allusion-book. A collection of allusions to Shakspere from 1591 to 1700, originally compiled by C. M. Ingleby, Miss L. Toulmin Smith, and by F. J. Furnivall, with the assistance of the New Shakspere Society, and now re-edited, revised, and rearranged, with an introd. by John Munro. 2 vols. London, 1909. (lxxvi, 527 and x, 558 pp.)

JOHN MUNRO: More Shakespeare allusions. In: Mod. Phil., vol. 13, 1915–16, pp. 497–544.

[GEORGE THORN-DRURY]: Some 17th century allusions to Shakespeare and his works not hitherto collected. London, 1920. (iv, 48 pp.)

HENRIETTA C. BARTLETT: Mr. William Shakespeare. Original and early editions of his quartos and folios, his source books and those containing contemporary notices. New Haven & London, 1922. (xxviii, 217 pp.)

(c) SHAKESPEARE'S SIGNIFICANCE FOR VARIOUS ENGLISH AUTHORS

ALWIN THALER: Shakespeare and Sir Thomas *Browne*. In his Shakespeare's silences, O.U.P. 1929, pp. 97–138.

G. R. ELLIOTT: Shakespeare's significance for *Browning*. Diss. Jena, 1909. (35 S.) Enlarged in: Anglia, Bd. 32, 1909, S. 90–162.

H. ENGEL: *Byron's* Stellung zu Shakespeare. Progr. Berlin, 1903. (25 S.)

E. ZABEL: Byrons Kenntnis von Shakespeare und sein Urteil über ihn. Diss. Halle, 1904. (69 S.)

J. D. E. WILLIAMS: Sir William *Davenant's* relation to Shakespeare. With an analysis of the chief characters of Davenant's plays. Diss. Strassburg, 1906. (120 pp.)

WILHELM DIBELIUS: *Dickens* und Shakespeare. In: Sh. Jb. Jg. 52, 1916, S. 76–83.

NICOLAUS DELIUS: *Dryden* und Shakespeare. In: Sh. Jb. Jg. 4, 1869, S. 6–40.

M. WOLFF: John *Ford*, ein Nachahmer Shakespeares. Diss. Heidelberg, 1880. (71 S.)

P. BIRCK: Literarische Anspielungen in den Werken Ben *Jonsons*. Diss. Strassburg, 1908. (xi, 121 S.)

MARY SUDDARD: *Keats, Shelley*, and Shakespeare. Studies and essays in English literature. Cambridge, 1912. (308 pp.)

JOHN MIDDLETON MURRY: Keats and Shakespeare. A study of Keats' poetic life from 1816 to 1820. O.U.P., 1925. (xii, 248 pp.) Rev.: Sh. Jb. 61, 1925, S. 146–7, W. Keller.

CAROLINE F. E. SPURGEON: Keats's Shakespeare. A descriptive study based on new material. O.U.P., 1928. (viii, 178 pp.) Rev.: Bbl. 40, 1929, S. 97–9, B. Fehr; Sh. Jb. 65, 1929, S. 215–16, Hel. Richter.

H. JUNG: Das Verhältnis von Thomas *Middleton* zu Shakespeare. Leipzig, 1904. (viii, 99 S.)=Münch. Beitr. z. rom. und engl. Philol., hrsg. von Breymann und Schick, H. 29. Rev.: E. St. 35, 1905, R. Fischer; Bbl. 15, 1904, Koeppel.

ALWIN THALER: The Shakespearean element in *Milton*. In: PMLA., vol. 40, 1925, pp. 645–91. Enlarged in his Shakespeare's silences, O.U.P. 1929, pp. 139–256. Rev.: Sh. Jb. 63, 1927, S. 223, Beckmann.

G. C. TAYLOR: Shakspere and Milton again. In: Stud. in Philol., vol. 23, 1926, pp. 189 seq.

H. W. GARROD: Milton's lines on Shakespeare. In: Essays and Studies, vol. 12, 1926, pp. 7–23.

GUSTAV HAGEMANN: Shakespeares Einfluss auf *Otways* künstlerische Entwicklung. Diss. Münster, 1917. (70 S.) Rev.: Sh. Jb. 55, 1919, S. 166–7, W. Keller.

MARGARETHE ROTHBARTH: *Pope* and Shakespeare. In: Anglia. Bd. 39, N.F. Bd. 27, 1916, S. 75–100.

JOHN WILMON BREWER: Shakespeare's influence on Sir Walter *Scott*. Boston, 1925. (xii, 508 pp.)

JOSEPH CARO: G. B. *Shaw* und Shakespeare. In: Festschr. z. 15. Neuphilologentage in Frankf. a. M., 1912. Frankf. a. M., 1912, S. 47–78. Rev.: Sh. Jb. 49, 1913, S. 249, M. Förster.

For influence on *Shelley*, cf. Keats.

WILH. MÜNCH: Gedanken eines Poeten [W. B. *Yeats*] in Shakespeares Stadt. In: Sh. Jb. Jg. 40, 1904, S. 204–12.

(2) SHAKESPEARE'S INFLUENCE OUTSIDE ENGLAND
(a) AMERICA

GEORGE B. CHURCHILL: Shakespeare in America. A lecture. In: Sh. Jb. Jg. 42, 1906, S. xiii–xlv.

WILLIAM B. CAIRNS: Shakespeare in America. In: Edda, Bd. 6, 1916, S. 189–208.

ASHLEY THORNDIKE: Shakespeare in America. London, 1927. (22 pp.)= Annual Shakespeare lecture of the Brit. Acad., 1927. Rev.: Bbl. 39, 1928, S. 109, W. Fischer.

RICHARD CLARENCE HARRISON: *Walt Whitman* and Shakespeare. In: PMLA., vol. 44, 1929, pp. 1201–38.

(b) THE CONTINENT IN GENERAL

J. G. ROBERTSON: The knowledge of Shakespeare on the continent at the beginning of the 18th century. In: MLR., vol. 1, 1905–6, pp. 312–21.

J. G. ROBERTSON: Shakespeare on the continent. In: CHEL., vol. 5, 1910, pp. 283–308.
With bibliography.

C. H. HERFORD: A sketch of the history of Shakespeare's influence on the continent. In: Bull. of John Rylands Libr., vol. 9, 1925, pp. 20–62.

(c) THE LATIN COUNTRIES
(α) FRANCE
(aa) *General Treatises*

A. LACROIX: Histoire de l'influence de Shakespeare sur le théâtre français jusqu'à nos jours. Bruxelles, 1856. (359 pp.)

G. PELLISSIER: Le drame shakespearien en France. In his Essais de littérature contemporaine. Paris, 1893, pp. 69–109.

J. J. JUSSERAND: Shakespeare en France sous l'ancien régime. Paris, 1898. (389 pp.) English translation: Shakespeare in France under the ancien régime. London, 1899. (xxviii, 496 pp.) Rev.: Sh. Jb. 35, 1899, S. 314–16, Schultz-Gora.

JAKOB ENGEL: Shakespeare in Frankreich. In: Sh. Jb. Jg. 34, 1898, S. 66–118.

E. FIERLINGER: Shakespeare in Frankreich. Progr. Olmütz, 1900. (36 S.)

F. BALDENSPERGER: Esquisse d'une histoire de Shakespeare en France. In his Études d'histoire littéraire. 2ᵉ sér. Paris, 1910, pp. 155–216.

C. M. HAINES: Shakespeare in France. Criticism: Voltaire to Victor Hugo. London, 1925. (viii, 170 pp.) Rev.: Bbl. 38, 1927, S. 113, H. T. Price; MLN. 42, 1927, pp. 539–46, W. D. Briggs.
With bibliography.

SIDNEY LEE: Shakespeare in France. In his Shakespeare and the modern stage. London, 1907.

(bb) Influence on Individual French Writers

CARL KÜHN: Über *Ducis* in seiner Beziehung zu Shakespeare. Diss. Jena, 1875. (37 S.)

PAUL STAPFER: *Molière* et Shakespeare. Paris, 1887.

EMIL FRICKE: Der Einfluss Shakespeares auf *Alfred de Mussets* Dramen. Diss. Basel, 1901. (62 S.)

GEORGES DUVAL: Shakespeare et Musset. In: Le Figaro, 1911 (8 avril).

J. C. CARPENTER: The *Abbé Prévost* and Shakespeare. In: MLR., vol. 10, 1915, pp. 196–202.

STENDHAL [Henri Beyle]: *Racine* et Shakespeare. Paris, 1823. Cf. Stendhal: Œuvres complètes, p. p. Pierre Martino. 2 vols. Paris, 1925.
Contains reprints of two polemic treatises by Stendhal (1823, 1825), which signalized his entry into the struggle between classicism and romanticism.

ANNIE SESSELY: L'influence de Shakespeare sur *Alfred de Vigny*. Berne, 1928. (124 pp.)

ALEXANDER SCHMIDT: *Voltaires* Verdienste um die Einführung Shakespeares in Frankreich. Königsberg, 1864.

WILHELM KÖNIG, JR.: Voltaire und Shakespeare. In: Sh. Jb. Jg. 10, 1875, S. 259–310.

THOMAS R. LOUNSBURY: Shakespeare and Voltaire. London, 1902. (476 pp.)

(β) SPAIN

RICARDO RUPPERT Y UJARAVI: Shakespeare en España. Traducciones, imitaciones e influencia de las obras de Shakespeare en la literatura española. Madrid, 1920. (107 pp.) Rev.: Litbl. 44, 1923, Sp. 247, Hämel.

WOLFGANG VON WURZBACH: Shakespeares 'Heinrich VIII' und *Calderóns* 'La Cisma de Inglaterra'. In: Sh. Jb. Jg. 32, 1896, S. 190–211.

MARIA SCHÜTT: Hat Calderón Shakespeare gekannt? Die Quellen von Calderóns 'La Cisma de Inglaterra'. In: Sh. Jb. Jg. 61, 1925, S. 94–107.

(γ) ITALY

VINZENZO REFORGIATO: Shakespeare e *Manzoni*. Catania, 1908.

P. BELLEZZA: Shakespeare e Manzoni. Milano, 1927. (191 pp.)

(d) GERMANY AND THE GERMANIC COUNTRIES

(α) GERMANY

(aa) *General Treatises*

AUGUST KOBERSTEIN: Shakespeare in Deutschland. In: Sh. Jb. Jg. 1, 1865, S. 1–17.

ALBERT COHN: Shakespeare in Germany in the 16th and 17th centuries. An account of English actors in Germany and the Netherlands and of the plays performed by them during the same period. London, 1865. (422 pp.)

R. GENÉE: Geschichte der Shakespeareschen Dramen in Deutschland. Leipzig, 1870.

C. C. HENSE: Deutsche Dichter in ihrem Verhältnis zu Shakespeare. I. II. In: Sh. Jb. Jg. 5, 1870, S. 107–47; Jg. 6, 1871, S. 83–128.

Deals chiefly with Shakespeare's influence on the dramatists of the Sturm und Drang period, and on Goethe, Schiller, Kleist, Tieck.

WILHELM OEHLMANN: Shakespeares Wert für unsere nationale Literatur. In: Sh. Jb. Jg. 5, 1870, S. 148–53.

B. SUPHAN: Shakespeare im Anbruch der klassischen Zeit unserer Literatur. Festvortrag. In: Sh. Jb. Jg. 25, 1890, S. 1–20.

E. WALTHER: Der Einfluss Shakespeares auf die Sturm- und Drangperiode unserer Literatur im 18. Jahrhundert. Progr. Chemnitz, 1890. (28 S.)

MARIE JOACHIMI-DEGE: Deutsche Shakespeare-Probleme im 18. Jahrhundert und im Zeitalter der Romantik. Leipzig, 1907. (296 S.)=Untersuchungen z. neueren Sprach- und Lit.gesch., hrsg. von Walzel, H. 12. Rev.: Sh. Jb. 44, 1908, S. 329–30, Dowden.

A. BÖHTLINGK: Shakespeare und unsere Klassiker. I: Lessing und Shakespeare. II: Goethe und Shakespeare. III: Schiller und Shakespeare. Leipzig, 1909, 1910. (xix, 303; xii, 320 und xiv, 457 S.) Rev.: Sh. Jb. 46, 1910, S. 279–82 und 47, 1911, S. 300–1, K. Jahn.

K. A. RICHTER: Beiträge zum Bekanntwerden Shakespeares in Deutschland. 3 Teile. Progr. Breslau, 1909 (48 S.), 1910 (31 S.), und 1912 (35 S.). Also: Oppeln, 1912. (116 S.) Rev.: Bbl. 24, 1913, S. 307–8, Aronstein.

F. GUNDELFINGER: Shakespeare und der deutsche Geist vor dem Auftreten Lessings. Hab. Schr. Heidelberg, 1911. (86 S.) Enlarged edition: FRIEDR. GUNDOLF: Shakespeare und der deutsche Geist. Berlin, 1911. (viii, 360 S.) 1920⁵, 1927⁸. Rev.: Sh. Jb. 48, 1912, S. 259–74, O. Walzel; JEGPh. 13, 1914, pp. 330–4, L. M. Kueffner.

K. A. RICHTER: Shakespeare in Deutschland in den Jahren 1739–1770. Oppeln, 1912. (116 S.)

ALOIS BRANDL: Shakespeare and Germany. London [1913]. (14 pp.)=The Brit. Acad. 3rd annual Shakespeare lecture. Rev.: Sh. Jb. 50, 1914, S. 209–10, M. Förster.

LAWRENCE M. PRICE: English>German literary influences. Bibliography and survey. Berkeley, 1920. (616 pp.)=Univ. of California Publ. in Mod. Philol., vol. 9. Rev.: Sh. Jb. 57, 1921, S. 102–3, W. Keller.

MAX FÖRSTER: Shakespeare und Deutschland. Festvortrag. In: Sh. Jb. Jg. 57, 1921, S. 7–27.

(bb) Shakespeare's Significance for Various German Authors

ARTHUR BÖHTLINGK: *Bismarck* und Shakespeare. Stuttgart & Berlin, 1908. (viii, 149 S.) Rev.: Sh. Jb. 45, 1909, S. 408, M. Förster.

ERNST GÖTZINGER: Das Shakespeare-Büchlein des Armen Mannes im Toggenburg [Ulrich *Bräker*] vom Jahre 1780. Nach der Originalhandschr. mitgeteilt. In: Sh. Jb. Jg. 12, 1877, S. 100–68.

KARL SCHNEIDER: Heinrich Wilhelm von *Gerstenberg* als Verkünder Shakespeares. In: Sh. Jb. Jg. 58, 1922, S. 39–45.

ERNST FRIEDRICHS: *Gottsched*—Shakespeare—Tolstoi. (Zu Gottscheds 150. Todestage—12 Dez. 1766). In: N. Spr. Bd. 24, 1917, S. 513.

F. A. LEO: Shakespeare und *Goethe*. Festvortrag. In: Sh. Jb. Jg. 24, 1889, S. 9–23.

C. B. WAGNER: Shakespeares Einfluss auf Goethe in Leben und Dichtung. I. Teil. Diss. Halle, 1890. (54 S.)

A. HUTHER: Goethes Götz von Berlichingen und Shakespeares historische Dramen. Progr. Cottbus, 1893. (22 S.)

A. R. A. BÖHTLINGK: Goethe und Shakespeare. Leipzig, 1909. (xii, 320 S.)

H. ECKERT: Goethes Urteile über Shakespeare aus seiner Persönlichkeit erklärt. Diss. Göttingen, 1918. (35 S.)

ALBERT LEITZMANN: Dodd's 'Beauties of Shakespeare' als Quelle für Goethe und Herder. In: Sh. Jb. Jg. 55, 1919, S. 59–74.

H. BARTMANN: *Grabbes* Verhältnis zu Shakespeare. Diss. Münster, 1898. (45 S.)

WILHELM BOLIN: *Grillparzers* Shakespeare-Studien. In: Sh. Jb. Jg. 18, 1883, S. 104–26.

EDGAR GROSS: Grillparzers Verhältnis zu Shakespeare. In: Sh. Jb. Jg. 51, 1915, S. 1–33.

HANS BRAUN: Grillparzers Verhältnis zu Shakespeare. Diss. München, 1916. (viii, 115 S.)

WILHELM ALBERTS: *Hebbels* Stellung zu Shakespeare. Diss. Freiburg, 1908. (39 S.) Reprinted in extended form: Berlin, 1908. (78 S.)=Forsch. z. neueren Lit.gesch., hrsg. von Muncker, H. 23. Rev.: Sh. Jb. 45, 1909, S. 356–7, R. Petsch; JEGPh. 7, 1907–8, pp. iii, 171–5, E. O. Eckelmann.

E. A. SCHALLES: *Heines* Verhältnis zu Shakespeare. Diss. Berlin, 1904. (69 S.)
Rev.: Sh. Jb. 41, 1905, S. 260–2, R. Petsch.

FRANZ ZINKERNAGEL: *Herders* Shakespeare-Aufsatz in dreifacher Gestalt.
Mit Anm. hrsg. Bonn, 1912. (41 S.)=Kleine Texte f. Vorles. und Übungen,
hrsg. von Lietzmann, No. 107.

META CORSSEN: *Kleists* und Shakespeares dramatische Gestalten. In: Sh. Jb.
Jg. 58, 1922, S. 46–67.

META CORSSEN: Kleist und Shakespeare. Weimar, 1930. (208 S.)=Forsch. z.
neueren Lit.gesch., hrsg. von W. Brecht, No. 61.

L. JACOBOWSKI: *Klinger* und Shakespeare. Ein Beitrag zur Shakespearomanie
der Sturm- und Drangperiode. Diss. Freiburg, 1891. (66 S.)

H. RAUCH: *Lenz* und Shakespeare. Ein Beitrag zur Shakespearomanie der
Sturm- und Drangperiode. Diss. Freiburg, 1892. (110 S.) Rev.: Bbl. 4,
1894, S. 133–5.

F. W. MEISNEST: *Lessing* und Shakespeare. In: PMLA., vol. 19, N.F. vol.
12, 1904, pp. 234–49.

GUSTAV KETTNER: Lessing und Shakespeare. In: Neue Jbb. f. d. klass. Altertum.
Bd. 19, 1907, 1. Abt., S. 267 ff.

OSKAR WALZEL: Der Kritiker Lessing und Shakespeare. In: Sh. Jb. Jg. 65,
1929, S. 23–48.

B. FISCHER: Otto *Ludwigs* Trauerspielplan 'Der Sandwirt von Passeier'
und sein Verhältnis zu den 'Shakespeare-Studien'. Diss. Greifswald, 1916.
(68 S.)

ALFRED STERN: Moses *Mendelssohn* und Shakespeare. In: Neue Schweizer
Rdsch. 1929.

ALBERT LUDWIG: *Nietzsche* und Shakespeare. In: Sh. Jb. Jg. 56, 1920,
S. 24–57.

K. H. KERN: Th. *Roetscher's* Stellung zu Shakespeare als Bühnendichter.
Diss. Marburg. (90 S.)

F. ENGEL: Spuren Shakespeares in *Schillers* dramatischen Werken. Progr.
Magdeburg, 1901. (24 S.)

MAX NUSSBERGER: Schiller als politischer Dichter. Shakespeare und das
deutsche Drama. Hab. Schr. Basel, 1919. (56 S.)

RICHARD GEBHARD: Shakespeare und *Schopenhauer*. In: Sh. Jb. Jg. 47, 1911,
S. 170–87.

DOMINIK ŻELAK: *Tieck* und Shakespeare. Ein Beitrag zur Geschichte der
Shakespearomanie in Deutschland. Progr. Tarnopol, 1900. Leipzig, 1902.
(72 S.) Rev.: Sh. Jb. 39, 1903, S. 288–9, R. Petsch.

HENRY LÜDEKE: Ludwig Tiecks Shakespeare-Studien. Zwei Kapitel zum
Thema: Ludwig Tieck und das alte englische Theater. Diss. Frankfurt,
1917. (62 S.)

HENRY LÜDEKE: Ludwig Tieck und das alte englische Theater. Ein Beitrag zur Geschichte der Romantik. Frankfurt a. M., 1922. (viii, 373 S.)=Dt. Forsch., hrsg. von Fr. Panzer und J. Petersen, H. 6. Rev.: Litbl. 48, 1927, Sp. 257-9; MLR. 18, 1923, pp. 234-6, J. G. Robertson.

LUDWIG TIECK: Das Buch über Shakespeare. Handschriftl. Aufzeichnungen, aus dem Nachlass hrsg. von HENRY LÜDEKE. Halle, 1920. (xxvi, 524 S.)= Neudr. dt. Lit.werke des 18. und 19. Jhrh., hrsg. v. A. Leitzmann und W. Oehlke, No. 1. Rev.: MLR. 17, 1922, pp. 103-5, M. Montgomery; Bbl. 35, 1924, S. 119-27, H. Huscher.

WERNER DEETJEN: Goethe und Tiecks elisabethanische Studien. Ein Fund im Goethe- und Schiller-Archiv. In: Sh. Jb. Jg. 65, 1929, S. 175-83.

W. HÜTTMANN: Christian Felix *Weisse* und seine Zeit in ihrem Verhältnis zu Shakespeare. Diss. Bonn, 1912. (95 S.)

(β) THE REMAINING GERMANIC COUNTRIES

THEODOR VETTER: Shakespeare und die deutsche Schweiz. In: Sh. Jb. Jg. 48, 1912, S. 21-36.

THOMAS J. I. ARNOLD: Shakespeare in de nederlandsche letterkunde en op het nederlandsch tooneel. Bibliographisch overzicht. 's-Gravenhage, 1879= Bibliographische Adversaria IV, No. 4 en 5. (36 S.)

TH. J. I. ARNOLD: Shakespeare-bibliography in the Netherlands. The Hague, 1879. Also in: Bibliographische Adversaria IV, 4 and 5.

LINA SCHNEIDER: Shakespeare in den Niederlanden. In: Sh. Jb. Jg. 26, 1891, S. 26-42.

WILHELM BOLIN: Zur Shakespeare-Literatur Schwedens. In: Sh. Jb. Jg. 15, 1880, S. 73-128.

HARRY V. E. PALMBLAD: Shakspere and *Strindberg*. In: The Germanic Rev. vol. 3, 1928, S. 1-22 and 168-77.

TRYGVE TONSTAD: *Wergeland* og Shakespeare. In: Edda. Jg. 15, Bd. 28, 1928, S. 345-93.

(e) THE SLAVONIC COUNTRIES
(a) RUSSIA

ANDRÉ LIRONDELLE: Shakespeare en Russie (1748-1840). Étude de littérature comparée. Paris, 1912. (248 pp.) 1927 (250 pp.). Rev.: Sh. Jb. 49, 1913, S. 249-50, M. Förster.

ERNST FRIEDRICHS: Shakespeare in Russland. In: E. St. 50, 1916, S. 106-36. Rev.: Sh. Jb. 53, 1917, S. 215-16, Grabau.

MICHAEL POKROWSKIJ: *Puschkin* und Shakespeare. In: Sh. Jb. Jg. 43, 1907, S. 169-209.

RICHARD GEBHARD: Iwan *Turgenjew* in seinen Beziehungen zu Shakespeare. In: Sh. Jb. Jg. 45, 1909, S. 171-84.

(β) POLAND

JOSEPHINE CALINA [i.e. Mrs. Allardyce Nicoll]: Shakespeare in Poland. A Shakespeare survey. I. O.U.P., 1923. (76 pp.) Rev.: Bbl. 35, 1924, S. 197–203, L. Masing.

(f) HUNGARY

A. GREGUSS: Shakespeare in Ungarn. Budapest, 1879.

ALBERT BERZEVICZY: Shakespeare és a magyar nemzetlélek. In: Magyar Shakespeare-Tár, Bd. 8, 1896. Rev.: Sh. Jb. 54, 1918, S. 156–7, A. Weber.

FRIEDRICH RIEDL: Shakespeare és a magyar irodalom (=Shakespeare and Hungarian literature). Budapest, 1916. (42 S.) Rev.: Sh. Jb. 54, 1918, S. 162–3, D. Rózsa.

ELEMÉR CZÁSZÁR: Shakespeare és a magyar költészet (=Shakespeare and Hungarian poetry). Budapest, 1917. (265 S.) Rev.: Sh. Jb. 54, 1918, S. 163, D. Rózsa.

Z. HARASZTI: Shakespeare in Hungary, his plays on the stage and his influence in literature and life. Boston, Trustees of the Public Library, 1929. (36 pp.)

(g) OTHER COUNTRIES (NOT INCLUDED ABOVE)

WILHELM WAGNER: Shakespeare in Griechenland. In: Sh. Jb. Jg. 12, 1877, S. 33–56.

ERWIN WALTER: Shakespeare in Japan. In: Sh. Jb. Jg. 51, 1915, S. 98–110.

V. POPOVIĆ: Shakespeare in Serbia. London, 1928. (vi, 128 pp.)

(3) ALTERATIONS AND ADAPTATIONS
(a) GENERAL TREATISES

RUDOLPH GENÉE: Geschichte der Shakespeareschen Dramen in Deutschland. Leipzig, 1870. (viii, 509 S.)

GISBERT FREIHERR VINCKE: Bearbeitungen und Aufführungen Shakespearescher Stücke vom Tode des Dichters bis zum Tode Garricks. In: Sh. Jb. Jg. 9, 1874, S. 41–54.
A bibliographical survey of the English stage versions of Shakespeare's plays in the XVIIth and XVIIIth centuries.

GISBERT FREIHERR VINCKE: Shakespeare auf der englischen Bühne seit Garrick. In: Sh. Jb. Jg. 22, 1887, S. 1–23.

O. GLÖDE: Shakespeare in der englischen Literatur des 17. und 18. Jahrhunderts. Progr. Doberan, 1902. (20 S.)

FREDERICK W. KILBOURNE: Alterations and adaptations of Shakespeare. Boston, 1906. (191 pp.) Rev.: Sh. Jb. 43, 1907, S. 279–81, F. Lindner.

WALTER KÜHN: Shakespeares Tragödien auf dem deutschen Theater im 18. Jahrhundert. Theaterbearbeitungen und Kritiken. (Teildr.) Diss. München, 1909. (45 S.)

ALFRED W. POLLARD: The improvers of Shakespeare. In: Libr., 3rd ser., vol. 7, 1916, pp. 265–90.

JOCZA SAVITS: Shakespeare und die Bühne des Dramas. Erfahrungen und Betrachtungen. Bonn, 1917. (viii, 724 S.)

Pp. 27–376 deal with the chief adapters of Shakespeare's works in the XVIIIth and XIXth centuries.

MONTAGUE SUMMERS: Shakespeare adaptations. Boston & London, 1922. (cviii, 282 pp.)

An anthology.

HAZELTON SPENCER: Improving Shakespeare. Bibliographical notes on the Restoration adaptations. In: PMLA., vol. 41, 1926, pp. 727–46. Rev.: Sh. Jb. 64, 1928, S. 219–20, Beckmann.

With careful bibliography.

HAZELTON SPENCER: Shakespeare improved. The Restoration versions in quarto and on the stage. Cambridge, Harv. Univ. Pr., & O.U.P., 1927. (xii, 406 pp.) Rev.: MLN. 43, 1928, pp. 400–2, A. Nicoll; Litbl. 1928, Sp. 237; JEGPh. 28, 1929, pp. 138–9, R. A. Law; RESt. 4, 1928, pp. 472–4, D. M. Walmsley; Sh. Jb. 64, 1928, S. 200–1, W. Keller; Bbl. 40, 1929, S. 299–304, A. Eichler.

The most exhaustive work on the subject.

(b) VARIOUS ADAPTERS OF SHAKESPEARE

M. ROSBUND: *Dryden* als Shakespeare-Bearbeiter. Diss. Halle, 1882. (72 S.)

ALLARDYCE NICOLL: Dryden as an adapter of Shakespeare. Oxford, 1921. (35 pp.)

With good bibliography of the Shakespeare adaptations between 1660 and 1700.

E. PRESTON DARGAN: Shakespeare and *Ducis*. In: Mod. Phil., vol. 10, 1912–13, pp. 137–78.

GISBERT FREIHERR VINCKE: *Garrick's* Bühnenbearbeitungen Shakespeares. In: Sh. Jb. Jg. 13, 1878, S. 267–73.

GISBERT FREIHERR VINCKE: Karl *Immermann's* Shakespeare-Einrichtungen. In: Sh. Jb. Jg. 22, 1887, S. 172–88.

ALEXANDER VON WEILEN: *Laube* und Shakespeare. Heinrich Laubes Bearbeitungen Shakespearescher Dramen. In: Sh. Jb. Jg. 43, 1907, S. 98–137.

OSCAR ZOLLINGER: Ein französischer Shakespeare-Bearbeiter des 18. Jahrhunderts [Louis-Sébastien *Mercier*]. In: Sh. Jb. Jg. 38, 1902, S. 98–117.

EUGEN KILIAN: *Schreyvogels* Shakespeare-Bearbeitungen. Ein Beitrag zur Bühnengeschichte der Shakespeareschen Dramen in Deutschland. In: Sh. Jb. Jg. 39, 1903, S. 87–120; 41, 1905, S. 135–62; 43, 1907, S. 53–69 (Merch.), 70–9 (Oth.), 80–97 (Haml.).

ELSE PFENNIGER: Friedrich Ludwig *Schröder* als Bearbeiter englischer Dramen. Diss. Zürich, 1919. (106 S.)

(4) TRANSLATIONS OF SHAKESPEARE

(a) GERMAN TRANSLATIONS

(α) GENERAL WORKS DEALING WITH GERMAN TRANSLATORS AND TRANSLATIONS

C. ASSMANN: Shakespeare und seine deutschen Übersetzer. Eine literarisch-linguistische Abhandlung. Progr. Liegnitz, 1843. (32 S.)

RUDOLPH GENÉE: Geschichte der Shakespeareschen Dramen in Deutschland. Leipzig, 1870. (viii, 509 S.)
A survey up to 1867.

GISBERT FREIHERR VINCKE: Zur Geschichte der deutschen Shakespeare-Übersetzungen. In: Sh. Jb. Jg. 16, 1881, S. 254–73 und Jg. 17, 1882, S. 82–99.
A sketch of the German translations of Shakespeare's collected works with synoptical table.

RUDOLF KRAUSS: Ludwig Schubart als Shakespeare-Übersetzer. In: Sh. Jb. Jg. 39, 1903, S. 69–73.

ARNOLD SCHRÖER: Über Shakespeare-Übersetzungen. In: N. Spr. Bd. 16, 1908–9, S. 577–99.

ALBERT LEITZMANN: Karl Lachmann als Shakespeare-Übersetzer. In: Sh. Jb. Jg. 56, 1920, S. 73–89.

For further bibliography, cf. GOEDEKE'S Grundriss zur Geschichte der deutschen Dichtung.

For bibliographical survey of the German translations of individual dramas, cf. LUDWIG UNFLAD: Die Shakespeare-Literatur in Deutschland. München, 1880.

(β) THE MOST IMPORTANT GERMAN TRANSLATIONS

Shakespears theatralische Werke. Aus dem Englischen übersetzt von HERRN WIELAND. 8 Bde. Zürich, 1762–6. Cf. also the collected works: WIELANDS gesammelte Schriften. Hrsg. von d. deutschen Kommission der Preuss. Akad. d. Wiss. 2. Abt.: Übersetzungen. 1.–3. Bd.: Shakespeares theatralische Werke. Hrsg. von ERNST STADLER. Berlin, 1909–11.
Prose translation.

Cf. also MARCUS SIMPSON: Eine Vergleichung der Wielandschen Shakespeare-Übersetzung mit dem Originale. Diss. München, 1898. (133 S.)

ERNST STADLER: Wielands Shakespeare. Strassburg, 1910. (vii, 133 S.)= Quellen und Forsch., H. 107. Rev.: Sh. Jb. 47, 1911, S. 301–2, G. Witkowski.

F. W. MEISNEST: Wieland's translation of Shakespeare. In: MLR., vol. 9, 1914, pp. 12–40. Rev.: Sh. Jb. 51, 1915, S. 234–5, Grabau.

William Shakespear's Schauspiele. Neue Ausgabe, von JOH. JOACHIM ESCHENBURG. 13 Bde. Zürich, 1775–82.
Prose translation.

Willhelm Shakespears Schauspiele. Von JOH. JOACHIM ESCHENBURG. Neue verbess. Auflage. 22 Bde. Strassburg, 1778–Mannheim, 1783. = The Strassburg-Mannheim reprint.

> Cf. also: HERMANN UHDE-BERNAYS: Der Mannheimer Shakespeare. Ein Beitrag zur Geschichte der ersten deutschen Shakespeare-Übertragungen. Berlin, 1902. (x, 90 S.)=Lit.histor. Forsch., hrsg. von Schick und von Waldberg, H. 25. Rev.: Sh. Jb. 40, 1904, S. 284–5, Leitzmann.
>
> H. SCHRADER: Eschenburg und Shakespeare. Diss. Marburg, 1911. (81 S.)

Shakspeares dramatische Werke, übersetzt von AUGUST WILHELM SCHLEGEL. 8 Bde. Berlin, 1797–1801. 9. Bd., 1. Abt. Berlin, 1810.

Translations of 17 plays.

> Cf. MICHAEL BERNAYS: Zur Entstehungsgeschichte des Schlegel'schen Shakespeare. Hab. Schr. Leipzig, 1872. (55 S.) Considerably enlarged: Leipzig, 1872. (vi, 260 S.)
>
> W. PAETOW: Die erste metrische deutsche Shakespeare-Übersetzung in ihrer Stellung zu ihrer Literaturepoche. Diss. Bern, 1893. (82 S.)
>
> RUDOLF GENÉE: A. W. Schlegel und Shakespeare. Ein Beitrag zur Würdigung der Schlegelschen Übersetzungen, mit 3 faksimilierten Seiten seiner Handschrift des Hamlet. Berlin, 1903. (43 S.) Rev.: Sh. Jb. 40, 1904, S. 283–4, W. Keller.
>
> B. ASSMANN: Studien zur A. W. Schlegelschen Shakespeare-Übersetzung. Die Wortspiele. Progr. Dresden, 1906. (26 S.)

Shakspeare's Schauspiele von JOHANN HEINRICH VOSS und dessen Söhnen Heinrich Voss und Abraham Voss. 9 Bde. Leipzig, 1818–29.

Shakspeares dramatische Werke, übersetzt und erläutert von J. W. O. BENDA. 19 Bde. Leipzig, Göschen, 1825–6.

The first German translation of the collected works by *one* translator.

Shakspeares dramatische Werke. Übersetzt von AUGUST WILHELM VON SCHLEGEL, ergänzt und erläutert von LUDWIG TIECK. 9 Teile. Berlin, 1825–33.

Shakespeares dramatische Werke. Übersetzt von August Wilhelm von Schlegel und Ludwig Tieck. 12 Bde. Berlin, 1839–40.

> The orthodox Schlegel-Tieck.

> Cf. MICHAEL BERNAYS: Der Schlegel-Tiecksche Shakespeare. In: Sh. Jb. Jg. 1, 1865, S. 396–405.
>
> W. WETZ: Zur Beurteilung der sog. Schlegel-Tieckschen Shakespeare-Übersetzung. In: E. St. Bd. 28, 1900, S. 321–65.
>
> ALOIS BRANDL: Ludwig Fulda, Paul Heyse und Adolf Wilbrandt über die Schlegel-Tiecksche Shakespeare-Übersetzung. In: Sh. Jb. Jg. 37, 1901, S. xxxvii–lv.
>
> F. DEIBEL: Dorothea Schlegel als Schriftstellerin im Zusammenhang mit der romantischen Schule. Diss. Greifswald, 1904. (61 S.)

HENRY LÜDEKE: Zur Tieckschen Shakespeare-Übersetzung. In: Sh. Jb. Jg. 55, 1919, S. 1–29.

HENRY LÜDEKE: Ludwig Tiecks erste Shakespeare-Übersetzung (1794). In: Sh. Jb. Jg. 57, 1921, S. 54–64.

HENRY LÜDEKE: Ludwig Tieck und das alte englische Theater. Ein Beitrag zur Geschichte der Romantik. Frankf. a. M., 1922. (373 S.)=Deutsche Forsch., hrsg. von Panzer und Petersen, H. 6. Rev.: Sh. Jb. 59–60, 1924, S. 193–5, W. Keller.
Indicates Tieck's essential collaboration in the Shakespeare-translation.

WALTHER FISCHER: Ludwig Tiecks Shakespeare. In: N. Spr. Bd. 34, 1926, S. 102–8.

W. Shakspeares dramatische Werke, übers. von ERNST ORTLEPP. 16 Bde. Stuttgart, 1838–9. New emended edition 1842.
The second German translation of the collected works by *one* translator.

W. Shakespeares sämtliche dramatische Werke, übers. von A. Böttger, H. Döring, Alex. Fischer, L. Hilsenberg, W. Lampadius, Th. Mügge, Th. Oelckers, E. Ortlepp, L. Petz, K. Simrock, E. Susemihl, E. Thein. 12 Bde. Leipzig, 1839.

William Shaksperes dramatische Werke, übers. und erläutert von ADELBERT KELLER und MORIZ RAPP. 37 Bdchen. Stuttgart, 1843–7. 2nd edition in 8 vols. Stuttgart, 1854.

Shakespeares dramatische Werke. Nach der Übers. von Aug. Wilh. Schlegel und Ludw. Tieck sorgfältig revid. von H. ULRICI, hrsg. durch die Deutsche Shakespeare-Gesellschaft. 12 Bde. Berlin, 1867–71, 1876–7².
The Schlegel-Tieck Edition of the German Shakespeare Society.

Shakespeare in deutscher Übersetzung [*Dingelstedt*]. 10 Bde. Hildburghausen, Bibliogr. Inst., 1867. Translators: K. Simrock, H. Viehoff, W. Jordan, F. Dingelstedt, L. Seeger, F. A. Gelbcke.

William Shakespeares dramatische Werke [*Bodenstedt*]. Übers. von Friedrich Bodenstedt, Nicolaus Delius, F. Freiligrath, Otto Gildemeister, Georg Herwegh, Paul Heyse, Hermann Kurz, Adolf Wilbrandt. Mit Einl. und Anm. hrsg. von Friedrich Bodenstedt. 9 Bde. Leipzig, Brockhaus, 1867–71, 1873², 1878–9³.

W. Shakespeares dramatische Werke. Deutsche Volksausgabe. Hrsg. von MAX MOLTKE. 12 Bde. Leipzig, 1868.

W. Shakespeares dramatische Werke. Nach den Schlegel-Tieckschen Übers. für die deutsche Bühne bearb. von WILH. OECHELHÄUSER. 27 Bdchen. Berlin, 1870–Weimar, 1878.
Expurgated edition.

Shakespeares dramatische Werke, übers. von Aug. Wilh. von Schlegel und Ludw. Tieck. Hrsg. von RICHARD GOSCHE und BENNO TSCHISCHWITZ. Erste illustr. Ausg. 3. verb. Aufl. 8 Bde. Berlin, 1877.

Shakespeares dramatische Werke nach der Übers. von Aug. Wilh. Schlegel, Philipp Kaufmann und Voss revid. und hrsg. von MAX KOCH. 12 Bde. Stuttgart, Cotta [1882–4].

Shakespeares dramatische Werke, übers. von Aug. Wilh. v. Schlegel und Ludw. Tieck, durchges. von MICHAEL BERNAYS. 12 Bde. Berlin, 1891.

W. Shakespeares dramatische Werke. Übers. von Aug. Wilh. von Schlegel und Ludw. Tieck. Im Auftrag d. Deutschen Shakespeare-Gesellschaft hrsg. von WILHELM OECHELHÄUSER. Stuttgart, Deutsche Verlags-Anstalt (1891). Popular edition.

Shakespeares dramatische Werke, übers. von A. W. von Schlegel und L. Tieck, hrsg. von ALOIS BRANDL. 10 Bde. Leipzig & Wien, Bibliogr. Inst., 1897–9. Rev.: Bbl. 10, 1900, S. 292–7, W. Wetz.

Shakespearedramen (Romeo und Julia, Othello, Lear, Macbeth). Nachgegelassene Übersetzungen von OTTO GILDEMEISTER. Hrsg. von HEINRICH SPIES. Berlin, 1904. (xv, 524 S.)

W. Shakespeares dramatische Werke. Übers. von Aug. Wilh. Schlegel und Ludw. Tieck. Revid. von HERMANN CONRAD. 5 Bde. Stuttgart & Leipzig, Deutsche Verlags-Anstalt (1905).
Popular edition in one volume, 1906.

> Cf. HERMANN CONRAD: Grundsätze und Vorschläge zur Verbesserung des Schlegelschen Shakespeare-Textes. I, II. In: Sh. Jb. Jg. 38, 1902, S. 212–23; 39, 1903, S. 179–201.

> HERMANN CONRAD: Schwierigkeiten der Shakespeare-Übersetzung. Erläuterung zweifelhafter Stellen. Halle, 1906. (xvi, 155 S.)

> HERMANN CONRAD: Unechtheiten in der ersten Ausgabe von Schlegels Shakespeare-Übersetzung (1797–1801). Nachgewiesen aus seinen Manuskripten. In: Z. f. e. U., Bd. 11, 1912, S. 289–321; 385–406; 481–506.

Shakespeare in deutscher Sprache. Hrsg., zum Teil neu übers. von FRIEDRICH GUNDOLF. 10 Bde. Berlin, Bondi, 1908–23. Rev.: Dt. Litztg. 1910, Sp. 1000–4, L. L. Schücking.

> ARTHUR BÖHTLINGK: Gundolfs 'Shakespeare in deutscher Sprache'. Ein Vademecum. Karlsruhe [1929]. (40 S.)
> Severe criticism.

Shakespeares Werke in 15 Teilen. Übersetzung der Dramen von Schlegel und Tieck, der Gedichte von Wilhelm Jordan und Max Josef Wolff. Hrsg., nach dem engl. Texte revid. und mit Einl. und Anm. versehen von WOLFGANG KELLER. 5 Bde. Berlin & Leipzig [1912].=Goldene Klassiker Bibliothek. Good popular edition.

Shakespeares Werke, englisch und deutsch. Hrsg. von L. L. SCHÜCKING u. a. Leipzig, Tempel-Klassiker, 1912 seq.

Neue Shakespeare-Übersetzung von HANS ROTHE. München.
Each volume bears the title of the play it contains (Lear 1922, Troil. 1922, As 1922, Macb. 1922, R. II 1923).

New edition: 1st vol.: Lustspiele. Leipzig [1928]. (xxxvi, 439 S.)

Cf. WALTHER FISCHER: Hans Rothes neue Shakespeare-Übersetzung. In: N. Spr. Bd. 31, 1923, S. 298–302.

William Shakespeare: Sämtliche Werke. Nach der Schlegel-Tieckschen Übers. in neuer Bearbeitung mit Einleitungen hrsg. von JULIUS BAB. 9 Bde. Stuttgart [1923]. Rev.: Sh. Jb. 59–60, 1924, S. 171–3, W. Keller.

Shakespeares sämtliche Werke. Die Übertragungen von Aug. Wilh. Schlegel und Ludw. Tieck, mit Anm. hrsg. von L. L. SCHÜCKING und E. VON SCHAU-BERT. 10 Bde. München, 1925–9. Rev.: Arch. 81, Jg. 150, 1296, S. 286–7.

Shakespeare: Meisterdramen. Vorwort von MAX J. WOLFF. 6 Bde. Leipzig, Inselverlag, 1927.

Shakespeares Werke in Einzelausgaben. Leipzig, Insel-Verlag, 1920 seq.

(b) TRANSLATIONS INTO OTHER GERMANIC LANGUAGES

Shakspeares dramatiska arbeten, efter C. A. HAGBERGS öfversättning med hänsyn till den sceniska framställningen och för läsning i hemmet bearbetade af W. BOLIN. Med illustrationer af Sir J. Gilbert. I–IV. Lund (1879–87).
Hagberg's monumental Swedish translation.

Shakespeares dramatiske værker oversat og kommenteret af V. ØSTERBERG. København, 1927 seq. Rev.: Sh. Jb. 65, 1929, S. 209–14, L. Magon.

FINNUR JÓNSSON: Shakespeare i Island. In: Edda, Bd. 6, 1916, S. 185–8.
Enumeration of the modern Icelandic translations.

(c) TRANSLATIONS INTO ROMANCE LANGUAGES
(α) FRENCH TRANSLATIONS

ALBERT DUBEUX: Les traductions françaises de Shakespeare. Paris, 1928. (81 pp.)=Études françaises XV. Rev.: Revue anglo-amér., vol. 6, 1928, pp. 64–5, A. Brulé.

———

PIERRE-ANTOINE DE LA PLACE: Théâtre anglais 1745–8.
Contains translations of the chief works.

Shakespeare, traduit de l'anglois par LE TOURNEUR. 20 vols. Paris, 1776–82.

Cf. PAUL HAAK: Die ersten französischen Shakespeare-Übersetzungen von La Place und Le Tourneur. Diss. Berlin, 1922. (94 S.) Rev.: Sh. Jb. 59–60, 1924, S. 196, W. Keller.

Œuvres dramatiques de Shakespeare. Traduction nouvelle par L. LAROCHE, précédée d'une introd. sur le génie de Shakespeare par A. DUMAS. 2 vols. Paris, 1839–40.

Œuvres complètes de W. Shakespeare, traduites par FRANÇOIS-VICTOR HUGO. 18 vols. Paris, 1856–67.

Œuvres complètes de Shakespeare, traduites par É. Montégut. 10 vols. Paris, 1889–94.

(β) SPANISH AND PORTUGUESE TRANSLATIONS

RICARDO RUPPERT Y UJARAVI: Shakespeare en España. Traducciones, imitaciones e influencia de las obras de Shakespeare en la literatura española. Madrid, 1920. (107 pp.)

CAROLINA MICHAËLIS DE VASCONCELLOS: Shakespeare in Portugal. In: Sh. Jb. Jg. 15, 1880, S. 266–97.

(d) SLAVONIC TRANSLATIONS

Шекспиръ. Библіотека великихъ писателей подъ редакціей С. А. Венгерова. Изданіе Брокгаузъ-Ефрона. С.-Петербургъ. 1902. Т. 1 и 2.
Russian translation of the collected works, with numerous illustrations.

William Shakespeare. Dzieła dramatyczne. [Shakespeares plays in Polish translation by J. Kasprowicz, J. Korzeniowski, St. Koźmian, K. Ostrowski, A. Pajgert, J. Paszkowski, E. Porębowicz and L. Ulrich. With an introd. by ROMAN DYBOSKI, and with a study on Shakespeare in Poland by L. BERNACKI. 6 vols. Warsaw, 1911–13. Rev.: Sh. Jb. 50, 1914, S. 171–2, W. Creizenach.
A collection of the best Polish translations.

JOSEPHINE CALINA: [i.e. Mrs. Allardyce Nicoll]: Shakespeare in Poland. Oxford, 1923. (76 pp.)

VLADETA POPOVIĆ: Shakespeare in Serbia. London, 1928. (viii, 128 pp.)

(5) SHAKESPEARE AND THE MODERN STAGE
(a) GENERAL DRAMATURGIC LITERATURE

EDUARD DEVRIENT: Geschichte der deutschen Schauspielkunst. Dresden, 1848. Neuausgabe in 2 Bden. Berlin, 1905. (xliii, 557 und xx, 605 S.)

KARL ELZE: Shakespeares Geltung für die Gegenwart. In: Sh. Jb. Jg. 2, 1867, S. 96–123.

HERMANN FREIHERR VON FRIESEN: Wie soll man Shakespeare spielen? I, II. In: Sh. Jb. Jg. 5, 1870, S. 154–82 und 6, 1871, S. 250–76.

ROB. PRÖLSS: Katechismus der Dramaturgie, 1877.

HEINRICH BULTHAUPT: Dramaturgie des Schauspiels. Bd. 2: Shakespeare. Oldenburg, 1894[5], 1903[8]. (xi, 508 S.) Rev.: Sh. Jb. 36, 1900, S. 321, E. Kilian; Bbl. 7, 1897, S. 7–12, R. Fischer.

EUGEN KILIAN: Die szenischen Formen Shakespeares in ihrer Beziehung zu der Aufführung seiner Dramen auf der modernen Bühne. In: Sh. Jb. Jg. 28, 1893, S. 90–110.

K. FRENZEL: Die szenischen Einrichtungen der Shakespeare-Dramen. In: Sh. Jb. Jg. 36, 1900, S. 256–66.

EUGEN KILIAN: Shakespeare auf der modernen Bühne. In: Sh. Jb. Jg. 36, 1900, S. 228–48.

JULIUS CSERWINKA: Shakespeare und die Bühne. Wiesbaden, 1902. (90 S.) Rev.: Sh. Jb. 39, 1903, S. 303–5, R. Petsch.

EUGEN KILIAN: Der Shakespearesche Monolog und seine Spielweise. Festvortrag. In: Sh. Jb. Jg. 39, 1903, S. xiv–xlii.

ADOLF WINDS: Die Technik der Schauspielkunst. Dresden (1904). (viii, 325 S.) Rev.: Lit. Zbl. 56, 1905, Sp. 1263, M. Seidel.

EUGEN KILIAN: Dramaturgische Blätter. Aufsätze und Studien aus dem Gebiete der praktischen Dramaturgie, der Regiekunst und der Theatergeschichte. München & Leipzig, 1905. (iv, 400 S.) Rev.: Sh. Jb. 42, 1906, S. 273–4, Gaehde.

SIDNEY LEE: Shakespeare and the modern stage, with other essays. London, 1907. (xv, 251 pp.) German translation: Shakespeare und die moderne Bühne, ins Deutsche übertr. von Jocza Savits. München, 1911. (38 S.)

CARL HAGEMANN: Über Versuche moderner Shakespeare-Inszenierungen. Festvortrag. In: Sh. Jb. Jg. 45, 1909, S. xv–xxxii.

HANS HECHT: Shakespeare und die deutsche Bühne der Gegenwart. I, II. In: GRM. Jg. 2, 1910, S. 288–99 und 348–57.

WILLIAM POEL: Shakespeare in the theatre. London, 1913. (vii, 247 pp.) Rev.: Sh. Jb. 50, 1914, S. 205–7, M. Förster.
Essays by the well-known founder of the Elizabethan Stage Society.

OSKAR WALZEL: Neue Bühnentechnik im Dienste Shakespeares. In: Sh. Jb. Jg. 50, 1914, S. 74–87.

PAUL MARX: Shakespeare und die modernen Bühnenprobleme (seit 1907). In: Sh. Jb. Jg. 51, 1915, S. 53–70.

ADOLF WINDS: Shakespeare als Bildner des Schauspielers. In: Sh. Jb. Jg. 52, 1916, S. 64–75.

MAX MARTERSTEIG: Shakespeare-Regie. Festvortrag. In: Sh. Jb. Jg. 53, 1917, S. x–xxvii.

JOCZA SAVITS: Shakespeare und die Bühne des Dramas. Erfahrungen und Betrachtungen. Bonn, 1917. (viii, 724 S.) Rev.: Sh. Jb. 54, 1918, S. 145–7, A. Winds.
Advocates a return to the simple stage without scenery.

WOLDEMAR JÜRGENS: Die Inszenierung von Shakespeares Lustspielen. Festvortrag. In: Sh. Jb. Jg. 56, 1920, S. 6–23.

MARTIN LUSERKE: Shakespeare-Aufführungen als Bewegungsspiele. Stuttgart, 1921. (168 S.)

EUGEN KILIAN: Shakespeare und die Mode des Tages. In: Sh. Jb. Jg. 61, N.F. 2, 1925, S. 7–38. Rev.: E. St. 62, 1928, S. 435–7, Eichler.

ADOLF WINDS: Geschichte der Regie. Stuttgart, 1925.

HUBERT GRIFFITH: Iconoclastes, or the future of Shakespeare. London (1927). (95 pp.)
Advocates performances of Shakespeare in modern dress.

(b) SHAKESPEAREAN ACTORS

(a) GENERAL WORKS

DR. DORAN: 'Their Majesties Servants', or, annals of the British stage from Thomas Betterton to Edmund Kean. 2 vols. London, 1864, 1865[2].

GISBERT FREIHERR VINCKE: Shakespeare auf der englischen Bühne seit Garrick. Festvortrag. In: Sh. Jb. Jg. 22, 1887, S. 1–23.

HEINRICH BULTHAUPT: Shakespeare und die Virtuosen. In: Sh. Jb. Jg. 24, 1889, S. 89–107.

GEORGE C. D. ODELL: Shakespeare from Betterton to Irving. 2 vols. London, 1921. (xiv, 456, and viii, 498 pp.)

(β) INDIVIDUAL SHAKESPEAREAN ACTORS

JOHN ADOLPHUS: Memoirs of John *Bannister*, comedian. 2 vols. London, 1839.

RICHARD ROSENBAUM: Alfred *Freiherr von Berger* (1853–1912). In: Sh. Jb. Jg. 49, 1913, S. 150–6.

ROBERT W. LOWE: Thomas *Betterton*. 1891.

THOMAS DAVIES: Memoirs of the life of David *Garrick*. 2 vols. London, 1780.

GISBERT FREIHERR VINCKE: Shakespeare und Garrick. Vortrag. In: Sh. Jb. Jg. 9, 1874, S. 1–24.

CHRISTIAN GAEHDE: David Garrick als Shakespeare-Darsteller und seine Bedeutung für die heutige Schauspielkunst. Berlin, 1904. (198 S.)= Schriften d. Dt. Shakespeare-Ges., Bd. 2. Rev.: Sh. Jb. 41, 1905, S. 256–8, Gregori.

THEODORE MARTIN: Monographs. Garrick, Macready, Rachel, and Baron Stockmar. London, 1906. (341 pp.) Rev.: Sh. Jb. 43, 1907, S. 282–3, R. Fischer.

FRANK A. HEDGCOCK: David Garrick et ses amis français. Paris, 1911. (283 pp.) English transl. entitled: A cosmopolitan actor, David Garrick and his French friends. London [1912]. (442 pp.) Rev.: Sh. Jb. 49, 1913, S. 217–19, Ch. Gaehde; MLR. 7, 1912, pp. 387–90, H. F. Stewart.

The Diary of DAVID GARRICK. Being a record of his memorable trip to Paris in 1751. Now first printed from the original MS. and ed. by R. C. ALEXANDER. O.U.P., 1928. (x, 118 pp.)

ADOLF WINDS: Friedrich *Haase* (1827–1911). In: Sh. Jb. Jg. 48, 1912, S. 155–63.

HELENE RICHTER: Ernst *Hartmann* (1844–1910). In: Sh. Jb. Jg. 48, 1912, S. 163–8.

ELIZABETH LEE: *Irving* as an interpreter of Shakespeare. In: Sh. Jb. Jg. 42, 1906, S. 224–7.

HELENE RICHTER: Josef *Kainz*. In: Sh. Jb. Jg. 47, 1911, S. 1–17.

JOHN WILLIAM COLE: The life and theatrical times of Charles *Kean*, including a summary of the English stage for the last 50 years. 2 vols. London, 1859.

F. W. HAWKINS: The life of Edmund *Kean*. 2 vols. London, 1869.

JAMES BOADEN: Memoirs of the life of John Philip *Kemble*, including a history of the stage from the time of Garrick. 2 vols. London, 1825.

EUGEN KILIAN: Rudolf *Lange*. In: Sh. Jb. Jg. 45, 1909, S. 233–7.

HELENE RICHTER: Josef *Lewinsky*. In: Sh. Jb. Jg. 44, 1908, S. 171–85.

HELENE RICHTER: Josef Lewinsky, 50 Jahre Wiener Kunst und Kultur. Zum 150jährigen Jubiläum des Burgtheaters. Wien, 1925. (vii, 320 S.) Rev.: Sh. Jb. 62, 1926, S. 170–1, W. Keller; Arch. 153, S. 117–18, A. Brandl.

J. T. KIRKMAN: Memoirs of the life of Charles *Macklin*, principally compiled from his own papers and memorandums. 2 vols. London, 1799.

WILLIAM COOKE: Memoirs of Charles Macklin. London, 1806.

E. A. PARRY: Charles Macklin. London, 1891.

FREDERICK POLLOCK: *Macready's* reminiscences and selections from his diaries and letters. 2 vols. London, 1875.

THEODORE MARTIN: Monographs. Garrick, Macready, Rachel, and Baron Stockmar. London, 1906. (341 pp.) Rev.: Sh. Jb. 43, 1907, S. 282–3, R. Fischer.

ALFRED KLAAR: Adalbert *Matkowsky* (1858–1909). In: Sh. Jb. Jg. 46, 1910, S. 140–53.

HELENE RICHTER: Alexander *Roempler* (1860–1909). In: Sh. Jb. Jg. 46, 1910, S. 153–5.

GISBERT FREIHERR VINCKE: Shakespeare und *Schröder*. Vortrag. In: Sh. Jb. Jg. 11, 1876, S. 1–29.

THOMAS CAMPBELL: Life of Mrs. *Siddons*. 2 vols. London, 1834.

FRIEDRICH BODENSTEDT: Mrs. Siddons. Nach Aufzeichnungen ihrer Tochter, Mrs. Combe, nebst einigen Bemerkungen über den Charakter der Lady Macbeth. In: Sh. Jb. Jg. 1, 1865, S. 341–61.

HELENE RICHTER: Adolf von *Sonnenthal*. In: Sh. Jb. Jg. 46, 1910, S. 130–9.

KARL ARNS: Ellen *Terry* (Nekrolog). In: Sh. Jb. Jg. 65, 1929, S. 184–8.

ALFRED FREIHERR VON BERGER: Charlotte *Wolter*. In: Sh. Jb. Jg. 34, 1898, S. 326–31.

HELENE RICHTER: Charlotte Wolter (1834–97). In: Sh. Jb. Jg. 45, 1909, S. 185–203.

JULIAN CHARLES YOUNG: A memoir of Charles Mayne *Young*, tragedian, with extracts from his son's journal. 2 vols. London, 1871.

HELENE RICHTER: Clara *Ziegler*. In: Sh. Jb. Jg. 47, 1911, S. 203–14.

(c) SHAKESPEARE PERFORMANCES

(a) GENERAL WORKS

[Various authors]: Statistischer Überblick Shakespearescher Werke auf den deutschen und einigen ausländischen Theatern im Jahre ... In: Sh. Jb. ...

The stage year book. London ....

Appears annually; discusses and reports performances in all countries.

RUDOLF GENÉE: Geschichte der Shakespeareschen Dramen in Deutschland. Leipzig, 1870. (viii, 509 S.)

A survey of performances of Shakespeare in Germany up to 1867.

EDWARD PAYSON MORTON: Shakspere in the 17th century. In: JEGPh., vol. I, 1897, pp. 31–44.

ROBERT F. ARNOLD: Bibliographie der deutschen Bühne seit 1830. Strassburg, 1909[2].

PAUL ALFRED MERBACH: Bibliographie für Theatergeschichte. 1913.=Schriften d. Gesellsch. f. Theatergeschichte, Bd. 21.

(β) VARIOUS THEATRES

KÄTHE STRICKER: Die Aufnahme Shakespeares am *Bremer* Stadttheater. In: Sh. Jb. Jg. 54, 1918, S. 22–41.

ROBERT PRÖLSS: Shakespeare-Aufführungen in *Dresden* (1778–1816). In: Sh. Jb. Jg. 12, S. 182 seq.; 1816–60: Jg. 15, 1880, S. 173–210; 1861 seq.: Jg. 8, 316 seq.

ELISABETH MENTZEL: Geschichte der Schauspielkunst in *Frankfurt a. M.* 1882.

MERSCHBERGER: Die Anfänge Shakespeares auf der *Hamburger* Bühne. Progr. Hamburg, 1890. (44 S.) Also in: Sh. Jb. Jg. 25, 1890, S. 205–72.

OTTO DEVRIENT: Statistik der *Karlsruher* Shakespeare-Aufführungen in den Jahren 1810–72. In: Sh. Jb. Jg. 8, 1873, S. 280–305.

EUGEN KILIAN: Die Königsdramen auf der Karlsruher Bühne, mit besonderer Berücksichtigung der Einrichtungen von Heinrich V. und Heinrich VI. In: Sh. Jb. Jg. 28, 1893, S. 111–56.

AUGUST HAGEN: Shakespeare und *Königsberg*. In: Sh. Jb. Jg. 15, 1880, S. 325–38.

R. GERICKE: Statistik der *Leipziger* Shakespeare-Aufführungen von 1817 bis 1871. In: Sh. Jb. Jg. I, 1872, S. 324–39.

R. GERICKE: Shakespeare-Aufführungen in Leipzig und Dresden, 1778–1817. In: Sh. Jb. Jg. 12, 1877, S. 182–221.

ANTON PICHLER: Die Shakespeare-Aufführungen der *Mannheimer* Hof- und Nationalbühne 1779–1870. In: Deutsche Bühnengenossenschaft, No. 23–6, 1873.

FRIEDRICH BODENSTEDT: Über einige Shakespeare-Aufführungen in *München*. In: Sh. Jb. Jg. 2, 1867, S. 244–76.

EUGEN KILIAN: Die Münchener Shakespeare-Bühne. In: Sh. Jb. Jg. 32, 1896, S. 109–32.

JOCZA SAVITS: Von der Absicht des Dramas. Dramaturgische Betrachtungen über die Reform der Szene, namentlich im Hinblick auf die Shakespeare-Bühne in München. München, 1908. (xi, 397 S.) Rev.: Sh. Jb. 44, 1908, S. 316–20, W. Bormann.

EUGEN KILIAN: Eine neue Shakespeare-Bühne [München]. In: Sh. Jb. Jg. 46, 1910, S. 69–83.

GERHARD AMUNDSEN: Die neue Shakespeare-Bühne des Münchener Hoftheaters. Hrsg. von G. Amundsen, unter Mitarbeit von JULIUS VIKTOR KLEIN und EUGEN KILIAN. München [1911]. (37 S. und 22 Szenenbilder.)

ERNST SIEPER: Shakespeare und das Künstlertheater [München]. In: Süddeutsche Monatshefte, 6, S. 463 ff.

F. MEISTER: Shakespeares Theater zu *Stratford*. In: Sh. Jb. Jg. 15, 1880, S. 156–63.

R. KRAUSS: Shakespeares Dramen auf der *Stuttgarter* Hofbühne (1783–1908). In: Sh. Jb. Jg. 45, 1909, S. 126–38.

C. A. H. BURCKHARDT: Das Repertoire des *Weimarischen* Theaters unter Goethes Leitung. Hamburg, 1901.

RUDOLF FISCHER: Shakespeare und das Burgtheater [*Wien*]. Eine Repertoirestudie. In: Sh. Jb. Jg. 37, 1901, S. 123–64.

ALEXANDER VON WEILEN: Shakespeare und das Burgtheater. In: Sh. Jb. Jg. 50, 1914, S. 60–73.

(6) ILLUSTRATIONS TO SHAKESPEARE'S WORKS

S. HARTMANN: Shakespeare in art. Boston, 1901. (v, 371 pp.) Contents: (1) Shakespearean portraits. (2) The Shakespearean illustrators. (3) The painters of the historical dramas. (4) The painters of the comedies. (5) Shakespeare in sculpture. (7) Portraits of actors in Shakespearean parts. (7) Bibliography.
Cf. the Russian Shakespeare Edition, 1902, p. 163.

MALCOLM C. SALAMAN: Shakespeare in pictorial art. Ed. by CHARLES HOLME. London, 1916. (viii, 183 pp.)

Shakespeare-Visionen. Eine Huldigung deutscher Künstler. Radierungen, Steindrucke, Holzschnitte. Mit Vorrede von GERHART HAUPTMANN. München, 1918.=Drucke der Marées-Gesellschaft. 3. Druck. Rev.: Sh. Jb. 55, 1919, S. 188–90, F. Servaes.

(7) MUSICAL SETTINGS OF SHAKESPEARE'S WORKS, SONGS, ETC.

(a) GENERAL TREATISES

J. GREENHILL, W. A. HARRISON, and F. J. FURNIVALL: A list of all the songs and passages in Shakespeare which have been set to music. London, for the New Shakspere Soc., 1884. (xxxv, 111 pp.)

MAX FRIEDLÄNDER: Shakespeares Werke in der Musik. Versuch einer Zusammenstellung. In: Sh. Jb. Jg. 37, 1901, S. 85–122.
A bibliographical list.

CAMILLE BELLAIGUE: Shakespeare et la musique. In: Revue des deux mondes, 73, 1903, pp. 428–45.

E. VON WIECKI: Shakespeare und die Tonkunst. I. Teil. Progr. Bromberg, 1913. (32 S.)

CHRISTOPHER WILSON: Shakespeare and music. London, 1922. (xiii, 170 pp.)
Discussion of the musical settings of Shakespeare's plays.

HERMANN W. VON WALTERSHAUSEN: Shakespeares Einfluss auf die Musik. Festvortrag. In: Sh. Jb. Jg. 64, N.F. Jg. 5, 1928, S. 13–42.

(b) INDIVIDUAL COMPOSERS

GEORGE SAMPSON: *Bach* and Shakespeare. In: Quart. Rev., vol. 239, 1923, pp. 360–79. Also in: The hundred best English essays, selected by the Earl of Birkenhead. London, 1929.

G. G. GERVINUS: *Händel* und Shakespeare. Leipzig, 1868.

HUGO DAFFNER: *Haydn* und Shakespeare. In: Sh. Jb. Jg. 50, 1914, S. 51–9.

FRIEDRICH SCHNAPP: Franz *Liszts* Stellung zu Shakespeare. In: Sh. Jb. Jg. 61, N.F. Jg. 2, 1925, S. 67–80. Rev.: E. St. 62, 1928, S. 437–8, A. Eichler.

GEORG RICHARD KRUSE: Shakespeare und Otto *Nicolai*. Zur Jahrhundertfeier von Otto Nicolais Geburtstag. In: Sh. Jb. Jg. 46, 1910, S. 84–91.

EDGAR ISTEL: *Verdi* und Shakespeare ('Macbeth'—Briefe über 'König Lear'—'Othello'—'Falstaff'). In: Sh. Jb. Jg. 53, 1917, S. 69–124.

KURT REICHELT: Richard *Wagner* und die englische Literatur. Leipzig, 1912. (179 S.) Rev.: Sh. Jb. 49, 1913, S. 248–9, M. Förster.

(c) SHAKESPEARE AND THE BALLET

AUGUST FRESENIUS: Der getanzte Shakespeare. In: Sh. Jb. Jg. 38, 1902, S. 144–52.

(8) PROSE VERSIONS OF SHAKESPEARE'S PLAYS

CHARLES and MARY ANN LAMB: Tales from Shakespeare. London, 1807 and later editions. German translations:

KARL LAMB: Shakespeare-Erzählungen. Übersetzt von F. W. DRALLE. Stuttgart, 1843. (viii, 272 S.)

3728   Z

CHARLES und MARY LAMB: Das Shakespeare-Geschichtenbuch. Neu übers. von H. E. HERLITSCHKA. Wien, 1928. (363 S.)

CHARLES und MARY LAMB: Shakespeare-Novellen. Auf Grund einer älteren Übersetzung bearbeitet von ELISABETH SCHÜCKING. Leipzig, 1928. (308 S.)=Hafis-Lesebücherei, 60.

LOIS GROSVENOR HUFFORD: Shakespeare in tale and verse. New York & London, 1902. (445 pp.) Rev.: Sh. Jb. 40, 1904, S. 294–5, H. Pigulla.

(9) TRAVESTIES OF SHAKESPEARE'S PLAYS

R. F. SHARP: Travesties of Shakespeare's plays. In: Libr., 4th ser., vol. 1, 1920, pp. 1–20.

(10) DICTIONARIES OF QUOTATIONS

WILLIAM DODD: Beauties of Shakespeare. 2 vols. London, 1752 and later editions.

S. AYSCOUGH: An index to the remarkable passages and words made use of by Shakespeare. London, 1827. (674 pp.)

J. B. MARSH: Familiar, proverbial, and select sayings from Shakspere. London, 1863. (viii, 162 pp.)

E. ROUTLEDGE: Quotations from Shakespeare. London, 1867. (iv, 175 pp.)

G. SOMERS BELLAMY: The new Shakespearian dictionary of quotations. (With marginal classification and reference.) London, 1875. (vii, 272 pp).

JOHN BARTLETT: The Shakespeare phrase book. London, 1881. (1034 pp.)

W. S. W. ANSON: Shakespearean quotations. A collection of the most familiar passages. . . . London [1906]. (160 pp.)

(11) SHAKESPEAREAN SOCIETIES AND THEIR PUBLICATIONS

F. S. BOAS: Shakespeare societies, past and present. In: Shakespeare Review 1, 1928, pp. 315–21.

———

Shakespeare Society, 1841–52: Publications, 1841–53.

For list of titles of the treatises see JAGGARD: Shakespeare bibliography, pp. 606–7.

Ungarische Shakespeare-Gesellschaft, gegr. 1860: Magyar Shakespeare-Tár. A vallás-és közoktatásügyi M. Kir. Minister támogatásával kiadja a Kisfaludy-Társaság Shakespeare-bizottsága, szerkeszti Ferenczi Zoltán. [Ungarisches Shakespeare-Archiv, hrsg. von der ungarischen Kisfaludy-Gesellschaft. Redigiert von ZOLTÁN FERENCZI.] Budapest, 1908 seq.

Deutsche Shakespeare-Gesellschaft, gegr. 1864: Jahrbuch der Deutschen Shakespeare-Gesellschaft. Jg. 1, 1865.

Complete list of the contents of the first 30 vols. is contained in Jg. 29–30, 1894, pp. 410–90.

Cf. F. A. LEO: Rückblick auf das 25jährige Bestehen der Deutschen Shakespeare-Gesellschaft. In: Sh. Jb. Jg. 24, 1889, S. 1–8.

ALBERT LUDWIG: Die Deutsche Shakespeare-Gesellschaft. Ein Rückblick anlässlich ihres 50jährigen Bestehens. In: Sh. Jb. Jg. 49, 1913, S. 1–96.

The New Shakspere Society Publications. London, 1874–84.
For list of titles of the treatises see JAGGARD: Shakespeare bibliography, pp. 228–31.

Cf. NICOLAUS DELIUS: Über die 'New Shakspere Society' und ihre bisherigen Leistungen. In: Sh. Jb. Jg. 10, 1875, S. 355–9.

NICOLAUS DELIUS: Die neuesten Publikationen der 'New Shakspere Society'. In: Sh. Jb. Jg. 18, 1883, S. 238–42.

New York Shakespeare Society Papers and Publications, 1885 seq.
For list of treatises see JAGGARD: Shakespeare bibliography, p. 232.

The Shakespeare Association Pamphlets. O.U.P., 1917 seq.:

1. Shakespeare Day. Report of meeting held on May 3, 1913, to promote the Annual Observance of Shakespeare Day. 1917.

2. J. M. ROBERTSON: The Problem of 'The Merry Wives of Windsor'. 1917. (32 pp.)

3. A. E. HUGHES: Shakespeare and his Welsh Characters. 1918. (34 pp.)

4. H. DUGDALE SYKES: The Authorship of 'The Taming of a Shrew', 'The Famous Victories of Henry V', and the additions to Marlowe's 'Faustus'. 1919. (36 pp.)

5. ERNEST LAW: Shakespeare's 'Tempest' as Originally Produced at Court. (36 pp.)

6. CHARLOTTE CARMICHAEL STOPES: The Seventeenth Century Accounts of the Masters of the Revels. 1922. (36 pp.)

7. ARTHUR W. REED: The Beginnings of the English Secular and Romantic Drama. 1922. (32 pp.)

8. ALLARDYCE NICOLL: Dryden as an Adapter of Shakespeare. 1922. (36 pp.)

9. ROMAN DYBOSKI: Rise and Fall in Shakespeare's Dramatic Art. 1923. (30 pp.)

10. THOMAS M. PARROTT: The Problem of Timon of Athens. 1923. (34 pp.)

11. A. E. MORGAN: Some Problems of Shakespeare's 'Henry the Fourth'. 1924. (44 pp.)

12. The Shakespeare Association, 1925–6. A series of papers on Shakespeare and the theatre. London, 1927. (239 pp.)

The Shakespeare Association Bulletin. Publ. by the Shakespeare Association of America. New York, vol. i, 1926.
With an annual Shakespeare bibliography by S. A. Tannenbaum.

Shakespeare Review, 1928 seq.

(12) SHAKESPEARE AS A HERO IN LITERATURE

(a) DRAMA

ALBERT LUDWIG: Shakespeare als Held deutscher Dramen. In: Sh. Jb. Jg. 54, 1918, S. 1–21.

M. H. SPIELMANN: Shakespeare treads the boards. In: TLS., Dec. 1, 1921 and Feb. 2, 1922.

Shakespeare as a stage figure in European and American dramatic literature.

RICHARD GARNETT: William Shakespeare, pedagogue and poacher. A drama. London, 1905. (111 pp.) Rev.: Sh. Jb. 41, 1905, S. 264–5, A. Brandl.

WILLIAM T. SAWARD: William Shakespeare, a play in 4 acts. London, 1907. (120 pp.) Rev.: Sh. Jb. 44, 1908, S. 363, M. Förster.

BERNARD SHAW: The Dark Lady of the sonnets. A play. London, 1910.

H. F. RUBINSTEIN and CLIFFORD BAX: Shakespeare. A play in 5 episodes. With a preface by A. W. Pollard. London, 1921. (x, 117 pp.)

Cf.: ALBERT EICHLER: Ein biographisches Drama 'Shakespeare'. In: Arch. 143, 1922, S. 252–4.

CLEMENCE DANE: Will Shakespeare. An invention in 4 acts. London, 1921. (viii, 131 pp.) Rev.: Bbl. 33, 1922, S. 232–40, A. Eichler.

Cf.: N. HARDY WALLIS: Two modern plays on Shakespeare [by Clifford Bax and Clemence Dane]. In the same author's: The ethics of criticism and other essays. London, 1924, pp. 15–51.

GEORGE MOORE: The making of an immortal. A play in one act. London [1928]. Rev.: TLS., Jan. 26, 1928, p. 58.

(b) NOVEL

PAUL ALFRED MERBACH: Shakespeare als Romanfigur. In: Sh. Jb. Jg. 58, 1922, S. 83–98.

LUDWIG TIECK: Dichterleben (1825–9).

Cf.: ALBERT EICHLER: Zur Quellengeschichte und Technik von L. Tiecks Shakespeare-Novellen. In: E. St. 56, 1922, S. 254–80.

HEINRICH KÖNIG: William's Dichten und Trachten. Roman. 1839.

Cf.: H. HALBEISEN: Heinrich Josef König. Ein Beitrag zur Geschichte des Romans im 19. Jahrhundert. Diss. Münster, 1915. (83 S.)

LÉON-ALPHONSE DAUDET: Le voyage de Shakespeare. Roman d'histoire et d'aventures. Paris, 1896. German translation: Fahrten und Abenteuer des jungen Shakespeare. Historischer Roman. Autoris. Übers. von A. BERGER. Stuttgart, 1898. (291 S.) Rev.: Sh. Jb. 36, 1900, S. 324–5, K. Weichberger.

A. T. QUILLER-COUCH: Shakespeare's Christmas and other stories. London, 1905. (344 pp.) Also: Tauchnitz Edition, vol. 3860. Rev.: Sh. Jb. 42, 1906, S. 284–5, A. Brandl.

DENTON JACQUES SNIDER [pseud. THEOPHILUS MIDDLING]: The rise of young Shakespeare. A biographic novel. St. Louis, 1925. (464 pp.)

ALBERT PETERSEN: Der Schwan vom Avon. Roman. Hamburg & Berlin, 1926. (236 S.) Rev.: Sh. Jb. 63, 1927, S. 213–14, W. Keller.

(13) SHAKESPEARE IN THE SCHOOLS AND UNIVERSITIES

LUDWIG FRÄNKEL: Die gegenwärtige Beschäftigung der akademisch-neu-philologischen Vereine Deutschlands mit Shakespeare. In: Sh. Jb. Jg. 26, 1891, S. 120–30.

LUDWIG FRÄNKEL: Shakespeare an den deutschen Hochschulen der Gegenwart. In: Sh. Jb. Jg. 32, 1896, S. 87–108.

JOHN D. JONES: Shakespeare in English schools. In: Sh. Jb. Jg. 42, 1906, S. 113–26.

XIII. CIVILIZATION IN SHAKESPEARE'S ENGLAND

(1) GENERAL WORKS

WILLIAM HARRISON: Description of Britaine and England. In: Holinshed's Chronicle, 1577. Reprints in: Sh. Soc. Publ. 1877–88, Scott Library 1899, and Everyman's Library.

JOHN STOW: Survey of London, 1598. Edited by WILLIAM J. THOMS. 1876. (xviii, 222 pp.) Reprinted from the text of 1603, with an introduction and notes by C. L. KINGSFORD. 2 vols. London, 1925. (c, 352 and iv, 476 pp.) Reprinted also in Everyman's Library.

―――

LUCY AIKIN: Memoirs of the court of Queen Elizabeth. 2 vols. 1818 and later editions.

LUCY AIKIN: Memoirs of the court of James I. 2 vols. 1822.

J. NICHOLS: The progresses and public processions of Queen Elizabeth. 3 vols. New edition, 1823.

J. NICHOLS: The progresses, processions and festivities of King James I and his court. 4 vols. 1828.

LUCY AIKIN: Memoirs of the court of King Charles I. 2 vols. Philadelphia, 1833.

JAMES A. FROUDE: History of England from the fall of Wolsey to the defeat of the Spanish Armada. 1856–70. Reprinted in Everyman's Library.

WILLIAM B. RYE: England as seen by foreigners in the days of Elizabeth and James. Journals of the two Dukes of Wirtemberg, 1592 and 1610, both illustrative of Shakespeare. London, 1865.

JOHN R. GREEN: A short history of the English people. London, 1876 and later editions.

JOHN R. GREEN: History of the English people. 4 vols. London, 1878–80 and later editions. In 8 vols. 1895–6.

THEODOR VATKE: Kulturbilder aus Altengland. Berlin, 1887. (326 S.) Rev.: Sh. Jb. 22, 1887, S. 217–19, G. Tanger.

EDWIN GOADBY: The England of Shakespeare. New edition, 1889.

MANDELL CREIGHTON: The age of Elizabeth. London, 1882 and later editions. (xx, 236 pp.) = Epochs of Mod. History.

WILLIAM WINTER: Shakespeare's England. Edinburgh, 1886. New ed. 1923. (270 pp.)

MANDELL CREIGHTON: The early Renaissance in England. Cambridge, 1895.

MANDELL CREIGHTON: Queen Elizabeth, 1896 and later editions.

ERICH MARCKS: Königin Elisabeth von England und ihre Zeit. Bielefeld & Leipzig, 1897, 1926². (135 S.) = Monographien z. Weltgeschichte, Bd. 2.

CLEMENS KLÖPPER: Shakespeare-Realien. Alt-Englands Kulturleben im Spiegel von Shakespeares Dichtungen. Dresden, 1902. (182 S.) Rev.: Sh. Jb. 38, 1902, S. 249–50, E. Vogel.

G. M. TREVELYAN: England under the Stuarts. [1904.]

The Cambridge modern history. Edited by A. W. WARD, G. W. PROTHERO and STANLEY LEATHES. 13 vols. Cambridge, 1904 seq. (vol. 3.)

ARTHUR D. INNES: England under the Tudors. London, 1905.

A. F. POLLARD: History of England, 1547–1603. London, 1910.

HENRY T. STEPHENSON: The Elizabethan people. New York & London, 1910. (xi, 230 pp.) Rev.: Sh. Jb. 47, 1911, S. 354, M. Förster.

JOHN DOVER WILSON: Life in Shakespeare's England. A book of Elizabethan prose. Cambridge, 1911, 1926. (xvi, 292 pp.) = The Cambridge Anthologies. Rev.: Sh. Jb. 48, 1912, S. 335–6, M. Förster; MLR. 7, 1912, pp. 249–51, Moore Smith.
A collection of sources.

Shakespeare's England. An account of the life and manners of his age. 2 vols. Oxford, 1917. (xxiv, 546 and xii, 610 pp.) Contains: SIR WALTER RALEIGH: The age of Elizabeth, vol. i, pp. 1–47.
With bibliography.

P. H. DITCHFIELD: The England of Shakespeare. London, 1917.

HENRY OSBORN TAYLOR: Thought and expression in the 16th century. 2 vols. New York, 1920. (xiv, 427 and 432 pp.) Rev.: Stud. in Phil. 18, 1921, pp. 365–8.
Vol. 2 deals with England.

LEWIS EINSTEIN: Tudor ideals. New York & London, 1921. (xiii, 366 pp.)

M. ST. CLARE BYRNE: Elizabethan life in town and country. London, 1925, (x, 294 pp.)

K. BURDACH: Reformation, Renaissance, Humanismus. Berlin, 1927. (270 S.)

(2) THE CHURCH AND THE MARPRELATE CONTROVERSY

Cf. also pp. 35–36.

(a) GENERAL WORKS ON THE STATE OF THE CHURCH

R. W. DIXON: History of the Church of England from the abolition of the Roman jurisdiction. 6 vols. 1879–1903. (vols. 5 and 6.)

DOUGLAS CAMPBELL: The Puritans in Holland, England and America. 2 vols. New York, 1892.

J. GAIRDNER: The English church in the 16th century from the accession of Henry VIII to the death of Mary. London, 1902.

W. H. FRERE: The English church in the reigns of Elizabeth and James I (1553–1625). In: W. HUNT and W. R. W. STEPHENS: History of the English church. 1904. Vol. 5.

SEDLEY LYNCH WARE: The Elizabethan parish in its ecclesiastical and financial aspects. Baltimore, 1908. (93 pp.)=Johns Hopkins Univ. Studies in history and political science. Ser. 26, nos. 7–8. Rev.: Sh. Jb. 45, 1909, S. 407, M. Förster.

GERHARD SEELIGER: Deutsche und englische Reformation. Vortrag. Leipzig, 1915. (28 S.) Rev.: Sh. Jb. 52, 1916, S. 243–5, M. Förster.

RONALD BAYNE: Religion. In: Shakespeare's England. Vol. I. O.U.P., 1917, pp. 48–78.
With bibliography.

ARTHUR J. KLEIN: Intolerance in the reign of Queen Elizabeth. London, 1917.

FRIEDRICH BRIE: Deismus und Atheismus in der englischen Renaissance. In: Anglia, Bd. 48, N.F. Bd. 36, 1924, S. 54–98 und 105–68.

A. F. SCOTT PEARSON: Thomas Cartwright and Elizabethan puritanism, 1535–1603. C.U.P., 1925. (xvi, 511 pp.)
Good introduction to the history of church politics in the time of Elizabeth.

S. B. LILJEGREN: The fall of the monasteries and the social changes in England leading up to the Great Revolution. Lund & Leipzig, 1925. (150 pp.)= Lunds Univ. Årsskrift, vol. 19, no. 10. Rev.: E. St. 8, 1926, S. 122 ff.

(b) THE MARPRELATE CONTROVERSY

(a) GENERAL TREATISES

WILLIAM PIERCE: An historical introduction to the Marprelate Tracts. A chapter in the evolution of civil and religious liberty in England. London, 1908. (xvii, 350 pp.) Rev.: Libr., N.S., vol. 10, 1909, pp. 214–18, J. D. Wilson.

J. DOVER WILSON: The Marprelate controversy. In: CHEL., vol. 3, 1909, pp. 374–98.
With extensive bibliography and list of sources.

RONALD B. MCKERROW: The Marprelate controversy. In: The works of Thomas Nashe. Ed. by R. B. MCKERROW. London (1910). Vol. 5, pp. 34–65.

G. BONNARD: La controverse de Martin Marprelate (1588–90). Épisode de l'histoire littéraire du puritanisme sous Élisabeth. Genève, 1916. (xv, 237 pp.)
Rev.: N. Spr. 26, 1919, S. 365–6, W. Fischer; Mod. Phil. 18, 1921, p. 507, Ch. R. Baskervill; Bbl. 31, 1920, S. 106–110, Th. Mühe.

(β) QUESTIONS OF AUTHORSHIP

J. DOVER WILSON: Martin Marprelate and Shakespeare's Fluellen. A new theory of the authorship of the Marprelate Tracts. In: Libr., 3rd ser., vol. 3, 1912, pp. 113–51 and 241–76.

Wilson regards the soldier-adventurer, Sir Roger Williams, the supposed prototype of Shakespeare's Fluellen, as the author of the Tracts.

WILLIAM PIERCE and R. B. MCKERROW: Did Sir Roger Williams write the Marprelate Tracts? In: Libr., 3rd ser., vol. 3, 1912, pp. 345–74.

J. DOVER WILSON: Did Sir Roger Williams write the Marprelate Tracts? A rejoinder. In: Libr., 3rd ser., vol. 4, 1913, pp. 92–104.

(3) POLITICAL, SOCIAL, AND ECONOMIC CONDITIONS

Cf. also p. 39.

(a) GENERAL WORKS

HUBERT HALL: Society in the Elizabethan age. 1901[4].

H. D. TRAILL and J. S. MAN: Social England. A record of the progress of the people. 6 vols. London, 1901–4. (Vols. 3 and 4.)

ANDREW LANG: Social England illustrated. A collection of 17th century tracts. In: The English Garner. Westminster, 1903.

W. CUNNINGHAM: Early writings on politics and economics. In: CHEL., vol. 4, 1909, pp. 295–315.

With valuable references to sources.

A. W. WARD: Some political and social aspects of the later Elizabethan and earlier Stuart period. In: CHEL., vol. 5, 1910, pp. 336–80.

With bibliography and list of sources.

F. J. C. HEARNSHAW: Social and political ideas of some great thinkers of the Renaissance and the Reformation. London, 1925. (216 pp.)

L. F. SALZMANN: England in Tudor times. An account of its social life and industries. London, 1926. (viii, 143 pp.)

J. W. ALLEN: A history of political thought in the 16th century. London, 1928. (xxii, 525 pp.)

(b) ECONOMIC CONDITIONS

THEODOR VATKE: Geld und Geldeswert in Shakespeares England. In: Sh. Jb. Jg. 20, 1885, S. 119–30.

R. H. TAWNEY: Agrarian problems of the 16th century, 1912.

W. CUNNINGHAM: The growth of English industry and commerce in modern times. Cambridge, 1912. (xxxviii, 1039 pp.)

R. E. PROTHERO: Agriculture and gardening. In: Shakespeare's England. Vol. I. O.U.P., 1917, pp. 346–80.

GEORGE UNWIN: Commerce and coinage. In: Shakespeare's England. Vol. I. O.U.P., 1917, pp. 311–45.

R. H. TAWNEY and EILEEN POWER: Tudor economic documents. Select documents illustrating the economic and social history of Tudor England. 3 vols. London, 1924. (397, 379, and 494 pp.)

(c) THE SOCIAL CLASSES

SIDNEY LEE: Elizabethan England and the Jews. In: Trans. New Shaksp. Soc. 1887–92, part ii, pp. 143–67.

H. SCHNAPPERELLE: Die bürgerlichen Stände und das Volk in England während des 16. und 17. Jahrhunderts, vornehmlich nach den Dramen Ben Jonsons. Diss. Halle, 1908. (83 S.)

E. K. CHAMBERS: The court. In: Shakespeare's England. Vol. I, 1917, pp. 79–111. With bibliography.

GERTRUD GÖTZE: Der Londoner Lehrling im literarischen Kulturbild der elisabethanischen Zeit. Diss. Jena, 1918. Rev.: Sh. Jb. 55, 1919, S. 178–9, W. Keller.

G. S. GARGÀNO: Scapigliatura italiana a Londra sotto Elisabetta e Giacomo I. Firenze, 1923. (193 pp.)

VIOLET A. WILSON: Society women of Shakespeare's time. London, 1924. (273 pp.)

(d) ROGUES AND VAGABONDS

The rogues and vagabonds of Shakespeare's youth: Awdeley's 'Fraternitye of Vagabondes' and HARMAN's 'Caveat', ed. with an introduction by EDWARD VILES and F. J. FURNIVALL. London, 1907. (xxx, 116 pp.)=The Shakespeare Library. Rev.: Sh. Jb. 44, 1908, S. 366, M. Förster.

FRANK AYDELOTTE: Elizabethan rogues and vagabonds. Oxford, 1913. (xii, 187 pp.)=Oxf. hist. and lit. studies, vol. I. Rev.: Sh. Jb. 50, 1914, S. 225–7, M. Förster; MLR. 9, 1914, pp. 391–4, F. P. Wilson.

CHARLES WHIBLEY: Rogues and vagabonds. In: Shakespeare's England. Vol. II. O.U.P. 1917, pp. 484–509.

GERHARD SCHEIDEGGER: Rogue and connycatcher. Ein Beitrag zur Kenntnis des elisabethanischen Proletariats und Gaunertums. Diss. Basel, 1927. (48 S.)

(4) THE ARTS

J. ALFRED GOTCH: Architecture of the Renaissance in England. 2 vols. London, 1891–4.

AYMER VALLANCE: Art in England during the Elizabethan and Stuart periods. In: The Studio. London, 1908. (120 pp.)=Spring Number.—Architecture and handicrafts.

J. ALFRED GOTCH: Architecture. In: Shakespeare's England. Vol. II. O.U.P., 1917, pp. 50–73.

———

LIONEL CUST: Painting, sculpture, and engraving. In: Shakespeare's England. Vol. II. O.U.P., 1917, pp. 1–14.

———

EDWARD W. NAYLOR: Shakespeare and music. With illustrations from the music of the 16th and 17th centuries. London, 1896. (vi, 225 pp.)=The Temple Shakespeare Manuals. Rev.: Sh. Jb. 36, 1900, S. 296–9, H. Hecht.

Oxford history of music, edited by W. H. HADOW. 6 vols. O.U.P., 1901–5.

W. BARCLAY SQUIRE: Music. In: Shakespeare's England. Vol. II. O.U.P., 1917, pp. 15–49.

———

FRANCIS DOUCE: On the ancient English morris dance. In Douce's Illustrations of Shakespeare. London, 1807. Vol. II, pp. 429–82.

A. FORBES SIEVEKING: Dancing. In: Shakespeare's England. Vol. II. O.U.P., 1917, pp. 437–50.

(5) SCIENCE AND PEDAGOGY

(a) SCIENCE

W. DILTHEY: Die Funktion der Anthropologie in der Kultur des 16. und 17. Jahrhunderts=Berliner Sitz.ber. 1904. Also in Dilthey's Gesammelte Schriften, Bd. 2.

Shakespeare's England. Vol. I, 1917, contains the following treatises with lists of sources and bibliography: SIR JOHN E. SANDYS: Scholarship, pp. 251–83; ALBAN H. G. DORAN: Medicine, pp. 413–43; E. B. KNOBEL: Astronomy and astrology, pp. 444–61; ROBERT STEELE: Alchemy, pp. 462–74.

(b) PEDAGOGY

J. BASS MULLINGER: The university of Cambridge, from 1535 to the accession of Charles I. 2 vols. Cambridge, 1873–84.

THEODOR VATKE: Bildung und Schule in Shakespeares England. In: Sh. Jb. Jg. 20, 1885, S. 172–89.

CORNELIE BENNDORF: Die englische Pädagogik im 16. Jahrhundert, wie sie dargestellt wird im Wirken und in den Werken von Elyot, Ascham und Mulcaster. Leipzig & Wien, 1905. (xi, 84 S.)=Wiener Beiträge, hrsg. von Schipper, 22. Rev.: Sh. Jb. 42, 1906, S. 233–5, E. Kröger.

W. H. WOODWARD: Studies in education during the age of the Renaissance, 1400–1600. Cambridge, 1906. (xx, 336 pp.) Rev.: Sh. Jb. 45, 1909, S. 381–6, S. Blach.

FOSTER WATSON: The English grammar schools to 1660, their curriculum and practice. Cambridge, 1908. (x, 548 pp.) Rev.: Sh. Jb. 45, 1909, S. 381–6, S. Blach.

W. H. WOODWARD: English universities, schools and scholarship in the 16th century. In: CHEL., vol. 3, 1909, pp. 418–38.
With bibliography.

WILHELM RUHMER: Pädagogische Theorien über Frauenbildung im Zeitalter der Renaissance, nebst einer kritischen Würdigung der Leistungen mittel-alterlicher Theoretiker. Diss. Bonn, 1915. (99 S.) Rev.: Sh. Jb. 52, 1916, S. 245–6, M. Förster.

SIR JOHN EDWIN SANDYS: Education. In: Shakespeare's England. Vol. I. O.U.P., 1917, pp. 224–50.
With bibliography.

CHARLES EDWARD MALLET: A history of the university of Oxford. Vol. II: The 16th and 17th centuries. London (1924). (xv, 502 pp.)

BRUNO DRESSLER: Geschichte der englischen Erziehung. Leipzig, 1928. (viii, 340 S.)

(6) OTHER ASPECTS OF ELIZABETHAN CIVILIZATION

(a) FOLKLORE

Cf. also pp. 36–38.

WALLACE NOTESTEIN: A history of witchcraft in England from 1558 to 1718. Washington, 1911. (xiv, 442 S.) Rev.: Sh. Jb. 49, 1913, S. 239–40, M. Förster.

H. LITTLEDALE: Folklore and superstitions; ghosts and fairies; witchcraft and devils. In: Shakespeare's England. Vol. I. O.U.P., 1917, pp. 516–46.
With bibliography.

GEORGE LYMAN KITTREDGE: Witchcraft in Old and New England. Harv. Univ. Pr., 1929. (641 pp.) Rev.: MLN. 45, 1930, pp. 257–9, H. W. Herrington.

(b) DOMESTIC LIFE

THEODOR VATKE: Gastmähler und Mahlzeiten in Shakespeares England. In: Sh. Jb. Jg. 23, 1888, S. 246–65.

PERCY MACQUOID: The home. Furniture, food and drink, christenings, weddings, funerals. In: Shakespeare's England. Vol. II, 1917, pp. 119–52.
With bibliography.

ELIZABETH GODFREY: Home life under the Stuarts, 1603–49. Illustrated. London (1925). (xx, 312 pp.)

(c) ARMY AND NAVY

J. W. FORTESCUE: The army; military service and equipment. In: Shakespeare's England. Vol. I. O.U.P., 1917, pp. 112–40.
With bibliography.

L. G. CARR LAUGHTON: The navy; ships and sailors. In: Shakespeare's England. Vol. I. O.U.P., 1917, pp. 141–69.
With bibliography.

(d) HERALDRY

ARTHUR HUNTINGTON NASON: Heralds and heraldry in Ben Jonson's plays, masques, and entertainments. New York, 1907. (146 pp.) Rev.: Sh. Jb. 45, 1909, S. 374–6, v. Mauntz; Bbl. 20, 1909, S. 169, K. Linke.
This work is at the same time a general reference-book on heraldry.

OSWALD BARRON: Heraldry. In: Shakespeare's England. Vol. II. O.U.P., 1917, pp. 74–90.
With bibliography.

(e) HYGIENE

F. P. WILSON: The plague in Shakespeare's London. Oxford, 1927. (228 pp.) Rev.: Sh. Jb. 63, 1927, S. 213, W. Keller.

(f) COSTUMES

DION CLAYTON CALTHROP: English costume. Vol. III: Tudor and Stuart. London, 1906. (viii, 142 pp. and 19 illustrations). Rev.: Sh. Jb. 44, 1908, S. 366–7, M. Förster.

F. W. FAIRHOLT: Costume in England to the end of the 18th century. 2 vols. London, 1910⁴ (revised by H. A. Dillon).

CH. H. ASHDOWN: British costume during nineteen centuries. London, 1910.

PERCY MACQUOID: Costume. In: Shakespeare's England. Vol. II. O.U.P., 1917, pp. 91–118.
With bibliography.

(g) LONDON AND STRATFORD

(Cf. also p. 31.)

(α) LONDON

WALTER BESANT: London in the time of the Stuarts. London, 1903.

WALTER BESANT: London in the time of the Tudors. London, 1904.

HENRY THEW STEPHENSON: Shakespeare's London, illustrated. New York, 1905. Rev.: Sh. Jb. 42, 1906, S. 255–6, W. Keller.

GEORGES DUVAL: Londres au temps de Shakespeare. Paris, 1907. (336 pp.) Rev.: Sh. Jb. 44, 1908, S. 335, W. Dibelius.

HENRY B. WHEATLEY: London and the life of the town. In: Shakespeare's England. Vol. II. O.U.P., 1917, pp. 153–81.

N. ZWAGER: Glimpses of Ben Jonson's London. Amsterdam, 1926. (xxii, 222 pp.) Rev.: E. St. 63, 1928, S. 119–20, M. J. Wolff.

(β) STRATFORD AND WARWICKSHIRE

SIDNEY LEE: Stratford-on-Avon from the earliest times to the death of Shakespeare. With 45 illustr. by Edward Hull. New ed. London, 1902. (viii, 304 pp.) Rev.: Sh. Jb. 42, 1906, S. 254–5.

c. j. ribton-turner: Shakespeare's land. Being a description of central and southern Warwickshire. With 13 maps and plans. London, 1893. (xxiv, 416 pp.)

(*h*) LAW

arthur underhill: Law. In: Shakespeare's England. Vol. I. O.U.P., 1917, pp. 381–412.
With bibliography.

(*i*) ELIZABETHAN VOYAGERS AND ADVENTURERS

h. r. fox bourne: English seamen under the Tudors (1485–1603). 2 vols. 1868.

charles n. robinson and john leyland: Seafaring and travel. The growth of professional text books and geographical literature. In: CHEL., vol. 4, 1909, pp. 86–108.
With bibliography and list of sources.

j. d. rogers: Voyages and exploration; geography, maps. In: Shakespeare's England. Vol. I. O.U.P., 1917, pp. 170–97.
With bibliography.

charles hughes: Land travel. In: Shakespeare's England. Vol. I. O.U.P., 1917, pp. 198–223.
With bibliography.

william paton ker: The Elizabethan voyagers. In his Collected essays. In 2 vols. London, 1925. (Vol. I, 1).

(*k*) SPORT AND PASTIMES

gervase markham: Writers on country pursuits and pastimes. In: CHEL., vol. 4, 1909, pp. 364–77.
With bibliography.

Shakespeare's England. Vol. II. O.U.P., 1917, contains the following treatises with lists of sources and bibliography: j. w. fortescue: Hunting, pp. 334–350; gerald lascelles: Falconry, pp. 351–66; a. forbes sieveking: Coursing, fowling, angling, pp. 367–75; h. walrond: Archery, pp. 376–88; a. forbes sieveking: Fencing and duelling, pp. 389–407, and Horsemanship, with farriery, pp. 408–27; sidney lee: Bearbaiting, bullbaiting, and cockfighting, pp. 428–36; a. forbes sieveking: Games, pp. 451–83.

(*l*) GREAT ELIZABETHANS

sidney lee: Great Englishmen of the 16th century. London, 1904. (337 pp.)

frederick j. harries: The Welsh Elizabethans. Pontypridd, 1924. Rev.: Sh. Jb. 61, 1925, S. 131–2, W. Keller.

XIV. THE SHAKESPEARE-BACON CONTROVERSY AND SIMILAR THEORIES

(1) THE SHAKESPEARE-BACON CONTROVERSY

W. H. WYMAN: Bibliography of the Bacon-Shakespeare controversy, with notes and extracts. Cincinnati, 1884. (124 pp.)

DELIA S. BACON: The philosophy of the plays of Shakespeare unfolded. With preface by N. HAWTHORNE. London, 1857. (680 pp.)
This work gave rise to the Shakespeare-Bacon controversy.

WILLIAM HENRY SMITH: Bacon and Shakespeare. An inquiry touching players, playhouses, and play-writers in the days of Elizabeth. London, 1857. (viii, 162 pp.)

NATHANIEL HOLMES: The authorship of Shakespeare. New York, 1866. (xvi, 602 pp.)

THOMAS D. KING: Bacon versus Shakespeare. A plea for the defendant. Montreal, 1875. (ii, 188 pp.)
Opposes Holmes's view.

E. O. VAILE: Shakespeare-Bacon controversy. In: Scribner's Monthly, 1875.
Vaile attempts to advance proofs of Bacon's authorship.

JAMES APPLETON MORGAN: The Shakespearean myth. William Shakespeare and circumstantial evidence. Cincinnati, 1881. (342 pp.)

MRS. HENRY POTT: The Promus of formularies and elegancies by Francis Bacon, illustrated and elucidated by passages from Shakespeare. London & Boston, 1883.
Claims that certain characteristic expressions in Bacon's Promus can all be found in Shakespeare.

MRS. HENRY POTT: Did Francis Bacon write Shakespeare? Thirty-two reasons for believing he did. 2 vols. London, 1884-5.

F. A. LEO: Die Baco-Gesellschaft. Neben einigen Exkursen über die Baco-Shakespeare-Affaire. In: Sh. Jb. Jg. 20, 1885, S. 190-227.

IGNATIUS DONNELLY: The great cryptogram. Francis Bacon's cipher in the so-called Shakespeare plays. 2 vols. London, 1888. (ix, 998 pp.)

JOHN ALDWELL NICHOLSON: No cipher in Shakespeare. A refutation of the Hon. Ignatius Donnelly's 'Great Cryptogram'. London, 1888. (68 pp.)

RICHARD WÜLKER: Die Shakspere-Bacon-Theorie. In: Ber. Sächs. Ges. d. Wiss. 1889, S. 217-300.

JACOB SCHIPPER: Zur Kritik der Shakespeare-Bacon-Frage. Wien, 1889.

KARL LENTZNER: Zur Shakespeare-Bacon-Theorie. Halle, 1890. (viii, 48 S.)

H. RAEDER: Über die behauptete Identität der Metaphern und Gleichnisse in Bacons und Shakespeares Werken. Ein Beitrag zur Bacon-Shakespeare-Frage. Progr. Grünberg, 1891. (26 S.)

EDWIN BORMANN: Das Shakespeare-Geheimnis. Leipzig, 1894.

KUNO FISCHER: Shakespeare und die Bacon-Mythen. Festvortrag. In: Sh. Jb. Jg. 32, 1896, S. 3–40.

JACOB SCHIPPER: Der Bacon-Bazillus. Zur Beleuchtung des Shakespeare-Bacon-Unsinns älteren und neuesten Datums. Wien & Leipzig, 1896.

A. TETZLAFF: Die Shakespeare-Bacon-Frage in ihrer historischen Entwicklung bis zum heutigen Stande populär-wissenschaftlich dargestellt. Hrsg. vom studentischen Shakespeare-Verein zu Halle a. S. (1896). (40 S.)

EDWARD JAMES CASTLE: Shakespeare, Bacon, Jonson and Greene. A study. London, 1897. (360 pp.)
Attempts to prove that Bacon assisted Shakespeare in the writing of certain dramas.

CHARLES ALLEN: Notes on the Bacon-Shakespeare question. Boston & New York, 1900. (xiv, 306 pp.) Rev.: Bbl. 12, 1901, S. 164 f., G. Sarrazin.
Complete rejection of the Bacon theory.

EDWIN BORMANN: Die Kunst des Pseudonyms. Zwölf literarhistorisch-bibliographische Essays. Leipzig, 1901. (xi, 135 S.)

EDWIN BORMANN: Der Shakespeare-Dichter. Wer war's und wie sah er aus? Eine Überschau alles Wesentlichen der Bacon-Shakespeare Forschung, ihrer Freunde und ihrer Gegnerschaft. Leipzig, 1902. (viii, 135 S. und 40 Abb.)

H. KÜSSWETTER: Beiträge zur Shakespeare-Bacon-Frage. Diss. Erlangen, 1906. (28 S.)

N. BØGHOLM: Bacon og Shakespeare. En sproglig sammenligning. København, 1906. (196 S.) Rev.: Sh. Jb. 45, 1909, S. 401–2, M. Förster.
A rejection of the Bacon theory on grammatical grounds.

KARL BLEIBTREU: Der wahre Shakespeare. (Das neue Shakespeare-Evangelium. Shakespeare-Tragikomödie in 5 Akten). München, 1907.

G. G. GREENWOOD: The Shakespeare problem restated. London, 1908. (xxx, 559 pp.)
An attempt to separate Shakespeare the actor from Shakespeare the dramatist.

H. C. BEECHING: William Shakespeare, player, playmaker, and poet. A reply to Mr. George Greenwood. London, 1908. (ix, 104 pp.)
Rejects Greenwood's view.

G. G. GREENWOOD: In re Shakespeare, Beeching v. Greenwood. Rejoinder on behalf of the defendant. London, 1909. (xi, 152 pp.) Rev.: Sh. Jb. 46, 1910, S. 318, M. Förster.

DURNING-LAWRENCE: Bacon is Shake-speare. Together with a reprint of Bacon's Promus of formularies and elegancies. London, 1910. (xiv, 286 pp.)

RICHARD WÜLKER: Zur sogenannten Shakespeare-Bacon-Frage. In: N. Spr. Bd. 18, 1910–11, S. 1–12.

ANDREW LANG: Shakespeare, Bacon, and the great unknown. London, 1912. (xxviii, 314 pp.) Rev.: Sh. Jb. 49, 1913, S. 244–5, M. Förster.
A rejection of the Bacon theory, and, in particular, of Greenwood's views.

MARY ROSE: Baconian myths. Notes on two great Englishmen and their defamers. Stratford-on-Avon [1913]. (39 pp.) Rev.: Sh. Jb. 50, 1914, S. 218–19, M. Förster.
A refutation of the Bacon theory.

J. M. ROBERTSON: The Baconian heresy. A confutation. London, 1913. (xx, 612 pp.) Rev.: Sh. Jb. 50, 1914, S. 219–20, M. Förster; MLR. 9, 1914, pp. 527–9, J. D. Wilson.

BRUNO EELBO: Bacon's entdeckte Urkunden. 3 Teile. Leipzig, 1914–16. (483 S.) Rev.: Sh. Jb. 52, 1916, S. 239–40, M. Förster.

JAMES THINNEY BAXTER: The greatest of literary problems. The authorship of the Shakespeare works. With illustrations. Boston & New York, 1915. (xxix, 686 pp.)
With extensive bibliography.

ALBERT EICHLER: Anti-Baconianus. Shakespeare-Bacon? Zur Aufklärung seines Anteils an der Erneuerung Österreichs. Wien & Leipzig, 1919. Rev.: Sh. Jb. 55, 1919, S. 179–80, W. Keller.

LEON KELLNER: Shakespeare-Bacon als Essayist. Wien, 1919. (16 S.) Also in: Neue Freie Presse, 9. Mai 1919.
A proof that the author of the plays cannot possibly have written the essays.

PAUL VULLIAND: Le mythe shakespearien. In: Mercure de France, vol. 139, 1920, pp. 5–33.

GEORGE HOOKHAM: Will o' the wisp, or the elusive Shakespeare. Oxford, 1921. (xi, 142 pp.)
Agrees with Greenwood.

CARTIER, général: Le mystère Bacon-Shakespeare, un document nouveau. In: Mercure de France 1922 and 1923.
Attempts to bring forward new proofs of Bacon's authorship.

ALBERT FEUILLERAT: Shakespeare est-il Shakespeare? In: Revue des deux mondes, 1922, pp. 166–200.
Rejects Cartier's views.

GUY DE POURTALÈS: N'y aurait-il plus d'affaire Shakespeare? In: Rev. hebdomadaire, Déc. 16, 1922.
Also rejects Cartier's views.

EMIL WOLFF: Die sogenannte Shakespeare-Bacon-Frage. Festvortrag. In: Sh. Jb. Jg. 59–60, N.F. Jg. 1, 1924, S. 130–58.

CLARA LONGWORTH-CHAMBRUN: L'existence de Shakespeare prouvée par ses contemporains. In: Rev. universelle, 1924, pp. 163–93.

GEORGES CONNES: Le mystère shakespearien. Paris, 1926. (264 pp.) Rev.: Revue anglo-amér. 6, 1928, pp. 170–2, R. Pruvost; E. St. 64, 1929, S. 129–30, M. J. Wolff.

(2) LITERATURE CONCERNING BACON AND BEARING ON THE SHAKESPEARE-BACON QUESTION

The essays or counsels civil and moral of FRANCIS BACON, Viscount St. Albans, Baron Verulam. From the final edition (1625), with notes and a glossary by LEON KELLNER. Leipzig, 1919.

JAMES SPEDDING: The life and letters of Francis Bacon. 7 vols. 1861–72.

A. ROHS: Syntaktische Untersuchungen zu Bacons Essays. Diss. Marburg, 1889. (53 S.)

EMIL WOLFF: Francis Bacons Verhältnis zu Platon. Diss. München, 1908. (159 S.) Rev.: Sh. Jb. 46, 1910, S. 189–90, Fr. Brie.

WALTER THOMAS: Le sentiment de l'amour chez Bacon et chez Shakespeare. In: Rev. des cours et confér., 18, 1909–10, série I, pp. 56–72.

EMIL WOLFF: Francis Bacon und seine Quellen. 1. Bd.: Bacon und die grie- chische Philosophie. Berlin, 1910. (xxx, 301 S.)=Lit.histor. Forsch., hrsg. von Schick und von Waldberg, H. 40. Rev.: Sh. Jb. 47, 1911, S. 325–9, Cl. Baeumker.

G. W. STEEVES: Medical allusions in the writings of Francis Bacon. Edin- burgh, 1913=Proc. Roy. Soc. of Medic. Rev.: Sh. Jb. 52, 1916, S. 225, M. Förster.

HELENE RICHTER: Bacon der Philosoph. In: Sh. Jb. Jg. 57, 1921, S. 28–55.

JOSEPH WILHELM KINDERVATER: Die Bildersprache in Francis Bacons Essays and Advancement of learning. MS. Diss. Göttingen, 1921. Summary in Jb. Philos. Fak. Gött. 1922, 1, S. 31–2.

J. ROGGENBURK: Untersuchungen über die Syntax des untergeordneten Satzes in Bacons englischen Schriften. Ein Beitrag zur Geschichte und Theorie der englischen Satzlehre. MS. Diss. Hamburg, 1925.

G. SEMPRINI: Francis Bacon. Milano, 1926. (100 pp.)

A. LEVI: Il pensiero di Francis Bacon. Torino, 1926. (436 pp.)

WILHELM RICHTER: Bacon als Staatsdenker. Diss. Berlin, 1928. (55 S.)

(3) THE DERBY THEORY

ABEL LEFRANC: Sous le masque de 'William Shakespeare'. 2 vols. Paris, 1919.

Lefranc considers William Stanley, sixth Earl of Derby, the author of Shakespeare's plays.

JACQUES BOULENGER: L'affaire Shakespeare. Paris, 1919. (75 pp.)

A defence of Lefranc's views.

SIDNEY LEE: More doubts about Shakespeare. In: Quart. Rev., 1919.
Severe refutation of Lefranc's thesis.

MAURICE CASTELAIN: Shakespeare ou Derby? In: Rev. germ. 1920, pp. 1–39.

(4) THE OXFORD THEORY

J. THOMAS LOONEY: 'Shakespeare' identified in Edward de Vere, the 17th Earl of Oxford. London, 1920. (551 pp.) Rev.: TLS., March 4, 1920, p. 149.

B. M. WARD: The 17th Earl of Oxford, 1550–1604. London, 1928. (xv, 408 pp.)

GEORGES CONNES: Du nouveau sur de Vere. In: Rev. anglo-amér. 6, 1928, pp. 144–54 (à suivre).

B. THE WORKS OF SHAKESPEARE EXAMINED INDIVIDUALLY

I. CHRONOLOGY OF THE DRAMAS

For Shakespeare chronology cp.:
  The most important treatises on Shakespeare's life and works, pp. 27–29.
  The introductions to the most important Shakespeare editions, pp. 53–58.
  Shakespeare's prosody, pp. 89–90.
  Shakespeare's literary style, pp. 92–98.
Further, the following treatises may be consulted:

EDMOND MALONE: An attempt to ascertain the order in which the plays attributed to Shakespeare were written.

First of all in Steevens's edition of Shakespeare 1778, then with emendations in Malone's own edition 1790, also printed in the 3rd Varior. Ed. 1821. Pioneer work. Malone's views are retained in the main unaltered to the present day.

JAMES HURDIS: Cursory remarks upon the arrangement of the plays of Shakespeare, occasioned by reading Malone's 'Essay on the chronological order of those celebrated pieces'. London, 1792. (56 pp.)

GEORGE CHALMERS: The chronology of Shakespeare's dramas. In his: A supplemental apology for the believers in the Shakespeare-papers, 1799.

This important work contributes the correction of some erroneous dates in Malone.

NICOLAUS DELIUS: Die Tieck'sche Shakespeare-Kritik. Bonn, 1846.

Gives a survey of the position at the time in the question of Shakespeare chronology.

F. J. FURNIVALL: The succession of Shakspere's works and the use of metrical tests in settling it. London, 1874.

J. K. INGRAM: On the weak endings of Shakespeare. In: Trans. New Shaksp. Soc. 1874.

F. G. FLEAY: Metrical tests as applied to dramatic poetry. In: Trans. New Shaksp. Soc. 1874.

WILHELM KÖNIG: Über den Gang von Shakespeares dichterischer Entwicklung und die Reihenfolge seiner Dramen nach demselben. In: Sh. Jb. Jg. 10, 1875, S. 193–258.

F. S. PULLING: Speech-ending test applied to twenty of Shakespeare's plays. In: Trans. New Shaksp. Soc. 1877–9.

HENRY P. STOKES: An attempt to determine the chronological order of Shakespeare's plays. London, 1878. (xvi, 220 pp.) Harness essay.

EDWARD DOWDEN: Evidence in the chronology of Shakspere's writings. In his Shakespeare. London, 1877. Chap. IV.

C. A. THEISEN: A chapter from an attempt of a critique of the chronologies of Shakespeare's plays. Progr. Giessen, 1885. (19 S.)

J. SCHIPPER: Englische Metrik. 2. Teil: Neuenglische Metrik. Bonn, 1888, S. 287–316: Shakespeares Blankvers.
A survey of the metrical criteria in the establishment of the chronology.

BERNHARD TEN BRINK: Shakspere. Fünf Vorlesungen. Strassburg, 1893, 1894². 2. Vorlesung: Die Zeitfolge von Shaksperes Werken. S. 31–66.

GREGOR SARRAZIN: Zur Chronologie von Shakespeares Jugenddramen. In: Sh. Jb. Jg. 29–30, 1894, S. 92–109.
Sarrazin makes use here and in his other works chiefly of stylistic criteria in setting up a chronology.

GREGOR SARRAZIN: Chronologie von Shakespeares Dichtungen. In: Sh. Jb. Jg. 32, 1896, S. 149–81.

HERM. CONRAD: Metrische Untersuchungen zur Feststellung der Abfassungszeit von Shakespeares Dramen. In: Sh. Jb. Jg. 31, 1896, S. 318–53.

GREGOR SARRAZIN: W. Shakespeares Lehrjahre. Eine literarhistorische Studie. Weimar, 1897.

A. W. WARD: A history of English dramatic literature. Vol. 2. London, 1899, pp. 43–54: Chronological order of Shakspere's plays.
A review of the tests.

RICHARD GARNETT: A Stratford tradition respecting Shakespeare. In: Sh. Jb. Jg. 37, 1901, S. 209–15.

HERMANN CONRAD: Kennen wir Shaksperes Entwicklungsgang? In: Preuss. Jbb. Bd. 122, 1905, S. 388–426.
Conrad recommends the consideration of metrical and stylistic peculiarities in the establishment of a chronology.

GREGOR SARRAZIN: Aus Shakespeares Meisterwerkstatt. Stilgeschichtliche Studien. Berlin, 1906. (vii, 226 S.) Rev.: Lit. Zbl. 1909, Sp. 95–8, H. Conrad.

MAX KALUZA: Englische Metrik in historischer Entwicklung. Berlin, 1909, S. 302–11.
A short survey of the metrical criteria.

HERM. CONRAD: Eine neue Methode der chronologischen Shakespeare-Forschung. I, II. In: GRM. Bd. 1, 1909, S. 232–48 und 307–20.
Use of parallel passages in the establishment of a chronology.

E. EKWALL: Die Shakespeare-Chronologie. In: GRM. Jg. 3, 1911, S. 90–108.
A good guide to and report on the investigations.

II. THE INDIVIDUAL DRAMAS

INTRODUCTION: *GENERAL TREATISES DEALING WITH THE VARIOUS TYPES OF DRAMA*

(a) TRAGEDY

CHARLES LAMB: On the tragedies of Shakespeare considered with reference to their fitness for stage representation. London, 1818 and numerous new impressions.

A. C. BRADLEY: Shakespearean tragedy. Lectures on Hamlet, Othello, King Lear, Macbeth. London, 1904. (xi, 498 pp.) Rev.: Sh. Jb. 41, 1905, S. 237–8, A. Brandl; MLR. 1, 1906, pp. 128–33, C. H. Herford.
The best presentation.

PAUL FENYVES: Studien zur dramatischen Technik in Shakespeares Tragödien. (Der Weg vom 'Höhepunkt' bis zur 'Katastrophe'). Diss. Prag. Summary in Jb. d. philos. Fak. 1925, S. 71–4.

(b) ROMAN PLAYS

F. BRINCKER: Poetik Shakespeares in den Römerdramen Coriolan, Julius Caesar und Antony and Cleopatra. Diss. Münster, 1884. (160 S.)

CARL MEINCK: Über das örtliche und zeitliche Colorit in Shakespeares Römerdramen und Ben Jonsons 'Catiline'. Diss. Göttingen, 1909. (59 S.) Enlarged: Halle, 1910 (xi, 75 S.) = Stud. z. engl. Phil., hrsg. von Morsbach, H. 38. Rev.: Sh. Jb. 46, 1910, S. 264–6, W. Keller; Sh. Jb. 48, 1912, S. 288–9, L. L. Schücking.

M. W. MacCALLUM: Shakespeare's Roman plays and their background. London, 1910. (xv, 666 pp.) Rev.: Sh. Jb. 47, 1911, S. 293–5, W. Keller; MLR. 7, 1912, pp. 110–13, F. S. Boas.
The best presentation.

(c) HISTORICAL PLAYS

TH. P. COURTENAY: Commentaries on the historical plays of Shakespeare. 2 vols. London, 1840, 1861².
Investigation into the historical backgrounds.

FRIEDRICH DINGELSTEDT: Shakespeares Historien. Deutsche Bühnenausgabe. 3 Bde. Berlin, 1867.

Cf. also LUDWIG ECKARDT: Shakespeares englische Historien auf der Weimarer Bühne. In: Sh. Jb. Jg. 1, 1865, S. 362–91.

HERMANN FREIHERR VON FRIESEN: Ein Wort über Shakespeares Historien. Festvortrag. In: Sh. Jb. Jg. 8, 1873, S. 1–27.

RICHARD SIMPSON: The politics of Shakespeare's historical plays. In: Trans. New Shaksp. Soc. 1874, ser. i, pt. 2, pp. 396–441.

RICHARD SIMPSON: The political use of the stage in Shakespeare's time. In: Trans. New Shaksp. Soc. 1874, ser. I, pt. 2, pp. 371–95.

WILHELM KÖNIG: Shakespeares Königsdramen, ihr Zusammenhang und ihr Wert für die Bühne. In: Sh. Jb. Jg. 12, 1877, S. 228–60.

A. S. G. CANNING: Thoughts on Shakespeare's historical plays. London, 1884.

W. WETZ: Die inneren Beziehungen zwischen Shakespeares 'Macbeth' und seinen Königsdramen. In: E. St. Bd. 16, 1892, S. 1–18.

BEVERLEY E. WARNER: English history in Shakespeare's plays. New York, 1894, 1903².

JULIUS CSERWINKA: Königsfrömmigkeit in Shakespeares Historien. In: Sh. Jb. Jg. 33, 1897, S. 57–84.

S. DAVEY: The relation of poetry to history, with special reference to Shakespeare's historical plays. In: Trans. Royal Soc. of Lit., 2nd ser., vol. 24, 1903, pp. 163–99.

L. OEHNINGER: Die Verbreitung der Königssagen der Historia Regum Britanniae von Geoffrey of Monmouth in der poetischen elisabethanischen Literatur. Diss. München, 1903. (118 S.)

W. BÜTTNER: Shakespeares Stellung zum Hause Lancaster. Diss. Freiburg, 1904, und Progr. Offenbach, 1904. (106 S.) Rev.: Bbl. 16, 1905, S. 307–10, Konr. Meier.

F. W. MOORMAN: Shakespeare's history-plays and Daniel's 'Civile Wars'. In: Sh. Jb. Jg. 40, 1904, S. 69–83.

J. A. R. MARRIOTT: English history in Shakespeare. London, 1918.

A. W. POLLARD: The York and Lancaster plays. In: TLS. Sept. 20 and 27, 1918, pp. 438 and 452.

MAX J. WOLFF: Der dramatische Begriff der 'history' bei Shakespeare. In: E. St. Bd. 54, 1920, S. 194–200.

ALFRED STEINITZER: Shakespeares Königsdramen. Geschichtliche Einführung. München, 1922. (viii, 348 S.) Rev.: Sh. Jb. 59–60, 1924, S. 200–5, J. Schick; Bbl. 36, 1925, S. 70–3, H. M. Flasdieck.

J. C. STOBART: Shakespeare's monarchs. London, 1926. (255 pp.) Rev.: TLS. Febr. 25, 1926, p. 143.

WOLFGANG KELLER: Shakespeares Königsdramen. Vortrag. In: Sh. Jb. Jg. 63, 1927, S. 35–54.

(d) COMEDY

EDWARD DOWDEN: Shakespeare as a comic dramatist. In: Representative English Comedies. Edited by C. M. GAYLEY. New York, 1903.

LUDWIG FULDA: Shakespeares Lustspiele und die Gegenwart. Festvortrag. In: Sh. Jb. Jg. 43, 1907, S. xii–xxxii.

W. P. KER: A note on the form of Shakespeare's comedies. In: Edda, 1916, S. 158–63.

H. B. CHARLTON: A note on Shakespeare's romantic comedies. In: Anglica, Festschr. Alois Brandl, 1924. Bd. 2, S. 144–9.

ARTHUR QUILLER-COUCH: Shakespeare's comedies. In his Studies in literature. 3rd ser. Cambridge, 1929, pp. 98–118.

(*e*) DOMESTIC DRAMA

ELISABETH SCHÄFER: Shakespeare und das Domestic Drama. I, II. In: GRM. Jg. 13, 1925, S. 202–18 und 286–95.

(*f*) THE MASQUE

J. W. CUNLIFFE: The masque in Shakespeare's plays. In: Arch. Bd. 125, 1910, S. 71–82.

(*g*) PASTORAL PLAYS

EDWIN GREENLAW: Shakespeare's pastorals. In: Stud. in Phil., vol. 13, 1916, pp. 122–54.

TITUS ANDRONICUS

Cp. also in particular the general surveys on Shakespeare, pp. 27–29, the critical editions, pp. 53–58, and the criticism, pp. 141–145.

(1) THE TEXT

The Shakspere quarto facsimiles (William Griggs): Titus Andronicus. Q 1600. With introduction by Arthur Symons. London, 1885. (xviii, 80 pp.)

WOLFGANG KELLER: Die neuaufgefundene Quarto des 'Titus Andronicus' von 1594. In: Sh. Jb. Jg. 41, 1905, S. 211–15.
Keller gives a comparison of Q 1594 and Q 1600, showing few variants.

JOSEF S. G. BOLTON: The authentic text of Titus Andronicus. In: PMLA., vol. 44, 1929, pp. 765–88.

(2) LITERARY GENESIS

HERMANN KURZ: Zu Titus Andronicus. In: Sh. Jb. Jg. 5, 1870, S. 82–106.

ARNOLD SCHRÖER: Über Titus Andronicus. Zur Kritik der neuesten Shakspereforschung. Marburg, 1891. (140 S.) Rev.: E. St. 17, 1892, S. 134–6, L. Proescholdt; Gött. Gel. Anz. 1891, S. 708–28, A. Brandl.
Atributes the play to Shakespeare alone.

E. KOEPPEL: Beiträge zur Geschichte des elisabethanischen Dramas. IV. Titus Andronicus. In: E. St. Bd. 16, 1892, S. 365–71.
Concerning the Aaron-Fable and its sources (Bandello, 21st short story in the 3rd vol., and perhaps a ballad, Ballad Soc., Roxburghe Ballads, ii. 49).

H. VARNHAGEN: Zur Vorgeschichte der Fabel von Shakespeares Titus Andronicus. In: E. St. Bd. 19, 1894, S. 163–4.
Points to a Latin story as source of the Aaron-Fable.

ALEXANDER B. GROSART: Was Robert Greene substantially the author of Titus Andronicus? In: E. St. Bd. 22, 1896, S. 389–436.
Affirmative answer.

GREGOR SARRAZIN: Germanische Heldensage in Shakespeares Titus Andronicus. In: Arch. Jg. 50, Bd. 97, 1896, S. 373–5.
Points to the Wieland Saga as possible source of the Aaron-Fable.

CHARLES CRAWFORD: The date and authenticity of Titus Andronicus. In: Sh. Jb. Jg. 36, 1900, S. 109–21.

Shakespeare the sole author. Date not earlier than 1593.

HAROLD DE W. FULLER: The sources of Titus Andronicus. In: PMLA., vol. 16, N.S. vol. 9, 1901, pp. 1–65.

Shakespeare revised an old play.

GEORGE P. BAKER: 'Tittus and Vespacia' and 'Titus and Ondronicus' in Henslowe's Diary. In: PMLA., vol. 16, N.S. vol. 9, 1901, pp. 66–76.

JOHN M. ROBERTSON: Did Shakespeare write 'Titus Andronicus'? A study in Elizabethan literature. London, 1905. (xi, 255 S.) Rev.: MLR., vol. 1, 1906, pp. 337–41, W. W. Greg; JEGPh. 6, 1906–7, pp. 446–55, A. H. Thorndike; Dt. Vjschr. 6, 1928, S. 182, L. L. Schücking.

Supposes at least the participation of Peele and Greene in the work.

R. SCHRECKHAS: Über Entstehungszeit und Verfasser des 'Titus Andronicus'. Diss. Rostock, 1906. (64 S.)

WILHELM DIBELIUS: Zur Stoffgeschichte des Titus Andronicus. In: Sh. Jb. Jg. 48, 1912, S. 1–12.

Attempts to prove historical origin of both principal characters.

HENRY DAVID GRAY: The authorship of 'Titus Andronicus'. In: Flügel Memorial Volume. Stanford Univ., 1916, pp. 114–26.

Supposes Shakespeare to be the author, but with revision by others (probably Greene and Peele).

T. M. PARROTT: Shakespeare's revision of 'Titus Andronicus'. In: MLR., vol. 14, 1919, pp. 16–37.

Supposes the revision by Shakespeare of an earlier play.

HENRY DAVID GRAY: The Titus Andronicus problem. In: Stud. in Philol., vol. 17, 1920, pp. 126–31.

JOHN M. ROBERTSON: An introduction to the study of the Shakespeare canon, proceeding on the problem of 'Titus Andronicus'. London, 1924. (viii, 494 pp.) Rev.: MLR. 21, 1926, pp. 86–9, A. E. Morgan.

Enlargement of his study of 1905.

HENRY DAVID GRAY: Shakespeare's share in Titus Andronicus. In: Phil. Quart., vol. 5, 1926, pp. 166–72.

Titus Andronicus written originally by Greene and Peele and revised by Shakespeare.

AUSTIN K. GRAY: Shakespeare and 'Titus Andronicus'. In: Stud. in Phil., vol. 25, 1928, pp. 295–311.

Supposes the revision by Shakespeare of an older play and attempts to ascertain his share.

(3) SHAKESPEARE'S ART IN TITUS ANDRONICUS

WILHELM VERSHOFEN: Charakterisierung durch Mithandelnde in Shakespeares Titus Andronicus. Diss. Bonn, 1905. (32 S.)

(4) SUBSEQUENT HISTORY OF THE PLAY

ALBERT COHN: König Lear 1692 und Titus Andronicus 1699 in Breslau aufgeführt. In: Sh. Jb. Jg. 23, 1888, S. 266–81.

Impression of both scenarios.

FR. BAKE: Ravenscrofts Bearbeitung des Shakespeareschen 'Titus Andronicus': 'Titus Andronicus, or the Rape of Lavinia', 1678. Diss. Rostock, 1907. (62 S.)

LOVE'S LABOUR'S LOST

Cp. also in particular the general surveys on Shakespeare, pp. 27–29, the critical editions, pp. 53–58, and the criticism, pp. 141–145.

(1) THE TEXT

The Shakspere quarto facsimiles (William Griggs): Love's Labour's Lost, Q 1598. With forewords by F. J. FURNIVAL. London, 1880.

The Bankside Shakespeare. Vol. 21. New York, 1906. Parallel impression of the text of Q and F.

H. B. CHARLTON: A textual note on 'Love's Labour's Lost'. In: Libr., 3rd ser., vol. 8, 1917, pp. 355–70.

H. B. CHARLTON: A disputed passage in 'Love's Labour's Lost'. In: MLR., vol. 12, 1917, pp. 279–85.

(2) LITERARY GENESIS

HERMANN FREIHERR VON FRIESEN: Bemerkungen zu den Altersbestimmungen für einige Stücke von Shakespeare. 3. Love's Labour's Lost. In: Sh. Jb. Jg. 2, 1867, S. 54–63.

Latest possible date: late eighties.

SIDNEY LEE: A new study of Love's Labour's Lost. In: Gentleman's Magazine, 1880, pp. 447–58.

GREGOR SARRAZIN: Die Entstehung von Shakespeares Verlorener Liebesmüh. In: Sh. Jb. Jg. 31, 1895, S. 200–30.

C. F. MCCLUMPHA: Parallels between Shakespeare's sonnets and Love's Labour's Lost. In: MLN., vol. 15, 1900, pp. 335–47.

Concludes that they are fairly contemporaneous productions because of similarity of phraseology and thought.

HENRY DAVID GRAY: The original version of 'Love's Labour's Lost' with a conjecture as to 'Love's Labour's Won'. California, 1918 = Leland Stanford junior Univ. Publ., Univ. series. Rev.: Sh. Jb. 56, 1920, S. 126–8, W. Keller.

Author raises objections to the uniformity of the play.

H. B. CHARLTON: The date of 'Love's Labour's Lost'. In: MLR., vol. 13, 1918, pp. 257–66 and 387–400.

Author supposes 1592.

C C

JOHN H. ROBERTS: The nine worthies. In: Mod. Philol., vol. 19, 1921–2, pp. 297–305.
Refutes Abel Lefranc (Sous le masque de Shakespeare. Paris, 1919) who sees in the Earl of Derby the author of L.L.L.

AUSTIN K. GRAY: The secret of Love's Labour's Lost. In: PMLA., vol. 39, 1924, pp. 581–611.

O. J. CAMPBELL: 'Love's Labour's Lost' re-studied. In: Studies in Shakespeare, Milton and Donne. New York, 1925, pp. 1–45.
Author supposes connexion with the Commedia dell' arte.

ALBERT EICHLER: Love's Labour's Lost und As you like it als Hofaufführungen. In: E. St. Bd. 64, 1929, S. 352–61.

(3) SUBSEQUENT HISTORY OF THE PLAY

F. SCHULT: Bühnenbearbeitungen von Shakespeares 'Love's Labour's Lost'. Diss. Rostock, 1910. (107 S.)

THE COMEDY OF ERRORS

Cp. also in particular the general surveys on Shakespeare, pp. 27–29, the critical editions, pp. 53–58, and the criticism, pp. 141–145.

(1) LITERARY GENESIS

The *Menaechmi*, the original of Shakespeare's 'Comedy of Errors'. The Latin text together with the Elizabethan translation, ed. by W. H. D. ROUSE. London, 1912. (xiv, 122 pp.) = The Shakespeare Classics.
The Elizabethan translation by W. W. [i.e. William Warner] is also printed in:
Collier-Hazlitt: Shakespeare's library. Part II, Vol. I.
The Arden Shakespeare: The Comedy of Errors. London, 1907. App. II, pp. 135–77.

_____

HERMANN FREIHERR VON FRIESEN: Bemerkungen zu den Altersbestimmungen für einige Stücke von Shakespeare. I. Comedy of Errors. In: Sh. Jb. Jg. 2, 1867, S. 37–48.

H. ISAAC: Shakespeares 'Comedy of Errors' und die Menächmen des Plautus. In: Archiv Bd. 70, 1883.

J. DOVER WILSON: The copy for 'The Comedy of Errors', 1623. In: The New Cambridge Shakespeare: Comedy of Errors. Cambridge, 1922.

J. M. ROBERTSON: The authorship of 'The Comedy of Errors'. In the same author's The Shakespeare canon. Vol. II, 1923, pp. 126–57.

ALLISON GAW: The evolution of the Comedy of Errors. In: PMLA., vol. 41, 1926, pp. 620–66. Rev.: Sh. Jb. 64, 1928, S. 206–7, Beckmann.

(2) ART OF CHARACTERIZATION

ERNA GILL: A comparison of the characters in 'The Comedy of Errors' with those in the 'Menaechmi'. Austin, 1925 = Univ. of Texas Stud. in English, No. 5.

(3) SUBSEQUENT HISTORY OF THE PLAY

FRIEDRICH LANG: Shakespeares 'Comedy of Errors' in englischer Bühnenbearbeitung mit besonderer Berücks. der vor der ersten Drucklegung von fremder Hand gemachten Interpolationen. Diss. Rostock, 1909. (103 S.) Rev.: Bbl. 21, 1910, S. 111–12, G. Becker.

THE TWO GENTLEMEN OF VERONA

Cp. also in particular the general surveys on Shakespeare, pp. 27–29, the critical editions, pp. 53–58, and the criticism, pp. 141–145.

(1) LITERARY GENESIS

COLLIER-HAZLITT: Shakespeare's library. London, 1875. Pt. I., vol. 1, pp. 275–312: MONTEMAYOR: The Shepherdess Felismena, transl. by Yonge.

JULIUS ZUPITZA: Über die Fabel in Shakespeares Beiden Veronesern. Festvortrag. In: Sh. Jb. Jg. 23, 1888, S. 1–17.

J. M. ROBERTSON: The authorship of 'The Two Gentlemen of Verona'. In the same author's The Shakespeare canon. Vol. II, 1923, pp. 1–44.

O. J. CAMPBELL: The Two Gentlemen of Verona and Italian comedy. In: Studies in Shakespeare, Milton and Donne. New York, 1925, pp. 47–63.
Attempts to connect the play with the Italian Commedia dell' arte.

(2) DRAMATIC ART

GRACE LATHAM: Julia, Silvia, Hero, and Viola. In: Trans. New Shaksp. Soc., 1887–92, Pt. 4, pp. 319–50.

GREGOR SARRAZIN: Der Räuberwald in der Lombardei (=Neue ital. Skizzen zu Shakespeare 6.). In: Sh. Jb. Jg. 39, 1903, S. 62–8.
Deals with local colour in the play.

HUGO NORPOTH: Metrisch-chronologische Untersuchung von Shakespeares Two Gentlemen of Verona. Diss. Bonn, 1916. (86 S.) Rev.: Sh. Jb. 55, 1919, S. 164–5, W. Keller.

(3) SUBSEQUENT HISTORY OF THE PLAY

GISBERT FREIHERR VINCKE: Die beiden Veroneser als Bühnenstück. In: Sh. Jb. Jg. 21, 1886, S. 149–58.

H. F. BRÜNDEL: Shakespeares Two Gentlemen of Verona in englischer Bühnenbearbeitung. Diss. Rostock, 1909. (74 S.)

KING HENRY VI (Parts I–III)

Cp. also in particular the general surveys on Shakespeare, pp. 27–29, the critical editions, pp. 53–58, and the criticism, pp. 141–145.

(1) LITERARY GENESIS

The first part of the *Contention* betwixt the two famous houses of Yorke and Lancaster (1594). Printed in:

Collier-Hazlitt: Shakspere's library. Pt. II, vol. 1. London, 1875.
The Shakspere quarto facsimiles. No. 37. 1889.
The Cambridge Shakespeare. London, 1893. Vol. 9, pp. 507–72.
The Bankside Shakespeare. Vol. 19. New York, 1892 = parallel impression of Contention and 2 H. VI.

The *True tragedy* of Richard Duke of Yorke (1595). Printed in:
The true tragedy of Richard III, to which is appended the Latin play of Richardus Tertius by Thomas Legge. With an introd. and notes by BARRON FIELD. London, 1844 = Shakespeare Soc. Publ.
Collier-Hazlitt: Shakspere's library. Pt. II, vol. 2. London, 1875.
The Shakspere quarto facsimiles. No. 38. 1889.
The Bankside Shakespeare. Vol. 20. New York, 1892 = Parallel impression of True trag. and 3 H. VI.
The Cambridge Shakespeare. London, 1893. Vol. 9, pp. 573–636.
The New Variorum Edition, ed. by H. H. Furness, jun., 1909[2]: Rich. III, pp. 505–48.

W. G. BOSWELL-STONE: Shakspere's Holinshed. 1896, 1907[2]. pp. 205–342.

EDMOND MALONE: A dissertation on the 3 parts of 'King Henry VI', tending to show that those plays were not originally written by Shakespeare. London, 1787, 1792[2]. Also in Malone's Shakespeare, vol. 18, pp. 555–96.

CHARLES KNIGHT: An essay on the three parts of King Henry VI, and King Richard III. In Knight's library edition of Shakespeare. London, 1843. Vol. 7, pp. 1–119.

RICHARD GRANT WHITE: An essay on the authorship of the three parts of King Henry VI. In White's Works of W. Shakespeare. Boston, 1859. Vol. 7, pp. 401–68.

HERMANN ULRICI: Christopher Marlowe und Shakespeares Verhältnis zu ihm. In: Sh. Jb. Jg. 1, 1865, S. 57 seq.

F. G. FLEAY: Who wrote Henry VI? In: Macmillan's Magazine, vol. 33, 1875, pp. 50–62.

JANE LEE: On the authorship of the 2nd and 3rd parts of Henry VI, and their originals. In: Trans. New Shaksp. Soc., 1875–6, pp. 219–313.

NICOLAUS DELIUS: Zur Kritik der Doppeltexte des Shakespeareschen King Henry VI (Part II und III). In: Sh. Jb. Jg. 15, 1880, S. 211–21. Also in: Abhandlungen zu Shakespeare. 2 Bde. Berlin, 1889.

JOHN BELL HENNEMAN: The episodes in Shakespeare's 1 Henry VI. In: PMLA., vol. 15, N.S. vol. 8, 1900, pp. 290–320. Rev.: Sh. Jb. 37, 1901, S. 280–1, Dibelius; Bbl. 13, 1902, S. 262–3, R. Ackermann.

HERMANN CONRAD: Entstehung des 2. und 3. Teiles von Shakespeares Heinrich VI. In: Z. f. e. U. Bd. 8, 1909, S. 481–515.

C. F. TUCKER BROOKE: The authorship of the 2nd and 3rd parts of King Henry VI. New Haven, 1912. (67 pp.) = Trans. Connecticut Acad. of arts and sciences. Vol. 17, 1912, pp. 141–211. Rev.: MLR. 8, 1913, pp. 220–2, E. W. Lummis.

PAUL SEYFERTH: In welchem Verhältnis steht H 6 B zu The Contention betwixt the two famous houses of Yorke and Lancaster und H 6 C zu The True tragedie of Richard Duke of Yorke, and the death of the good King Henrie VI? In: Anglia, Bd. 40, 1916, S. 322–42. Rev.: Sh. Jb. 53, 1917, S. 195–6, Grabau.

HENRY DAVID GRAY: The purport of Shakespeare's contribution to 1 Henry VI. In: PMLA., vol. 32, N.S. vol. 25, 1917, pp. 367–82.

ELSE VON SCHAUBERT: Drayton's Anteil an 'Heinrich VI', 2. und 3. Teil. Cöthen, 1920. (xvi, 219 S.) = Neue anglist. Arb., hrsg. von Schücking und Deutschbein, H. 4. Rev.: Sh. Jb. 57, 1921, S. 97–100, W. Keller; MLR. 17, 1922, pp. 301–3, H. B. Charlton.

WOLFGANG KELLER: Noch einmal Draytons angebliche Mitarbeit an Heinrich VI. In: E. St. Bd. 57, 1923, S. 141–5.

PETER ALEXANDER: '2 Henry VI' and the copy for 'The Contention', 1594. In: TLS. Oct. 9, 1924, pp. 629–30.

PETER ALEXANDER: '3 Henry VI' and 'Richard, Duke of York'. In: TLS. Nov. 13, 1924, p. 730.

A. W. POLLARD: The quartos of the 'Contention' and 'Richard, Duke of York'. In: TLS., 1924, p. 797.

J. GOURVITCH: Drayton and 'Henry VI'. In: N. & Q., vol. 151, 1926, pp. 201–4, 219–21, 239–41, 256–8. Rev.: Sh. Jb. 63, 1927, S. 223, Beckmann.

ALLISON GAW: The origin and development of 1 Henry VI in relation to Shakespeare, Marlowe, Peele, and Greene. Los Angeles, 1926. (viii, 173 pp.) = Univ. of South California Studies, 1st ser., no. 1. Rev.: Bbl. 39, 1928, S. 94–8, H. T. Price; Sh. Jb. 63, 1927, S. 202–3, W. Keller; E. St. 63, 1929, S. 266–9, M. J. Wolff; MLN. 44, 1929, pp. 55–6, R. A. Law; RESt. 4, 1928, pp. 100–6, H. D. Sykes; JEGPh. 28, 1929, pp. 557–61, T. W. Baldwin.

PETER ALEXANDER: Shakespeare's Henry VI and Richard III. With an introduction by A. W. Pollard. C.U.P., 1929. (viii, 230 pp.) = Shakespeare Problems III. Rev.: TLS. Dec. 12, 1929, p. 1053.
Attributes H. VI to Shakespeare alone and considers the Contention and True Tragedy to be inferior quartos put together from actors' parts.

MADELEINE DORAN: Henry VI, parts II and III, their relation to the Contention and the True Tragedy. Univ. of Iowa, 1929. (88 pp.) = Univ. of Iowa Humanistic Studies, vol. 4, no. 4.

(2) LANGUAGE

EMMA PHIPSON: The natural history similes in Henry VI. In: Trans. New Shaksp. Soc., 1877-9, Pt. III, pp. 354-83.

(3) ART OF CHARACTERIZATION

KARL SCHMIDT: Margareta von Anjou vor und bei Shakespeare. Kap. I: Lancaster-freundliche Chroniken der Rosenzeit. Diss. Berlin, 1905. (29 S.) Enlarged in: Palaestra 54. Berlin, 1906. (xi, 286 S.) Rev.: Sh. Jb. 44, 1908, S. 336-7, Churchill; Bbl. 20, 1909, S. 244-5, Konr. Meier.

EDUARD VAN JAN: Das literarische Bild der Jeanne d'Arc (1429-1926). Halle, 1928. (xi, 199 S.) = Zs. f. rom. Philol. Beih. 76.

(4) SUBSEQUENT HISTORY OF THE PLAY

WILHELM OECHELHÄUSER: König Heinrich VI. In *ein* Stück zusammengezogen und für die Bühne bearbeitet. In: Sh. Jb. Jg. 5, 1870, S. 292-309.

EUGEN KILIAN: Eine neue Bühnenbearbeitung von König Heinrich VI. In: Sh. Jb. Jg. 32, 1896, S. 212-34.

G. KRECKE: Die englischen Bühnenbearbeitungen von Shakespeares 'King Henry VI'. Diss. Rostock, 1911. (216 S.)

KING RICHARD III

Cp. also in particular the general surveys on Shakespeare, pp. 27-29, the critical editions, pp. 53-58, and the criticism, pp. 141-145.

(1) THE TEXT

The Shakspere quarto facsimiles: Richard III:

No. 11 = Q 1 (1597). London, 1886 ⎫
No. 42 = Q 3 (1602). London, 1888 ⎬ With introductions by
No. 43 = Q 6 (1622). London, 1889 ⎭ P. A. DANIEL

The Bankside Shakespeare: Richard III. New York, 1891.
Parallel impression of the text of Q I and F I.

Treatises on the History of the Text:

R. KOPPEL: Textkritische Studien über Shakespeares Richard III. und King Lear. Hab. Schr. Dresden, 1877. (102 S.)

W. D. MORIARTY: The bearing on dramatic sequence of the varia in Richard III and King Lear. In: Mod. Phil., vol. 10, 1912-13, pp. 451-71.

(2) LITERARY GENESIS

W. G. BOSWELL-STONE: Shakspere's Holinshed, 1896, 1907², pp. 342–424.

The *true tragedy* of Richard III.
For information regarding new impressions see H. VI.

———

NICOLAUS DELIUS: Über den ursprünglichen Text des King Richard III. In: Sh. Jb. Jg. 7, 1872, S. 124–69.

JAMES SPEDDING: On the corrected edition of Richard III. In: Trans. New Shaksp. Soc., 1875–6, pp. 1–76.

EDWARD H. PICKERSGILL: On the quarto and folio of Richard III. In: Trans. New Shaksp. Soc., 1875–6, pp. 77–124.

ALEXANDER SCHMIDT: Quartos und Folio von Richard III. In: Sh. Jb. Jg. 15, 1880, S. 301–24. Also in his: Ges. Abhandlungen. Berlin, 1889, S. 253–80.

GEORGE B. CHURCHILL: Richard III. bis Shakespeare (The true tragedy of Richard III). Diss. Berlin, 1897. (84 S.) Enlarged as: Richard III up to Shakespeare. Berlin, 1900. (xiii, 548 S.)=Palaestra X. Rev.: Sh. Jb. 37, 1901, S. 256–8, W. Keller.

OTTO PAPE: Über die Entstehung der ersten Quarto von Shakespeares Richard III. Diss. Erlangen, 1906. (49 S.) Rev.: Sh. Jb. 52, 1916, S. 206, M. Förster; Bbl. 19, 1908, S. 100–1, R. Ackermann.
Q I based on a stenographic report of a performance of the play written by six stenographers.

K. KOEPPEL: Shakespeares 'Richard III.' und Senecas 'Troades'. In: Sh. Jb. Jg. 47, 1911, S. 188–90.

FRIEDRICH WILHELM: Zu Seneca und Shakespeare ('Richard III.'). In: Arch. Jg. 66, Bd. 129, 1912, S. 69–73.

J. M. ROBERTSON: The authorship of 'Richard III'. In the same writer's The Shakespeare canon. Vol. 1, 1922, pp. 155–200.

ROBERT W. BABCOCK: An introduction to the study of the text of Richard III. In: Studies in Phil., vol. 24, 1927, pp. 243–60.

PETER ALEXANDER: Shakespeare's Henry VI and Richard III. With an introduction by A. W. POLLARD. C.U.P., 1929. (viii, 230 pp.) = Shakespeare Problems III. Rev.: TLS. Dec. 12, 1929, p. 1053.
Attributes sole authorship of R. III to Shakespeare.

(3) DRAMATIC ART

(a) *Dramatic Structure of the Play and the Separate Scenes*

WILHELM OECHELHÄUSER: Essay über Richard III. In: Sh. Jb. Jg. 3, 1868, S. 27–149.

ELEANOR P. HAMMOND: The tent scene in Richard III. In: MLN., vol. 17, 1902, pp. 129–31.

ROBERT ADGER LAW: Richard the Third, act I, scene 4. In: PMLA., vol. 27, N.S. vol. 20, 1912, pp. 117–41.

GERTRUD GOETZE: Die Richard-Anna-Szene in Shakespeares Richard III. (I, 2). In: Anglia, Bd. 41, 1917, S. 1–9.

(b) *Art of Characterization*

F. SCHÖNE: Über den Charakter Richards III. bei Shakespeare. Progr. Dresden, 1856. (36 S.)

KUNO FISCHER: Shakespeares Charakterentwicklung Richards III. Heidelberg, 1868, 1889².

C. WESSEL: Richard III in Shakespeare's plays compared with Richard III in history. Progr. Eschwege, 1876. (32 S.)

H. MÜLLER: Grundlegung und Entwicklung des Charakters Richards III. bei Shakespeare. Progr. Dortmund, 1889. (68 S.) Also printed (with comments) in: Sh. Jb. Jg. 26, 1891, S. 150–257.

(4) SUBSEQUENT HISTORY OF THE PLAY

The ghost of Richard III. A poem, printed in 1614, and founded upon Shakespeare's historical play. Reprinted from the only known copy in the Bodleian Library. With an introd. and notes by J. PAYNE COLLIER. London, 1844. (xv, 79 pp.) = Shakespeare Soc. Publ.

OSCAR J. CAMPBELL, JR.: A Dutch analogue of Richard III, 1651. In: Shakespeare Studies by Members of the Dep. of English of the University of Wisconsin. Madison, 1916. (300 pp.)
Deals with Lambert van den Bosch's 'Roode en witte roos of Lankaster en York'.

OSCAR J. CAMPBELL: The position of 'The roode en witte roos' in the saga of King Richard III. Madison, 1919. (169 pp.) Univ. of Wisconsin stud. in language and lit. No. 5. Rev.: JEGPh. 20, 1921, pp. 407–10, H. N. Hillebrand; MLR. 16, 1921, pp. 191–2, P. Geyl.

———

WILHELM OECHELHÄUSER: Über eine neue Bühnenbearbeitung von König Richard III. In: Sh. Jb. Jg. 4, 1869, S. 327–48.

R. DOHSE: Colley Cibbers Bühnenbearbeitung von Shakespeares Richard III. Diss. Rostock, 1897. (61 S.) Also in: Bonner Beitr. z. Anglistik, hrsg. von M. Trautmann, H. 2, 1899. Rev.: Bbl. 14, 1903, S. 353–6, G. Binz.

JULIUS CSERWINKA: Regiebemerkungen zum Shakespeare. IV. Die Erscheinungen in 'Richard III'. In: Sh. Jb. Jg. 37, 1901, S. 175–80.

ALICE I. PERRY WOOD: The stage history of Shakespeare's King Richard III. New York, 1909. (xi, 186 pp.) Rev.: Sh. Jb. 46, 1910, S. 278–9, Churchill; JEGPh. 11, 1912, pp. 497–9, R. A. Law.

KING RICHARD II

Cp. also in particular the general surveys on Shakespeare, pp. 27–29, the critical editions, pp. 53–58, and the criticism, pp. 141–145.

(1) THE TEXT

The Shakspere quarto facsimiles (William Griggs): King Richard II:

Q 1597. With introd. by w. A. HARRISON. London, 1888. (76 pp.)
Q 1608. With introd. by w. A. HARRISON. London, 1888. (iv, 78 pp.)
Q 1634. With introd. by P. A. DANIEL. London, 1887. (iv, 80 pp.)

The tragedy of King Richard II, printed for the 3rd time by Valentine Simmes in 1598. Reproduction in facsimile from the unique copy in the library of William Augustus White. With an introduction by ALFRED W. POLLARD. London, 1916. (104 pp. and facs.)

KARL ELZE: Notes on King Richard II. In: E. St. Bd. 12, 1889, S. 186–97.

(2) LITERARY GENESIS

Richard II. Erster Teil. Ein Drama aus Shakespeares Zeit. Hrsg. von WOLFGANG KELLER. In: Sh. Jb. Jg. 35, 1899, S. 3–121.

W. G. BOSWELL-STONE: Shakespeare's Holinshed. London, 1907², pp. 77–130.

———

M. DAMETZ: Marlowes Edward II. und Shakespeares Richard II. Ein literarhistorischer Vergleich. Progr. Wien, 1904. (23 S.)

F. W. MOORMAN: Shakespeare's history-plays and Daniel's 'Civile Wars'. In: Sh. Jb. Jg. 40, 1904, S. 69–83. Includes: 'The Civile Wars' and Richard II. S. 72–6.

PAUL KÜHL: Das Verhältnis von Shaksperes Richard II. zu Marlowes Edward II. MS. Diss. Greifswald, 1920. Summary: Greifswald, 1923. (8 S.)

J. M. ROBERTSON: The authorship of 'Richard II'. In his The Shakespeare canon. Vol. 2, 1923, pp. 45–125.

(3) MISCELLANEOUS TREATISES ON RICHARD II

KARL ELZE: Alexandrines in The Winter's Tale and King Richard II. Halle, 1882.

CHRISTIAN EIDAM: Über die Einleitung in Shakespeares Richard II. In: N. Spr. Bd. 19, 1911–12, S. 277–95.

JOSEF KOHLER: Die Staatsidee Shakespeares in 'Richard II'. In: Sh. Jb. Jg. 53, 1917, S. 1–12.

EVELYN MAY ALBRIGHT: Shakespeare's Richard II and the Essex conspiracy. In: PMLA., vol. 42, 1927, pp. 686–720.

(4) SUBSEQUENT HISTORY OF THE PLAY

WILHELM ALLWARDT: Die englischen Bühnenbearbeitungen von Shakespeares 'King Richard II'. Diss. Rostock, 1909. (131 S.)

ROMEO AND JULIET

Cp. also in particular the general surveys on Shakespeare, pp. 27–29, the critical editions, pp. 53–58, and the criticism, pp. 141–145.

(1) THE TEXT

Shakespeares Romeo und Julie. Eine kritische Ausgabe des überlieferten Doppeltextes mit vollständiger *varia lectio* bis auf Rowe. Nebst einer Einleitung über den Wert der Textquellen und den Versbau Shakespeares von TYCHO MOMMSEN. Oldenburg, 1859.
Parallel impression of Q 1 and Q 2.

Romeo and Juliet. Reprints for the New Shaksp. Soc.:
Q 1 (1597). Ed. by P. A. DANIEL. London, 1874.
Q 2 (1599). Ed. by P. A. DANIEL. London, 1874.
Parallel texts of the first two quartos (Q 1) 1597, (Q 2) 1599. Ed. by P. A. DANIEL. London, 1874.
Revised edition of the second or 1599 quarto. Ed. by P. A. DANIEL. London, 1875.

The Shakspere quarto facsimiles (William Griggs): Romeo and Juliet:
Q 1 (1597.) With introd. by H. A. EVANS. London, 1886. (xvi, 78 pp.)
Q 2 (1599). With introd. by H. A. EVANS. London, 1886. (viii, 92 pp.)
The undated quarto. With introd. by H. A. EVANS. London, 1887. (iv, 88 pp.)

The most excellent tragedie of Romeo and Juliet (Q 1599). Printed in: The Cambridge Shakespeare. Vol. 9. London, 1893, pp. 638–96.

A New Var. Ed. (Furness): Reprint of Q 1597.

The first quarto edition of Shakespeare's Romeo and Juliet. Ed. with introd. and notes by FRANK G. HUBBARD. Madison, 1924 = Univ. of Wisconsin Studies in lang. and lit. no. 19. Rev.: JEGPh. 24, 1925, pp. 434–6, R. A. Law.
Q 1 with modern spelling.

J. DOVER WILSON and A. W. POLLARD: The 'stolne and surreptitious' Shakespearian texts. Romeo and Juliet (1597). In: TLS. Aug. 14, 1919, p. 434.

B. A. P. VAN DAM: Did Shakespeare revise 'Romeo and Juliet'? In: Anglia, Bd. 51, 1927, S. 39–63. Rev.: Sh. Jb. 63, 1927, S. 223–4, W. Keller.

(2) LITERARY GENESIS

RUDOLF FISCHER: Quellen zu Romeo und Julia. Bonn, 1922. (viii, 251 S.) = Shakespeares Quellen in der Originalsprache und deutsch hrsg. im Auftrag der Deutschen Shakespeare-Ges. 2. Bändchen. Rev.: JEGPh. 22, 1923, pp. 463–5, R. A. Law.
CONTENTS: I. Masuccio's Mariotto and Gianozza. II. Da Porto's Giulietta. III. Bandello's Romeo and Giulietta. IV. Boisteau's Rhomeo and Juliette. V. Brooke's Romeus and Juliet.

Brooke's 'Romeus and Juliet' being the original of Shakespeare's 'Romeo and Juliet', newly ed. by J. J. MUNRO. London, 1908. (lxix, 167 pp.)＝The Shakespeare Classics.

Cf. also E. REDDIG: Die epische Technik A. Brookes in seiner Tragicall historye of Romeus and Juliet. Diss. Göttingen, 1927. (79 S.)

KARL PAUL SCHULZE: Die Entwicklung der Sage von Romeo und Julia. In: Sh. Jb. Jg. 11, 1876, S. 140–225.

THOMAS ALFRED SPALDING: On the first quarto of Romeo and Juliet. Is there any evidence of a second hand in it? In: Trans. New Shaksp. Soc., 1877–9, pp. 58–87.
Defends the sole authorship of Shakespeare.

KARL PAUL SCHULZE: The Jolly Goshawk. In: Sh. Jb. Jg. 13, 1878, S. 205–11.
Identifies certain reminiscences of this ballad in Romeo and Juliet.

ROBERT GERICKE: Romeo und Juliet nach Shakespeares Manuskript. In: Sh. Jb. Jg. 14, 1879, S. 207–73.

NICOLAUS DELIUS: Brookes episches und Shakespeares dramatisches Gedicht von Romeo und Juliet. In: Sh. Jb. Jg. 16, 1881, S. 213–27.

ALBERT COHN: Adrian Sevin's Bearbeitung der Sage von Romeo und Julia. In: Sh. Jb. Jg. 24, 1889, S. 122–30.
Reprint of the story from A. Sevin's translation of Boccaccio's Philocolo [1542].

LUDWIG FRÄNKEL: Untersuchungen zur Entwicklungsgeschichte des Stoffes von Romeo und Julia. Ein Beitrag zur vergleichenden Literaturgeschichte. I. Teil. Diss. Leipzig, 1889. (40 S.) Enlarged in: Zs. f. vgl. Lit. gesch., N.F. Bd. 3, 1890, S. 171–210 und Bd. 4, 1891, S. 48–91.

LUDWIG FRÄNKEL: Neue Beiträge zur Geschichte des Stoffes von Shakespeares 'Romeo and Juliet'. In: E. St. Bd. 19, 1894, S. 183–206.

HAROLD DE WOLF FULLER: Romeo and Juliette. In: Mod. Phil., vol. 4, 1906–7, pp. 75–120.
Tries to prove that the Dutchman Jacob Struijs used in his drama the lost pre-Shakespearean Romeo play.

ADOLF SCHÖTTNER: Über die mutmassliche stenographische Entstehung der ersten Quarto von Shakespeares Romeo und Julia. Diss. Leipzig, 1918. (vi, 111 S.) Also printed in: Arch. f. Schriftkunde I, 1914–18. Leipzig, 1918. Rev.: Sh. Jb. 55, 1919, S. 163–4, W. Keller; Bbl. 30, 1919, S. 122–5, Ph. Aronstein.

J. M. ROBERTSON: 'Romeo and Juliet'. In his The Shakespeare canon. Vol. 3, 1925, pp. 113–202.

OLIN H. MOORE: Le rôle de Boaistuau dans le développement de la légende de 'Roméo et Juliette'. In: Rev. de litt. comp., 9, 1929, pp. 637–43.

ROBERT EDGAR LAW: On Shakespeare's changes of his source material in Romeo and Juliet. In: Univ. of Texas Stud. in English. No. 9, 1929, pp. 87–102.

(3) SHAKESPEARE'S ART IN ROMEO AND JULIET

TH. STRÄTER: Die Komposition von Shakespeares Romeo und Julia. 3 Vorlesungen. Bonn, 1861.

HELENE HÜLSMANN: Die Metaphern in Shakespeares 'Romeo and Juliet'. Diss. München, 1928. (93 S.) Rev.: Sh. Jb. 65, 1929, S. 194, W. Keller.

(4) MISCELLANEOUS TREATISES ON ROMEO AND JULIET

EDUARD VON HARTMANN: Shakespeares Romeo und Julia. Leipzig, 1874. (38 S.)

MAX GÜNTHER: A defence of Shakespeare's 'Romeo and Juliet' against modern criticism. Diss. Halle, 1876. (31 S.)

C. F. MCCLUMPHA: Shakespeare's sonnets and Romeo and Juliet. In: Sh. Jb. Jg. 40, 1904, S. 187–203.
Points out parallel passages.

RICHARD STECHER: Erläuterungen zu Shakespeares Romeo. Leipzig, 1922.

ALLISON GAW: Actors' names in basic Shakespearean texts, with special reference to 'Romeo and Juliet' and 'Much Ado'. In: PMLA., vol. 40, 1925, pp. 530–50.

LEVIN L. SCHÜCKING: Neuere Shakespeareliteratur. In: Dt. Vjschr. Jg. 6, 1928, S. 187–8.

(5) SUBSEQUENT HISTORY OF THE PLAY

(a) Adaptations and Translations

L. H. FISCHER: Die Sage von Romeo und Julia in deutschen Prosadarstellungen des 17. Jahrhunderts. In: Sh. Jb. Jg. 25, 1890, S. 124–31.

JOHANNES BOLTE: Die Oxforder Tragödie Thibaldus (1640). In: Sh. Jb. Jg. 27, 1892, S. 228–9.

EUGEN KILIAN: Zu Goethes Bearbeitung von 'Romeo und Julia'. In: Beil. z. Allgem. Ztg., 1892, No. 297.

KARL HOLTERMANN: Vergleichung der Schlegelschen und Voss'schen Übersetzung von Shakespeares 'Romeo und Juliet'. Progr. Münster, 1892. (30 S.)

WILLY SCHRAMM: Thomas Otways 'The history and fall of Caius Marius' und Garricks 'Romeo and Juliet' in ihrem Verhältnis zu Shakespeares 'Romeo and Juliet' und den übrigen Quellen. Diss. Rostock, 1898. (76 S.)

J. MINOR: Die Lesarten zu Goethes Bearbeitung von Romeo und Julia. In: Festschr. z. 8. allgem. dt. Neuphilologentage in Wien, 1898, S. 3–15.

JOHANNES GRUBER: Das Verhältnis von Weisses Romeo und Julia zu Shakespeare und den Novellen. Berlin, 1905 = Stud. z. vgl. Lit. gesch., Bd. 5.

EUGEN KILIAN: Schreyvogels Shakespeare-Bearbeitungen. Ein Beitrag zur Bühnengeschichte der Shakespeareschen Dramen in Deutschland. 3. Romeo und Julia. In: Sh. Jb. Jg. 41, 1905, S. 135–62.

G. R. HAUSCHILD: Das Verhältnis von Goethes 'Romeo und Julia' zu Shakespeares gleichnamiger Tragödie. Progr. Frankfurt a. M., 1907. (57 S.) Rev.: Sh. Jb., 45, 1909, S. 279–80, Fr. Brie.

E. WENDLING: Goethes Bühnenbearbeitung von 'Romeo und Julia'. Progr. Zabern, 1907. (22 S.)

REINHOLD BÖSSER: Shakespeares Romeo and Juliet in französischer Bearbeitung. Diss. Rostock, 1907. (132 S.)

W. SMITH: A comic version of Romeo and Juliette. In: Mod. Phil., vol. 7, 1909–10, pp. 217–20.
Translation of the scenario of an Italian Commedia dell' arte (1611).

MAX J. WOLFF: Die Tragödie von Romio and Julietta. In: Sh. Jb. Jg. 47, 1911, S. 92–105. (Reprinted in: COHN, Shakespeare in Germany. London, 1865, pp. 310 seq.)
Deals with the German Romeo-play.

ANNA E. MILLER: Die erste deutsche Übersetzung von Shakespeares 'Romeo and Juliet'. In: JEGPh., vol. 11, 1912, pp. 30–60.

A. SAUER: Shakespeares 'Romeo und Julia' in den Bearbeitungen und Übersetzungen der deutschen Literatur. Diss. Greifswald, 1915. (122 S.)

H. HAUVETTE: Une variante française de la légende de Roméo et Juliette. In: Rev. de litt. comp., 1921.

KARL BRUNNER: Die erste deutsche Romeo-Übersetzung. In: Arch. Jg. 83, Bd. 153, 1928, S. 188–201.

(b) Romeo and Juliet on the stage

HERMANN FREIHERR VON FRIESEN: Wie soll man Shakespeare spielen? III. Romeo und Julie. In: Sh. Jb. Jg. 7, 1872, S. 7–28.

K. TRAUTMANN: Die älteste Nachricht über eine Aufführung von Shakespeares 'Romeo und Julia'. In: Arch. f. Lit. gesch. Bd. 11, 1882.
Refers to Nördlingen (1604).

JULIUS CZERWINKA: Regiebemerkungen zum Shakespeare. III. Die Apothekerszene in 'Romeo und Julia'. In: Sh. Jb. Jg. 37, 1901, S. 165–75.

FERDINAND GREGORI: Shakespeare auf der deutschen Bühne. II. Josef Kainz: Romeo. In: Sh. Jb. Jg. 40, 1904, S. 89–94.

A MIDSUMMER NIGHT'S DREAM

Cp. also in particular the general surveys on Shakespeare, pp. 27–29, the critical editions, pp. 53–58, and the criticism, pp. 141–145.

(1) THE TEXT

The Shakspere quarto facsimiles: A Midsummer Night's Dream.

No. 3: Q 1 (Fisher quarto), 1600 ⎱ With introductions by J. W. EBSWORTH.
No. 4: Q 2 (Roberts quarto), 1600 ⎰　London, 1880.

The Bankside Shakespeare: A Midsummer Night's Dream. New York, 1890.
Parallel impression of Q 1 and F 1.

Treatises on the History of the Text:

ALEXANDER SCHMIDT: Die ältesten Ausgaben des Sommernachtstraums. Progr. Königsberg, 1881. (21 S.) Also in his Gesammelte Abhandlungen. Berlin, 1889, S. 281–312.

B. KRAUSE: Die drei ältesten Drucke des Sommernachtstraums. (Q A ist der einzig glaubwürdige unter den dreien.) In: Sh. Jb. Jg. 21, 1886, S. 159–74.

E. FLÜGEL: Pyramys and Tysbe. In: Anglia, Bd. 12, 1889, S. 13–20.
Reprint of two settings of the Pyramus story.

A. WÜRZNER: Die Orthographie der beiden Quarto-Ausgaben von Shaksperes Sommernachtstraum. Progr. Wien, 1893. (31 S.) Rev.: Bbl. 5, 1895, S. 7, L. Proescholdt.

ALFRED E. THISELTON: Some textual notes on 'A Midsummer Night's Dream.' London, 1904.

W. W. GREG: On certain false dates in Shakespearian quartos. In: Libr., N.S. vol. 9, 1908, pp. 113–31 and 381–409.
According to Greg, the Roberts-Quarto is a reprint of the Fisher-Quarto of 1619, purposely wrongly dated. Pollard (in: Shakespeare folios and quartos, 1909) supports this opinion.

(2) LITERARY GENESIS

The sources and analogues of 'A Midsummer Night's Dream', compiled by FRANK SIDGWICK. London, 1908. (196 pp.) = The Shakespeare Library. Rev.: Sh. Jb. 45, 1909, S. 393–4, M. Förster.
Compilation of similar subject-matter.

———

JAMES O. HALLIWELL: An introduction to Shakespeare's 'Midsummer Night's Dream'. London, 1841. (iv, 104 pp.)

NICHOLAS J. HALPIN: Oberon's vision in the 'Midsummer Night's Dream' illustrated by a comparison with Lyly's 'Endymion'. In: Shakespeare Soc., 1843.

KARL ELZE: Zum Sommernachtstraum. In: Sh. Jb. Jg. 3, 1868, S. 150–74.
Presumes the marriage of the Earl of Essex with Lady Sidney to be the date of production.

HERMANN KURZ: Nachlese. 2. Zum Sommernachtstraum. In: Sh. Jb. Jg. 4, 1869, S. 268–307.

FRITZ KRAUSS: Eine Quelle zu Shakespeares Sommernachtstraum. In: Sh. Jb. Jg. 11, 1876, S. 226–44.

L. PRÖSCHOLDT: On the sources of Shakespeare's Midsummer Night's Dream. Diss. Halle, 1878. (34 pp.)
Points above all to Chaucer's Knight's Tale.

BERNHARD TEN BRINK: Über den Sommernachtstraum. Vortrag. In: Sh. Jb. Jg. 13, 1878, S. 92–110.

JAMES O. HALLIWELL: Memoranda on Shakespeare's 'Midsummer Night's Dream'. London, 1879. (48 pp.)

ADOLF SCHÖLL: Über Shakespeares Sommernachtstraum. In: Sh. Jb. Jg. 17, 1882, S. 100–27.

G. FINKENBRINK: An essay on the date, plot and sources of Shakespeare's 'A Midsummer Night's Dream'. Part I: On the date. Progr. Mühlheim a. d. R., 1884. (20 pp.)

GREGOR SARRAZIN: Die Abfassungszeit des 'Sommernachtstraums'. In: Arch. Bd. 95, 1895, S. 291–300.
Presumes the date of production to have been the marriage-ceremony of the Countess of Southampton, mother of Henry Wriothesley, with Sir Thomas Heneage (2 May 1594). For further evidence cp.:

CHARLOTTE C. STOPES: Shakespeare's environment. London, 1918², pp. 156 ff.

R. TOBLER: Shakespeares Sommernachtstraum und Montemayors Diana. In: Sh. Jb. Jg. 34, 1898, S. 358–66.

W. VOLLHARDT: Die Beziehungen des Sommernachtstraums zum italienischen Schäferdrama. I. Progr. Leipzig, 1899. (32 S.) Rev.: Bbl. 10, 1900, S. 140–1, Ph. Wagner.

GREGOR SARRAZIN: Szenerie und Staffage im 'Sommernachtstraum'. In: Arch. Bd. 104, 1900, S. 67–74.
Sarrazin continues to support the date of production (2 May 1594) suggested by himself, as against Fleay who contends for the wedding of Lord Derby and Lady Elizabeth Vere (26 Jan. 1595).

F. P. VON WESTENHOLZ: Shakespeares 'Gewonnene Liebesmüh'. In: Beil. Allg. Ztg. No. 10 vom 14. Jan. 1902.
Attempts to identify it with Mids.

HERMANN REICH: Der Mann mit dem Eselskopf. Ein Mimodrama vom klassischen Altertum verfolgt bis auf Shakespeare. In: Sh. Jb. Jg. 40, 1904, S. 109–28.

GERHARD HEINE: Shakespeares 'Sommernachtstraum' und 'Romeo und Julia'. Progr. Bernburg, 1907. (32 S.) Rev.: Z. f. e. U. 7, 1908, S. 556 ff., O. Glöde.

EDITH RICKERT: Political propaganda and satire in 'A Midsummer Night's Dream.' In: Mod. Phil., vol. 21, 1923, pp. 53–89 and 133–55.

ALBERT EICHLER: Das Hofbühnenmässige in Shakespeares 'Midsummer Night's Dream'. In: Sh. Jb. Jg. 61, N.F. 2, 1925, S. 39–51. Also in: Neusprachliche Studien. Festgabe für K. Luick=N. Spr. Beiheft 6.

(3) SUBSEQUENT HISTORY OF THE PLAY

W. GOERNER: Das Verhältnis von Garricks 'The Fairies' zu Shakespeares 'A Midsummer Night's Dream'. Diss. Halle, 1902. (50 S.)

N. FEIN: Die deutschen Nachahmer des Rüpelspiels aus Shakespeares 'Sommernachtstraum'. I. Progr. Brünn, 1914. (16 S.)

A. KÖLLMANN: Wieland und Shakespeare, mit besonderer Berücksichtigung der Übersetzung des Sommernachtstraums. Progr. Remscheid, 1896. (17 S.)

LEOPOLD WURTH: Zu Wielands, Eschenburgs und A. W. von Schlegels Übersetzungen des Sommernachtstraums. Progr. Budweis, 1897. (16 S.)

WILHELM OECHELHÄUSER: Über die Darstellung des Sommernachtstraums auf der deutschen Bühne. In: Sh. Jb. Jg. 5, 1870, S. 310–24.

EUGEN KILIAN: Zur Aufführung des Sommernachtstraums. In: Sh. Jb. Jg. 34, 1898, S. 52–65.

THE TAMING OF THE SHREW

Cp. also in particular the general surveys on Shakespeare, pp. 27–29, the critical editions, pp. 53–58, and the criticism, pp. 141–145.

(1) THE TEXT

FLORENCE H. ASHTON: The revision of the folio text of 'The Taming of the Shrew'. In: Philol. Quart., vol. 6, 1927, pp. 151–60.

(2) LITERARY GENESIS

The old 'Taming of a Shrew', upon which Shakespeare founded his comedy, reprinted from the edition of 1594, and collated with the subsequent editions of 1596 and 1607. Edited by THOMAS AMYOT. London, 1844. (xii, 92 pp.)

The Shakspere quarto facsimiles (William Griggs): The Taming of a Shrew. Q I (1594). With foreword by F. J. FURNIVALL. London, 1886. (xiv, 52 pp.)

'The Taming of a Shrew', being the original of Shakespeare's 'Taming of the Shrew', ed. by F. S. BOAS. London, 1908. (xl, 128 pp.)=The Shakespeare Classics. Rev.: Sh. Jb. 45, 1909, S. 392–3, M. Förster.

Cf. also H. DUGDALE SYKES: The authorship of 'The Taming of a Shrew', 'The Famous Victories of Henry V', and the additions to Marlowe's 'Faustus'. London, for the Shakespeare Assoc., 1920.

Sykes attributes these plays to Sam. Rowley.

B. A. P. VAN DAM: The Taming of a Shrew. In: Engl. Studies, vol. 10, 1928, pp. 97–106.

Estimates the play later than Shakespeare's Shrew

GEORGE GASCOIGNE: Poems. The Supposes. Ed. by W. C. Hazlitt, 1869.

Early plays from the Italian: Supposes, The Buggbears, Misogonus. Edited with introduction, notes, and glossary by R. WARWICK BOND. Oxford, 1911. (cxviii, 332 pp.)
Contains Gascoigne's Supposes, pp. 1–73.

———

NICOLAUS DELIUS: Shakespeares 'Taming of the Shrew'. Elberfeld, 1864.

REINHOLD KÖHLER: Zu Shakespeares The Taming of the Shrew. In: Sh. Jb. Jg. 3, 1868, S. 397–401.
Contains information about a Danish fairy-tale with similar subject-matter.

F. G. FLEAY: On the authorship of 'The Taming of the Shrew', with remarks on 'Titus Andronicus.' In: Trans. New Shaksp. Soc., 1874.
Considers a Shrew to be an early work of Shakespeare.

ALEXANDER VON WEILEN: Shakespeares Vorspiel zu der Widerspänstigen Zähmung. Ein Beitrag zur vergleichenden Literaturgeschichte. Frankf. a. M., 1884. (93 S.) Rev.: E. St. 9, 1886, S. 301–5, M. Koch.

R. URBACH: Das Verhältnis des Shakespeareschen Lustspiels 'The Taming of the Shrew' zu seinen Quellen. Diss. Rostock, 1887. (44 S.)

ALBERT H. TOLMAN: Shakspere's part in 'The Taming of the Shrew'. Diss. Strassburg, 1891. (82 S.)

ALBERT H. TOLMAN: What has become of Shakespeare's play 'Love's Labour's Won'? Chicago, 1902. (34 pp.) = Decennial Publ. Univ. Chicago, vol. 7. Rev.: Bbl. 16, 1905, S. 193–4, R. Ackermann.
Tolman maintains that an anonymous poet remodelled it into a Shrew.

ELIAS HUGO SCHOMBURG: The Taming of the Shrew. Eine Studie zu Shaksperes Kunst. Halle a. S., 1904. (123 S.) = Studien z. engl. Phil., hrsg. von Morsbach, H. 20.

ERNEST P. KUHL: The authorship of The Taming of the Shrew. In: PMLA., vol. 40, 1925, pp. 551–618. Rev.: Sh. Jb. 63, 1927, S. 224, Beckmann; MLR. 22, 1927, pp. 328–30, H. D. Sykes; Bbl. 38, 1927, S. 115–17, W. Vollhardt.
Supports the sole authorship of Shakespeare.

B. A. P. VAN DAM: The Taming of the Shrew. In: Engl. Studies, vol. 10, 1928, pp. 161–77.

(3) SUBSEQUENT HISTORY OF THE PLAY

JOHANNES BOLTE: Eine holländische Bearbeitung von Shakespeares Taming of the Shrew vom Jahre 1654. In: Sh. Jb. Jg. 26, 1891, S. 78–86.

JOHANNES BOLTE: Eine Parallele zu Shakespeares The Taming of the Shrew. In: Sh. Jb. Jg. 27, 1892, S. 130–4.
Reimpression of a German farce (1667).

JOHANNES BOLTE: Der Widerspenstigen Zähmung als Görlitzer Schulkomödie. In: Sh. Jb. Jg. 27, 1892, S. 125–9.

E. MOOSMANN: John Lacy's Sauny the Scot. Eine Bearbeitung von Shakespeares 'The Taming of the Shrew' aus der Restaurationszeit (1667). Diss. Halle, 1901. (70 S.)

FRANZ WEBER: Lacy's Sauny the Scot und Garrick's Catharine and Petruchio im Verhältnis zu ihren Quellen. Diss. Rostock, 1901. (85 S.)

C. SCHNAUS: Über das Verhältnis von David Garrick's 'Catharine and Petruchio' zu Shakespeares 'The Taming of the Shrew'. Diss. Halle, 1902. (46 S.)

M. RÖSSLER: Die Beziehungen von Fletchers 'The Tamer Tamed' zu Shakespeares 'Taming of the Shrew'. Progr. Brünn, 1907. (13 S.)

EUGEN KILIAN: Der Widerspenstigen Zähmung. Vorschläge für eine neue szenische Einrichtung des Stückes. In: Sh. Jb. Jg. 31, 1895, S. 55–82.

KING JOHN

Cp. also in particular the general surveys on Shakespeare, pp. 27–29, the critical editions, pp. 53–58, and the criticism, pp. 141–145.

(1) LITERARY GENESIS

The Life and Death of King John by William Shakespeare together with The Troublesome Reign of King John, ed. by F. G. FLEAY. London, 1878. (224 pp.)

The Shakspere quarto facsimiles (William Griggs): The Troublesome Raigne of John, King of England. The 1st quarto, 1591, parts I and II. London, 1888.

The Troublesome Reign of King John, being the original of Shakespeare's 'Life and Death of King John'. Ed. by F. J. FURNIVALL and JOHN MUNRO. O.U.P., 1913. (xlviii, 186 pp.) = The Shakespeare Classics.

The Troublesome Raigne of John, King of England. London, 1591. Reprinted in: A New Var. Ed. of Shakespeare: King John. Philadelphia, 1919, pp. 471–537.

> H. DUGDALE SYKES: 'The Troublesome Reign of King John.' In his Sidelights on Shakespeare. Stratford, 1919, pp. 99–125.
> Sykes attributes authorship to George Peele.

W. G. BOSWELL-STONE: Shakespeare's Holinshed. London, 1907[2], pp. 45–77.

FERDINAND STÜMCKE: Studien zu Shakespeares King John. Progr. Otterndorf, 1889. (10 S.)

GEORG KOPPLOW: Shakespeares 'King John' und seine Quellen. Diss. Kiel, 1900. (86 S.) Rev.: Sh. Jb. 37, 1901, S. 258, W. Keller.

ANNA KERRL: Unterschiede in der Behandlung von Satzschluss und Versschluss in Shakespeares King John und Julius Caesar. Diss. Bonn, 1913. (x, 43 S.) Enlarged under the title: Die metrischen Unterschiede von Shakespeares

King John und Julius Caesar. Eine chronologische Untersuchung. Bonn, 1913. (x, 189 S.) = Bonner Studien z. engl. Philol., hrsg. von K. D. Bülbring, H. 10. Rev.: Sh. Jb. 50, 1914, S. 222, M. Förster; Bbl. 25, 1914, S. 109–13, E. Ekwall.

FELIX LIEBERMANN: Shakespeare als Bearbeiter des King John. I, II, III. In: Arch. Bd. 142, 1921, S. 177–202; 143, 1922, S. 17–46 und 190–203.

E. W. SIEVERS: Shakespeare und der Gang nach Canossa. In: E. St. Bd. 20, 1895, S. 220–65.

(2) SUBSEQUENT HISTORY OF THE PLAY

K. KÖPPE: Das Verhältnis von Cibbers 'Papal tyranny in the reign of King John' zu Shakespeares 'King John'. Diss. Halle, 1901. (100 S.)

THE MERCHANT OF VENICE

Cp. also in particular the general surveys on Shakespeare, pp. 27–29, the critical editions, pp. 53–58, and the criticism, pp. 141–151.

(1) THE TEXT

The Shakspere quarto facsimiles (William Griggs): Merchant of Venice.

Q 1600 (Roberts). With foreword by F. J. FURNIVALL. London, 1881. (xii, 78 pp.)

Q 1600 (Heyes). With foreword by F. J. FURNIVALL. London, 1887. (xiv, 76 pp.)

WALTER W. GREG: On certain false dates in Shakespearian quartos. In: Libr. N.S., vol. 9, 1908, pp. 113–31 and 381–409.

Greg maintains that the Roberts Q 1600 was published in 1619 and was purposely wrongly dated.

B. A. P. VAN DAM: The text of the Merchant of Venice. In: Neophilologus, Jg. 13, 1927, S. 33–51.

(2) LITERARY GENESIS

For material as to questions of sources see: New Var. Ed. (Furness): The Merchant of Venice. Philadelphia, 1888.

R. A. C. HEBLER: Shakespeares Kaufmann von Venedig. Ein Versuch über die sogenannte Idee dieser Komödie. Bern, 1854. (iii, 132 S.)

W. BERNHARDI: Shakespeares Kaufmann von Venedig. Eine kritische Skizze. Altona, 1859.

KARL ELZE: Zum Kaufmann von Venedig. In: Sh. Jb. Jg. 6, 1871, S. 129–68.

H. GRÄTZ: Shylock in der Sage, im Drama und in der Geschichte. Krotoschin, 1880, 1888².

JOHANNES BOLTE: Jakob Rosefeldt's Moschus, eine Parallele zum Kaufmann von Venedig. In: Sh. Jb. Jg. 21, 1886, S. 187–210.

Reprint of a part of this Latin comedy (1599).

JOHANNES BOLTE: Zur Shylock-Fabel. In: Sh. Jb. Jg. 27, 1892, S. 225–7.
Reprint of a divergent Dutch version of the story of the pound of flesh.

E. MORY: Marlowes Jude von Malta und Shakespeares Kaufmann von Venedig.
Progr. Basel, 1897. (27 S.)

FRIEDRICH BRIE: Zur Entstehung des 'Kaufmanns von Venedig'. In: Sh. Jb.
Jg. 49, 1913, S. 97–121.
With a reprint of Anthony Munday's Zelanto, the Fountaine of Fame (1580).

WILHELM CREIZENACH: Betrachtungen über den 'Kaufmann von Venedig'. In:
Sh. Jb. Jg. 51, 1915, S. 171–82.

BERTA VIKTORIA WENGER: Shylocks Pfund Fleisch. Eine stoffgeschichtliche
Untersuchung. Diss. München. Also printed in: Sh. Jb. Jg. 65, 1929,
S. 92–174.

BEATRICE DAW BROWN: Medieval prototypes of Lorenzo and Jessica. In:
MLN., vol. 44, 1929, pp. 227–32.

(3) ART OF CHARACTERIZATION

D. HONIGMANN: Über den Charakter des Shylock. In: Sh. Jb. Jg. 17, 1882,
S. 201–29.

H. HEINEMANN: Shylock und Nathan. Vortrag. Frankfurt a. M., 1886. (14 S.)

ELMER EDGAR STOLL: Shylock. In: JEGPh., vol. 10, 1911, pp. 236–79. Enlarged in: Shakespeare studies. New York, 1927, pp. 255–336. Rev.: Sh. Jb.
48, 1912, S. 223, Grabau.

ARNOLD SCHRÖER: Zur Beurteilung des Shylock. In: E. St. Bd. 50, 1916–17,
S. 51–62.

C. R. BASKERVILL: Bassanio as an ideal lover. In: The Manly Anniversary
Stud. in Lang. and Lit. Chicago Univ. Pr., 1923, pp. 90–103.

SAMUEL A. SMALL: Shaksperean character interpretation: The Merchant of
Venice. Göttingen, 1927. (126 pp.)=Hesperea, Ergänzungsreihe, H. 10.
Rev.: E. St. 63, 1929, S. 273–6, E. Eckhardt; MLN. 44, 1929, pp. 54–5,
R. A. Law.
With detailed review of the literature on the subject up to date.

R. VOLBEDA: Over de Shylockfiguur. I, II, III. In: Neophilologus, Jg. 14,
1929, S. 120–6, 196–204 und 274–81.

(4) THE SHYLOCK PACT

JOSEF KOHLER: Shakespeare vor dem Forum der Jurisprudenz. Berlin &
Leipzig, 1883–4, 1919^2. (xi, 366 S.) Rev.: Bbl. 28, 1927, S. 200–2, M.
Förster.

FRITZ FREUND: Shakespeare als Rechtsphilosoph. Kaufmann von Venedig und
Mass für Mass. In: Sh. Jb. Jg. 28, 1893, S. 54–71.

WLADIMIR STASSOW: Über Shakespeares Kaufmann von Venedig und das Shylock-Problem. Autor. Übers. aus dem Russ. von WILHELM HENCKEL. München, 1905. (50 S.) Rev.: Dt. Litztg. 26, 1905, Sp. 479–80, Fr. Dukmeyer.

J. STRASSER: Shakespeare als Jurist. Versuch einer Studie über Shakespeares 'Kaufmann von Venedig'. Halle, 1907. (32 S.) Rev.: Sh. Jb. 44, 1908, S. 332–5, R. Eberstadt.

RUDOLF EBERSTADT: Der Shylockvertrag und sein Urbild. In: Sh. Jb. Jg. 44, 1908, S. 1–35.

THEODOR NIEMEYER: Der Rechtsspruch gegen Shylock im 'Kaufmann von Venedig'. Ein Beitrag zur Würdigung Shakespeares. Leipzig, 1912. (32 S.) Rev.: Lit. Zbl. 1912, Sp. 1484–5, M. J. Wolff; Sh. Jb. 49, 1913, S. 206–9, Fr. Oetker.

(5) SUBSEQUENT HISTORY OF THE PLAY

(a) *Adaptations*

JOHANNES BOLTE: Der Jude von Venetien. Die älteste deutsche Bearbeitung des Merchant of Venice [um 1690]. In: Sh. Jb. Jg. 22, 1887, S. 189–201.

EUGEN KILIAN: Dalbergs Bühnenbearbeitungen des Kaufmanns von Venedig und Coriolans. In: Sh. Jb. Jg. 26, 1891, S. 4–25.

K. TREUTEL: Shakespeares Kaufmann von Venedig in französischer Bühnenbearbeitung. Diss. Rostock, 1901. (80 S.)

OTTO BURMEISTER: Nachdichtungen und Bühneneinrichtungen von Shakespeares Merchant of Venice. Diss. Rostock, 1902. (143 S.) Rev.: Sh. Jb. 39, 1903, S. 303, Rud. Fischer; Bbl. 14, 1903, S. 334–5, Ph. Wagner.
With a further chapter on travesties of the Merch. of Ven.

(b) *The Merchant of Venice on the Stage*

HERMANN FREIHERR VON FRIESEN: Wie soll man Shakespeare spielen? IV. Der Kaufmann von Venedig. In: Sh. Jb. Jg. 8, 1873, S. 138–70.

LUDWIG MALYOTH: Shakespeare auf der deutschen Bühne. VI. Ernst von Possart: Shylock. In: Sh. Jb. Jg. 42, 1906, S. 94–107.

WOLFGANG STAMMLER: Zur Darstellung Shylocks und Hamlets auf der deutschen Bühne. In: Sh. Jb. Jg. 49, 1913, S. 137–44.
The actor Friedrich Haase as interpreter of Shylock and Hamlet.

KING HENRY IV (Parts I and II)

Cp. also in particular the general surveys on Shakespeare, pp. 27–29, the critical editions, pp. 53–58, and the criticism, pp. 141–145.

(1) THE TEXT

The Shakspere quarto facsimiles (William Griggs): King Henry IV.
Part I, Quarto 1598 (XIII, 79 pp.). ⎫
Part II, Quarto 1600 (XII, 85 pp.). ⎭ With foreword by Herbert A. Evans.

R. P. COWL: Notes on the text of 'King Henry IV'. London, 1927. (21 pp.)

(2) LITERARY GENESIS

The famous victories of King Henry V. Reprint in: COLLIER-HAZLITT: Shakspere's library. Vol. 5. London 1875. *The Shakspere quarto facsimiles* (William Griggs): Q 1 (1598). With introd. by P. A. DANIEL. London, 1887.

W. G. BOSWELL-STONE: Shakspere's Holinshed. London, 1907², pp. 130–64.

———

E. A. STRUVE: Studien zu Shakespeares Heinrich IV. Kiel, 1851.

F. W. MOORMAN: Shakespeare's history-plays and Daniel's 'Civile Wars'. In: Sh. Jb. Jg. 40, 1904, S. 69–83.

H. AX: The relation of Shakespeare's Henry IV to Holinshed. Diss. Freiburg i. B., 1912. (115 S.)

A. E. MORGAN: Some problems of Shakespeare's 'Henry IV.' O.U.P., 1924. (43 pp.) = The Shakespeare Assoc. Papers. Rev.: Bbl. 36, 1925, S. 364–7, E. Deckner.

R. P. COWL: Some 'echoes' in Elizabethan drama of Shakespeare's 'King Henry IV', part I and II, considered in relation to the text of those plays. Helsingfors and London, 1926. (27 pp.) Rev.: MLR. 23, 1928, pp. 74–5, W. W. Greg.

R. P. COWL: King Henry IV and other plays. An experiment with echoes. London, 1927. (19 pp.)

(3) DRAMATIC ART

ROBERT A. LAW: Structural unity in the two parts of Henry IV. In: Stud. in Phil., vol. 24, 1927, pp. 223–42.

J. W. CUNLIFFE: The character of Henry V as prince and king. In: Columbia Univ. Shakespearian Studies. New York, 1916.

The Character of Falstaff:

MAURICE MORGANN: An essay on the dramatic character of Sir John Falstaff. London, 1777. Reprint: MORGANN'S essay on . . ., ed. by WILLIAM ARTHUR GILL. London, 1912. (xvi, 185 pp.)

JAMES O. HALLIWELL: On the character of Sir John Falstaff, as originally exhibited by Shakespeare in the two parts of 'King Henry IV'. London, 1841. (56 pp.)

J. GAIRDNER: On the historical elements in Shakespeare's Falstaff. In: The Fortn. Rev. 1872, and in: Gairdner's and Speeding's Studies in English history. Edinburgh, 1881.

WILH. BAESKE: Oldcastle-Falstaff in der englischen Literatur bis zu Shakespeare (Teil I: bis zum Beginn der Reformation). Diss. Berlin, 1905. (44 S.) Enlarged: Berlin, 1905 (vi, 119 S.)=Palaestra, Bd. 50. Rev.: Sh. Jb. 43, 1907, S. 274-5, A. K. Potter; MLR. 2, 1907, S. 72-3, G. C. Moore Smith; Bbl. 20, 1909, S. 243-4, Konr. Meier.

A. AINGER: Sir John Falstaff. In his Lectures and essays. London, 1905. Vol. 1, pp. 119-55.

A. C. BRADLEY: The rejection of Falstaff. In his Oxford lectures on poetry. London, 1909, pp. 247-75.

A. LESCHTSCH: Der Humor Falstaffs. Berlin, 1912. (155 S.)=Neue Shakespeare-Bühne X. Rev.: Sh. Jb. 48, 1912, S. 280-2, R. Fischer.

ELMER E. STOLL: Falstaff. In: Mod. Phil., vol. 12, 1914, pp. 197-240.

HARRY T. BAKER: The two Falstaffs. In: MLN., vol. 34, 1919, pp. 470-4.

ALBERT H. TOLMAN: Why did Shakespeare create Falstaff? In: PMLA., vol. 34, N.S. vol. 27, 1919, pp. 1-13.

JAMES MONAGHAN: Falstaff and his forebears. In: Stud. in Phil., vol. 18, 1921, pp. 353-61.

JOHN W. SPARGO: An interpretation of Falstaff. In: Washington Univ. Stud., Human. ser., vol. 9, 1922, pp. 119-33.

E. C. KNOWLTON: Falstaff redux. In: JEGPh., vol. 25, 1926, pp. 193-215.

ELMER E. STOLL: Falstaff. In his Shakespeare studies. New York, 1927, pp. 403-90.

JOHN DAWTREY: The Falstaff saga, being the life and opinions of Captain Nicholas Dawtrey, sometime Senechal of Clandebrye and Warden of the Palace of Carrickfergus, immortalized by Shakespeare as Sir John Falstaff. London, 1927. (226 pp.) Rev.: Sh. Jb. 63, 1927, S. 204, W. Keller; TLS. June 2, 1927, p. 388.

Cp. also literature on miles gloriosus, p. 113.

(4) SUBSEQUENT HISTORY OF THE PLAY

JOSEF KAINZ: Shakespeare auf der deutschen Bühne. III. Bernhard Baumeister: Falstaff. In: Sh. Jb. Jg. 41, 1905, S. 1-12.

W. WRAGE: Englische Bühnenbearbeitungen von Shakespeares King Henry IV, part I. Diss. Rostock, 1910. (x, 78 S.)

KING HENRY V

Cp. also in particular the general surveys on Shakespeare, pp. 27–29, the critical editions, pp. 53–58, and the criticism, pp. 141–145.

(1) THE TEXT

King Henry V. Parallel texts of the first quarto (1600) and the first folio (1623) editions. Ed. by B. NICHOLSON. With an introduction by P. A. DANIEL. London, for the New Shakspere Soc. 1877. (xv, 216 pp.)

Daniel considers F 1 to be alone authentic and the quarto to be stolen.

The life of Henry the Fift, written by William Shakespeare. The edition of 1623, newly revised and corrected, with notes and an introduction by WALTER G. STONE. London, for the New Shakspere Soc. 1880. (cvi, 180 pp.)

The Shakspere quarto facsimiles (William Griggs): King Henry V.
Q 1 (1600). London, 1886 ⎱ With introd. by ARTHUR SYMONS.
Q 3 (1608). London, 1886 ⎰

The chronicle historie of Henry the Fift (Q 1600). Reprint in: The Cambr. Shakespeare. London, 1893. Vol. 9, pp. 461–506.

King Henry V. Parallel texts of the first and third quartos and the first folio. Ed. by ERNEST ROMAN. Marburg, 1908. (viii, 198 pp.) = Shakespeare reprints. General editor: Wilhelm Viëtor. III.

———

A. W. POLLARD and J. DOVER WILSON: The 'stolne and surreptitious' Shakespearian texts. Henry V (1600). In: TLS. March 13, 1919, p. 134.

HEREWARD T. PRICE: The text of Henry V. Newcastle-under-Lyme (1920). (55 pp.) Rev.: Bbl. 34, 1923, S. 230–2, H. Flasdieck; E. St. 57, 1923, S. 300–2, L. L. Schücking; MLR. 16, 1921, pp. 339–40, A. W. Pollard.

(2) LITERARY GENESIS

The famous victories of King Henry V. Reprint in:
Collier-Hazlitt: Shakspere's library. Vol. 5. London, 1875.
The Shakspere quarto facsimiles (William Griggs): Q 1 (1598). With introd. by P. A. DANIEL. London, 1887.

W. G. BOSWELL-STONE: Shakespeare's Holinshed, 1907², pp. 165–205.

———

G. A. SCHMEDING: Essay on Shakspere's Henry V. Diss. Jena, 1874. (36 S.)

BRINSLEY NICHOLSON: The relation of the quarto to the folio version of Henry V. In: Trans. New Shakspere Soc., 1880–2. Pt. I, pp. 77–102.

Takes Q 1 to be a first sketch of the play.

PAUL KABEL: Die Sage von Heinrich V. bis zu Shakespeare. Kap. I–IV. Diss. Berlin, 1907. (47 S.) Enlarged: Berlin, 1908. (142 S.)=Palaestra 69. Rev.: Sh. Jb. 46, 1910, S. 268–9, Churchill.

A. WIELERT: Quartos und Folios von Shakespeares 'Henry V'. Diss. Königsberg, 1913. (91 S.)

J. M. ROBERTSON: The origination of 'Henry V'. In his The Shakespeare canon. Vol. I, 1922, pp. 1–65.

Maintains that the play is based on a sketch of Marlowe's.

WERNER KRANER: Die Entstehung der ersten Quarto von Shakespeares 'Heinrich V.' Diss. Leipzig, 1924. (36 S.) Also in: Zs. d. dt. Vereins f. Buchwesen und Schrifttum, 1923, No. 3–4.

Q I based on a shorthand copy.

N. HARDY WALLIS: Some aspects of Shakespeare's 'Richard II' and 'Henry V'. In the same author's The ethics of criticism and other essays. London, 1924, pp. 55–77.

HARDIN CRAIG: The relation of the first quarto version to the first folio version of Shakespeare's Henry V. In: Phil. Quart., vol. 6, 1927, pp. 225–34.

Maintains that Q I is neither based on a shorthand copy nor a stolen edition.

EVELYN MAY ALBRIGHT: The folio version of 'Henry V' in relation to Shakespeare's times. In: PMLA., vol. 43, 1928, pp. 722–56.

She sees allusions to Essex in the passages in the Folio which are missing in the quartos.

———

H. DUGDALE SYKES: The authorship of 'The Taming of a Shrew', 'The Famous Victories of Henry V' and the additions to Marlowe's 'Faustus'. London, 1920.

Attributes these plays to Rowley.

B. M. WARD: 'The Famous Victories of Henry V', its place in Elizabethan dramatic literature. In: RESt., vol. 4, 1928, pp. 270–94.

(3) DRAMATIC ART

WILLIAM POEL: The five act divisions in Henry V. In: TLS. Oct. 6, 1927, p. 694.

(4) SUBSEQUENT HISTORY OF THE PLAY

GERHARDT DAMES: Roger Boyles 'Henry V', besonders verglichen mit dem gleichnamigen Stücke von Shakespeare. Diss. Rostock, 1904. (84 S.)

THE MERRY WIVES OF WINDSOR

Cp. also in particular the general surveys on Shakespeare, pp. 27–29, the critical editions, pp. 53–58, and the criticism, pp. 141–145.

(1) THE TEXT

The Shakspere quarto facsimiles (William Griggs): The Merry Wives of Windsor. Q 1602. With introd. by P. A. DANIEL. London, 1881. (xvi, 54 pp.)

A pleasant conceited comedy of Syr John Falstaffe and the merry wives of Windsor. (Q 1602.) Reprint in: The Cambr. Shakespeare. Vol. 9. London, 1893, pp. 421–60.

Shakespeare's Merry Wives of Windsor, 1602. Ed. by w. w. GREG. Oxford, 1910. (lvi, 100 pp.)＝Tudor and Stuart Library. Rev.: Sh. Jb. 47, 1911, S. 333–4, M. Förster; MLR. 7, 1912, pp. 547–8, E. K. Chambers; Bbl. 23, 1912, S. 113–14, Ph. Aronstein.

Facsimile edition. Greg tries to prove that the Quarto goes back to the part belonging to the actor who played the host.

A. W. POLLARD and J. DOVER WILSON: The 'stolne and surreptitious' Shakespearian texts. The Merry Wives of Windsor (1602). In: TLS. Aug. 7, 1919, p. 420.

(2) LITERARY GENESIS

PAUL FRIEDRICH: Studien zur englischen Stenographie im Zeitalter Shakespeares. Timothe Brights Characterie entwicklungsgeschichtlich und kritisch betrachtet. Mit einem Anhang: Neue Gesichtspunkte für stenographische Untersuchungen von Shakespeare-Quartos, dargelegt an der ersten Quarto der 'Merry Wives of Windsor', 1602. Diss. Leipzig, 1914. (95 S.) Rev.: Sh. Jb. 52, 1916, S. 206–10, M. Förster.

Maintains that Q 1 of Wiv. is of stenographic origin.

JOHN M. ROBERTSON: The problem of 'The Merry Wives of Windsor'. Oxford, 1917. (32 pp.)＝The Shakespeare Assoc. Pamphl. No. 2.

ROBERT S. FORSYTHE: A Plautine source of The Merry Wives of Windsor. In: Mod. Phil., vol. 18, 1920–1, pp. 401–21.

LEVIN L. SCHÜCKING: The fairy scene in 'The Merry Wives' in folio and quarto. In: MLR., vol. 19, 1924, pp. 338–40.

ROBERT S. FORSYTHE: The Merry Wives of Windsor. Two new analogues. In: Phil. Quart., vol. 7, 1928, pp. 390–8.

For the character of Falstaff, cp. pp. 214–215.

JULIUS CAESAR

Cp. also in particular the general surveys on Shakespeare, pp. 27–29, the critical editions, pp. 53–58, and the criticism, pp. 141–145.

(1) THE TEXT

HENRIETTA BARTLETT: Quarto editions of 'Julius Caesar'. In: Libr., 3rd ser., vol. 4, 1913, pp. 122–32.

Deals with six of the Quarto editions following on F 1.

(2) LITERARY GENESIS

Shakespeare's Plutarch, ed. by c. f. TUCKER BROOKE. Vol. I: containing the main sources of Julius Caesar. O.U.P., 1909. (xxiv, 212 pp.)＝The Shakespeare Classics.

———

F. SCHÖNE: Über Shakespeares Julius Caesar mit besonderer Berücksichtigung des Verhältnisses zur Quelle des Stückes. Progr. Dresden, 1873. (32 S.)

NICOLAUS DELIUS: Shakespeares Julius Caesar und seine Quellen im Plutarch. In: Sh. Jb. Jg. 17, 1882, S. 67–81.

PAUL KANNENGIESSER: Eine Doppelredaktion in Shakespeares 'Julius Caesar'. In: Sh. Jb. Jg. 44, 1908, S. 51–64.

GREGOR SARRAZIN: Shakespeare und Orlando Pescetti. In: E. St. Bd. 46, 1913, S. 347–54.
Treats of the possibility of a connexion between Shakespeare's play and Pescetti's Il Cesare (1594).

ALEXANDER BOECKER: A probable Italian source of Shakespeare's 'Julius Caesar'. Diss. New York, 1913. Rev.: E. St. 48, 1915, S. 441–3, M. J. Wolff.
Also investigates the connexion with Pescetti's Il Cesare.

ADOLFO FAGGI: Il Giulio Cesare di Shakespeare. Roma, 1916.

J. M. ROBERTSON: The origination of 'Julius Caesar'. In his The Shakespeare canon. Vol. I, 1922, pp. 66–154.
Attributes the basis of the play to Marlowe and presumes revisions by Chapman, Drayton, Shakespeare, and Ben Jonson.

WILLIAM WELLS: The authorship of Julius Caesar. London, 1923. (viii, 225 pp.)
Basis by Marlowe, revisions by Shakespeare and Beaumont.

E. H. C. OLIPHANT: The plays of Beaumont and Fletcher. New Haven & London, 1927. (xviii, 553 pp.)
Presumes collaboration of Beaumont.

Contemporary Caesar-Dramas:

The tragedie of Caesar and Pompey, or, Caesar's revenge [1607]. Ein Drama aus Shakespeares Zeit zum 1. Male neugedruckt von WILHELM MÜHLFELD. In: Sh. Jb. Jg. 47, 1911, S. 132–55.

SIR WILLIAM ALEXANDER: The tragedy of Julius Caesar. Reprint of the 1637 edition in: A New Var. Ed. (H. H. Furness): The tragedie of Julius Caesar. Philadelphia, 1913, pp. 317–85.

———

A. KERN: George Chapman's Tragödie Caesar and Pompey und ihre Quellen. Diss. Halle, 1901. (44 S.)

F. GUNDELFINGER: Caesar in der deutschen Literatur. Diss. Berlin, 1903. (42 S.) Enlarged: Berlin, 1922. (viii, 129 S.)

HARRY M. AYRES: Shakespeare's 'Julius Caesar' in the light of some other versions. In: PMLA., vol. 25, N.S. vol. 18, 1910, pp. 183–227.

WILHELM MÜHLFELD: The tragedie of Caesar and Pompey, or, Caesar's revenge. Ein Beitrag zur Geschichte der englischen Caesar-Dramen zur Zeit Shakespeares. Diss. Münster, 1912. (lxvi, 60 S.)

FRIEDRICH GUNDOLF: Caesar, Geschichte seines Ruhms. Berlin, 1924, 1926².

(3) DRAMATIC ART

ALBERT LINDNER: Die dramatische Einheit im Julius Caesar. In: Sh. Jb. Jg. 2, 1867, S. 90–5.

HEINRICH VIEHOFF: Shakespeares Julius Caesar. In: Sh. Jb. Jg. 5, 1870, S. 6–36.

FRIEDRICH VON WESTENHOLZ: Idee und Charaktere in Shakespeares Julius Caesar. Stuttgart, 1897. (39 S.) Rev.: Bbl. 10, 1900, S. 200–3, W. Wetz.

J. GROAG: Der Charakter des Julius Caesar nach Shakespeares gleichnamigem Trauerspiele. Progr. Linz, 1893. (29 S.)

W. ZOLLMANN: Marcus Brutus in Shakespeares Julius Caesar. Progr. Nürnberg, 1867. (26 S.)

P. KREUTZBERG: Brutus in Shakespeares Julius Caesar. Progr. Neisse, 1894. (16 S.)

HERMANN CONRAD: Was erkennen wir von Shakespeares Wesen in seinem Brutus? In: Preuss. Jbb. Bd. 125, 1906, S. 462–92.

(4) EXPLANATORY WORKS

GEORGE L. CRAIK: The English of Shakespeare, illustrated in a philological commentary on his 'Julius Caesar'. London, 1857 and later editions.

(5) CHRONOLOGY

ANNA KERRL: Unterschiede in der Behandlung von Satzschluss und Versschluss in Shakespeares King John und Julius Caesar. Diss. Bonn, 1913. (x, 43 S.) Enlarged under the title: Die metrischen Unterschiede von Shakespeares King John und Julius Caesar. Eine chronologische Untersuchung. Bonn, 1913. (x, 189 S.) = Bonner Stud. z. engl. Phil., hrsg. von Bülbring, H. 10. Rev.: Bbl. 25, 1914, S. 109–13, E. Ekwall; Sh. Jb. 50, 1914, S. 222, M. Förster.

(6) SUBSEQUENT HISTORY OF THE PLAY

OTTO MIELCK: John Sheffield Duke of *Buckingham's* Zweiteilung und Bearbeitung des Shakespeareschen Julius Caesar. In: Sh. Jb. Jg. 24, 1889, S. 27–71. Also: Diss. Halle, 1889. (55 S.)

WOLFGANG KELLER: Eine Bearbeitung des 'Julius Caesar' von *Friedrich Hebbel*. In: Sh. Jb. Jg. 39, 1903, S. 247–9.

LUDWIG BERNACKI: *Stanislaus August Poniatowski* als Shakespeare-Übersetzer. In: Sh. Jb. Jg. 42, 1906, S. 187–202.

WENDELIN VON MALTZAHN: Julius Caesar. Für die Bühne eingerichtet von *A. W. Schlegel*. In: Sh. Jb. Jg. 7, 1872, S. 48–81.

H. F. T. BEHNE: Comparaison entre le 'Jules César' de *Voltaire* et celui de Shakspeare. Diss. Rostock, 1872. (42 S.)

M. ASCH: Shakespeare's and Voltaire's Julius Caesar compared. Progr. Gardelegen, 1881. (18 S.)

J. PETKOVIC: Voltaires Tragödie 'La mort de César' verglichen mit Shaksperes 'Julius Caesar'. Progr. Wien, 1909. (21 S.)

W. BRIESE: Shakespeares 'Julius Caesar' und 'La mort de César' von Voltaire. In: Z. f. e. U. Bd. 15, 1916, S. 253–69.

W. VON BORCKE: Versuch einer gebundenen Übersetzung des Trauerspiels von dem Tode des Julius Cäsar. Aus dem englischen Werke des Shakespeare übers. von CASPAR WILHELM VON BORCKE [1741]. Hrsg. von MAX J. WOLFF. Berlin [1929]. (120 S.)=Weltgeist-Bücher, Nr. 369–70.

MUCH ADO ABOUT NOTHING

Cp. also in particular the general surveys on Shakespeare, pp. 27–29, the critical editions, pp. 53–58, and the criticism, pp. 141–145.

(1) THE TEXT

The Shakspere quarto facsimiles (William Griggs): Much adoe about nothing. Q 1600. With introd. by P. A. DANIEL. London, 1886. (xii, 72 pp.)

(2) LITERARY GENESIS

Source material printed in: A New Var. Ed. (Furness).

JAKOB AYRER: Schöne Phönicia. Reprint in: Deutsche Dichter des 16. Jahrhunderts, hrsg. von Goedeke und Tittmann, Bd. 2, Teil 1. Leipzig, 1868.

___

K. LÜTZELBERGER: Jakob Ayrer's Foenicia und Shakespeares Viel Lärm um nichts. In: Album d. Lit. Ver. in Nürnberg, 1868.

HERMANN ISAAC: Die Hamletperiode in Shaksperes Leben. II. In: Arch. Bd. 74, 1885, S. 45–68.
Contains treatise on the date of Much ado on pp. 45–56. Suggested date: 1595–6.

KONRAD WEICHBERGER: Die Urquelle von Shakespeares 'Much ado about nothing'. In: Sh. Jb. Jg. 34, 1898, S. 339–45.

GREGOR SARRAZIN: Die Abfassungszeit von 'Viel Lärm um nichts'. In: Sh. Jb. Jg. 35, 1899, S. 127–35.
Date suggested: 1598–9.

MARY AUGUSTA SCOTT: The book of the courtyer: a possible source of Benedick and Beatrice. In: PMLA., vol. 16, N.S. vol. 9, 1901, pp. 475–502.

FRITZ HOLLECK-WEITHMANN: Zur Quellenfrage von Shakespeares Lustspiel 'Much ado about nothing'. Diss. Kiel, 1902. (49 S.) Enlarged: Heidelberg, 1902. (92 S.)=Kieler Stud. z. engl. Phil., hrsg. von Holthausen, H. 3. Rev.: Sh. Jb. 39, 1903, S. 301–2, A. Hauffen; Bbl. 13, 1902, S. 228–30, v. Westenholz.

MAX J. WOLFF: Zur Geschichte des Stoffes von Much ado about nothing. In: E. St. Bd. 48, 1914–15, S. 342–8.

(3) MISCELLANEOUS TREATISES ON THE PLAY

LAWRENCE MASON: A new stage-direction for Much ado, act I, sc. I. In: Mod. Phil., vol. 11, 1913–14, pp. 379–89.

ALLISON GAW: Actors' names in basic Shakespearean texts, with special reference to 'Romeo and Juliet' and 'Much ado'. In: PMLA., vol. 40, 1925, pp. 530–50.

(4) SUBSEQUENT HISTORY OF THE PLAY

G. ILLIES: Das Verhältnis von Davenants 'The law against lovers' zu Shakespeares 'Measure for measure' und 'Much ado about nothing'. Diss. Halle, 1900. (90 S.)

AS YOU LIKE IT

Cp. also in particular the general surveys on Shakespeare, pp. 27–29, the critical editions, pp. 53–58, and the criticism, pp. 141–145.

(1) LITERARY GENESIS

LODGE'S Rosalynde. Reprint in: *Collier-Hazlitt*: Shakespeare's library. London, 1875.

LODGE'S Rosalynde. Reprint in: A New Var. Ed., ed. H. H. Furness. Philadelphia (1890), pp. 316–87.

LODGE'S Rosalynde, being the original of Shakespeare's 'As you like it'. Edited by W. W. GREG. O.U.P., 1907. (xxx, 210 pp.)=The Shakespeare Classics.

The Tale of Gamelyn from the Harleian MS. No. 7334, collated with 6 other MSS., edited with notes and a glossarial index by WALTER W. SKEAT. Also in German translation in:

JULIUS ZUPITZA: Die mittelenglische Vorstufe von Shakespeares As you like it. In: Sh. Jb. Jg. 21, 1886, S. 69–148.

———

NICOLAUS DELIUS: Lodges Rosalynde und Shakespeares As you like it. In: Sh. Jb. Jg. 6, 1871, S. 226–49.

W. G. STONE: Shakspere's 'As you like it' and Lodge's Rosalynde compared. In: Trans. New Shaksp. Soc., 1880–5. Pt. II, pp. 277–93.

C. A. WURTZBURG: Die Handlung in 'Wie es euch gefällt'. Eine induktive Studie. In: Sh. Jb. Jg. 27, 1892, S. 230–7.

Deals with the structure of the play and its relation to sources.

ASHLEY H. THORNDIKE: The relation of 'As you like it' to Robin Hood plays. In: JEGPh., vol. 4, 1901, pp. 59–69. Rev.: Sh. Jb. 39, 1903, S. 330–1, W. Dibelius.

ELMER EDGAR STOLL: Shakspere, Marston, and the Malcontent type. In: Mod. Phil., vol. 3, 1905–6, pp. 281–3.

Comparison of Jaques with Marston's 'Malcontent'.

JOHN D. REA: Jaques in praise of folly. In: Mod. Phil., vol. 17, 1919, pp. 465–9.
Assumes the influence of Erasmus' 'Praise of folly'.

L. LANDAU: Some parallels to Shakespeare's 'Seven ages'. In: JEGPh., vol. 19, 1920, pp. 382–96.

ALBERT H. TOLMAN: Shakespeare's manipulation of his sources in 'As you like it'. In: MLN., vol. 37, 1922, pp. 65–76.

ALBERT EICHLER: Love's Labour's Lost und As you like it als Hofaufführungen. In: E. St. Bd. 64, 1929, S. 352–61.

(2) SUBSEQUENT HISTORY OF THE PLAY

GISBERT FREIHERR VINCKE: 'Wie es euch gefällt' auf der Bühne. In: Sh. Jb. Jg. 13, 1878, S. 186–204.

W. BIBELJE: Die englischen Bühnenbearbeitungen von Shakespeares 'As you like it.' Diss. Rostock, 1911. (86 S.)

TWELFTH NIGHT

Cp. also in particular the general surveys on Shakespeare, pp. 27–29, the critical editions, pp. 53–58, and the criticism, pp. 141–145.

(1) THE TEXT

WILLIAM SHAKESPEARE: Twelfth Night. A facsimile of the first folio text. Boston & New York, 1928.

(2) LITERARY GENESIS

For sources see: A New Var. Ed. (Furness): Twelfe Night. Philadelphia, 1901.

Collier-Hazlitt: Shakespeare's library. London, 1875. Contains Rich: Apolonius and Silla.

RICH'S 'Apolonius and Silla', an original of Shakespeare's 'Twelfth Night'. Ed. by MORTON LUCE. London, 1912. (xi, 96 pp.) = The Shakespeare Classics. Rev.: Sh. Jb. 49, 1913, S. 232, M. Förster; MLR. 7, 1912, p. 552, Moore Smith.

Laelia. A comedy acted at Queen's College, Cambridge, probably on March 1st, 1595, now first printed with an introduction and notes by G. C. MOORE SMITH. Cambridge, 1910. (xxviii, 115 pp.) Rev.: MLR. 6, 1911, pp. 528–9, W. W. Greg; Bbl. 22, 1911, S. 197–201, A. Klotz.

Cp. also GEORGE B. CHURCHILL und WOLFGANG KELLER: Die lateinischen Universitätsdramen in der Zeit der Königin Elisabeth. In: Sh. Jb. Jg, 34, 1898, S. 291–4.

———

HERMANN CONRAD: Über die Entstehungszeit von 'Was ihr wollt'. In: Sh. Jb. Jg. 31, 1895, S. 177–99.

H. MEISSNER: Die Quellen zu Shakespeares 'Was ihr wollt'. I. Progr. Lyck, 1895. (26 S.)

HERMANN CONRAD: Zu den Quellen von Shaksperes Twelfth Night. In: E. St. Bd. 46, 1912–13, S. 73–85.

(3) MISCELLANEOUS TREATISES

WILHELM KÖNIG: 'Was ihr wollt' als komisches Gegenstück zu Romeo und Julia. In: Sh. Jb. Jg. 8, 1873, S. 202–23.

C. H. COOTE: Shakspere's new map in Twelfth Night. In: Trans. New Shaksp. Soc., London, 1878.

MORRIS P. TILLEY: The organic unity of 'Twelfth Night'. In: PMLA., vol. 29, N.S. vol. 22, 1914, pp. 550–66.

F. G. BLANDFORD: Shakespeare's pronunciation. A transcription of 'Twelfth Night', act I, scene 5. Made for the Festival Theatre Company, Cambridge. Cambridge, 1927. (20 pp.)

(4) SUBSEQUENT HISTORY OF THE PLAY

JOS. DE PERROT: Eine portugiesische Parallele zum Heiligen Dreikönigsabend. In: Anglia, Bd. 38, 1914, S. 255–60.

GEORGE E. STRUBLE: Schlegel's translation of Twelfth Night. In: Quart. Journ. of the Univ. of North Dakota. vol. 19, 1929, pp. 148–67.

HAMLET

Cp. also in particular the general surveys on Shakespeare, pp. 27–29, the critical editions, pp. 53–58, and the criticism, pp. 141–145.

(1) THE TEXT

(a) *Reprints of Earliest Editions*

Hamlet, 1603, and Hamlet, 1604, being exact reprints of the first and second editions of Shakespeare's great drama . . . the two texts printed on opposite pages . . . by SAMUEL TIMMINS. London, 1860. (xvi, 200 pp.)
Parallel reprint of Q1 and Q2.

Hamlet. The first quarto, 1603. A facsimile . . . by WILLIAM GRIGGS. With foreword by F. J. FURNIVALL. London, 1880. (xii, 64 pp.)=Shakspere quarto facsimiles, No. 1.

Hamlet. The second quarto, 1604. A facsimile . . . by WILLIAM GRIGGS. With foreword by F. J. FURNIVALL. London, 1880. (xx, 100 pp.)=Shakspere quarto facsimiles, No. 2.

Hamlet. Parallel texts of the first and second quartos and the first folio. Edited by WILHELM VIËTOR. Marburg, 1891, 1913². (319 pp.)=Shakespeare Reprints II.
Parallel reprint of Q 1, Q 2, and F 1.

The tragicall historie of Hamlet, prince of Denmarke [1603]. In: The Cambridge Shakespeare. London, 1893. Vol. 9, pp. 697–749.

The first quarto edition of Shakespeare's *Hamlet*, edited with an introduction and notes by FRANK G. HUBBARD. Madison, 1920. (120 pp.)=Univ. of Wisconsin Stud. in lang. and lit. No. 8. Rev.: Sh. Jb. 58, 1922, S. 121–2, W. Keller; Bbl. 34, 1923, S. 288–300, M. Förster.
Reprint of Q 1 with detailed introduction.

The tragicall historie of *Hamlet*, Prince of Denmarke, 1603, edited by G. B. HARRISON. London, 1924. (xxxi, 73 pp.)=Bodley Head Quartos.
Reprint of Q 1 with good introduction.

The tragedie of Hamlet, Prince of Denmarke. A study, with the text of the folio of 1623. Ed. by George Macdonald. London, 1924. (xxxi, 73 pp.)
Reprint of F 1.

(b) *Later Editions*

The tragicall historie of Hamlet, Prince of Denmarke, by William Shakespeare. Edited according to the first printed copies, with the various readings, and critical notes by F. H. STRATMAN. (London &) Krefeld, 1869.
Critical edition with variants.

Shakespeare's tragedy of Hamlet. Ed. by KARL ELZE. Halle, 1882. (xvi, 258 S.)
With detailed explanations of the text.

Cp. also GUSTAV TANGER: Prof. Elze's Hamletausgabe. In: Sh. Jb. Jg. 18, 1883, S. 218–37.

The tragedy of Hamlet, edited by EDWARD DOWDEN. London, 1899. (xxviii, 237 pp.) Rev.: Sh. Jb. 36, 1900, S. 306–7, A. Brandl.
Edition with important commentary.

(c) *Treatises on the History of the Text*

C. H. HERFORD: The first quarto edition of Hamlet, 1603. London, 1880.

GUSTAV TANGER: The first and second quartos and the first folio of Hamlet, their relation to each other. In: Trans. New Shakspere Soc., 1880–2. Pt. I, pp. 109–97.

GUSTAV TANGER: Hamlet, nach Shakespeares Manuskript. In: Anglia, Bd. 4, 1881, S. 211–36.
Investigation of Q 1 which is held to be printed directly from the poet's own MS.

F. P. VON WESTENHOLZ: Die Hamlet-Quartos. In: E. St. Bd. 34, 1904, S. 337–50.
Considers Q 2 to be the original Shakespeare version; Q 1, on the other hand, to be an abbreviated stage copy for the provinces.

WILHELM CREIZENACH: Hamletfragen. In: Sh. Jb. Jg. 42, 1906, S. 76–85.

AURA MILLER: The 6th quarto of Hamlet in a new light. In: Mod. Phil., vol. 4, 1906–7, pp. 501–5.
Gives variants as against the other Quartos.

ELISE DECKNER: Die beiden ersten Hamlet-Quartos. Berlin, 1909. (48 S.)= Normannia, hrsg. von Kaluza und Thurau, Bd. 4. Rev: Sh. Jb. 46, 1910, S. 305–6, M. Förster.

The author, in opposition to Westenholz, considers Q 1 to be the original Shakespeare version.

HENRY DAVID GRAY: The first quarto of 'Hamlet'. In: MLR., vol. 10, 1915, pp. 171–80.

Marcellus-theory according to which Q 1 is a stage-version, obtained by the printer from the player of Marcellus.

JOHN DOVER WILSON: The copy for Hamlet, 1603. In: Libr., 3rd ser., vol. 9, 1918, pp. 153–85.

JOHN DOVER WILSON: The copy for 'Hamlet', 1603, and the 'Hamlet transcript', 1593. London, 1918. (64 pp.)

JOHN DOVER WILSON: The 'Hamlet' transcript, 1593. In: Libr., 3rd ser., vol. 9, 1918, pp. 217–47.

FRANK G. HUBBARD: The 'Marcellus' theory of the first quarto of Hamlet. In: MLN., vol. 33, 1918, pp. 73–9.

The author opposes this theory.

T. B. RUDMOSE-BROWN: The Hamlet quartos. In: TLS. Febr. 13, 1919, p. 83.

V. ØSTERBERG: Studier over Hamlet-texterne I. København, 1920. (74 S.) Rev.: Sh. Jb. 57, 1921, S. 100–1, W. Keller; MLR. 15, 1920, pp. 434–40, J. D. Wilson; Bbl. 34, 1923, S. 300–6, M. Förster; E. St. 55, 1921, S. 100–1, S. B. Liljegren.

Investigation of Q 1.

H. DE GROOT: Hamlet, its textual history. An inquiry into the relations between the first and second quartos and the first folio of Hamlet. Diss. Amsterdam, 1923. (143 S.) Rev.: MLR. 19, 1924, pp. 228–30, W. W. Greg; Bbl. 35, 1924, S. 141–5, B. Fehr.

FRANK G. HUBBARD: The readings of the first quarto of Hamlet. In: PMLA., vol. 38, 1923, pp. 792–822.

B. A. P. VAN DAM: The text of Shakespeare's Hamlet. London, 1924. (vii, 380 pp.) Rev.: Sh. Jb. 61, 1925, S. 138–9, W. Keller; Bbl. 37, 1926, S. 360–72, E. Deckner; Z. f. e. U. 27, 1928, S. 467–9, J. Hedbavny; JEGPh. 25, 1926, pp. 142–3, K. Malone; MLR. 20, 1925, pp. 83–8, W. W. Greg.

Important contribution.

JOHN DOVER WILSON: Spellings and misprints in the 2nd quarto of Hamlet. In: Essays and Studies by members of the English Association, vol. 10, 1924.

W. J. LAWRENCE: The date of Hamlet. In: TLS. April 8, 1926, p. 263.

W. J. LAWRENCE: The mystery of the Hamlet first quarto. In: The Monthly Criterion, vol. 5, 1927, pp. 191–201.

Shakespeare held to have no part in Q 1.

HENRY DAVID GRAY: Thomas Kyd and the first quarto of Hamlet. In: PMLA., vol. 42, 1927, pp. 721–35.

(2) LITERARY GENESIS

(a) *General Works on Genesis*

GREGOR SARRAZIN: Die Entstehung der Hamlet-Tragödie. In: Anglia, Bd. 12, 1889, S. 143–57; Bd. 13, 1891, S. 117–39, und Bd. 14, 1892, S. 322–45.

JOSEF SCHICK: Die Entstehung des Hamlet. Festvortrag. In: Sh. Jb. Jg. 38, 1902, S. xiii–xlviii.

C. M. LEWIS: The genesis of Hamlet. New York, 1907. (vi, 133 pp.)

MAX J. WOLFF: Zum Werden des Hamlet. In: Intern. Mschr. f. Wiss., Kunst und Techn. Jg. 6, 1912, Sp. 585–94.

V. ØSTERBERG: Studier over Hamlet-Teksterne. I. København, 1920. (74 S.)

CLARA LONGWORTH-CHAMBRUN: Hamlet de Shakespeare. Paris, 1929. Rev.: Rev. anglo-amér. 7, 1930, pp. 440–1, É. Legouis.

(b) *Sources and related material*

ADOLF ZINZOW: Die Hamletfrage an und mit verwandten Sagen erläutert. Ein Beitrag zum Verständnis nordisch-deutscher Sagendichtung. Halle, 1877. (xii, 418 S.)

KARL SILBERSCHLAG: Shakespeares Hamlet, seine Quellen und politischen Beziehungen. In: Sh. Jb. Jg. 12, 1877, S. 261–89.

ROBERT GERICKE: Shakespeares Hamlet-Quellen: Saxo Grammaticus (lateinisch und deutsch), Belleforest und The hystorie of Hamlet. Mit Vorw., Einl. und Nachträgen hrsg. von MAX MOLTKE. Leipzig, 1881. (104 S.)

JOHN CORBIN: The Elizabethan Hamlet. A study of the sources, and of Shakspere's environment, to show that the mad scenes had a comic aspect now ignored. London, 1895. Rev.: Bbl. 6, 1896, S. 296–9, Rud. Fischer.

OTTO L. JIRICZEK: Die Amlethsage auf Island. In: Beiträge zur Volkskunde. Festschr. f. Karl Weinhold. Breslau, 1896.

ISRAEL GOLLANCZ: Hamlet in Iceland. Being the Icelandic romantic Ambales Saga, edited and translated, with extracts from five Ambales Rimur and other illustrative texts for the most part now first printed, and an introductory essay. London, 1898. (xcviii, 284 pp.) Rev.: Sh. Jb. 35, 1899, S. 335–6, A. Brandl; Bbl. 9, 1899, S. 224–6, E. Mogk.

AXEL OLRIK: Amledsagnet på Island. In: Arkiv för nordisk filologi, Jg. 15, 1899, S. 360 ff.

OTTO L. JIRICZEK: Hamlet in Iran. In: Zs. des Vereins f. Volkskunde, Bd. 10, 1900, S. 353–64.

PAUL HERRMANN: Erläuterungen zu den ersten neun Büchern der dänischen Geschichte des Saxo Grammaticus. 1. Teil: Übersetzung. Leipzig, 1901. 2. Teil: Kommentar. Die Heldensagen des Saxo Grammaticus. Leipzig, 1922. (508 und 668 S.) Rev.: Sh. Jb. 59–60, 1924, S. 181–2, W. Keller.

RUDOLF ZENKER: Boeve-Amlethus. Das altfranzösische Epos von Boeve de Hamtone und der Ursprung der Hamletsage. Berlin, 1905=Literarhistor. Forsch., hrsg. von Schick und von Waldberg, H. 32. Rev.: Sh. Jb. 42, 1906, S. 285–95, Anders.

E. N. SETÄLÄ: Kullervo-Hamlet, ein sagenvergleichender Versuch. Helsingfors & Leipzig, 1911. (vi, 197 S.) Also in: Finnisch-Ugrische Forsch. III, VII, X. Rev.: Sh. Jb. 48, 1912, S. 283–5, M. Deutschbein.
Deals with the relation of Hamlet to the Finnish Kullervo-Saga.

CORPUS HAMLETICUM. Hamlet in Sage und Dichtung, Kunst und Musik. Hrsg. von JOSEF SCHICK. Abt. I, Bd. 1: JOS. SCHICK: Das Glückskind mit dem Todesbrief. Orientalische Fassungen. Berlin, 1912. (xv, 418 S.) Rev.: Sh. Jb. 50, 1914, S. 166–70, W. Keller.
Compilation of sources.

JOSEF SCHICK: Hamlet in China. In: Sh. Jb. Jg. 50, 1914, S. 31–50.
The text of a Chinese version of the fairy-tale of the lucky child with the death-letter in the original and in translation.

LORENZ MORSBACH: Der Weg zu Shakespeare und das Hamletdrama. Eine Umkehr. Halle, 1922. Rev.: Dt. Vjschr. Jg. 6, 1928, S. 190–1, L. L. Schücking; JEGPh. 24, 1925, pp. 432–4, K. Malone; MLR. 18, 1923, pp. 486–7, Moore Smith.

PAUL HERRMANN: Heldensagen des Saxo Grammaticus. Leipzig, 1922.

KEMP MALONE: The literary history of Hamlet. I: The early tradition. Heidelberg, 1923. (xii, 268 pp.)=Anglist. Forsch., hrsg. von J. Hoops, H. 59. Rev.: Sh. Jb. 61, 1925, S. 139–40, W. Keller; Arch. Jg. 78, Bd. 146, 1923, S. 287–8; JEGPh. 24, 1925, pp. 413–24, W. D. Briggs.

ISRAEL GOLLANCZ: The sources of Hamlet, with an essay on the legend. O.U.P., 1926. (xii, 321 pp.)=The Shakespeare Classics, vol. XII. Rev.: JEGPh. 26, 1927, pp. 275–6, K. Malone; MLR. 22, 1927, pp. 462–3, F. S. Boas.

ALFRED NORDFELT: Om det äldre Hamletproblemet. Namnet och typen. Uppsala, 1927. In: Språkvetenskapliga sällskapets i Uppsala förhandligar 1925–7, S. 53–94.
Connects with the Roman story of Brutus.

(c) *The Ur-Hamlet*

ALBERT E. JACK: Thomas Kyd and the Ur-Hamlet. In: PMLA., vol. 20, N.S. vol. 13, 1905, pp. 729–48.

O. L. HATCHER: The Ur-Hamlet problem. In: MLN., vol. 21, 1906, pp. 177–80.

MAX J. WOLFF: Zum Urhamlet. In: E. St. Bd. 45, 1912, S. 9–29.

HENRY DAVID GRAY: Reconstruction of a lost play. In: Phil. Quart., vol. 7, 1928, pp. 254–74.

(d) *The 'Bestrafte Brudermord'*

Tragoedia der bestrafte Brudermord oder: Prinz Hamlet aus Dänemark. In: Die Schauspiele der englischen Komödianten, hrsg. von w. CREIZENACH = Dt. National-Literatur, Bd. 23, S. 148–86.

WILHELM CREIZENACH: Die Tragödie 'Der bestrafte Brudermord oder Prinz Hamlet von Dänemark' und ihre Bedeutung für die Kritik des Shakespeareschen Hamlet. Leipzig, 1887 = Ber. Sächs. Ak. Wiss., phil.-hist. Kl., Bd. 39, 1887.

GUSTAV TANGER: 'Der bestrafte Brudermord oder Prinz Hamlet aus Dänemark' und sein Verhältnis zu Shakespeares Hamlet. In: Sh. Jb. Jg. 23, 1888, S. 224–45.

M. B. EVANS: Der bestrafte Brudermord. Sein Verhältnis zu Shakespeares Hamlet. I. Diss. Bonn, 1902. (x, 49 S.) Enlarged in: Theatergeschichtl. Forsch., hrsg. von Litzmann, xix, 1910. (145 S.) Rev.: Bbl. 14, 1903, S. 109–12, R. Ackermann.
Contains as a supplement: Belleforests Amleterzählung.

M. B. EVANS: 'Der bestrafte Brudermord' and Shakespeares 'Hamlet'. In: Mod. Phil., vol. 2, 1904–5, pp. 433–49.

WILHELM CREIZENACH: 'Der bestrafte Brudermord' and its relation to Shakespeare's 'Hamlet.' In: Mod. Phil., vol. 2, 1904–5, pp. 249–60.

WILHELM CREIZENACH: Hamletfragen. In: Sh. Jb. Jg. 42, 1906, S. 76–85.

(e) *Further Literary Relations*

BENNO TSCHISCHWITZ: Shakespeares Hamlet in seinem Verhältnis zur Gesamtbildung, namentlich zur Theologie und Philosophie der Elisabeth-Zeit. Halle, 1867. (21 S.)

NICOLAUS DELIUS: Chettles Hoffman und Shakespeares Hamlet. In: Sh. Jb. Jg. 9, 1874, S. 166–94.

B. LEONHARDT: Über die Beziehungen von Beaumont und Fletchers Philaster, or, Love lies a-bleeding zu Shakespeares Hamlet und Cymbeline. In: Anglia, Bd. 8, 1885, S. 424–47.

ASHLEY H. THORNDIKE: The relations of Hamlet to contemporary revenge plays. In: PMLA., vol. 17, N.S. vol. 10, 1902, pp. 125–220. Rev.: Sh. Jb. 39, 1903, S. 331–2, W. Dibelius.
Important contribution.

GREGOR SARRAZIN: Shakespeares 'Hamlet' und Ben Jonsons 'The case is altered'. In: Sh. Jb. Jg. 40, 1904, S. 222–3.

KONRAD MEIER: Klassisches im Hamlet. Progr. Dresden, 1907. (56 S.) Rev.: Bbl. 20, 1909, S. 73–6, R. Hauschild.

FRIEDRICH RADEBRECHT: Shakespeares Abhängigkeit von John Marston. Cöthen, 1918. (xv, 122 S.) = Neue anglist. Arb., hrsg. von L. L. Schücking und M. Deutschbein, No. 3. Rev.: Bbl. 30, 1919, S. 95–8, Ph. Aronstein; MLR. 17, 1922, pp. 301–3, H. B. Charlton.

W. VOLLHARDT: Italienische Parallelstellen zu Shakespeares Hamlet. In: Sh. Jb. Jg. 62, 1926, S. 132–57.

J. DOVER WILSON: The ghost-scenes in Hamlet in the light of Elizabethan spiritualism. In LEWES LAVATER: Of ghostes and spirites walking by nyght, 1572. Ed. by J. DOVER WILSON and MAY YARDLEY. Oxford, 1929, pp. vii–xxxi.

ELSE VON SCHAUBERT: Die Stelle vom 'rauhen Pyrrhus' (Hamlet II, 2, 460–551) in ihrem Verhältnis zu Marlowe-Nashe's 'Dido', zu Seneca und dem 'Ur-hamlet' und damit ihrer Bedeutung für Datierungsfragen, Quarto-Problem und Nashe's Angriff auf Thomas Kyd. In: Anglia, Bd. 53, N.F. Bd. 41, 1929, S. 374–439.

(3) DRAMATIC ART

(a) *General Essays*

EDWARD ROSE: The division into acts of Hamlet. In: Trans. New Shakspere Soc., 1877–9, pp. 1–10.

WILHELM VERSHOFEN: Gedanken zur Technik des Dramas, erläutert an Shakespeares Hamlet. Progr. Jena, 1907, und Bonn, 1907. Rev.: Sh. Jb. 45, 1909, S. 274–5, F. Brie.

B. KÖHLER: Die Schilderung des Milieus in Shakespeares Hamlet, Macbeth und King Lear. Halle a. S., 1912. (xi, 65 S.) = Stud. z. engl. Phil., hrsg. von Morsbach, H. 46.

ARNOLD E. BERGER: Zur Technik des 'Hamlet'. In: Sh. Jb. Jg. 59–60, N.F. Bd. 1, 1924, S. 109–22.

(b) *Art of Characterization*

For the character of *Hamlet* see pp. 231–235.

GRACE LATHAM: O arme Ophelia. In: Sh. Jb. Jg. 22, 1887, S. 131–63.

F. A. LEO: Rosenkrantz und Güldenstern. In: Sh. Jb. Jg. 25, 1890, S. 281–6 und 26, 1891, S. 325–36.

W. T. LYNN: Rosencrantz and Guildenstern. In: N. & Q., 10th ser., vol. iii, 1905.

WOLFGANG PFLEIDERER: Das seelische Verhältnis zwischen Hamlet und Ophelia. Diss. Tübingen, 1908. (85 S.) Rev.: Sh. Jb. 45, 1909, S. 346, A. von Weilen; Arch. 122, 1909, S. 215, A. Brandl.

J. HUIZINGA: Rosenkranz und Güldenstern. In: Sh. Jb. Jg. 46, 1910, S. 60–8.

GERTRUD LANDSBERG: Ophelia. Die Entstehung der Gestalt und ihre Deutung. Diss. Breslau, 1918. (40 S.) Enlarged in: Neue anglist. Arb., hrsg. von Schücking und Deutschbein, H. 1. Rev.: Sh. Jb. 55, 1919, S. 154–6, W. Keller; MLR. 17, 1922, pp. 301–3, H. B. Charlton; Bbl. 30, 1919, S. 89–95, Ph. Aronstein.

HOWARD MUMFORD JONES: The King in Hamlet. In: Univ. of Texas Bull. No. 1865, 1918. (100 pp.) Rev.: Bbl. 35, 1924, S. 12–14, B. Fehr.

WILHELM MARSCHALL: Die Quellen der Polonius-Gestalt im 'Hamlet'. In: GRM. Jg. 16, 1928, S. 86–9.

(4) STAGE PRODUCTIONS DURING SHAKESPEARE'S LIFETIME

WILLIAM J. LAWRENCE: 'Hamlet' as Shakespeare staged it. In his Pre-Restoration stage studies. Harv. Univ. Pr., 1927, pp. 102–21.

(5) AESTHETIC CRITICISM OF THE PLAY AND ANALYSIS OF THE CHARACTER
OF THE HERO

WOLFGANG GOETHE in: Wilhelm Meisters Lehrjahre. 1795. In: Jub. Ausg., Cotta, Bd. 17 und 18.

Cf. also W. DIAMOND: Wilhelm Meister's interpretation of 'Hamlet'. In: Mod. Phil., vol. 23, 1925–26, pp. 89–101.

AUGUST WILHELM SCHLEGEL in: Die Horen, 1796, and in: Vorlesungen über dramatische Kunst und Literatur, Bd. 3, 1811.

LUDWIG TIECK in: Dramaturgische Blätter ii, 1826.

Cf. also K. H. HERMES: Über Shakespeares Hamlet und seine Beurteiler Goethe, A. W. Schlegel und Tieck. Stuttgart & München, 1827.

TRAHNDORFF: Über den Orestes der alten Tragödie und den Hamlet des Shakespeare. Berlin, 1833.

EDUARD GANS: Der Hamlet des Ducis und der des Shakespeare. In his Vermischte Schriften, Bd. 2. Berlin, 1834, S. 269 ff.

HERMANN ULRICI in: Über Shakespeares dramatische Kunst und sein Verhältnis zu Calderon und Goethe. Halle, 1839, 1868³.

HEINRICH THEODOR RÖTSCHER in: Cyklus dramatischer Charaktere. 1844.

G. G. GERVINUS in: Shakespeare. 4 Bde. Leipzig, 1849–50.

E. VEHSE in: Shakespeare als Protestant, Politiker, Psycholog und Dichter. 2 Bde. Hamburg, 1851.
Conception of Hamlet as a melancholy character.

LUDWIG ECKARDT: Vorlesungen über Shakespeares Hamlet. Versuch einer psychologischen Entwicklung. Aarau, 1853. (xiv, 197 S.) In the same author's Dramaturgische Studien I.

H. FREIHERR VON FRIESEN: Briefe über Shaksperes Hamlet. Leipzig, 1864.

A. DÖRING: Shakespeares Hamlet seinem Grundgedanken und Inhalte nach erläutert. Hamm, 1865.

G. RÜMELIN in: Shakespeare-Studien. Stuttgart, 1866, S. 74–97.
Contrasts the avenger and the doubter in Hamlet.

W. OEHLMANN: Die Gemütsseite des Hamlet-Charakters. In: Sh. Jb. Jg. 3, 1868, S. 205–28.

H. A. WERNER: Über das Dunkel in der Hamlet-Tragödie. In: Sh. Jb. Jg. 5, 1870, S. 37–81.

WILHELM KÖNIG: Die Grundzüge der Hamlet-Tragödie. In: Sh. Jb. Jg. 6, 1871, S. 277–316.

OTTO LUDWIG in: Shakespeare-Studien [written in the 'fifties and 'sixties]. Leipzig, 1872.

MERCADE: Hamlet, or, Shakespeare's philosophy of history. London, 1875. (xxix, 208 pp.)

KARL WERDER: Vorlesungen über Shakespeares Hamlet, gehalten an der Universität zu Berlin. Berlin, 1875. (252 S.)

Cf. also ROBERT PRÖLSS: Werders Hamlet-Vorlesungen. In: Sh. Jb. Jg. 14, 1879, S. 115–55.

HERMANN BAUMGART: Die Hamlet-Tragödie und ihre Kritik. Königsberg, 1877.
Strong criticism of Werder.

TH. GESSNER: Von welchen Gesichtspunkten ist auszugehen, um einen Einblick in das Wesen des Prinzen Hamlet zu gewinnen? Progr. Quakenbrück, 1877, and in: Sh. Jb. Jg. 20, 1885, S. 228–81.
Stresses Hamlet's melancholy temperament.

ROBERT PRÖLSS: Hamlet, erläutert. Leipzig, 1878.

KARL THIERSCH: Medizinische Glossen zum Hamlet. In: Nord und Süd, Jg. 6, 1878, S. 231 ff.

JOSEF KOHLER: Shakespeare vor dem Forum der Jurisprudenz. Würzburg, 1883.
Hamlet's hesitation explained by his feeling that revenge is unlawful.

HERMANN TÜRCK: Hamlet ein Genie. 2 Vorträge. Leipzig, 1888.

BERNHARD TEN BRINK in: Shakespeare. 5 Vorlesungen aus dem Nachlass. Strassburg, 1893.

F. PAULSEN: Hamlet, die Tragödie des Pessimismus. In: Dt. Rdsch., Bd. 59, 1888–9, S. 237–59.
Stresses Hamlet's malicious nature.

HERMANN TÜRCK: Das psychologische Problem in der Hamlet-Tragödie. Diss. Leipzig, 1890. (84 S.)

J. LIEPERT: Shakespeares Hamlet. Progr. Straubing, 1892. (34 S.)

RICHARD LOENING: Die Hamlet-Tragödie Shakespeares. Stuttgart, 1893. (x, 418 S.) Rev.: Bbl. 4, 1894, S. 11–12, R. Wülker.
Author denies Hamlet's will to carry out his revenge. Gives a survey of Hamlet-criticism since Goethe.

ALOIS BRANDL: Shakespeare. Dresden 1894. (VIII, 232 S.)

ERNST TRAUMANN: Hamlet, die Tragödie des Menschengeistes. In: Sh. Jb. Jg. 29–30, 1894, S. 255–75.

KARL ROSNER: Shaksperes Hamlet im Lichte der Neuropathologie. Vortrag. Berlin & Prag, 1895. (51 S.)

GEORG BRANDES: William Shakespeare. 1895–6.

KUNO FISCHER: Shakespeares Hamlet. Heidelberg, 1896. (330 S.)=Kleine Schriften 5.

The author approaches Goethe's conception.

Cf. also A. DÖRING: Der Türck-Kuno Fischersche Hamletstreit. In: Die Kritik, No. 139, 1897.

FR. RUBINSTEIN: Hamlet als Neurastheniker. Leipzig, 1896.

HERMANN CONRAD: Shakespeares Selbstbekenntnisse. Hamlet und sein Urbild. Stuttgart, 1897=Reprint of papers in: Preuss. Jbb., 1885 and 1895.

HERMANN TÜRCK: Der geniale Mensch. Jena & Leipzig, 1897.

A. DÖRING: Hamlet. Ein neuer Versuch zur ästhetischen Erklärung der Tragödie. Berlin, 1898. Rev.: Sh. Jb. 34, 1898, S. 411–15, E. Penner; Bbl. 8, 1898, S. 357–72, H. Conrad.

Appendix II: A century of German criticism of Hamlet.

ERWIN HEUSE: Zur Lösung des Hamlet-Problems. Elberfeld, 1898.

ALBERT H. TOLMAN: A view of the views about Hamlet. In: PMLA., vol. 13, N.S. vol. 6, 1898, pp. 155–84.

GUSTAV FRIEDRICH: Hamlet und seine Gemütskrankheit. Heidelberg, 1899. (v, 207 S.) Rev.: Sh. Jb. 37, 1901, S. 251–4, Th. Ziehen.

Accepts the idea of Hamlet's lack of will-power.

FRIEDRICH THEODOR VISCHER: Shakespeare-Vorträge. 1. Bd.: Einleitung; Hamlet, Prinz von Dänemark. Stuttgart, 1889. (xxii, 510 S.) Rev.: Sh. Jb. 36, 1900, S. 299–300, A. Schröer.

Analysis, partial translation.

FRIEDRICH PAULSEN: Schopenhauer, Hamlet, Mephistopheles. Drei Aufsätze zur Naturgeschichte des Pessimismus. Berlin, 1900. (ix, 259 S.) Rev.: Sh. Jb. 37, 1901, S. 254–6, J. Volkelt.

A. C. BRADLEY: Hamlet. In his Shakespearean tragedy. London, 1904, pp. 79–174.

ALBERT H. TOLMAN: The views about Hamlet, and other essays. Boston & New York, 1904. (403 pp.) Rev.: Sh. Jb. 41, 1905, S. 248–9, W. Keller.

LÜDEMANN: Über den Begriff Tragik und die Tragik im Hamlet. Progr. Pankow, 1906. (7 S.)

SAMUEL LUBLINSKI: Shakespeares Problem im Hamlet. Leipzig, 1908. (88 S.) Rev.: Sh. Jb. 45, 1909, S. 345–6, A. von Weilen; Arch. 121, 1908, S. 477, A. Brandl.

ERNEST JONES: The Oedipus-complex as an explanation of Hamlet's mystery. In: The Amer. Journal of Psychology, vol. 21, pp. 72 seq. German translation: Das Problem des Hamlet und der Ödipus-Komplex. Übers. von PAUL TAUSIG. Leipzig & Wien, 1911. (65 S.) Rev.: Sh. Jb. 47, 1911, S. 264–5, Grabau.

A. RÜEGG: Shakespeares Hamlet. Basel, 1912. (68 S.)

EMERSON VENABLE: The Hamlet problem and its solution. Cincinnati, 1912. (107 pp.)

FRANZ HAHNE: Das Hamletproblem. In: GRM. Jg. 5, 1913, S. 442–56.

GUSTAV A. BIEBER: Der Melancholikertypus Shakespeares und sein Ursprung. Heidelberg, 1913. (92 S.)=Anglist. Arbeiten, hrsg. von L. L. Schücking, H. 3. Rev.: Euph. 23, 1921, S. 115–19.

WILBRAHAM FITZJOHN TRENCH: Shakespeare's Hamlet. A new commentary, with a chapter on first principles. London, 1913. (xv, 274 pp.) Rev.: Sh. Jb. 50, 1914, S. 199–200, M. Förster.

ERICH WULFFEN: Shakespeares Hamlet, ein Sexualproblem. Berlin [1913]. (186 S.) Rev.: Sh. Jb. 50, 1914, S. 200–1, M. Förster.

GILBERT MURRAY: Hamlet and Orestes. A study in traditional types. Oxford, 1914. (26 pp.)

GUSTAV WOLFF: Der Fall Hamlet. Ein Vortrag mit einem Anhang: Shakespeares Hamlet in neuer Verdeutschung. München, 1914. (180 S.) Rev.: Sh. Jb. 52, 1916, S. 215–17, M. Förster.

JOHAN MORTENSEN: Hamlet. Några utvecklingslinjor. In: Edda, Bd. 6, 1916, S. 58–74. Rev.: Sh. Jb. 54, 1918, S. 150, Jantzen.

GUSTAV MAI-RODEGG: Hamlet-Entdeckungen eines Schauspielers. Berlin. 1916. (107 S.) Rev.: Bbl. 29, 1918, S. 325–7, L. Kellner.
Connects the Hamlet-problem with the bella vendetta of the Italian Renaissance.

ALEXANDER W. CRAWFORD: Hamlet, an ideal prince, and other essays in Shakespearean interpretation. Boston, 1916.

ELMER E. STOLL: Hamlet. An historical and comparative study. Minneapolis, 1919=Publ. Univ. Minnesota, VIII, 5. Rev.: Sh. Jb. 56, 1920, S. 125–6, W. Keller; MLR. 15, 1920, pp. 434–40, J. D. Wilson.
Conception of Hamlet as hero.

LEVIN L. SCHÜCKING: Die Charakterprobleme bei Shakespeare. Leipzig, 1919, 1927[2] (various passages).

J. M. ROBERTSON: The problem of 'Hamlet'. London, 1919. (90 pp.) Rev.: MLR. 15, 1920, pp. 434–40, J. D. Wilson; TLS. Oct. 2, 1919, p. 528.

JOSEF WIHAN: Die Hamlet-Frage. Ein Beitrag zur Geschichte der Renaissance in England. Leipzig, 1921. (89 S.)=Leipziger Beitr. z. engl. Phil., hrsg. von M. Förster, H. 3. Rev.: Sh. Jb. 58, 1922, S. 131–2, W. Keller; Bbl. 35, 1924, S. 1–2, B. Fehr.

LORENZ MORSBACH: Der Weg zu Shakespeare und das Hamlet-Drama. Eine Umkehr. Halle, 1922. (viii, 111 S.) Rev.: Sh. Jb. 59–60, 1924, S. 178–81, W. Keller; Bbl. 35, 1924, S. 14–16, B. Fehr; Euphorion 26, S. 300–3, J. Wihan.

CLUTTON BROCK: Shakespeare's Hamlet. London, 1922. (viii, 126 pp.)

ERNEST JONES: A psycho-analytic study of Hamlet. London, 1922. (98 pp.)

J. M. ROBERTSON: 'Hamlet' once more. London, 1923. (196 pp.)

HERMANN TÜRCK: Der Totenschädel in Hamlets Hand. In: Sh. Jb. Jg. 61, N.F. Bd. 2, 1925, S. 81–8. Rev.: E. St. 62, 1928, S. 438, A. Eichler.

CHRISTIAN JANENTZKY: Shakespeares Weltbild, das Tragische und Hamlet. In: Die Ernte. Franz Muncker z. 70. Geb. Halle, 1926, S. 241–63. Rev.: Euph. 30, 1928, S. 272.

The author sees in Hamlet a 'Tragik der versagten Tragik'.

CUMBERLAND CLARK: A study of Hamlet. Stratford-upon-Avon, 1926. (167 pp.)

BERNARD R. CONRAD: Hamlet's delay. A restatement of the problem. In: PMLA., vol. 41, 1926, pp. 680–7.

Summarizes previous explanations of Hamlet's hesitation.

MARY I. O'SULLIVAN: Hamlet and Dr. Timothy Bright. In: PMLA., vol. 41, 1926, pp. 667–79.

Points out parallels between Shakespeare's Hamlet and Bright's 'Treatise of melancholie', 1586. (Type of melancholy man.)

ANNA BENEDETTI: Il problema psicologico di Amleto. In: Nuova Antologia 255, 1927, pp. 346–364.

H. DE GROOT: De geschiedenis van het Hamlet-problem. In: Neophilologus, Jg. 13, 1928, S. 282–93.

G. F. BRADBY: The problems of 'Hamlet'. London, 1928. (60 pp.) Rev.: Dt. Litztg., N.F. 5, 1928, Sp. 2507–9, B. Fehr; Arch. 154, 1928, S. 146–7; Sh. Jb. 64, 1928, S. 196–7, W. Keller; Bbl. 40, 1929, S. 116–17, Ph. Aronstein.

Deals with the contradictions in the characters and the progress of the action.

Appendix: *The Play within the play*

GREGOR SARRAZIN: Neue italienische Skizzen zu Shakespeare. 2. Das Gonzaga-Schauspiel im Hamlet. In: Sh. Jb. Jg. 31, 1895, S. 169–76.

W. W. GREG: Hamlet's hallucination. In: MLR., vol. 12, 1917, pp. 393–421.

JOHN DOVER WILSON: The parallel plots in 'Hamlet'. A reply to Dr. W. W. Greg. In: MLR., vol. 13, 1918, pp. 129–56.

JOHN DOVER WILSON: The play-scene in Hamlet restored. In: Athenaeum, 1918.

WILLIAM W. LAWRENCE: The play-scene in Hamlet. In: JEGPh., vol. 14, 1919, pp. 1–22.

ETHELWYN L. FERGUSON: The play-scene in 'Hamlet'. In: MLR., vol. 14, 1919, pp. 370–9.

(6) SYMBOLISM IN HAMLET

KARL SILBERSCHLAG: Shakespeares Hamlet. Quellen, Beziehungen auf Zeitgenossen, gleichzeitige Ereignisse der Abfassungszeit. In: Morgenblatt 1860, No. 46 und 47.

G. F. STEDEFELD: Hamlet, ein Tendenzdrama Shakespeares gegen die skeptische und kosmogonische Weltanschauung des Michael de Montaigne. Berlin, 1871.

M. KRUMMACHER: Geschichtliche und literarhistorische Beziehungen in Shakespeares Hamlet. Progr. Elberfeld, 1877.

KARL SILBERSCHLAG: Shakespeares Hamlet, seine Quellen und politischen Beziehungen. In: Sh. Jb. Jg. 12, 1877, S. 261–89.

HERMANN ISAAC: Hamlet's Familie. In: Sh. Jb. Jg. 16, 1881, S. 274–323.

JACOB FEIS: Shakespeare and Montaigne. An endeavour to explain the tendency of Hamlet from allusions in contemporary works. London, 1884. (viii, 210 pp.)
Hamlet a propaganda-play in opposition to Montaigne's mysticism.

J. SPANIER: Der 'Papist' Shakespeare im Hamlet. Trier, 1890.
Hamlet an anti-reformation propaganda-play.

HERMANN CONRAD: Shakespeares Selbstbekenntnisse. Hamlet und sein Urbild. Stuttgart, 1897. (vi, 321 S.) Rev.: Sh. Jb. 34, 1898, S. 411–15, E. Penner.
The Earl of Essex put forward as original of Hamlet.

A. DÖRING: Hamlet. Ein neuer Versuch zur ästhetischen Erklärung der Tragödie. Berlin, 1898. Contains: Das Urbild Hamlets, S. 29–54.
The Earl of Pembroke taken to be original of Hamlet.

P. HEINRICH: Die Namen der Hamlettragödie. Leipzig, 1904. (90 S.) Rev.: Sh. Jb. 42, 1906, S. 258–9, Anders; Dt. Litztg. 1905, Sp. 1976–7, W. Franz.
Attempts to ascertain the symbolic meaning of the names in the play.

LILIAN WINSTANLEY: Hamlet and the Scottish succession, being an examination of the relations of the play of Hamlet to the Scottish succession and the Essex conspiracy. C.U.P., 1921. (x, 188 pp.) Rev.: Sh. Jb. 58, 1922, S. 132–4, W. Keller; Bbl. 35, 1924, S. 2–6, B. Fehr.

J. W. THOMPSON: Hamlet and the mystery of Amy Robsart. In: North American Review, 1922.

LILIAN WINSTANLEY: 'Hamlet' and the Essex conspiracy = Aberystwyth Stud. VI and VII, 1924–5.

(7) HAMLET'S AGE AND NAME

(a) *Hamlet's Age*

HERMANN TÜRCK: Das Alter Hamlets. In: Sh. Jb. Jg. 36, 1900, S. 267–73. Also as special chapter in: Hamlet ein Genie. Berlin, 1902.

V. ØSTERBERG: Prinz Hamlets alder. In: Edda, 1920. Enlarged as: Prince Hamlet's age. København, 1924. (66 S.) Rev.: Sh. Jb. 59–60, 1924, S. 185–6, W. Keller.

(b) *Hamlet's Name*

ALFRED NORDFELT: Om det äldre Hamletproblemet. Namnet och typen. Uppsala, 1927. In: Språkvetenskapliga sällskapets i Uppsala förhandligar, 1925–7, S. 53–94.

R. MEISSNER: Der Name Hamlet. In: Idg. Forsch., Bd. 45, 1927, S. 370–94.

KEMP MALONE: Etymologies for Hamlet. In: RESt. 3, 1927, pp. 257–71.

KEMP MALONE: More etymologies for Hamlet. In: RESt. 4, 1928, pp. 257–69.

ED. BERGDOL: Hamlet's name. In: Scandinavian studies and notes. Vol. 10, 1929, pp. 159–75.

(8) SUBSEQUENT HISTORY OF THE PLAY.
Stage Adaptations and productions

KARL ELZE: Hamlet in Frankreich. In: Sh. Jb. Jg. 1, 1865, S. 86–126.

W. ROSSMANN: Eine Charakteristik Hamlets für Schauspieler. In: Sh. Jb. Jg. 2, 1867, S. 305–25.

CAROLINE MICHAËLIS: Hamlet in Spanien. In: Sh. Jb. Jg. 10, 1875, S. 311–54.

WILHELM BOLIN: Hamlet in Schweden. In: Sh. Jb. Jg. 14, 1879, S. 23–86.

KARL FRENZEL: Die Darsteller des Hamlet. In: Sh. Jb. Jg. 16, 1881, S. 324–48.

GISBERT FREIHERR VINCKE: Immermanns Einrichtung des Hamlet. In: Sh. Jb. Jg. 21, 1886, S. 175–86.

JOHANNES BOLTE: Hamlet als deutsches Puppenspiel. In: Sh. Jb. Jg. 28, 1893, S. 157–76.

FERDINAND GREGORI: Das Schaffen des Schauspielers. I: Wesentliches und Unwesentliches seiner Kunst. II: Die Bühnendarstellung der Hamlet-Rolle. Berlin, 1899. (155 S.) Rev.: Sh. Jb. 36, 1900, S. 323–4, E. Kilian.

EUGEN ZABEL: Weibliche Hamlets. In: Sh. Jb. Jg. 36, 1900, S. 249–55.

CLEMENT SCOTT: Some notable 'Hamlets' of the present time (Sarah Bernhardt, Henry Irving, Wilson Barrett, Beerbohm Tree, and Forbes Robertson). New ed. with a new chapter on Mr. H. B. Irving by W. L. Courtney. London, 1905. (183 pp.) Rev.: Sh. Jb. 42, 1906, S. 274–5, Gregori.

FERDINAND GREGORI: Shakespeare auf der deutschen Bühne. IV. Josef Kainz: Hamlet. In: Sh. Jb. Jg. 41, 1905, S. 13–21.

ADOLF WINDS: Shakespeare auf der deutschen Bühne. V. Paul Wiecke: Hamlet. In: Sh. Jb. Jg. 42, 1906, S. 86–94.

HELENE RICHTER: Shakespeare auf der deutschen Bühne. VIII. Stella von Hohenfels: Ophelia. In: Sh. Jb. Jg. 43, 1907, S. 138–46.

ALEXANDER VON WEILEN: Hamlet auf der deutschen Bühne bis zur Gegenwart. Berlin, 1908. (ix, 200 S.)= Schriften d. Dt. Shakespeare-Ges., Bd. 3. Rev.: Sh. Jb. 45, 1909, S. 347–9, E. Kilian; Bbl. 22, 1911, S. 111–19, R. Brotanek; E. St. 40, 1909, S. 420–2, Hel. Richter.

ADOLF WINDS: Hamlet auf der deutschen Bühne bis zur Gegenwart. Berlin, 1909. (234 S.)= Schriften der Ges. f. Theatergeschichte, Bd. 12. Rev.: Sh. Jb. 46, 1910, S. 292–5, E. Kilian.

KONRAD FALKE: Kainz als Hamlet. (Ein Abend im Theater.) Zürich, 1911. (xvi, 276 S.) Rev.: Sh. Jb. 47, 1911, S. 303–6, A. Winds.

EUGEN KILIAN: Hamlet in neuer Inszenierung. In: Sh. Jb. Jg. 47, 1911, S. 106–23.

HANS DAFFIS: Hamlet auf der deutschen Bühne bis zur Gegenwart. Berlin, 1912. (x, 154 S.)= Literarhistor. Forsch., hrsg. von Schick und von Waldberg, H. 50. Rev.: Sh. Jb. 49, 1913, S. 249, M. Förster.

E. PÜNDTER: Englische Hamlet-Darsteller und -Darstellung im 17. und 18. Jhrh. Beiträge zur engl. Theatergeschichte. Diss. München, 1912. (177 S.)

WOLFGANG STAMMLER: Zur Darstellung Shylocks und Hamlets auf der deutschen Bühne. In: Sh. Jb. Jg. 49, 1913, S. 137–44.
Friedrich Haase as Hamlet.

Der erste deutsche Bühnen-Hamlet. Die Bearbeitungen Heufelds und Schröders, hrsg. und eingeleitet von ALEXANDER VON WEILEN. Wien, 1914. (xlvii, 196 S.) Rev.: Sh. Jb. 55, 1919, S. 147, W. Keller; Bbl. 28, 1917, S. 105–7, R. Brotanek.
Publication of the three oldest German adaptations: Heufeld 1772, Schröder 1777 und 1778.

BRUNO VOELKER: Die Hamlet-Darstellungen Daniel Chodowieckis und ihr Quellenwert für die deutsche Theatergeschichte des 18. Jahrhunderts. (III. Teil: Schauspielkunst.) Diss. Greifswald, 1915. (x, 114 S.)

ELLA HORN: Zur Geschichte der ersten Aufführung von Schlegels Hamlet-Übersetzung auf dem Kgl. Nationaltheater zu Berlin. In: Sh. Jb. Jg. 51, 1915, S. 34–52.

G. L. VAN ROOSBROECK: Hamlet in France in 1663. In: PMLA., vol. 37, 1922, pp. 228–42.
Shows the similarity of plot of Montfleury's Trasibule to that of Hamlet.

HAZELTON SPENCER: Hamlet under the Restoration. In: PMLA., vol. 38, 1923, pp. 770–91.

CURT DEHNE: Welche hörbaren Ausdrucksmittel wenden ausgewählte Meistersprecher an zur Auswertung des Hamlet-Monologes 'Sein oder Nichtsein'. Diss. Halle, 1926. (56 S. und 2 Taf.)

TROILUS AND CRESSIDA

Cp. also in particular the general surveys on Shakespeare, pp. 27–29, the critical editions, pp. 53–58, and the criticism, pp. 141–145.

(1) THE TEXT

The Shakspere Quarto facsimiles (William Griggs): Troilus and Cressida. Q 1609. Introd. by H. P. STOKES. London, 1886. (xii, 91 pp.)

JOSEPH QUINCY ADAMS: Timon of Athens and the irregularities in the First Folio. In: JEGPh., vol. 7, 1907–8, pp. 53–63.
Deals also with the special circumstances attending the inclusion of Troilus in F 1.

PETER ALEXANDER: 'Troilus and Cressida', 1609. In: Libr., N.S. vol. 9, 1928, pp. 267–86.

(2) LITERARY GENESIS

KARL EITNER: Die Troilus-Fabel in ihrer literaturgeschichtlichen Entwicklung, und die Bedeutung des letzten Aktes von Shakespeares Troilus und Cressida im Verhältnis zum gesamten Stücke. In: Sh. Jb. Jg. 3, 1868, S. 252–300.

W. HERTZBERG: Die Quellen der Troilus-Sage in ihrem Verhältnis zu Shakespeares Troilus und Cressida. In: Sh. Jb. Jg. 6, 1871, S. 169–225.

E. STACHE: Das Verhältnis von Shakespeares Troilus and Cressida zu Chaucers gleichnamigem Gedicht. Progr. Nordhausen, 1893. (14 S.)

ROSCOE A. SMALL: The stage-quarrel between Ben Jonson and the so-called poetasters. Breslau, 1899. (ix, 204 pp.)
Detailed inquiry into the genesis of Troilus.

ROBERT BOYLE: Troilus and Cressida. In: E. St. Bd. 30, 1902, S. 21–59.

JOHN S. P. TATLOCK: The siege of Troy in Elizabethan literature, especially in Shakespeare and Heywood. In: PMLA., vol. 30, N.S. vol. 23, 1915, pp. 673–770.

ANNA THELEMANN: Dictys als Mitquelle von Shakespeares Troilus. In: Arch. Jg. 69, Bd. 133, 1915, S. 91–6.

J. H. HANFORD: A Platonic passage in Shakespeare's Troilus and Cressida. In: Stud. in Phil., vol. 13, 1916, pp. 100 seq.

WILLIAM W. LAWRENCE: The love-story in Troilus and Cressida. In: Shaksperian Studies, Columbia Univ. New York, 1916, pp. 187–211. Short notice in Arch. 135, 1916, S. 467.

F. LÜTGENAU: Troilus und Cressida. In: E. St. Bd. 50, 1916–17, S. 63–79.

HERMANN CONRAD: Shakespeares 'Troilus und Cressida'. Eine Rettung. Berlin, 1917. Also in: Preuss. Jbb. Bd. 169. Rev.: Sh. Jb. 54, 1918, S. 118–19, Grabau.

HYDER E. ROLLINS: The Troilus-Cressida story from Chaucer to Shakespeare. In: PMLA., vol. 32, N.S. vol. 25, 1917, pp. 383–429.

(3) MISCELLANEOUS LITERATURE

HERMANN ULRICI: Ist Troilus und Cressida comedy oder tragedy oder history? In: Sh. Jb. Jg. 9, 1874, S. 26–40.
Conclusion: a comedy.

TH. BRUNS: Der Epilog zu Troilus and Cressida. In: Sh. Jb. Jg. 12, 1877, S. 222–7.

EDUARD ECKHARDT: Zur Rolle des Thersites in Shakespeares Troilus and Cressida. In: E. St. Bd. 64, 1929, S. 370–9.

(4) SUBSEQUENT HISTORY OF THE PLAY

H. ZENKE: Drydens Troilus und Cressida im Verhältnis zu Shakespeares Drama und die übrigen Bearbeitungen des Stoffes in England. Diss. Rostock, 1904. (47 S.)

MEASURE FOR MEASURE

Cp. also in particular the general surveys on Shakespeare, pp. 27–29, the critical editions, pp. 53–58, and the criticism, pp. 141–145.

(1) THE TEXT

Measure for Measure. The text of the folio of 1623 with that of 'Law against Lovers' by Sir William D'Avenant, 1622, by FRANK CARPENTER. New York, 1908.

ALFRED EDWARD THISELTON: Some textual notes on 'Measure for Measure'. London, 1901.

(2) LITERARY GENESIS

COLLIER-HAZLITT: Shakspere's library. London, 1875. Contains: WHETSTONE, Historie of Promos and Cassandra.

K. FOTH: Shakespeares Mass für Mass und die Geschichte von Promos und Cassandra. In: Sh. Jb. Jg. 13, 1878, S. 163–85.

GREGOR SARRAZIN: Neue italienische Skizzen zu Shakespeare. 1. Herzog Vincentio in 'Mass für Mass' und sein Urbild, Herzog Vincenzio Gonzaga. In: Sh. Jb. Jg. 31, 1895, S. 165–9.

E. LEGOUIS: Shakespeare: 'Mesure pour Mesure'. In: Rev. des cours et conférences, t. 18, 1910, No. 7.

FRITZ LEDERBOGEN: Die inneren Beziehungen von Shakespeares 'Measure for Measure' mit den übrigen Dramen der Hamletperiode. Diss. Halle, 1912. (xii, 119 S.) Rev.: Sh. Jb. 49, 1913, S. 175–6, H. Weyhe.

LOUIS ALBRECHT: Neue Untersuchungen über die Quellen von Shakespeares Mass für Mass, über Zeit und Anlass der Entstehung des Stückes und über seine Bedeutung. 1. Die Quellen von Shakespeares Mass für Mass. Diss.

Königsberg, 1914. (163 S.) Enlarged under the title: Neue Untersuchungen zu Shakespeares Mass für Mass. Quellen, Zeit und Anlass der Entstehung des Stückes und seine Bedeutung als Offenbarung der persönlichen Weltanschauung des Dichters. Berlin, 1914. (xxiii, 302 S.) Rev.: Sh. Jb. 51, 1915, S. 264–8, Creizenach; Magyar Shakespeare-Tár 8, 1916. (Ludwig Bodrogi: Contra librum et pro domo); Bbl. 26, 1915, S. 360–6, L. Kellner.

J. P. WICKERSHAM CRAWFORD: A 16th century Spanish analogue of Measure for Measure. In: MLN., vol. 35, 1920, pp. 330–4.

J. M. ROBERTSON: The problem of 'Measure for Measure'. In his The Shakespeare canon, vol. 2, 1923, pp. 158–212.

F. E. BUDD: Rouillet's Philanira and Whetstone's Promos and Cassandra. In: RESt., vol. 6, 1930, pp. 31–48.
Looks upon Rouillet's Philanira as an indirect source of Shakespeare's play.

(3) SHAKESPEARE'S ART IN MEASURE FOR MEASURE

A. KOSZUL: La technique dramatique de Shakespeare, étudiée dans le 1er acte de 'Measure for Measure'. In: Rev. de l'enseignement des langues vivantes, 44, 1927, pp. 145–52.

(4) MISCELLANEOUS LITERATURE

FRITZ FREUND: Shakespeare als Rechtsphilosoph. Kaufmann von Venedig und Mass für Mass. In: Sh. Jb. Jg. 28, 1893, S. 54–71.

MARY SUDDARD: Measure for Measure as a clue to Shakespeare's attitude towards Puritanism. In her Studies and essays. C.U.P., 1912.

(5) SUBSEQUENT HISTORY OF THE PLAY

G. ILLIES: Das Verhältnis von Davenants 'The Law against Lovers' zu Shakespeares 'Measure for Measure' und 'Much Ado'. Diss. Halle, 1900. (90 S.)

EUGEN KILIAN: 'Mass für Mass' als deutsches Bühnenstück. In: Sh. Jb. Jg. 56, 1920, S. 58–72.

ALL'S WELL THAT ENDS WELL

Cp. also in particular the general surveys on Shakespeare, pp. 27–29, the critical editions, pp. 53–58, and the criticism, pp. 141–145.

(1) THE TEXT

ALFRED E. THISELTON: Some textual notes on 'All's well that ends well'. London, 1900. (32 pp.)

(2) LITERARY GENESIS

PAYNTER: Giletta of Narbonne. Repr. in: COLLIER-HAZLITT: Shakspere's library. London, 1875. Pt. i, vol. iii, pp. 140–51.

HERMANN FREIHERR VON FRIESEN: Bemerkungen zu den Altersbestimmungen für einige Stücke von Shakespeare. 2. All's well that ends well. In: Sh. Jb. Jg. 2, 1867, S. 48–54.
Considers it a very early work and assumes a later revision.

KARL ELZE: Zu 'Ende gut, alles gut'. An Gisbert Freiherrn Vincke. In: Sh. Jb. Jg. 7, 1872, S. 214–37.

H. VON DER HAGEN: Über die altfranzösische Vorstufe des Shakespeareschen Lustspiels 'Ende gut, alles gut'. Diss. Halle, 1879. (39 S.)

NICOLAUS DELIUS: Shakespeares 'All's well that ends well', and Paynter's Giletta of Narbonne. In: Sh. Jb. Jg. 22, 1887, S. 26–44.

ROBERT BOYLE: All's well that ends well and Love's Labour's Won. In: E. St. Bd. 14, 1890, S. 408–21.

JUTTA RUGENSTEIN: Shakespeares Vorlagen für 'Ende gut, alles gut'. MS. Diss. Rostock, 1922. Summary: Rostock, 1923. (1 S.)

ELISABETH SCHAEFER: Zur Datierung von Shakespeares 'All's well that ends well'. In: Sh. Jb. Jg. 59–60, N.F. Bd. 1, 1924, S. 86–108.

J. M. ROBERTSON: 'All's well that ends well.' In his Shakespeare canon, vol. iii, 1925, pp. 28–112.
Attributes the main share in the play to Chapman.

Supplement: *Love's Labour's Won*

F. P. VON WESTENHOLZ: Shakespeares 'Gewonnene Liebesmüh'. In: Allgem. Ztg. Beil. 10 vom 14. 1. 1902, S. 72–9.

ALBERT H. TOLMAN: What has become of Shakespeare's play 'Love's Labour's Won'? Chicago, 1902. (34 pp.)
Summary of the theories as to the whereabouts of the play.

(3) DRAMATIC ART

L. KELLNER: Exegetische Bemerkungen zu All's well that ends well. In: Sh. Jb. Jg. 53, 1917, S. 35–48.

WILLIAM WITHERLE LAWRENCE: The meaning of 'All's well that ends well'. In: PMLA., vol. 37, 1922, pp. 418–69.

KING LEAR

Cp. also in particular the general surveys on Shakespeare, pp. 27–29, the critical editions, pp. 53–58, and the criticism, pp. 141–145.

(1) THE TEXT

The Shakspere quarto facsimiles (William Griggs): King Lear.
1st Q 1608. With introd. by P. A. DANIEL. London, 1885. (xxii, 80 pp.)
2nd Q 1608. With introd. by P. A. DANIEL. London, 1885. (88 pp.)

King Lear. Parallel texts of the first quarto and the first folio. Ed. by WILHELM VIËTOR. Revised edition. Marburg, 1892. (vi, 178 pp.)=Shakespeare Reprints I.

_____

NICOLAUS DELIUS: Über den ursprünglichen Text des King Lear. In: Sh. Jb. Jg. 10, 1875, S. 50–74.

RICHARD KOPPEL: Textkritische Studien über Shakespeares Richard III. und King Lear. Hab. Schr. Dresden, 1877. (102 S.)

ALEXANDER SCHMIDT: Zur Textkritik des 'King Lear'. Progr. Königsberg, 1879. (21 S.) Also in: Anglia, Bd. 3, 1880, S. 1–34, and in the author's Gesammelte Abhandlungen. Berlin, 1889, S. 222–52.

RICHARD KOPPEL: Verbesserungsvorschläge zu den Erläuterungen und der Textlesung des 'Lear'. 2. Reihe der Shakespeare-Studien. Berlin, 1899. (156 S.) Rev.: Sh. Jb. 36, 1900, S. 300–1, W. Franz.

WALTER W. GREG: On certain false dates in Shakespearian quartos. In: Libr. N.S. vol. 9, 1908, pp. 113–31 and 381–409.

One of the Lear quartos claimed to be falsely dated and only published in 1619.

R. H. CUNNINGTON: The revision of 'King Lear'. In: MLR., vol. 5, 1910, pp. 445–53.

W. D. MORIARTY: The bearing on dramatic sequence of the varia in Richard III and King Lear. In: Mod. Phil., vol. 10, 1912–13, pp. 451–71.

(2) LITERARY GENESIS

RUDOLF FISCHER: Quellen zu König Lear. Bonn, 1914. (viii, 185 S.)=Shakespeares Quellen in der Originalsprache und deutsch hrsg. im Auftrag d. Dt. Shakespeare-Ges. 1. Bändchen. Rev.: Sh. Jb. 51, 1915, S. 263–4, Creizenach.

CONTENTS: I. Galfrid's history of the Britons. II. Holinshed's Chronicle. III. The mirror of Magistrates. IV. Spenser's Faerie Queene. V. The Chronicle-Play of King Leir. VI. Sidney's Arcadia.

The history of King Leir, 1605=The Malone Soc. Reprints, 1907. (viii, 72 pp.)

Reprint in facsimile.

The chronicle history of King Leir, the original of Shakespeare's 'King Lear'. Ed. by SIDNEY LEE. London, 1909. (xlvii, 131 pp.)=The Shakespeare Classics. Rev.: Sh. Jb. 46, 1910, S. 306–8, M. Förster.

Reprint in modernized spelling with valuable critical introduction.

Cf. also H. DUGDALE SYKES: The pre-Shakespearean King Leir. In his Sidelights on Shakespeare. Stratford, 1919, pp. 126–42.

Sykes attributes authorship to George Peele.

King Leir and his three daughters. (Ballad from Percy's Reliques.) Reprint in: Furness' New Var. Ed., King Lear. Philadelphia (1880), pp. 403–7.

Cf. also A. G. VAN HAMEL: The ballad of King Lear. In: GRM. Jg. 5, 1913, S. 307–18.

W. G. BOSWELL-STONE: Shakespeare's Holinshed. London, 1907², pp. 1–6.

HERMANN FREIHERR VON FRIESEN: Über Shakespeares Quellen zu King Lear. Ein berichtigender Nachtrag zu meinen 'Shakespeare-Studien'. Bd. 3. In: Sh. Jb. Jg. 12, 1877, S. 169–81.

CHRISTIAN EIDAM: Über die Sage von König Lear. Progr. Würzburg, 1880. (41 S.)

WILFRID PERRETT: The story of King Lear from Geoffrey of Monmouth to Shakespeare. Diss. Jena, 1903. (33 S.) Enlarged: Berlin, 1904. (x, 308 S.)= Palaestra 35. Rev.: Sh. Jb. 41, 1905, S. 253–4, R. Fischer; MLR. 1, 1906, pp. 69–72, F. W. Moorman; Bbl. 17, 1906, S. 42–9, Konr. Meier.

EMIL BODE: Die Learsage vor Shakespeare mit Ausschluss des älteren Dramas und der Ballade. Diss. Göttingen, 1904. (150 S.) Also in: Stud. z. engl. Philol., hrsg. von Morsbach, Bd. 17. Rev.: Sh. Jb. 41, 1905, S. 252–3, R. Fischer.

ROBERT ADGER LAW: On the date of King Lear. In: PMLA., vol. 21, N.S. vol. 14, 1906, pp. 462–77.

LEVIN L. SCHÜCKING: Eine Anleihe Shakespeares bei Tourneur. In: E. St. Bd. 50, 1916, S. 80–105.

FRIEDRICH RADEBRECHT: Shakespeares Abhängigkeit von John Marston. Cöthen, 1918. (xv, 122 S.)=Neue anglist. Arbeiten, hrsg. von L. L. Schücking und M. Deutschbein, No. 3. Rev.: MLR. 17, 1922, pp. 301–3, H. B. Charlton; Bbl. 30, 1919, S. 95–8, Ph. Aronstein.

Part II asserts close dependence of Lear on Marston's Malcontent.

EDUARD SIEVERS: Shakespeares Anteil am King Lear. Eine schallanalytische Untersuchung. In: Anglica. Alois Brandl z. 70. Geburtstag. Bd. 2. Leipzig, 1925, S. 173–210=Palaestra 148. Rev.: Sh. Jb. 61, 1925, S. 137, W. Keller.

Shakespeare has adapted a previous work, not identical with King Leir, and composed by two authors.

(3) DRAMATIC ART

THOMAS R. PRICE: King Lear. A study of Shakspere's dramatic method. In: PMLA., vol. 9, N.S. vol. 2, 1894, pp. 165–81.

A. C. BRADLEY: King Lear. In his Shakespearean tragedy. London, 1904, pp. 243–330.

BRINUS KÖHLER: Die Schilderung des Milieus in Shakespeares Hamlet, Macbeth und King Lear. Halle a. S., 1912. (xi, 65 S.)=Stud. z. engl. Philol., hrsg. von Morsbach, H. 46.

C. STARK: König Lear. Eine psychiatrische Shakespeare-Studie. Stuttgart, 1871.

HARDIN CRAIG: The ethics of King Lear. In: Philol. Quart., vol. 4, 1925, pp. 97–109.

W. OEHLMANN: Cordelia als tragischer Charakter. In: Sh. Jb. Jg. 2, 1867, S. 124–31.

H. ENGEL: Zu Shakespeares Edgar. In: Z. f. e. U., Bd. 21, 1922, S. 29–33.

(4) SYMBOLISM IN LEAR

LILIAN WINSTANLEY: Macbeth, King Lear and contemporary history. Being a study of the relations of the play of Macbeth to the personal history of James I, the Darnley murder and the St. Bartholomew massacre and also of King Lear as symbolic mythology. Cambridge, 1922. (228 pp.) Rev.: Sh. Jb. 58, 1922, S. 134–6, W. Keller; MLR. 18, 1923, pp. 209–13, C. H. Herford; Bbl. 35, 1924, S. 6–12, B. Fehr.

H. PRAGER: Deutung von Shakespeares Lear im Sinne einer Philosophie der Familie. In: Logos 18, 1929.

(5) SUBSEQUENT HISTORY OF THE PLAY

(a) *Adaptations*

WILHELM BOLIN: Zur Bühnenbearbeitung des König Lear. In: Sh. Jb. Jg. 20, 1885, S. 131–48.

RUDOLF ERZGRAEBER: Nahum Tate's und George Colman's Bühnenbearbeitungen des Shakespeareschen King Lear. Diss. Rostock, 1897. (69 S.) Also in: Sh. Jb. Jg. 33, 1897, S. 166–230.

ALBERT SAUR: Shaksperes 'König Lear' in Frankreich bis zum Jahre 1827. Diss. München, 1910. (viii, 48 S.) Rev.: Sh. Jb. Jg. 48, 1912, S. 210, H. Weyhe.

Shakespearian adaptations: The Tempest, The Mock Tempest, and King Lear. With an introd. and notes by MONTAGUE SUMMERS. London, 1922. (cviii, 282 pp.) Repr. of Nahum Tate's The history of King Lear (1681).

KARL BRUNNER: Der König-Lear-Text des Wiener Burgtheaters von 1780. In: E. St. Bd. 64, 1929, S. 362–9.

(b) *Stage-Productions*

HERMANN ULRICI: Ludwig Devrient als König Lear. In: Sh. Jb. Jg. 2, 1867, S. 292–7.

ALBERT COHN: König Lear 1692 und Titus Andronicus 1699 in Breslau aufgeführt. In: Sh. Jb. Jg. 23, 1888, S. 266–81.
With a reprint of the scenarios of the two plays.

EUGEN KILIAN: Vorschläge zur Bühnenaufführung des König Lear. In: Sh. Jb. Jg. 29–30, 1894, S. 148–71.

FERDINAND GREGORI: Shakespeare auf der deutschen Bühne. I. Adolf von Sonnenthal: König Lear. In: Sh. Jb. Jg. 40, 1904, S. 85–9.

HELENE RICHTER: Shakespeare auf der deutschen Bühne. VII. Josef Kainz: Narr im Lear. In: Sh. Jb. Jg. 42, 1906, S. 107–12.

OTHELLO

Cp. also in particular the general surveys on Shakespeare, pp. 27–29, the critical editions, pp. 53–58, and the criticism, pp. 141–145.

(1) THE TEXT

The Shakspere quarto facsimiles (William Griggs): Othello.
Q 1 (1622). Introd. by H. A. EVANS. London, 1885. (xvi, 92 pp.)
Q 2 (1630). Introd. by H. A. EVANS. London, 1885. (viii, 94 pp.)

Shakespeare's Othello in Paralleldruck nach der ersten Quarto und ersten Folio mit den Lesarten der zweiten Quarto und einer Einleitung hrsg. von ARNOLD SCHRÖER. Heidelberg, 1909. (xvi, 211 S.)=Engl. Textbibl., hrsg. von J. Hoops, 14. Rev.: Sh. Jb. 46, 1910, S. 300, M. Förster.

CÄCILIE NOLTE: Die Überlieferung von Shakespeares Othello. MS. Diss. Köln, 1923. (104 S.) Rev.: Sh. Jb. 61, 1925, S. 149, W. Keller.

(2) LITERARY GENESIS

For sources see A New Var. Ed. (Furness). Philadelphia (1886).

WILLIAM R. TURNBULL: Othello, a critical study. Edinburgh, 1892. (xii, 392 pp.)

ELMER E. STOLL: Othello, an historical and comparative study. Minneapolis, 1915. (70 pp.) Rev.: MLR. 11, 1916, pp. 466–7, E. K. Chambers; Bbl. 35, 1924, S. 145–7, B. Fehr.

FRIEDRICH RADEBRECHT: Shakespeares Abhängigkeit von John Marston. Cöthen, 1918. (xv, 122 S.)=Neue anglist. Arb., hrsg. von L. L. Schücking und M. Deutschbein, No. 3. Rev.: MLR. 17, 1922, pp. 301–3, H. B. Charlton; Bbl. 30, 1919, S. 95–8, Ph. Aronstein.
Part II shows Shakespeare's dependence in Othello on Marston's Malcontent.

LOIS WHITNEY: Did Shakespeare know 'Leo Africanus'? In: PMLA., vol. 37, 1922, pp. 470–83.
Accepts John Pary's translation of Leo's Geographical historie of Africa as source.

ALEXANDER H. KRAPPE: A Byzantine source of Shakespeare's Othello. In: MLN., vol. 39, 1924, pp. 156–61.

W. A. BULLOCK: The sources of 'Othello'. In: MLN., vol. 40, 1925, pp. 226–8.

(3) SHAKESPEARE'S ART IN OTHELLO

R. G. MOULTON: 'Othello' as a type of plot. In: Trans. New Shaksp. Soc., 1887–92, xix.

ERNST TRAUMANN: Die künstlerische Arbeit Shakespeares im Othello. In: Sh. Jb. Jg. 31, 1895, S. 231–61.

A. C. BRADLEY: Othello. In his Shakespearean tragedy. London, 1904, pp. 175–242.

A. H. GILBERT: Scenes of discovery in Othello. In: Philol. Quart., vol. 5, 1926, pp. 119–30.

w. WETZ: Othello. In the same author's Shakespeare vom Standpunkte der vergleichenden Literaturgeschichte. Worms, 1890, S. 262–387.

RUDOLF MEISSNER: Lieutenant Cassio und Fähnrich Jago. In: E. St. Bd. 30, 1902, S. 59–81.

D. E. OPPENHEIM: Othello. Ein Beitrag zur vergleichenden Psychologie Shakespearescher Gestalten. In the same writer's Dichtung und Menschenkenntnis. Psychologische Streifzüge durch alte und neue Literatur. München, 1926, S. 42–142.

(4) SYMBOLISM

LILIAN WINSTANLEY: Othello as the tragedy of Italy, showing that Shakespeare's Italian contemporaries interpreted the story of the Moor and the Lady of Venice as symbolizing their country in the grip of Spain. London, 1924. (152 pp.) Rev.: Marzocco 30, 1925, p. 45, G. S. Gargano.

(5) MISCELLANEOUS LITERATURE

ALBERT TESCH: Zum Namen Desdemona. In: GRM. Jg. 17, 1929, S. 387–8.

(6) SUBSEQUENT HISTORY OF THE PLAY

GISBERT FREIHERR VINCKE: Schillers Bühnenbearbeitung des Othello. In: Sh. Jb. Jg. 15, 1880, S. 222–9.

O. BOBSIN: Shakespeares Othello in englischer Bühnenbearbeitung. Diss. Rostock, 1904. (99 S.)

JOS. FEST: Othello in Frankreich. Diss. Erlangen, 1906. (30 S.)

MARGARET GILMAN: Othello in French. Diss. Bryn Mawr, 1924. Paris, 1925. (viii, 197 pp.) = Bibl. de la Revue de litt. comp., No. 21.

T. P. HARRISON, JR.: 'Othello' as a model for Dryden in 'All for Love'. In: Univ. of Texas Stud. in English. vii, 1927, pp. 136–43.

EDMOND ESTÈVE: Banville et Shakespeare. Une dernière variation sur la 'romance du saule'. In: Mélanges . . . offerts à Fernand Baldensperger. Paris, 1930. T. I, pp. 263–70.

MACBETH

Cp. also in particular the general surveys on Shakespeare, pp. 27–29, the critical editions, pp. 53–58, and the criticism, pp. 141–145.

(1) THE TEXT

Shaksperes Macbeth aus der Folioausgabe von 1623 abgedruckt, mit den Varianten der Folioausgaben von 1632, 1664 und 1687 und kritischen Anmerkungen zum Text hrsg. von NICOLAUS DELIUS. Bremen, 1841. (viii, 86 S.)

Shakespeares Macbeth nach der Folio von 1623 mit den Varianten der anderen Folios hrsg. von ALBRECHT WAGNER. Halle, 1890. (iv, 95 S.)

RICHARD KOPPEL: Shakespeare-Studien. I. Reihe: Ergänzungen zu den Macbeth-Kommentaren. Textkritisches.—Lexikalisches. Berlin, 1896. (122 S.)

(2) LITERARY GENESIS

W. G. BOSWELL-STONE: Shakespeare's Holinshed. London, 1907[2], pp. 18–45.

ERNST KRÖGER: Macbeth bis auf Shakspere. I: Macbeth in der Geschichte. Diss. Berlin, 1904. (28 S.) Enlarged under the title: Die Sage von Macbeth bis zu Shakespere. Berlin, 1904. (ix, 273 S.)=Palaestra 39. Rev.: Sh. Jb. 41, 1905, S. 254–6, Potter; Bbl. 16, 1905, S. 293–302, Konrad Meier.

A. BRANDL: Die Vorgeschichte der Schicksalsschwestern in Macbeth.=Sitzber. Preuss. Akad. Wiss. 1919. Also in: Texte und Forschungen z. engl. Kulturgeschichte, Festgabe f. Max Liebermann. Halle, 1921, S. 252–70.

(3) DRAMATIC ART

J. JEKELI: Die Gesetze der Tragödie, nachgewiesen an Shakespeares Macbeth. Progr. Mediasch, 1873. (46 S.)

THOMAS ALFRED SPALDING: On the witch-scenes in Macbeth. In: Trans. New Shaksp. Soc., 1877–9, pp. 27–40.

R. U. ZERBST: Die dramatische Technik des Macbeth. Jena, 1888.

A. WAGNER: Metrische Bemerkungen zu Shakespeares Macbeth. In: Anglia, Bd. 13, 1891, S. 352–7.

W. WETZ: Die inneren Beziehungen zwischen Shakespeares 'Macbeth' und seinen Königsdramen. In: E. St. Bd. 16, 1892, S. 1–18.

AUGUST VORDIECK: Parallelismus zwischen Shakespeares 'Macbeth' und seiner epischen Dichtung 'Lucrece'. Progr. Neisse, 1901. (36 S.) Rev.: E. St. 31, 1902, S. 121–3, O. Glöde.

RUDOLF FISCHER: Der Monolog im 'Macbeth' als formales Mittel zur Figuren-Charakterisierung. In: Beitr. z. neueren Philologie. Jakob Schipper z. 19. Juli 1902. Wien & Leipzig, 1902.

DAVID L. CHAMBERS: The metre of Macbeth, its relation to Shakespeare's earlier and later work. Princeton, 1903. (70 pp.) Rev.: Sh. Jb. 40, 1904, S. 300–1, A. Brandl.

B. SIBURG: Schicksal und Willensfreiheit bei Shakespeare, dargelegt am Macbeth. Diss. Göttingen, 1906. (73 S.) Enlarged: Halle, 1906. (xvi, 128 S.)= Stud. z. engl. Philol., hrsg. von Morsbach, H. 27. Rev.: Sh. Jb. 43, 1907, S. 269–74, R. Petsch.

WALTER BORMANN: Sinnbildliches im 'Macbeth'. In: Sh. Jb. Jg. 47, 1911, S. 124–7.

BRINUS KÖHLER: Die Schilderung des Milieus in Shakespeares Hamlet, Macbeth und King Lear. Halle a. S., 1912. (xi, 65 S.)=Stud. z. engl. Phil., hrsg. von Morsbach, H. 46.

GREGOR VON GLASENAPP: Die Dämonologie in Shakespeares Macbeth: Banquos Geist. In: Sh. Jb. Jg. 61, 1925, S. 52–66.

GREGOR VON GLASENAPP: Die Dämonologie in Shakespeares Macbeth: Die Hexen. In: Sh. Jb. Jg. 64, N.F. Bd. 5, 1928, S. 63–76.

(4) EXPLANATORY LITERATURE

HERMANN FREIHERR VON FRIESEN: Über Shakespeares Macbeth. In: Sh. Jb. Jg. 4, 1869, S. 198–245.

O. TIMME: Kommentar über die 1. Szene des 2. Aktes von Shakespeares Macbeth. Diss. Jena, 1873. (46 S.)

KARL WERDER: Vorlesungen über Shakespeares Macbeth, gehalten an der Universität zu Berlin. Berlin, 1885. (292 S.)

ERNST TRAUMANN: Macbeth. In: Sh. Jb. Jg. 32, 1896, S. 235–67.

A. C. BRADLEY: Macbeth. In his Shakespearean tragedy. London, 1904, pp. 331–400.

KONRAD MEIER: Über Shakespeares Macbeth. In: N. Spr. Bd. 13, 1905–6, S. 65–81 und 142–59.

OTTOMAR PETERSEN: Shakespeares Macbeth. In: Z. f. e. U., Bd. 11, 1912, S. 223–47.

H. HERRMANN: Macbeth, eine Interpretation. In: Zs. f. Aesth. und allgem. Kunstwiss. Bd. 22, 1928.

(5) SYMBOLISM

LILIAN WINSTANLEY: Macbeth, King Lear, and contemporary history, being a study of the relations of the play of Macbeth to the personal history of James I, the Darnley murder, and the St. Bartholomew massacre, and also of King Lear as symbolic mythology. C.U.P., 1922. (viii, 228 pp.) Rev.: Sh. Jb. 58, 1922, S. 134–6, W. Keller; MLR. 18, 1923, pp. 209–13, C. H. Herford; Bbl. 35, 1924, S. 6–12, B. Fehr.

(6) SUBSEQUENT HISTORY OF THE DRAMA

R. GERICKE: Zu einer neuen Bühnenbearbeitung des Macbeth. In: Sh. Jb. Jg. 6, 1871, S. 19–82.

Includes summary and review of the most important adaptations up to date of publication.

NICOLAUS DELIUS: Shakespeares Macbeth und Davenants Macbeth. In: Sh. Jb. Jg. 20, 1885, S. 69–84.

H. BECKHAUS: Shakespeares Macbeth und die Schillersche Bearbeitung. Progr. Ostrowo, 1889. (25 S.)

G. SCHATZMANN: Schillers Macbeth, nach dem englischen Originale verglichen. Progr. Trautenau, 1889. (30 S.)

H. FIETKAU: Schillers Macbeth unter Berücksichtigung des Originals und seiner Quelle. Progr. Königsberg, 1897. (46 S.)

J. MINOR: Zu Bürgers Macbeth-Übersetzung. In: Sh. Jb. Jg. 36, 1900, S. 122–7.

G. WEBER: Davenants Macbeth im Verhältnis zu Shakespeares gleichnamiger Tragödie. Diss. Rostock, 1903. (77 S.)

KURT KAUENHOWEN: Gottfried August Bürgers Macbeth-Bearbeitung. Diss. Königsberg, 1915. (89 S.)

KURT KAUENHOWEN: J. K. G. Wernichs 'Macbeth'-Bearbeitung. Die 1. Aufführung des 'Macbeth' in Berlin 1778. In: Sh. Jb. Jg. 54, 1918, S. 50–72.

HAZELTON SPENCER: D'Avenant's Macbeth and Shakespeare's. In: PMLA., vol. 40, 1925, pp. 619–44.

ANTONY AND CLEOPATRA

Cp. also in particular the general surveys on Shakespeare, pp. 27–29, the critical editions, pp. 53–58, and the criticism, pp. 141–145.

(1) THE TEXT

K. ELZE: Notes and conjectural emendations on 'Antony and Cleopatra' and 'Pericles'. In: E. St. Bd. 9, 1886, S. 267–90.

M. A. BAYFIELD: A study of Shakespeare's versification, with an inquiry into the trustworthiness of the early texts ... including a revised text of Antony and Cleopatra. C.U.P., 1920. (xii, 521 pp.)

(2) LITERARY GENESIS

Shakespeare's Plutarch, ed. by C. F. TUCKER BROOKE. Vol. II: containing the main sources of Antony and Cleopatra and of Coriolanus. London, 1909. (xix, 230 pp.)=The Shakespeare Classics.

SAMUEL DANIEL: The tragedy of Cleopatra, reprinted from the edition of 1611 by M. LEDERER. Louvain, 1911. (xvi, 99 pp.)=Mat. z. Kunde d. ält. engl. Dramas, 31.

———

THEODOR VATKE: Shakespeares Antonius und Kleopatra und Plutarchs Biographie des Antonius. In: Sh. Jb. Jg. 3, 1868, S. 301–40.

FRITZ ADLER: Das Verhältnis von Shakespeares 'Antony and Cleopatra' zu Plutarchs Biographie des Antonius. Diss. Halle, 1895. (55 S.) Also in: Sh. Jb. Jg. 31, 1895, S. 262–317.

GEORG HERMANN MÖLLER: Beiträge zur dramatischen Cleopatra-Literatur. Progr. Schweinfurt, 1907. (39 S.) Rev.: Sh. Jb. 45, 1909, S. 280, Brie.

A. C. BRADLEY: Shakespeare's Antony and Cleopatra. In his Oxford lectures on poetry. London, 1909, pp. 279–308.

A. BUBERT: Samuel Daniels 'Cleopatra' und 'Philotas' und Samuel Brandons 'The Virtuous Octavia'. Diss. Königsberg, 1913. (95 S.)

AMANDUS MÜLLER: Studien zu Samuel Daniels Tragödie 'Cleopatra'. Quellen-frage und literarischer Charakter. Diss. Leipzig, 1914. (ix, 56 S.) Rev.: Sh. Jb. 51, 1915, S. 271–2, W. Creizenach.

ERNST VON WILDENBRUCH: Einleitende Worte zu einer Vorlesung von 'Antonius und Cleopatra'. In: Sh. Jb. Jg. 50, 1914, S. 1–3.

FRIEDRICH GUNDOLF: Antonius und Cleopatra. Festvortrag. In: Sh. Jb. Jg. 62, 1926, S. 7–35.

LUCIE SIMPSON: Shakespeare's 'Cleopatra'. In: Fortnightly Rev., vol. 129, 1928, pp. 332–42.

(3) ART OF CHARACTERIZATION

ADOLF STAHR: Cleopatra. Berlin, 1879.

G. HERMANN MOELLER: Die Auffassung der Kleopatra in der Tragödienliteratur der romanischen und germanischen Nationen. Ulm, 1888.

L. L. SCHÜCKING: Szenenweise verschieden aufgefasster Charakter (Cleopatra). In his Die Charakterprobleme bei Shakespeare. Leipzig, 1927², S. 117–39.

ELMER EDGAR STOLL: Cleopatra. In: MLR., vol. 23, 1928, pp. 145–63.

(4) SUBSEQUENT HISTORY OF THE PLAY

WILHELM BOLIN: Antonius und Cleopatra in deutscher Bühnenbearbeitung. In: Sh. Jb. Jg. 17, 1882, S. 128–64.

FRIEDRICH HANNMANN: Drydens Tragödie 'All for love; or, the world well lost' und ihr Verhältnis zu Shakespeares 'Antony and Cleopatra'. Diss. Rostock, 1903. (82 S.)

Cf. Reprint of Dryden's play in: A New Var. Ed., ed. H. H. FURNESS: The tragedy of Anthony and Cleopatra. 1907.

EUGEN KILIAN: Antonius und Kleopatra auf der deutschen Bühne. In: Sh. Jb. Jg. 51, 1915, S. 82–97.

CORIOLANUS

Cp. also in particular the general surveys on Shakespeare, pp. 27–29, the critical editions, pp. 53–58, and the criticism, pp. 141–145.

(1) THE TEXT

William Shakespeare's Coriolanus, ed. by F. A. LEO. With a quarto-facsimile of the Tragedy of Coriolanus from the folio of 1623 and with extracts from North's Plutarch. London, 1864. (IX, 127+30+10 pp.)

CATHLEEN H. HAYHURST: A history of the text of Coriolanus. Chicago, 1924.

(2) LITERARY GENESIS

Shakespeare's Plutarch, ed. by C. F. TUCKER BROOKE. Vol. II: containing the main sources of Antony and Cleopatra and of Coriolanus. O.U.P., 1909. (xx, 230 pp.)=The Shakespeare Classics.

NICOLAUS DELIUS: Shakespeares Coriolanus in seinem Verhältnis zum Coriolanus des Plutarch. In: Sh. Jb. Jg. 11, 1876, S. 32–58.

OSCAR KARLOWA: Zu Shakespeares Coriolan. Progr. Pless. 1904. (15 S.)

RICHARD BÜTTNER: Zu 'Coriolan' und seiner Quelle. In: Sh. Jb. Jg. 41, 1905, S. 45–53.

A. C. BRADLEY: Coriolanus. London [1912]. (19 S.)=Brit. Acad. annual Shakespeare Lecture. Rev.: Sh. Jb. 49, 1913, S. 237–8, M. Förster.

(3) DRAMATIC ART

HEINRICH VIEHOFF: Shakespeares Coriolan. In: Sh. Jb. Jg. 4, 1869, S. 41–61.

FRIEDRICH VON WESTENHOLZ: Die Tragik in Shakespeares Coriolan. Stuttgart, 1895. (31 S.) Rev.: Bbl. 8, 1898, S. 47–8, L. Wurth.

MARTIN WOHLRAB: Ästhetische Erklärung von Shakespeares Coriolan. Berlin & Dresden, 1902. (96 S.)

ALBERT H. TOLMAN: The structure of Shakespeare's tragedies, with special reference to Coriolanus. In: MLN., vol. 37, 1922, pp. 449–58.

GRACE LATHAM: Volumnia. In: Sh. Jb. Jg. 23, 1888, S. 201–23.

WILHELM MÜNCH: Aufidius. In: Sh. Jb. Jg. 42, 1906, S. 127–47.

TIMON OF ATHENS

Cp. also in particular the general surveys on Shakespeare, pp. 27–29, the critical editions, pp. 53–58, and the criticism, pp. 141–145.

(1) THE TEXT

JOSEPH QUINCY ADAMS: Timon of Athens and the irregularities of the First Folio. In: JEGPh., vol. 7, 1907–8, pp. 53–63.

(2) LITERARY GENESIS

NICOLAUS DELIUS: Über Shakespeares Timon of Athens. In: Sh. Jb. Jg. 2, 1867, S. 335–61.
Revision by Shakespeare of an old play.

B. TSCHISCHWITZ: Timon von Athen. Ein kritischer Versuch. In: Sh. Jb. Jg. 4, 1869, S. 160–97.

ADOLF MÜLLER: Über die Quellen, aus denen Shakespeare den Timon von Athen entnommen hat. Diss. Jena, 1873. (30 S.)

FREDERICK G. FLEAY: On the authorship of Timon of Athens. In: Trans. New Shaksp. Soc., 1874, pp. 130 seq.
A fragmentary sketch of Shakespeare's revised by another.

GEORG KULLMANN: Shakespeares Anteil an dem unter seinem Namen veröffentlichten Trauerspiele Timon mit Berücksichtigung der von Knight, Delius, Tschischwitz, Fleay und Ulrici aufgestellten Hypothesen kritisch beleuchtet. In: Archiv f. Lit. gesch., Bd. 11, 1882, S. 196–245.

WILHELM WENDLANDT: Shakespeares Timon von Athen. In: Sh. Jb. Jg. 23, 1888, S. 107–92.
Shakespeare claimed as sole author.

HERMANN CONRAD: Shakesperes Timon. Urheberschaft, Abfassungszeit und Entstehung. In: Zs. f. vgl. Lit. gesch. N.F. Bd. 17, 1909, S. 337–84.

ERNEST HUNTER WRIGHT: The authorship of Timon of Athens. New York, 1910. (ix, 104 pp.)=Columbia Univ. Studies in English. Rev.: Sh. Jb. 47, 1911, S. 296–8, W. Keller; JEGPh. 10, 1911, pp. 492–8, J. Q. Adams; MLR. 6, 1911, pp. 257–9, R. C. Brooke.

Agrees on essential points with Fleay.

J. M. ROBERTSON: Shakespeare and Chapman. A thesis of Chapman's authorship of 'A Lover's Complaint' and his origination of 'Timon of Athens', with indications of further problems. London, 1917. (302 pp.) Rev.: MLR. 13, 1918, pp. 244–50, H. D. Sykes.

Revision by Shakespeare of a Chapman play.

H. DUGDALE SYKES: The problem of 'Timon of Athens'. In: N. & Q., 13th ser., vol. i, 1923, 4th Aug.–15th Sept., pp. 83–6, 105–7, 123–6, 145–9, 166–8, 188–90, 208–10.

Asserts that the earlier play comes from the pen of Middleton.

THOMAS MARC PARROTT: The problem of Timon of Athens. London, 1923. (34 pp.)=The Shakespeare Assoc. Papers, No. 10.

A Shakespeare play revised and completed by Chapman and another author.

DIXON WECTER: Shakespeare's purpose in Timon of Athens. In: PMLA., vol. 43, 1928, pp. 701–21.

Shakespeare the sole poet, but the play was included in F 1 in a mutilated condition. The author sees allusions to the Earl of Essex.

FRANZ BERTRAM: Die Timonlegende, eine Entwicklungsgeschichte des Misanthropentypus in der antiken Literatur. Diss. Heidelberg, 1906. (99 S.)

(3) SUBSEQUENT HISTORY OF THE PLAY

EUGEN KILIAN: Die Dalberg'sche Bühnenbearbeitung des Timon von Athen. Nach dem handschriftlichen Soufflierbuch des Mannheimer Theaterarchivs veröffentlicht. In: Sh. Jb. Jg. 25, 1890, S. 24–76.

HERMANN CONRAD: Shakespeares und Bulthaupts 'Timon'. In: Sh. Jb. Jg. 29–30, 1894, S. 110–47.

AUGUST FRESENIUS: Shakespeares 'Timon von Athen' auf der Bühne. In: Sh. Jb. Jg. 31, 1895, S. 83–125.

With a chronological table of the German translations of Timon from 1763 to 1867.

OSCAR BEBER: Thomas Shadwells Bearbeitung des Shakespeareschen 'Timon of Athens'. Diss. Rostock, 1897. (55 S.)

EUGEN KILIAN: 'Timon von Athen' auf der heutigen Bühne. In: Sh. Jb. Jg. 49, 1913, S. 122–36.

STANLEY T. WILLIAMS: Some versions of Timon of Athens on the stage. In: Mod. Phil., vol. 18, 1920, pp. 269–85.

CYMBELINE

Cp. also in particular the general surveys on Shakespeare, pp. 27–29, the critical editions, pp. 53–58, and the criticism, pp. 141–145.

(1) THE TEXT

The tragedie of Cymbeline. Reprinted from the first folio, 1623, with collations of the second, third and fourth folios, by w. j. craig. London, 1883. (145 pp.) = Publ. New Shaksp. Soc.

K. ELZE: A letter to C. M. Ingleby, Esq., containing notes and conjectural emendations on Shakespeare's 'Cymbeline'. In: Anglia, Bd. 8, 1885, S. 263–97.

LEON KELLNER: Cymbeline. Eine textkritische Studie. In: Anglica. Festschr. f. Alois Brandl, Bd. 2, S. 150–72. Leipzig, 1925 = Palaestra 148.

(2) LITERARY GENESIS

W. G. BOSWELL-STONE: Shakspere's Holinshed. London, 1907², pp. 6–18.

BOCCACCIO: The story of Ginevra (Ninth tale of the second day). English translation in: A New Var. Ed. (H. H. FURNESS): Cymbeline. Philadelphia, 1913, pp. 455–69.

B. LEONHARDT: Über die Quellen Cymbelines. In: Anglia, Bd. 6, 1883, S. 1–45.

S. LEVY: Eine neue Quelle zu Shakespeares Cymbeline. In: Anglia, Bd. 7, 1884, S. 120–7.
The author adds as source Boccaccio's 8th tale of the 2nd day.

B. LEONHARDT: Über Beziehungen von Beaumont und Fletcher's Philaster, or, Love lies a-bleeding zu Shakespeares Hamlet und Cymbeline. In: Anglia, Bd. 8, 1885, S. 424–47.

R. W. BOODLE: Die Quelle zu Cymbeline und eventuell zum Sturm. In: Sh. Jb. Jg. 23, 1888, S. 344–7.

R. OHLE: Shakespeares Cymbeline und seine romanischen Vorläufer. Diss. Leipzig, 1890. (60 S.)

HERMANN REICH: Zur Quelle des 'Cymbeline'. In: Sh. Jb. Jg. 41, 1905, S. 177–81.
Proposes 'The Golden Ass' of Apuleius as source.

ALOIS BRANDL: Imogen auf den Aran-Inseln. In: Sh. Jb. Jg. 53, 1917, S. 13–34.

PAUL REYHER: La date de 'Cymbeline'. In: Rev. anglo-amér., vol. 2, 1924–5, pp. 428–30.
Play dated between July and end of 1610.

ELISE RICHTER: Juan Timoneda und das Imogen-Portia-Motiv. In: Sh. Jb. Jg. 64, N.F. Bd. 5, 1928, S. 141–58.
Refers to the 15th patraña of Timoneda's 'El Patrañuelo'.

(3) DRAMATIC ART

WILLIAM W. LAWRENCE: The wager in Cymbeline. In: PMLA., vol. 35, N.S. vol. 28, 1920, pp. 391–430.

(4) SUBSEQUENT HISTORY OF THE PLAY

A. LINDNER: Die Einrichtung des Cymbeline für die Bühne. In: Sh. Jb. Jg. 3, 1868, S. 370–82.

Cymbeline in Ungarn. 'Aschenhans', ein ungarisches Volksmärchen, mitgeteilt von ELISABET RONA-SKLAREK. In: Sh. Jb. Jg. 44, 1908, S. 118–25.

FRIEDRICH LÜCKE: Über Bearbeitungen von Shakespeares 'Cymbeline'. Diss. Rostock, 1909. (178 S.) Rev.: Sh. Jb. 46, 1910, S. 192–3, F. Brie.

THE WINTER'S TALE

Cp. also in particular the general surveys on Shakespeare, pp. 27–29, the critical editions, pp. 53–58, and the criticism, pp. 141–145.

(1) THE TEXT

SAMUEL A. TANNENBAUM: Textual and other notes on The Winter's Tale. In: Philol. Quart., vol. 7, 1928.

(2) LITERARY GENESIS

GREENE'S 'Pandosto', or 'Dorastus and Fawnia', being the original of Shakespeare's 'Winter's Tale'. Newly edited by P. G. THOMAS. O.U.P., 1907. (xxx, 148 pp.)=The Shakespeare Classics.

J. CARO: Die historischen Elemente in Shakespeares Sturm und Wintermärchen. In: E. St. Bd. 2, 1879, S. 141–85.

NICOLAUS DELIUS: Greenes Pandosto und Shakespeares Winter's Tale. In: Sh. Jb. Jg. 15, 1880, S. 22–43.

R. BOYLE: Shakespeares Wintermärchen und Sturm. St. Petersburg, 1885. (40 S.) Rev.: E. St. 9, 1886, S. 305–8, M. Koch.

JOHANNES BOLTE: Zur Schlussszene des Wintermärchens. In: Sh. Jb. Jg. 26, 1891, S. 87–90.
A Dutch parallel to Hermione's resuscitation, 1671.

EMIL KOEPPEL: Ein Vorbild für Shaksperes Statue der Hermione. In: Arch. Jg. 50, Bd. 97, 1896, S. 329–32.

HERMANN CONRAD: Das 'Wintermärchen' als Abschluss von Shaksperes Denken und Schaffen. In: Preuss. Jbb. Bd. 130, 1907, S. 1 ff.

JOSEF DE PEROTT: Die Hirtendichtung des Feliciano de Silva und Shakespeares Wintermärchen. In: Arch. Bd. 130, 1913, S. 53–6.

NIELS MØLLER: Shakespeare ved sit arbejde. Særlig i 'Winter's Tale'. In: Edda, Bd. 6, 1916, S. 44–57. Rev.: Sh. Jb. 54, 1918, S. 149, Jantzen.

(3) MISCELLANEOUS TREATISES

KARL ELZE: Alexandrines in The Winter's Tale and King Richard II. Halle, 1882.

F. BOAS: Der Sturm und das Wintermärchen, zwei Shakespearesche Dramen, in ihrer symbolischen Bedeutung. Stettin, 1882.

EDMUND VON LIPPMANN: 'Die Küste von Böhmen.' In: Sh. Jb. Jg. 27, 1892, S. 115–23.

LUDWIG FRÄNKEL: Der Streit um die Küste von Bohemia im Wintermärchen. In: Sh. Jb. Jg. 34, 1898, S. 346–57.

RICHARD KRALIK: Shakespeares Böhmen im Wintermärchen. In: Sh. Jb. Jg. 37, 1901, S. 230–3.

(4) SUBSEQUENT HISTORY OF THE PLAY

W. SCHNEIDER: Über das Verhältnis von David Garricks 'Florizel and Perdita' zu Shakespeares 'The Winter's Tale'. Diss. Halle, 1902. (112 S.)

ERNST LEOPOLD STAHL: Ellen Terry als Hermione. In: Sh. Jb. Jg. 43, 1907, S. 147–54.

H. KRAUSE: Umarbeitungen und Bühneneinrichtungen von Shakespeares 'The Winter's Tale'. Ein Beitrag zur Geschichte der Shakespeare-Dramen auf der Londoner Bühne. Diss. Rostock, 1913. (76 S.)

THE TEMPEST

Cp. also in particular the general surveys on Shakespeare, pp. 27–29, the critical editions, pp. 53–58, and the criticism, pp. 141–145.

(1) THE TEXT

The Tempest. A reduced Dallastype facsimile from the 1st folio (1623) edition and facing each page thereof the modern text as determined by Charles Knight. Introd. by F. J. FURNIVALL. Ed. by FRED. A. HYNDMAN and D. C. DALLAS. London, 1895.

Shakespeare's Tempest nach der Folio von 1623 mit den Varianten der anderen Folios und einer Einleitung hrsg. von ALBRECHT WAGNER. Berlin, 1900. (xxv, 108 S.)=Englische Textbibl., hrsg. von J. Hoops, No. 6. Rev.: Sh. Jb. 37, 1901, S. 259–61, H. Logeman; Bbl. 17, 1906, S. 257–60, Rud. Fischer.

(2) LITERARY GENESIS

For sources see A New Var. Ed. (FURNESS). Philadelphia, 1892. Containing also AYRER: The Fair Sidea (in English translation).

JAKOB AYRER: Dramen. Hrsg. von A. VON KELLER=Bibl. d. Lit. Ver. i. Stuttg. Bd. 76–80. 1865.

K. J. CLEMENT: Shakespeares Sturm historisch beleuchtet. Leipzig, 1846.

KARL ELZE: Die Abfassungszeit des Sturms. In: Sh. Jb. Jg. 7, 1872, S. 29–47.
Estimates 1604 as date of play.

MARCUS LANDAU: Le fonti della 'Tempesta' di W. Shakspeare. In: Nuova Antologia, 1878. Rev.: E. St. 9, 1886, S. 306–8, M. Koch.
Refers to Greene's Alphonsus and demonstrates two historical sources.

J. CARO: Die historischen Elemente in Shakespeares Sturm und Winter-märchen. In: E. St. Bd. 2, 1879, S. 141–85.

R. BOYLE: Shakespeares Wintermärchen und Sturm. St. Petersburg, 1885. Rev.: E. St. 9, 1886, S. 305–8, M. Koch.

R. W. BOODLE: Die Quelle zu Cymbeline und eventuell zum Sturm. In: Sh. Jb. Jg. 23, 1888, S. 344–7.

RICHARD GARNETT: Die Entstehung und Veranlassung von Shakespeares Sturm. In: Sh. Jb. Jg. 35, 1899, S. 166–79.

W. W. NEWELL: Sources of Shakespeare's Tempest. In: Journ. of Amer. Folk-lore, Boston, vol. 16, 1903.

JOSEF DE PEROTT: The probable source of the plot of Shakespeare's 'Tempest'. Worcester, Mass., 1905 = Publ. Clark Univ. Libr., vol. i, no. 8.
Accepts the 'Mirrour of Knighthood', a translation of 'Espejo de principes y caballeros', as source of Tempest.

GREGOR SARRAZIN: Neue italienische Skizzen zu Shakespeare. 7. Die Vertrei-bung des Herzogs Prospero. In: Sh. Jb. Jg. 42, 1906, S. 179–86.

GUSTAV BECKER: Zur Quellenfrage von Shakespeares Sturm. In: Sh. Jb. Jg. 43, 1907, S. 155–68.
Containing the translation of a tale from Antonio de Eslava's Noches de invierno (1610).

JOSEF DE PEROTT: Die Magelonen- und die Sturmfabel. In: Sh. Jb. Jg. 47, 1911, S. 128–31.

JOHN D. REA: A source for the storm in the Tempest. In: Mod. Phil., vol. 17, 1919–20, pp. 279–86.

ERNEST LAW: Shakespeare's Tempest as originally produced at court. London, for the Shakespeare Assoc., 1920. (35 pp.)

W. J. LAWRENCE: The masque in the Tempest. In: Fortn. Rev. 1920, June.

HENRY DAVID GRAY: The sources of the Tempest. In: MLN., vol. 35, 1920, pp. 321–30.

HENRY DAVID GRAY: Some indications that the Tempest was revised. In: Stud. in Phil., vol. 28, 1921, pp. 129–40.

E. K. CHAMBERS: The integrity of 'The Tempest'. In: RESt., vol. 1, 1925, pp. 129–50.
Attributes, in opposition to Robertson, sole authorship to Shakespeare.

A. EICHLER: Shakespeares 'The Tempest' als Hofaufführung. In: Neusprachl. Studien. Festgabe f. Karl Luick zu s. 60. Geb. Marburg, 1925. S. 227–38 = Die Neueren Sprachen, Beiheft 6.

CLARA LONGWORTH-CHAMBRUN: Influences françaises dans la Tempête de Shakespeare. In: Rev. de litt. comp. 1925, pp. 37–59.

W. VOLLHARDT: Zur Quellenkunde von Shakespeares 'Sturm'. In: Bbl. Jg. 37, 1926, S. 337–42.

ROBERT R. CAWLEY: Shakspere's use of the Voyagers in the Tempest. In: PMLA., vol. 41, 1926, pp. 688–726.

KARL FOUQUET: Jakob Ayrers 'Sidea', Shakespeares Tempest und das Märchen. Marburg, 1929. (115 S.)=Beitr. z. dt. Lit. wiss., hrsg. von E. Elster, No. 32. Rev.: Sh. Jb. 65, 1929, S. 194–5, W. Keller; Bbl. 51, 1930, S. 26–7, Hel. Richter.

(3) EXPLANATORY LITERATURE

JOHANNES MEISSNER: Aphorismen über Shakespeares Sturm. In: Sh. Jb. Jg. 5, 1870, S. 183–226.

JOHANNES MEISSNER: Untersuchungen über Shakespeares 'Sturm'. Dessau, 1872. (vii, 151 S.)

C. C. HENSE: Das Antike in Shakespeares Drama 'Der Sturm'. In: Sh. Jb. Jg. 15, 1880, S. 129–55.

OLIVER COOPER: Explanatory notes on Shakespeare's 'Tempest'. London, 1889.

PAUL RODEN: Shakespeares Sturm. Ein Kulturbild. Leipzig o. J. (62 S.)

RICHARD GARNETT: 'The still-vexed Bermoothes' in 'The Tempest.' In: Sh. Jb. Jg. 40, 1904, S. 231.

KONRAD MEIER: Über Shakespeares Sturm. I, II, III. In: N. Spr. Bd. 15, 1907–8, S. 193–210, 271–9 und 321–36.

ALLAN H. GILBERT: The Tempest, parallelism in characters and situations. In: JEGPh., vol. 14, 1915, pp. 63–74.

ERICH ISRAEL: Die Grundzüge von Shakespeares Weltanschauung in seinem Kulturdrama 'Der Sturm'. Diss. Marburg, 1917. (86 S.) Rev.: Sh. Jb. 55, 1919, S. 156–7, W. Keller.

LEON KELLNER: Einige grundsätzliche Bemerkungen zu Shakespeares Sturm. In: E. St. Bd. 62, 1927, S. 170–86.
Concerning the artistic technique of Shakespeare's style in the Tempest.

(4) SYMBOLISM

F. BOAS: Der Sturm und das Wintermärchen, zwei Shakespearesche Dramen in ihrer symbolischen Bedeutung. Stettin, 1882.

(5) SUBSEQUENT HISTORY OF THE PLAY

HERMANN GRIMM: Shakespeares Sturm in der Bearbeitung von Dryden und Davenant. In the same author's Fünfzehn Essays, 1875, S. 183–224.

ERNEST RENAN: Caliban, suite de la Tempête, drame philosophique. Paris, 1878. English translation by ELEANOR G. VICKERY in: New York Shakespeare Soc. Papers and Publ., 1896.

JOHN DRYDEN and WILLIAM DAVENANT: The Tempest, or, the Enchanted Island. Reprint in: A New Var. Ed., ed. H. H. Furness. The Tempest. 1892, pp. 389-449.

O. WITT: The Tempest, or the Enchanted Island, a comedy by John Dryden, 1670, The Sea-Voyage, a comedy by Beaumont and Fletcher, 1647, The Goblins' Tragi-Comedy by Sir John Suckling, 1646, in ihrem Verhältnis zu Shakespeares Tempest und den übrigen Quellen. Diss. Rostock, 1899. (138 S.)

N. KRASSNIG: Fletcher's Sea-Voyage and Shakespeare's Tempest. Progr. Marburg, 1900. (17 S.)

WILLIAM J. LAWRENCE: Did Thomas Shadwell write an opera on 'The Tempest'? In his The Elizabethan playhouse and other studies. 1st ser. Stratford, 1912, pp. 193-206.

WERNER DEETJEN: Immermann's Bearbeitung des 'Sturms' als Operntext. In: Sh. Jb. Jg. 57, 1921, S. 65-76.

Shakespearian adaptations. The Tempest, The Mock Tempest, and King Lear. With an introd. and notes by MONTAGUE SUMMERS. London, 1922. (cviii, 282 pp.)

WERNER DEETJEN: Der 'Sturm' als Operntext bearbeitet von Einsiedel und Gotter. In: Sh. Jb. Jg. 64, N.F. Bd. 5, 1928, S. 77-89.

KING HENRY VIII

Cp. also in particular the general surveys on Shakespeare, pp. 27-29, the critical editions, pp. 53-58, and the criticism, pp. 141-145

(I) LITERARY GENESIS

W. G. BOSWELL-STONE: Shakespeare's Holinshed. London, 1907², pp. 424-507.

KARL ELZE: Zu Heinrich VIII. In: Sh. Jb. Jg. 9, 1874, S. 55-86.

JAMES SPEDDING: On the several shares of Shakspere and Fletcher in the play of Henry VIII. In: Trans. New Shaksp. Soc., 1874, Appendix.

NICOLAUS DELIUS: Fletchers angebliche Beteiligung an Shakespeares King Henry VIII. In: Sh. Jb. Jg. 14, 1879, S. 180-206.
Attributes sole authorship to Shakespeare.

W. ZEITLIN: Shakespeares 'King Henry VIII' und Rowleys 'When you see me, you know me'. In: Anglia, Bd. 4, 1881, S. 73-96.
Considers them as competitive plays.

ROBERT BOYLE: Über die Echtheit Heinrichs VIII. von Shakespeare. St. Petersburg, 1884.

ROBERT BOYLE: 'King Henry VIII.' An investigation into the origin and authorship of the play. In: Trans. New Shaksp. Soc., 1880–6, xxi.

HERMANN CONRAD: Henry VIII, Fletchers Werk, überarbeitet von Shakespeare. In: E. St. Bd. 52, 1918, S. 204–64.
[Reprinted from posthumous papers.]

H. DUGDALE SYKES: King Henry VIII. In his Sidelights on Shakespeare. Stratford, 1919, pp. 18–47.
Attributes the play to Massinger and Fletcher.

A. H. CRUICKSHANK: Philip Massinger. Oxford, 1920.
Denies Massinger any participation in H. VIII.

KARL EGE: Shakespeares Anteil an 'Heinrich VIII.' MS. Diss. Münster, 1922. (23 S.) Also in: Sh. Jb. Jg. 58, 1922, S. 99–119.
Rejects Fletcher's participation for stylistic reasons, but assumes double authorship.

MARJORIE H. NICHOLSON: The authorship of Henry VIII. In: PMLA., vol. 37, 1922, pp. 484–502.
Attributes authorship to Shakespeare and Fletcher.

———

FELIX LIEBERMANN: Shakespeares Anschauung von Staat, Gesellschaft und Kirche in Heinrich VIII. In: Beitr. z. Lit.- und Theatergeschichte, Ludwig Geiger z. 70. Geb. Berlin, 1918, S. 13 seq. Rev.: Sh. Jb. 55, 1919, S. 158–9, W. Keller.

(2) SUBSEQUENT HISTORY OF THE PLAY

WOLFGANG VON WURZBACH: Shakespeares 'Heinrich VIII.' und Calderóns 'La cisma de Inglaterra'. In: Sh. Jb. Jg. 32, 1896, S. 190–211.
Considers Calderón to have been influenced by Shakespeare's play.

PERICLES

Cp. also in particular the general surveys on Shakespeare, pp. 27–29, the critical editions, pp. 53–58, and the criticism, pp. 141–145.

(1) THE TEXT

The Shakspere quarto facsimiles: Pericles (1609).
> No. 21 = The earlier Quarto, 1609 ⎫ With introduction by
> No. 22 = The later Quarto, 1609 ⎭   P. Z. ROUND

Shakespeare's Pericles. Being a reproduction in facsimile of the 1st edition, 1609, from the copy in the Malone Collection in the Bodleian library. With introduction and bibliography by SIDNEY LEE. Oxford, 1905. (48 pp. and facs.)

KARL ELZE: Notes and conjectural emendations on 'Antony and Cleopatra' and 'Pericles'. In: E. St. Bd. 9, 1886, S. 267–90.

(2) LITERARY GENESIS

COLLIER-HAZLITT: Shakespeare's library. London, 1875. Reprint of the sources:
1. GOWER: Apollonius of Tyre. From: Confessio amantis, ll. 281–2018.
2. LAURENCE TWINE: The patterne of painfulle adventures of Apollonius of Tyre.

NICOLAUS DELIUS: Über Shakespeares Pericles, Prince of Tyre. In: Sh. Jb. Jg. 3, 1868, S. 175–204.
Considers George Wilkins to be the original author.

F. G. FLEAY: On the play of Pericles. In: Trans. New Shaksp. Soc., 1874, pp. 195 seq.
Only the last three acts attributed to Shakespeare.

ROBERT BOYLE: Pericles. In: E. St. Bd. 5, 1882, S. 363–9.
Boyle assumes treble authorship: Shakespeare, Wilkins, and Rowley.

ROBERT BOYLE: On Wilkins's share in the play called Shakspere's Pericles. In: Trans. New Shaksp. Soc., 1882, pp. 321 seq.

ALBERT H. SMYTH: Shakespeare's Pericles and Apollonius of Tyre. A study of comparative literature. Philadelphia, 1898. (112 pp.) Rev.: Sh. Jb. 35, 1899, S. 338–9, W. Keller; Bbl. 10, 1900, S. 115, Singer.
Inquiry into the connexion between the drama and Twine's tale.

DANIEL L. THOMAS: On the play Pericles. In: E. St. Bd. 39, 1908, S. 210–39.
Attributes original authorship to Thomas Heywood.

HARRY T. BAKER: The relation of Shakspere's Pericles to George Wilkins's novel 'The painfull adventures of Pericles, Prince of Tyre'. In: PMLA., vol. 23, N.S. vol. 16, 1908, pp. 100–18.

ROBERT MAX GARRETT: Gower in 'Pericles'. In: Sh. Jb. Jg. 48, 1912, S. 13–20.

T. S. GRAVES: On the date and significance of Pericles. In: Mod. Phil., vol. 13, 1915–16, pp. 545–56.

KAROLINA STEINHÄUSER: Die neueren Anschauungen über die Echtheit von Shakespeares Pericles. Diss. Würzburg, 1917. Enlarged, with an appendix on stylistic criteria: Heidelberg, 1918. (iv, 136 S.)=Würzburger Beitr. z. engl. Lit. gesch., hrsg. von Jiriczek, No. 4. Rev.: Sh. Jb. 55, 1919, S. 157–8, W. Keller.

H. DUGDALE SYKES: Wilkins and Shakespeare's 'Pericles, Prince of Tyre'. In his Sidelights on Shakespeare. Stratford, 1919, pp. 143–203.

HENRY DAVID GRAY: Heywood's 'Pericles' revised by Shakespeare. In: PMLA., vol. 40, 1925, pp. 507–29. Rev.: Sh. Jb. 63, 1927, S. 225, Beckmann.
Agrees with the opinion of D. L. Thomas.

R. P. COWL: The authorship of 'Pericles', and the date of 'The life and death of Lord Cromwell'. London, 1927. (7 pp.)

(3) SUBSEQUENT HISTORY OF THE PLAY

ALFRED MEISSNER: Shakespeares Seitenstück zum 'Wintermärchen'. In: Sh. Jb. Jg. 17, 1882, S. 282–8.

Thorough revision would make of Pericles an effective stage-play.

Pericles, Fürst von Tyrus. Schauspiel in 5 Aufzügen von Shakespeare. Für die deutsche Bühne frei bearb. von ERNST POSSART. Musik von KARL PERFALL. München, 1883.

Cf. also: ALFRED MEISSNER: Shakespeares 'Pericles, Fürst von Tyrus' auf der Münchener Bühne. In: Sh. Jb. Jg. 18, 1883, S. 209–17.

SHAKESPEARE: Perikles, Fürst von Tyrus. In deutscher Übersetzung von H. STEINITZER. In: Shakespeares sämtliche Werke, hrsg. von L. L. Schücking. Bd. 10. München 1929. (S. 1–106).

III. SHAKESPEARE'S POEMS

Cp. also in particular the general surveys on Shakespeare, pp. 27–29, the critical editions, pp. 53–58, and the criticism, pp. 141–145.

(1) SHAKESPEARE'S POEMS IN GENERAL

(a) ENGLISH EDITIONS

The poems of Shakespeare, edited with an introduction and notes by GEORGE WYNDHAM. London, 1898. (cxlvii, 343 pp.) Rev.: Sh. Jb. 35, 1899, S. 325–6, A. Brandl.

Containing a good introduction and notes.

The poems and sonnets of Shakspere. With an introduction by EDWARD DOWDEN. London, 1903.

Shakespeare's poems and Pericles. Collotype facsimiles, with introductions and bibliographies by SIDNEY LEE, of the earliest editions. 5 vols. O.U.P., 1905. Containing: Ven. (1593), Lucr. (1594), Pilgr. (1599), Sonn. and Compl. (1609), Per. (1609).

(b) GERMAN TRANSLATIONS

William Shakspeares sämtliche Gedichte, übersetzt von E. VON BAUERNFELD und A. SCHUMACHER. Wien, 1827.

William Shakspeares sämtliche Gedichte, im Versmass des Originals übersetzt von E. WAGNER. Königsberg, 1840. (xii, 237 S.)

Shakespeares Gedichte. Deutsch von WILHELM JORDAN. Berlin, 1861. (liii, 422 S.)

Shakespeares Gedichte. Deutsch von KARL SIMROCK. Stuttgart, 1867. (xxvi, 376 S.)

Gedichte von *William Shakespeare*, ins Deutsche übertragen durch A. VON MAUNTZ. Berlin, 1894. (xvi, 362 S.)

(c) TREATISES

HERMANN ISAAC: Wie weit geht die Abhängigkeit Shakespeares von Daniel als Lyriker? Eine Studie zur englischen Renaissancelyrik. In: Sh. Jb. Jg. 17, 1882, S. 165–200.

R. SACHS: Shakespeares Gedichte. In: Sh. Jb. Jg. 25, 1890, S. 132–84.

HANS REIMER: Der Vers in Shakespeares nichtdramatischen Werken. Diss. Bonn, 1908. (60 S.) Rev.: Sh. Jb. 45, 1909, S. 276–7, Fr. Brie.

GEORGE SAINTSBURY: Shakespeare, poems. In: CHEL., vol. 5, 1910, pp. 223–35.
Containing a detailed bibliography.

KARL GROOS und ILSE NETTO: Psychologisch-statistische Untersuchungen über die visuellen Sinneseindrücke in Shakespeares lyrischen und epischen Dichtungen. In: E. St. Bd. 43, 1910, S. 27–51.

HELEN KATE FURNESS: A concordance to Shakespeare's poems, an index to every word therein contained. Philadelphia, 1874. (iv, 422 pp.)

(2) THE SONNETS

For the sonnets the following abbreviations will be used:
Fr. = The friend of Shakespeare.
D.L. = The Dark Lady.
R.P. = The Rival Poet.
Mr. W. H.

(a) ENGLISH EDITIONS

The sonnets of William Shakespeare, edited by EDWARD DOWDEN. London, 1881. (lxii, 251 pp.)
Large critical edition, with introduction, good notes, and critical survey of previous research.

The Shakespeare quarto facsimiles (William Griggs): Shakespeare's sonnets and A lover's complaint. Q 1 (1609). With introd. by THOMAS TYLER. London, 1886. (xxxii, 80 pp.)

Shakespeare's sonnets, edited with notes and introduction by THOMAS TYLER. London, 1890. (xx, 316 pp.) Rev.: Bbl. 1, 1891, S. 193–5, E. R.

Cp. also CHARLOTTE STOPES: Shakespeare's sonnets, edited by Thomas Tyler. In: Sh. Jb. Jg. 25, 1890, S. 185–204.

Shakespeare's sonnets, reconsidered and in part re-arranged, with introductory chapters, notes and a reprint of the original 1609 edition, by SAMUEL BUTLER. London, 1899. (340 pp.) Rev.: Sh. Jb. 38, 1902, S. 266–7, W. Dibelius.
Reproduction in facsimile of Q 1609.

The sonnets of Shakespeare, with an introduction and notes by H. C. BEECHING. Boston & London, 1904. (lxvii, 145 pp.) Rev.: Sh. Jb. 42, 1906, S. 272, A. Brandl.
Advocates the Pembroke theory.

Shakespeare's sonnets. With introduction and notes by C. C. STOPES. London, 1904. (lvi, 242 pp.) Rev.: Sh. Jb. 41, 1905, S. 245–6, Moorman.

Fr.=Southampton, D. L.=Mrs. Jacqueline Field, Mr. W. H.=Sir William Harvey.

Shakespeare's sonnets, being a reproduction in facsimile of the first edition, 1609. With introduction and bibliography by SIDNEY LEE. Oxford, 1905. (71 pp. and facs.)

Shakespeare's sonnets and A lover's complaint. An exact reprint of the first edition of 1609, with an introduction by W. H. HADOW. O.U.P., 1907. (xxiv, 104 pp.)=Tudor and Stuart Library. Rev.: Sh. Jb. 44, 1908, S. 358–9, M. Förster; Bbl. 19, 1908, S. 144, K. Lincke.

Fr.=Pembroke, D. L.=Mary Fitton.

The sonnets of Shakespeare, from the quarto of 1609 with variorum readings and commentary. Edited by RAYMOND M. ALDEN. Boston & New York, 1916. (xix, 542 pp.) Rev.: E. St. 57, 1923, S. 298–9.

Reliable edition with very detailed bibliography of text-editions, translations, and commentaries.

The sonnets of Shakespeare, edited from the quarto of 1609, with introduction and commentary by T. G. TUCKER. Cambridge, 1924. (lxxxviii, 239 pp.)

Containing valuable linguistic commentary.

Shakespeare's sonnets. A facsimile, with a note by A. T. B. London, 1925.

A facsimile of Q 1 (1609) of the Grenville copy in the Brit. Mus.

(b) GERMAN TRANSLATIONS

Shakespeares Sonette, übersetzt von KARL LACHMANN. Berlin, 1820. (153 S.)

Cp. also A. LEITZMANN: Karl Lachmann als Shakespeare-Übersetzer. In: Sh. Jb. 56, 1920, S. 73–89.

William Shakespeares Sonette in deutscher Nachbildung von FRIEDRICH BODENSTEDT. Berlin, 1862. (246 S.)

Shakespeares Sonette, übersetzt von HERMANN FREIHERR VON FRIESEN. Dresden, 1869. (154 S.)

Shaksperes Sonette, deutsch von BENNO TSCHISCHWITZ. Halle, 1870. (xviii, 156 S.)

Shakespeares Sonette, übersetzt von OTTO GILDEMEISTER. Mit Einleitung und Anmerkungen. Leipzig, 1871. (xxxii, 181 S.)

Die Sonette von William Shakespeare ins Deutsche übertragen von ALEXANDER NEIDHARDT. Leipzig, 1902². (199 S.) Rev.: Sh. Jb. 40, 1904, S. 295–8, Meyerfeld.

Shakespeares Sonette, übersetzt von MAX J. WOLFF. Berlin, 1903. (xix, 162 S.) Rev.: Sh. Jb. 40, 1904, S. 298, Meyerfeld.

Shakespeare-Sonette. Umdichtung von STEPHAN GEORGE. Berlin, 1909. (160 S.) Rev.: Sh. Jb. 46, 1910, S. 266–8, M. Gothein; Arch. 122, 1909, S. 212, A. Brandl; Bbl. 22, 1911, S. 242–6, L. Petry.

Shakespeares Sonette, übertragen von EDUARD SÄNGER. Jubiläumsausgabe, 1609–1909. Leipzig, 1909. (82 S.) 1914². Rev.: Sh. Jb. 46, 1910, S. 266–8, M. Gothein; Bbl. 22, 1911, S. 242–6, L. Petry.

Shakespeares Sonette, erläutert von ALOIS BRANDL, übersetzt von LUDWIG FULDA. Stuttgart & Berlin, 1913. (lv, 156 S.) Rev.: Sh. Jb. 50, 1914, S. 182–4, M. Förster; E. St. 49, 1915–16, S. 161, M. J. Wolff; Bbl. 37, 1926, S. 271–86, E. Deckner; Die Geisteswissenschaften, Jg. 1, 1913–14, S. 787–92, L. L. Schücking (Alois Brandls neuste Shakespeare-Forschungen.)

Detailed introduction: Fr.=Southampton, D. L.=uncertain, R. P.=Chapman, Mr. W. H. =(possibly) Sir William Harvey.

Shakespeares Sonette, ins Deutsche übertragen von FRIEDRICH HUCH. München, 1921. (44 S.) Rev.: Sh. Jb. 58, 1922, S. 126, W. Keller.

Only 30 sonnets.

Shakespeares Sonette, ins Deutsche übertragen von THERESE ROBINSON. In: Shakespeares sämtliche Werke, hrsg. von L. L. Schücking. Bd. 10. München 1929. (S. 107–153).

Shakespeares Sonette. Ins Deutsche übertragen und hrsg. von KARL HAUER. Graz, 1929. (91 S.) Rev.: Bbl. 41, 1930, S. 136–40, E. Groth.

(c) TREATISES

JAMES BOADEN: On the sonnets of Shakespeare, identifying the person to whom they were addressed and elucidating several points in the poet's history. London, 1837. (iv, 62 pp.)

Fr.=Lord Pembroke.

NICOLAUS DELIUS: Über Shakespeares Sonette. Ein Sendschreiben an Friedrich Bodenstedt. In: Sh. Jb. Jg. 1, 1865, S. 18–56.

Denies autobiographical value.

GERALD MASSEY: Shakespeare's sonnets, never before interpreted, his private friends identified, together with a recovered likeness of himself. London, 1866. (xii, 604 pp.)

HERMANN FREIHERR VON FRIESEN: Über Shakespeares Sonette. In: Sh. Jb. Jg. 4, 1869, S. 94–120.

HERMANN ISAAC: Zu den Sonetten Shakspéres. In: Arch. Bd. 59, 1878, S. 155–204 und 241–72; Bd. 60, 1878, S. 33–64; Bd. 61, 1879, S. 177–200 und 393–426; Bd. 62, 1879, S. 1–30 und 129–72.

Theory of two sonnet-periods based on parallel passages in dramas.

W. HERTZBERG: Eine griechische Quelle zu Shakespeares Sonetten. In: Sh. Jb. Jg. 13, 1878, S. 158–62.

A Greek epigram by Scholasticus Marianus as source of Son. 153 and 154. M. J. Wolff points to an Italian translation (Sh. Jb. 47, 1911, S. 191–2).

E. STENGEL: Bilden die ersten 126 Sonette Shakespeares einen Sonettzyklus, und welches ist die ursprüngliche Reihenfolge derselben? In: E. St. Bd. 4, 1881, S. 1–34.

FRITZ KRAUSS: Die Schwarze Schöne der Shakespeare-Sonette. In: Sh. Jb. Jg. 16, 1881, S. 144–212.
D. L.=Lady Rich, Sidney's Stella.

HERMANN ISAAC: Die Sonett-Periode in Shakespeares Leben. In: Sh. Jb. Jg. 19, 1884, S. 176–264.
Points out 41 parallel passages in the dramas and uses them for chronological purposes.

F. A. LEO: Hilfsmittel bei Untersuchungen über Shakespeares Sonette. In: Sh. Jb. Jg. 23, 1888, S. 304–17.

ALFRED VON MAUNTZ: Shakespeares lyrische Gedichte. In: Sh. Jb. Jg. 28, 1893, S. 273–331.
Deals chiefly with the sonnets.

GREGOR SARRAZIN: Shakespeares Lehrjahre. Eine literarhistorische Studie. Weimar, 1897.
Fr.=Southampton, D. L.=Italian.

HERMANN CONRAD: Shaksperes Selbstbekenntnisse. Hamlet und sein Urbild. Stuttgart, 1897. (321 S.) Rev.: E. St. 25, 1898, S. 430–8, G. Sarrazin; Bbl. 8, 1898, S. 227–31, Ph. Wagner.
Fr.=The Earl of Essex (who is also the original of Hamlet).

WILLIAM ARCHER: Shakespeare's sonnets. In: Fortn. Rev., vol. 68, 1897, pp. 817 seq.
Fr.=Pembroke.

ALFRED VON MAUNTZ: Einige Glossen zu Shakespeares Sonett 121. In: Anglia, Bd. 19, 1897, S. 291–6.

SIDNEY LEE: Shakespeare and the Earl of Pembroke. In: Fortn. Rev., vol. 69, 1898, pp. 210–23.

SIDNEY LEE: A life of William Shakespeare. London, 1898[1].
Fr.=Southampton, D. L.=unknown. Points out the conventional character of the sonnets and attaches accordingly little autobiographical value to them.

THOMAS TYLER: The Herbert-Fitton theory of Shakespeare's sonnets. A reply. London, 1898. (23 pp.)
Fr.=Pembroke, D. L.=Mary Fitton. Defends his opinion in opposition to Sidney Lee.

AUGUSTIN FILON: Les sonnets de Shakespeare. In: RDM. 71, 1901, pp. 795–830.

ARTHUR ACHESON: Shakespeare and the rival poet. Displaying Shakespeare as a satirist and proving the identity of the patron and the rival of the sonnets. London & New York, 1903. (viii, 360 pp.)
Fr.=Southampton, R. P.=Chapman.

C. F. MCCLUMPHA: Shakespeare's sonnets and Romeo and Juliet. In: Sh. Jb. Jg. 40, 1904, S. 187–203.
Shows parallel passages.

GREGOR SARRAZIN: Aus Shakespeares Meisterwerkstatt. Stilgeschichtliche Studien. Berlin, 1906. (vii, 226 S.)
Detailed inquiry into style of Sonnets.

SIDNEY LEE: Ovid and Shakespeare's sonnets. In: Quart. Rev., vol. 210, 1909, pp. 455–76.

ERNEST SUTHERLAND BATES: The sincerity of Shakespeare's sonnets. In: Mod. Phil., vol. 8, 1910–11, pp. 87–106.

J. E. G. DE MONTMORENCY: The 'other poet' of Shakespeare's sonnets. In: Contemp. Rev., vol. 101, 1912, pp. 885–9.
R.P.=Spenser.

ARTHUR ACHESON: Mistress Davenant, the dark lady of Shakespeare's sonnets. Demonstrating the identity of the dark lady of the sonnets, and the authorship and satirical intention of Willobie his Avisa. With a reprint of Willobie his Avisa (in part), Penelope's Complaint, An elegy, Constant Susanna, Queen Dido, Pyramus and Thisbe, The Shepherd's Slumber, and sundry other poems by the same author. London, 1913. (v, 332 pp.) Rev.: Sh. Jb. 50, 1914, S. 201–5, M. Förster.
D. L.=Mrs. Davenant, the hostess of the Crown Inn at Oxford.

PAUL ROEDDER: Shakespeares Sonette im Lichte der neueren Forschung. Progr. Gollnow, 1913. (20 S.)

RAYMOND M. ALDEN: The quarto arrangement of Shakespeare's sonnets. In: Anniversary papers by colleagues and pupils of G. L. Kittredge. Boston, 1913, pp. 279–88. Rev.: Sh. Jb. 51, S. 247, A. Brandl.

LORENZ MORSBACH: Die Sonette Shakespeares im Lichte der Überlieferung. In: Nachr. Ges. Wiss. Göttingen, phil.-histor. Kl. 1915, S. 137–66. Rev.: Sh. Jb. 53, 1917, S. 203–4, Grabau; E. St. 50, 1916, S. 162–3, M. J. Wolff.

HENRY DAVID GRAY: The arrangement and the date of Shakespeare's sonnets. In: PMLA., vol. 30, NS. vol. 23, 1915, pp. 629–44.

MAX J. WOLFF: Petrarkismus und Antipetrarkismus in Shakespeares Sonetten. In: E. St. Bd. 49, 1915–16, S. 161–89. Rev.: Sh. Jb. 53, 1917, S. 202–3, Grabau.
Demonstrates the Petrarchian models for the main characteristics of Shakespeare's sonnets. Important essay.

ALBERT WIETFELD: Die Bildersprache in Shakespeares Sonetten. Diss. Göttingen, 1914. (xii, 62 S.) Enlarged in: Stud. z. engl. Phil., hrsg. von L. Morsbach, H. 54. Halle, 1916. (ix, 132 S.) Rev.: Sh. Jb. 55, 1919, S. 159–61, W. Keller; Bbl. 28, 1917, S. 257–9, L. Kellner.

RAYMOND M. ALDEN: The 1640 text of Shakespeare's sonnets. In: Mod. Phil., vol. 14, 1916–17, pp. 17–30.

MAX J. WOLFF: Shakespeare und der Petrarkismus. In: N. Spr. Bd. 28, 1921, S. 193–203.

HUBERT ORD: Chaucer and the rival poet in Shakespeare's sonnets. A new theory. London, 1921. (63 pp.)

ARTHUR ACHESON: Shakespeare's sonnet story, 1592–8. With an appendix, including a monograph on 'The Crosse Inn and the Tavern of Oxford', by E. Thurlow Leeds. London, 1922. (xxxii, 676 pp.)

D. L.=Mrs. Davenant, R. P.=Chapman.

MATS REDIN: The friend in Shakespeare's sonnets. In: E. St. Bd. 56, 1922, S. 390–407.

H. T. S. FORREST: The five authors of Shakespeare's sonnets. London, 1924.

J. A. FORT: The two dated sonnets of Shakespeare. [Nos. 104 and 107.] O.U.P., 1924. (47 pp.) Rev.: Bbl. 36, 1925, S. 367–72, E. Deckner.

RUDOLF FISCHER: Shakespeares Sonette (Gruppierung, Kunstform). Hrsg. von K. BRUNNER. Wien, 1925. (vi, 182 S.)=Wiener Beitr. z. engl. Phil., hrsg. von Karl Luick, H. 53. Rev.: E. St. 63, 1928, S. 110–12, M. J. Wolff; Bbl. 39, 1928, S. 102–8, J. Hedbavny; RESt. 2, 1926, pp. 350–4.

The classification of the Sonnets on a psychological basis and investigation of the various Sonnets according to their artistic form.

DENYS BRAY: The original order of Shakespeare's sonnets. London, 1925. (xiv, 130 pp.) Rev.: Sh. Jb. 63, 1927, S. 215–17, O. Reinecke; Bbl. 39, 1928, S. 99–102, Marschall.

Rearrangement of the Sonnets according to rhyme-links and according to meaning.

EDUARD SIEVERS: Shakespeares Anteil am King Lear. Eine schallanalytische Untersuchung. In: Anglica. Alois Brandl z. 70. Geb. Bd. 2. Leipzig, 1925. =Palaestra 148.

Containing pp. 203–6, a phono-analytical inquiry into Shakespeare's non-dramatic works. Attributes Sonnets to two authors.

JOHN M. ROBERTSON: The problems of the Shakespeare sonnets. London, 1926. (xii, 291 pp.) Rev.: Sh. Jb. 64, 1928, S. 197–8, W. Keller; Rev. anglo-amér. 5, 1928, pp. 260–2, Ch.-M. Garnier; Engl. Studies 10, 1928, pp. 22–6, M. Praz; MLR. 22, 1927, pp. 330–3, A. Nicoll.

Attributes only part-authorship to Shakespeare. Survey of previous solutions of the Sonnet problems.

J. A. FORT: Thorpe's text of Shakespeare's sonnets. In: RESt., vol. 2, 1926, pp. 439–45. Rev.: Sh. Jb. 63, 1927, S. 225–6, Beckmann.

Investigation into the arrangement of the Sonnets.

W. MARSCHALL: Aus Shakespeares poetischem Briefwechsel. Heidelberg, 1926. (50 S.) Rev.: Bbl. 38, 1927, S. 248–53, E. Deckner.

Shakespeare's Sonnets=poetic correspondence between Bacon and Rutland.

ELIZABETH BECKWITH: On the chronology of Shakespeare's sonnets. In: JEGPh., vol. 25, 1926, pp. 227–42. Rev.: Sh. Jb. 63, 1927, S. 225, Beckmann.

J. A. FORT: The story contained in the 2nd series of Shakespeare's sonnets. In: RESt., vol. 3, 1927, pp. 406–14.

DENIS BRAY: The art-form of the Elizabethan sonnet sequence and Shakespeare's sonnets. In: Sh. Jb. Jg. 63, 1927, S. 159–82.

THEODOR SPIRA: Shakespeares Sonette im Zusammenhang seines Werkes. Königsberg, 1929. (47 S.)= Schriften d. Kgl. Dt. Ges. zu Königsberg, H. 1.

J. A. FORT: The date of Shakespeare's 107th sonnet. In: Libr., vol. 9, 1929, pp. 381–4.

J. A. FORT: A time-scheme for Shakespeare's sonnets. London, 1929.
Considers the arrangement in Q 1609 to be chronologically correct.

(3) SHAKESPEARE'S EPIC POEMS

(a) GENERAL TREATISES

ALOIS WÜRZNER: Die Orthographie der ersten Quarto-Ausgaben von Shakespeares 'Venus and Adonis' und 'Lucrece'. Progr. Wien, 1887. (19 S.) Rev.: Bbl. 5, 1895, S. 7, L. Proescholdt.

BENNO TSCHISCHWITZ: Über die Stellung der epischen Dichtungen Shakespeares in der englischen Literatur. In: Sh. Jb. Jg. 8, 1873, S. 32–45.

WILHELM MARSCHALL: Shakespeares Orthographie. In: Anglia, Bd. 51, 1927, S. 307–22.
Tries to prove that the orthography changes in Ven. l. 1027 and that the new method continues in Lucr.

(b) VENUS AND ADONIS

The Shakespeare quarto facsimiles (William Griggs): Shakespeare's Venus and Adonis. Q 1 (1593). With introd. by A. SYMONS. London, 1886. (xx, 52 pp.)

Shakespeare's Venus and Adonis, being a reproduction in facsimile of the 1st edition, 1593. With introduction and bibliography by SIDNEY LEE. Oxford, 1905. (75 pp. and facs.)

Venus und Adonis, übersetzt von FERDINAND FREILIGRATH. Düsseldorf, 1849. (73 S.)

Venus und Adonis, deutsch nebst Einleitung von BENNO TSCHISCHWITZ. Halle, 1875.

Shakespeare: Venus and Adonis. Deutsche Übertragung von BRUNO E. WERNER. Leipzig, 1924. (54 S.)

M. DÜRNHÖFER: Shakespeares 'Venus und Adonis' im Verhältnis zu Ovids Metamorphosen und Constables Schäfergesang. Diss. Halle, 1890. (47 S.)

GREGOR SARRAZIN: Die Abfassungszeit von Shakespeares Venus und Adonis. In: E. St. Bd. 19, 1894, S. 352–9.
Between winter 1591–2 and spring 1593.

E. BROHM: Essay on Shakespeare's 'Venus and Adonis'. Progr. Zeitz, 1899. (22 S.)

CARLETON BROWN: Shakespeare and the horse. In: Libr., 3rd ser., vol. 3, 1912, pp. 152–220. Rev.: Bbl. 29, 1918, S. 9–10, B. Fehr.
Study of the sources of the description of the horse.

BRUNO E. WERNER: Venus und Adonis. Beitrag zur stilgeschichtlichen Betrachtung Shakespeares. In: Das Inselschiff 6, 1925, S. 99–114.

(c) THE RAPE OF LUCRECE

The Shakspere quarto facsimiles (William Griggs): Shakespeare's Lucrece. Q I (1594). With foreword by F. J. FURNIVALL. London, 1886. (xxvi, 94 pp.)

Shakespeare's Lucrece, being a reproduction in facsimile of the 1st edition, 1594. With introduction and bibliography by SIDNEY LEE. Oxford, 1905. (56 pp. and facs.)

William Shakespeare: Die Schmach der Lucretia. Deutsch von MAX KAHLEN-BERG. Berlin, 1920. (95 S.) Rev.: Sh. Jb. 57, 1921, S. 93, W. Keller.

W. EWIG: Shakespeares Lucrece. Eine literarhistorische Untersuchung. Diss. Kiel, 1899. (32 S.) Enlarged in: Anglia, Bd. 22, 1899, S. 1–32, 343–63 und 393–455.

A. VORDIECK: Parallelismus zwischen Shakespeares Macbeth und seiner epischen Dichtung Lucrece. Progr. Neisse, 1901. (36 S.)

WILHELM MARSCHALL: Das 'Argument' zu Shakespeares 'Lucrece'. In: Anglia, Bd. 53, 1929, S. 102–22.

(4) SHAKESPEARE'S LYRIC POEMS

(a) A LOVER'S COMPLAINT

The Shakspere quarto facsimiles (William Griggs): Shakespeare's sonnets and A Lover's Complaint. Q I (1609). With introd. by THOMAS TYLER. London, 1886. (xxxii, 80 pp.)

NICOLAUS DELIUS: Shakespeare's A Lover's Complaint. In: Sh. Jb. Jg. 20, 1885, S. 41–53. Also in the same author's Abhandlungen zu Shakespeare. Berlin, 1889.

J. W. MACKAIL: A Lover's Complaint. In: Essays and Studies by Members of the English Association, vol. 3, 1912, pp. 51–70. Rev.: Sh. Jb. 49, 1913, S. 238–9, M. Förster.
Attributes it to the 'rival poet' of the Sonnets.

JOHN M. ROBERTSON: Shakespeare and Chapman. A thesis of Chapman's authorship of 'A Lover's Complaint' and his origination of 'Timon of Athens', with indication of further problems. London, 1917. (302 pp.) Rev.: MLR. 13, 1918, pp. 244–50, H. D. Sykes.

(b) THE PASSIONATE PILGRIM

The Shakspere quarto facsimiles (William Griggs): The Passionate Pilgrim Q I (1599). With introd. by EDWARD DOWDEN. London, 1883.

The Passionate Pilgrim, being a reproduction in facsimile of the 1st edition, 1599. With introduction and bibliography by SIDNEY LEE. Oxford, 1905. (57 pp. and facs.)

A. HÖHNEN: Shakespeare's Passionate Pilgrim. Diss. Jena, 1867. (31 S.)

(c) THE PHOENIX AND THE TURTLE

F. J. FURNIVALL: On Chester's Love's Martyr: Essex is not the turtle-dove of Shakspere's Phoenix and the Turtle. In: Trans. New Shaksp. Soc., 1877–9. Pt. III, pp. 451–5.

ARTHUR H. R. FAIRCHILD: The Phoenix and Turtle. A critical and historical interpretation. In: E. St. Bd. 33, 1904, S. 337–84.

IV. THE SHAKESPEARE APOCRYPHA

Cp. also in particular the general surveys on Shakespeare, pp. 27–29, the critical editions, pp. 53–58, and the criticism, pp. 141–145.

(1) THE SHAKESPEARE APOCRYPHA IN GENERAL

(a) ENGLISH EDITIONS

The doubtful plays of Shakspeare, revised from the original editions by HENRY TYRRELL. London, 1851.

Pseudo-Shakspersche Dramen. Hrsg. von NICOLAUS DELIUS. Elberfeld, 1854–74.

The following plays with short introductions: Edw. III 1854, Arden 1855, Merl. 1856, Muced. 1874, Em 1874.

Doubtful plays of William Shakespeare, ed. by MAX MOLTKE. Leipzig, 1869. (vi, 352 pp.) = Tauchn. Ed. 1041.

Pseudo-Shakespearian plays. Ed. by KARL WARNKE and LUDWIG PROESCHOLDT. Halle, 1883–8.

The following plays with introduction and notes: Em 1883, Merry D. 1884, Edw. III 1886, Merl. 1887, Arden 1888.

Shakespeare's doubtful plays, ed. with an introduction to each play by A. F. HOPKINSON. 3 vols. London, 1891–5.

The Shakespeare Apocrypha. Being a collection of 14 plays which have been ascribed to Shakespeare. Edited by C. F. TUCKER BROOKE. Oxford, 1908. (lvi, 456 pp.) Rev.: Sh. Jb. 45, 1909, S. 410–12, M. Förster; MLR. 5, 1910, pp. 119–20, F. W. Moorman; Bbl. 19, 1908, S. 289–92, E. Koeppel.

Valuable introduction, reprint from the oldest prints with old spelling, variants from the other original editions, and detailed bibliography.

(b) GERMAN TRANSLATIONS

Shakespeare-Vorschule. Hrsg. und mit Vorreden begleitet von LUDWIG TIECK. 2 Bde. Leipzig, 1823, 1829.

Containing: Arden, Em, Merl.

Vier Schauspiele von Shakspeare, übersetzt von LUDWIG TIECK. Stuttgart & Tübingen, 1836.

Containing: Edw. III, Cromw., Oldc., Prod. S.

Shakespeares sämtliche Schauspiele. Supplemente zu allen Ausgaben, übersetzt von H. DÖRING. 2 Bde. Erfurt, 1840.
Containing: Merry D., Merl., Yorksh., Prod. S., Cromw., Arden, Oldc., Em.

Shakespeares Werke. Nachträge. Übersetzt von ERNST ORTLEPP. 4 Bde.
Stuttgart, 1840.
Containing: Prod. S., Cromw., Merl., Oldc., Yorksh., Per., Edw. III, Merry D.,
Locr., Arden.

(c) TREATISES

GISBERT FREIHERR VINCKE: Die zweifelhaften Stücke Shakespeares. In: Sh. Jb.
Jg. 8, 1873, S. 368–76.

KARL ELZE: Notes on Elizabethan dramatists. Halle, 1880.
Deals with nine apocryphal plays.

R. SACHS: Die Shakespeare zugeschriebenen zweifelhaften Stücke. In: Sh. Jb.
Jg. 27, 1892, S. 135–99.

A. F. HOPKINSON: Essays on Shakespeare's doubtful plays. London, 1900.
Reprinted from author's edition, 1891–5.

F. W. MOORMAN: Plays of uncertain authorship attributed to Shakespeare. In:
CHEL., vol. 5, 1910, pp. 236–58.
Containing bibliography.

OTTOMAR PETERSEN: Pseudoshakespearesche Dramen. In: Anglia, Bd. 37,
1913, S. 424–62.

H. DUGDALE SYKES: Sidelights on Shakespeare, being studies of The Two
Noble Kinsmen, Henry VIII, Arden of Feversham, A Yorkshire Tragedy,
The Troublesome Reign of King John, King Leir, Pericles Prince of Tyre.
Stratford-on-Avon, 1919. (xiii, 207 pp.)

(2) THE INDIVIDUAL PLAYS

ARDEN OF FEVERSHAM

Arden of Feversham, a tragedy, reprinted from the edition of 1592. With an
introduction by A. H. BULLEN. London, 1887. (xx, 108 pp.)
With critical introduction.

Arden of Feversham. Edited with a preface, notes and glossary by RONALD
BAYNE. London, 1897 = The Temple Dramatists.

CHARLES CRAWFORD: The authorship of Arden of Feversham. In: Sh. Jb. Jg.
39, 1903, S. 74–86.
Author = Kyd, date of production 1591–2.

WALTHER MIKSCH: Die Verfasserschaft des Arden of Feversham. Ein Beitrag
zur Kydforschung. Diss. Breslau, 1907. (83 S.) Rev.: Sh. Jb. 45, 1909,
S. 277, F. Brie.

H. DUGDALE SYKES: Arden of Feversham. In his Sidelights on Shakespeare.
Stratford, 1919, pp. 48–76.
Also attributes it to Kyd.

MAX J. WOLFF: Zu Arden von Feversham. In: N. Spr. Bd. 35, 1927, S. 424–7.

A play based on the model of the classics, Shakespearian authorship impossible.

LOCRINE

KÖNIG LOKRIN. Ein Trauerspiel in 5 Aufzügen von William Shakespeare. Deutsche Übersetzung mit literar-ästhetischer Einl. und Anm. von ALFRED NEUBNER. Berlin, 1908. (li, 138 S.) = Neue Shakespeare-Bühne, hrsg. von Erich Paetel, IV. Rev.: Sh. Jb. 45, 1909, S. 355, Rud. Fischer; Bbl. 20, 1909, S. 147–52, Ph. Aronstein.

RUDOLF BROTANEK: Plagiate im Locrine. In: Bbl. Bd. 11, 1900, S. 202–7.

Points out the author of Locrine's serious plagiarisms from Spenser's Complaints, noted by L. Tieck in his Shakespeare F 4.

CHARLES CRAWFORD: Spenser, 'Locrine', and 'Selimus'. In: N. & Q., ser. 9, vol. 7, 1901, pp. 61 seq., 101 seq., 142 seq., 203 seq., 261 seq., 324 seq., 384 seq. Rev.: Sh. Jb. 38, 1902, S. 297–8, W. Dibelius.

Affirms the opinion of Tieck-Brotanek.

W. S. GAUD: The authorship of Locrine. In: Mod. Phil., vol. 1, 1903–4, pp. 409–22.

Attributes authorship to Peele.

E. KOEPPEL: 'Locrine' und 'Selimus'. In: Sh. Jb. Jg. 41, 1905, S. 193–200.

TH. ERBE: Die Locrinesage und die Quellen des Pseudo-Shakespeareschen Locrine. Textausgabe mit einer Einleitung (I). Diss. Göttingen, 1904. (72 S.) Also Halle, 1904. (72 S.) = Stud. z. engl. Phil., hrsg. von Morsbach, H. 16. Rev.: Sh. Jb. 42, 1906, S. 239–40, Rud. Fischer.

Cp. also ALGERNON CHARLES SWINBURNE: Locrine. A tragedy. 1887.

KING EDWARD III

King Edward III, edited with a preface, notes and glossary by G. C. MOORE SMITH. London, 1897. (xxii, 128 pp.)

Eduard III., ein Trauerspiel (nach Shakespeare) von CHRISTIAN FELIX WEISSE. Leipzig, 1776.

Eduard III. Trauerspiel in 5 Aufzügen von William Shakespeare. Nach der Übersetzung von Ludwig Tieck frei bearbeitet von AUGUST HAGEN. Leipzig, 1879. (iv, 136 S.)

HERMANN FREIHERR VON FRIESEN: Eduard III., angeblich ein Stück von Shakespeare. In: Sh. Jb. Jg. 2, 1867, S. 64–89.

Refutes Shakespearian authorship.

J. PAYNE COLLIER: King Edward III, a historical play by William Shakespeare. An essay in vindication of Shakespeare's authorship of the play. Maidenhead, 1874.

ALEXANDER TEETGEN: Shakespeare's 'King Edward III' absurdly called and scandalously treated as a 'doubtful play'. An indignation pamphlet. London, 1875. (iv, 52 pp.)

GISBERT FREIHERR VINCKE: König Eduard III.—ein Bühnenstück? In: Sh. Jb. Jg. 14, 1879, S. 304–18.

GUSTAV LIEBAU: König Eduard III. von England und die Gräfin von Salisbury. Dargestellt in ihren Beziehungen nach Geschichte, Sage und Dichtung, unter besond. Berücks. des pseudo-Shakespeareschen Schauspiels 'The Raigne of King Edward III'. Diss. Heidelberg, 1900. (60 S.) 2. Aufl. Berlin, 1901 = Lit.histor. Forsch., hrsg. von Schick und von Waldberg, H.13. Rev.: Sh. Jb. 38, 1902, S. 268–9, W. Keller; Bbl. 15, 1904, S. 299–300, Rud. Fischer.

GUSTAV LIEBAU: König Eduard III. von England im Lichte europäischer Poesie. Heidelberg, 1901. (viii, 100 S.) = Anglist. Forsch., hrsg. von J. Hoops, H. 6. Rev.: Sh. Jb. 38, 1902, S. 269–71, A. L. Stiefel; Bbl. 15, 1904, S. 299–300, Rud. Fischer.

ROBERT METCALF SMITH: Edward III. A study of the authorship of the drama in the light of a new source. In: JEGPh., vol. 10, 1911, pp. 90–104.

S. R. GOLDING: The authorship of 'Edward III'. In: N. & Q., vol. 154, 1928, pp. 313–15.
Probable author = Robert Wilson.

V. ØSTERBERG: The 'Countess-scenes' of 'Edward III.' In: Sh. Jb. Jg. 65, 1929, S. 49–91.

MUCEDORUS

Mucedorus, ein englisches Drama aus Shakespeares Zeit, übersetzt von Ludwig Tieck, hrsg. von JOHANNES BOLTE. Berlin, 1893. (xxxix, 67 S.)

WILHELM WAGNER: Über und zu Mucedorus. Neue Konjekturen zu Mucedorus. In: Sh. Jb. Jg. 11, 1876, S. 56–69 und Jg. 14, 1879, S. 274–84.

KARL ELZE: Nachträgliche Bemerkungen zu 'Mucedorus' und 'Fair Em'. In: Sh. Jb. Jg. 15, 1880, S. 339–52.
Suggested improvements in the text.

KARL ELZE: Last notes on 'Mucedorus'. In: E. St. Bd. 6, 1883, S. 311–21.

E. SOFFÉ: Ist 'Mucedorus' ein Schauspiel Shakespeares? Progr. Brünn, 1887. (11 S.)

W. W. GREG: On the editions of 'Mucedorus'. A study of printers and compositors in the time of Shakespeare. In: Sh. Jb. Jg. 40, 1904, S. 95–108.

SIR JOHN OLDCASTLE

WILHELM BAESKE: Oldcastle-Falstaff in der englischen Literatur bis zu Shakespeare (Teil I: bis zum Beginn der Reformation). Diss. Berlin, 1905. (44 S.) Enlarged: Berlin, 1905. (vi, 119 S.) = Palaestra, Bd. 50. Rev.: Sh. Jb. 43, 1907, S. 274–5, A. K. Potter; MLR. 2, 1907, pp. 72–3, Moore Smith; Bbl. 20, 1909, S. 243–4, Konr. Meier.

THE LIFE AND DEATH OF THOMAS CROMWELL

WILLY STREIT: The Life and Death of Thomas Lord Cromwell. Eine literar-historische Untersuchung. Diss. Jena, 1904. (64 S. und 1 Taf.)

THE LONDON PRODIGAL SON

William Shakespeare: Der Londoner verlorene Sohn. Ein historisches Schauspiel. Nach der Übersetzung von Ludwig Tieck bearbeitet und szenisch ergänzt von E. KAMNITZER. Berlin, 1926. (171 S.)

A YORKSHIRE TRAGEDY

Ein Trauerspiel in Yorkshire von William Shakespeare. Übersetzt und mit Vorwort von ALFRED NEUBNER. Berlin, 1907. (ix, 49 S.) Rev.: Bbl. 20, 1909, S. 147–52, Ph. Aronstein.

———

H. DUGDALE SYKES: The authorship of 'A Yorkshire Tragedy'. In: JEGPh., vol. 16, 1917, pp. 437–53.
Attributes sole or main authorship to George Wilkins.

H. DUGDALE SYKES: A Yorkshire Tragedy. In his Sidelights on Shakespeare. Stratford, 1919, pp. 77–98.

FAIR EM

KARL ELZE: Nachträgliche Bemerkungen zu 'Mucedorus' und 'Fair Em'. In: Sh. Jb. Jg. 15, 1880, S. 339–52.

G. STEINSCHNEIDER: Das pseudo-Shaksperesche Drama Fair Em. Progr. Prossnitz, 1892. (16 S.)

PAUL LOHR: Le Printemps d'Yver und die Quelle zu Fair Em. Diss. München, 1912. (57 S.)=Lit.histor. Forsch., hrsg. von Schick und von Waldberg, H. 49. Rev.: Sh. Jb. 48, 1912, S. 346, M. Förster.

THE TWO NOBLE KINSMEN

The Two Noble Kinsmen. Reprint of the first quarto, 1634, with a collation of the second edition, folio 1679. Ed. by HAROLD LITTLEDALE. Publ. for the New Shakspere Soc., London, 1876. (xiv, 112 pp.)

The Two Noble Kinsmen. Ed. with a preface, notes and glossary by C. H. HERFORD. London, 1897. (xvi, 148 pp.)=The Temple Dramatists.

———

SAMUEL HICKSON: The shares of Shakespeare and Fletcher in 'The Two Noble Kinsmen'. In: Trans. New Shaksp. Soc., 1874, pp. 25*–61*.

W. SPALDING: A letter on Shakespeare's authorship of 'The Two Noble Kinsmen.' In: New Shaksp. Soc., ser. viii, 1876.
Defends Shakespearian collaboration.

NICOLAUS DELIUS: Die angebliche Shakespeare-Fletchersche Autorschaft des Dramas 'The Two Noble Kinsmen'. In: Sh. Jb. Jg. 13, 1878, S. 16–44.
Denies the collaboration of both Shakespeare and Fletcher.

ROBERT BOYLE: Shakespeare und die 'Beiden edlen Vettern'. Eine metrisch-kritische Abhandlung. St. Petersburg, 1880. Also in: E. St. Bd. 4, 1881, S. 34–68.
Makes Massinger's authorship highly probable.

ROBERT BOYLE: On Massinger and 'The Two Noble Kinsmen'. In: Trans. New Shaksp. Soc., 1882, pp. 371–99.

THEODOR BIERFREUND: Palamon og Arcite. En literaturhistorisk undersøgeke som bidrag til Shakespearekritiken. København, 1891. (80 S.) Rev.: E. St. 16, 1892, S. 98–100, E. Kölbing.
Fletcher and Beaumont taken as probable authors.

E. H. OLIPHANT: The works of Beaumont and Fletcher. In: E. St. Bd. 15, 1891, S. 321–60. Includes: The Two Noble Kinsmen, S. 323–6.
Still believes in Shakespeare's collaboration.

A. KRUSENBAUM: Das Verhältnis von Davenants Drama The Rivals zu The Two Noble Kinsmen. Diss. Halle, 1895. (65 S.)

B. LEUSCHNER: Über das Verhältnis von The Two Noble Kinsmen zu Chaucers Knightes Tale. Diss. Halle, 1903. (45 S.)

OTTOMAR PETERSEN: The Two Noble Kinsmen. In: Anglia, Bd. 38, 1914, S. 213–26.

H. DUGDALE SYKES: The authorship of 'The Two Noble Kinsmen'. In: MLR., vol. 11, 1916, pp. 136–48. Also in: Sidelights on Shakespeare. Stratford, 1919, pp. 1–17.
Authorship attributed to Massinger and possibly to Fletcher.

A. H. CRUICKSHANK: Philip Massinger. Oxford, 1920.
Denies Massinger's collaboration.

W. J. LAWRENCE: New light on 'The Two Noble Kinsmen'. In: TLS. July 14, 1921.

A. H. CRUICKSHANK: Massinger and The Two Noble Kinsmen. Oxford, 1922. (32 pp.)
Considers Beaumont and Fletcher as authors of the play, Shakespeare contributed a few scenes and Massinger revised the whole.

KARL EGE: Der Anteil Shakespeares an 'The Two Noble Kinsmen'. In: Sh. Jb. Jg. 59–60, N.F. Bd. 1, 1924, S. 62–85.
Assumes joint authorship of Shakespeare and Fletcher.

E. H. C. OLIPHANT: The plays of Beaumont and Fletcher. An attempt to determine their respective shares and the shares of others. London, 1927. (xviii, 553 pp.)
Attributes a share to Shakespeare.

THE BIRTH OF MERLIN

FRED ALLISON HOWE: The authorship of 'The Birth of Merlin'. In: Mod. Phil., vol. 4, 1906, pp. 193–205.
Defends the authorship of Middleton and Rowley.

WILLIAM WELLS: The Birth of Merlin. In: MLR., vol. 16, 1921, pp. 129–37
Attributes authorship to Beaumont and Fletcher.

THE BOOK OF SIR THOMAS MORE

[Cp. also literature on Shakespeare's handwriting, p. 24, and on Elizabethan palaeography, p. 47.]

Sir Thomas More. A play, now first printed. Ed. by ALEXANDER DYCE. London, 1844. (xxvi, 102 pp.) = Shakespeare Soc. Publ., vol. 23.

Sir Thomas More. Edited with an introduction by A. F. HOPKINSON. London, 1902. (xxiv, 122 pp.) Privately printed.

Sir Thomas More. Edited by J. S. FARMER. London, 1910 = Tudor Facsimile Texts.

The Book of Sir Thomas More. Edited by W. W. GREG = The Malone Soc. Reprints, 1911. (xxxi, 93 pp.) Rev.: Sh. Jb. 48, 1912, S. 342–3, M. Förster.
Very careful edition complete with critical introduction.

RICHARD SIMPSON: Are there any extant MSS. in Shakespeare's handwriting? In: N. & Q., 4th ser., vol. 8, 1871, pp. 1 seq.
The first to attribute the insurrection-scene to Shakespeare.

JAMES SPEDDING: Shakespeare's handwriting. In: N. & Q., 4th ser., vol. 10, 1872, pp. 227 seq.
Joins Simpson on essential points.

LEVIN L. SCHÜCKING: Das Datum des pseudo-shakespeareschen Thomas More. In: E. St. Bd. 46, 1912–13, S. 228–51.
Probably 1604–5.

W. W. GREG: Autograph plays by Anthony Munday. In: MLR., vol. 8, 1913, pp. 89–90.
Considers Munday to be writer of the 'Addition'.

SIR EDWARD M. THOMPSON: Shakespeare's handwriting. A study. Oxford, 1916. (63 pp.) Rev.: Libr., 3rd ser., vol. 8, 1917, pp. 97–100, J. A. Herbert; Sh. Jb. 55, 1919, S. 183–4, A. Schröer; Bbl. 35, 1924, S. 97–102, B. Fehr.
The 'Addition' in Shakespeare's own handwriting.

PERCY SIMPSON: The play of 'Sir Thomas More', and Shakespeare's hand in it. In: Libr., 3rd ser., vol. 8, 1917, pp. 79–96.

E. H. C. OLIPHANT: Sir Thomas More. In: JEGPh., vol. 18, 1919, pp. 226–35.

W. J. LAWRENCE: Was 'Sir Thomas More' ever acted? In: TLS. July 1, 1920.

Shakespeare's hand in 'The play of Sir Thomas More'. Papers by A. W. POLLARD, W. W. GREG, E. MAUNDE THOMPSON, J. DOVER WILSON and R. W. CHAMBERS. With the text of the Ill May Day Scenes, ed. by W. W. GREG. Cambridge, 1923. (viii, 243 pp. and 7 plates.) Rev.: E. St. 59, S. 444–50, Ph. Aronstein; Bbl. 35, 1924, S. 97–102, B. Fehr.

SIR GEORGE GREENWOOD: The Shakespeare signatures and 'Sir Thomas More'. London, 1924. (xvii, 112 pp.)
Opposes Thompson's thesis.

LEVIN L. SCHÜCKING: Shakespeare and Sir Thomas More. In: RESt., vol. 1, 1925, pp. 40–59.

Opposes Shakespeare's authorship of the insurrection-scene on grounds of content and language. Date: 1601–2.

A. W. POLLARD: Verse tests and the date of 'Sir Thomas More'. In: RESt., vol. 1, 1925, pp. 441–3.

G. B. HARRISON: The date of 'Sir Thomas More'. In: RESt., vol. 1, 1925, pp. 337–9.

SAMUEL A. TANNENBAUM: Shakspere's unquestioned autographs and the Addition to SIR THOMAS MOORE. In: Stud. in Phil., vol. 22, 1925, pp. 133–60. Rev.: Dt. Vjschr. Jg. 6, 1928, S. 180, L. L. Schücking.

Criticism of Thompson's thesis.

EDUARD SIEVERS: Shakespeares Anteil an King Lear. In: Anglica. Brandl Festschr. Bd. 2. Leipzig, 1925, S. 207–10=Palaestra 148.

Neither the writer nor the author of the insurrection-scene can be connected with Shakespeare.

ARTHUR ACHESON: Shakespeare, Chapman et 'Sir Thomas More', avec un avant-propos de Franck L. Schoell. In: Rev. anglo-amér., vol. 3, 1926, pp. 428–39 et 514–31. Rev.: Sh. Jb. 63, 1927, S. 225, Beckmann.

Chapman taken to be author of the 'Addition', Shakespeare the reviser.

R. W. CHAMBERS: The saga and the myth of Sir Thomas More. O.U.P., 1927. (52 pp.)=Brit. Acad. Lecture.

Does not touch the drama.

SAMUEL A. TANNENBAUM: 'The Booke of Sir Thomas Moore.' A bibliotic study. New York, 1927. (vii, 135 pp.) Rev.: MLR. 23, 1928, pp. 231–4, Ch. Sisson; E. St. 63, 1929, S. 428–9, E. Eckhardt; Sh. Jb. 63, 1927, S. 204, W. Keller; Bbl. 48, 1929, S. 362–4, E. Ekwall; JEGPh. 28, 1929, pp. 555–7, R. A. Law.

Thorough investigation of the MS.

SAMUEL A. TANNENBAUM: Problems in Shakspere's penmanship, including a study of the poet's will. New York, 1927. (xvi, 241 pp.) Rev.: MLR. 23, 1928, pp. 231–4, Ch. Sisson.

W. W. GREG: Shakespeare's hand once more. In: TLS. Nov. 24 and Dec. 1, 1927, pp. 871 and 908.

WILHELM MARSCHALL: Das 'Sir Thomas Moore'-Manuskript und die englische 'Commedia dell' arte'. In: Anglia, Bd. 52, 1928, S. 193–241.

S. R. GOLDING: Robert Wilson and 'Sir Thomas More'. In: N. & Q., vol. 154, 1928, pp. 237–9, 259–62; vol. 155, pp. 237–40.

Attributes authorship of 'Addition' to R. Wilson.

SAMUEL A. TANNENBAUM: More about the 'Booke of Sir Thomas Moore'. In: PMLA., vol. 43, 1928, pp. 767–78.

Refutation of Greg's assumption that the MS. is a prompter's copy.

INDEX

PRINTED IN GREAT BRITAIN AT THE UNIVERSITY PRESS, OXFORD
BY JOHN JOHNSON, PRINTER TO THE UNIVERSITY